A JUST
& TRUE
LOVE

A JUST & TRUE LOVE

Feminism at the Frontiers
of Theological Ethics:

Essays in Honor of
Margaret A. Farley

Edited by Maura A. Ryan *and* Brian F. Linnane, S.J.

Foreword by Francine Cardman

University of Notre Dame Press

Notre Dame, Indiana

Copyright © 2007 by University of Notre Dame
Notre Dame, Indiana 46556
www.undpress.nd.edu
All Rights Reserved

Manufactured in the United States of America

Library of Congress Cataloging-in-Publication Data
A just and true love : feminism at the frontiers of theological ethics :
essays in honor of Margaret Farley / edited by Maura A. Ryan and
Brian F. Linnane.
p.   cm.
Includes bibliographical references and index.
ISBN-13: 978-0-268-04025-3 (Cloth : alk. paper)
ISBN-10: 0-268-04025-7 (Cloth : alk. paper)
1. Feminist ethics.   2. Feminist theology.   3. Christian ethics.
4. Sexual ethics.   5. Medical ethics.   I. Farley, Margaret A.
II. Ryan, Maura A., 1957–   III. Linnane, Brian F.
BJ1395.J86   2007
241.082—dc22

                                    2007033424

∞ *The paper in this book meets the guidelines for permanence*
and durability of the Committee on Production Guidelines for
Book Longevity of the Council on Library Resources.

Contents

Foreword

Francine Cardman

Margaret Farley brings to the interwoven relationships of her life and work the gift of compassionate regard for the deep reality of persons and unfailing respect for the complexities of their lives. Long before she articulated the virtue of "compassionate respect," she lived it. Her willingness to sit with patient presence and contemplate the tangled skein of existence is a crucial source of the careful insights, the revelatory questions, the emphatic hope that characterize her teaching, preaching, writing, being. Her ability to listen, to consider, and then to arise and act—to comfort, to challenge, to stand with, to urge on, to struggle, to mourn, to pray, to begin again—has its roots in that loving regard for human and, ultimately, divine complexity.

As teacher, scholar, mentor, friend, as Sister of Mercy and sister in the struggle, Margaret has inhabited the borderlands of intersecting institutions and movements, commitments and communities. From her appointment to the faculty of Yale Divinity School in 1971, to her appointment to the Gilbert L. Stark Chair in Christian Ethics in 1986, to the milestone marked by this *Festschrift,* Margaret has embodied the best of Roman Catholic and ecumenical traditions of theology and ethics. As one of the pioneers of feminist ethics and theology she has labored persistently at the frontiers of these traditions, pushing back their boundaries while drawing from and drawing together their hearts.

For Margaret the life of teaching and scholarship is profoundly relational. At its source and in its practice it is a life of ministry, rooted in a contemplative dialogue of prayer and intellect that seeks the just, the merciful word and action. Her teaching, preaching, writing, listening, and accompaniment are as rigorous in their attention to this inner dialogue as they are to the particularities of personal and communal contexts. In all these undertakings she neither begins nor ends with the theoretical but instead with the concrete realities of human relationships, and searches out the ways that lead toward greater freedom and love.

Thus students, friends, and colleagues share vocational and personal quandaries with her and are gently encouraged to attend to their own inner dialogue, to discern the truth in their desires. Gay and lesbian Catholics find their lives and love, their faith and faithfulness affirmed in Margaret's clear-sighted proposal of norms for "just love" in same-sex as well as heterosexual relationships. Persons making new commitments or confronting changes in long-standing ones discover in her book the insight they need in order to let go of uncertainty or fear, judgment or defeat, and move toward the beginnings of new life. Women and men living with HIV/AIDS and those who stand with them take heart from her integrated analysis and advocacy, which honors their agency and experience as she joins her voice with theirs in demanding both mercy and justice in the face of their suffering.

What follows from this attentive listening and speaking, this action and reflection, is Margaret's uncanny ability to make a way where there appears to be no way through the dilemmas of human relatedness, the constrictions of doctrinal authoritarianism and ecclesiastical politics, the ultimately deadly antagonism of truth and charity. Three brief examples from Margaret's writings over the past three decades reveal the relational method of her theological ethics at work in just such kinds of apparent "limit" situations. In each instance she finds a path through the gridlock of issues by reframing the question and asking what is fundamentally at stake for human and divine, personal and communal relationships in the matter at hand. Each of these examples arises from the life of the churches and takes on particular significance and forms of expression in the context of theological education, where Margaret has lived her vocation to teaching and scholarship for more than thirty years. All remain points of contention in the churches, presenting critical challenges to those who teach, learn, and practice theology and ministry. Margaret's pathfinding through these difficult questions is a vital source of hope for those who labor and long for life-giving resolutions to these quandaries.

In 1975 Margaret was one of the plenary speakers at the Detroit Women's Ordination Conference, the first national gathering to explore the question of ordination for Roman Catholic women that followed on and was emboldened by the ordinations of eleven women to the priesthood in the Episcopal Church in Philadelphia the previous summer. Margaret refused to get tangled in questions of absolute ordinations, licit or illicit, regular or irregular, that were being raised in the Anglican communion and had strong resonances in the Roman Catholic church. She set to one side doctrinal debates about the maleness of Christ and therefore the priesthood, as well as assertions about unbroken tradition and the will of God or the intention of Jesus. Instead she asked the deeper ethical questions that point the way toward answers that respect the gifts of ministry, community, and the ways in which we image the divine for each other. In place of deadlocked doctrinal absolutes she opened a new horizon for exploring the moral imperatives for the ordination of women.[1]

I have already mentioned the second example—Margaret's thoughtful, humane, and loving consideration of an ethic of same-sex relations. Here I simply note the way in which she went about reframing the question so that it honors the deep reality of human experience and the giftedness of human connection. Looked at from this perspective, the question is not a matter of intrinsically disordered acts or lack of generativity in sexual relationships. What is at stake, that is to say, is not sin but love. The deeper question is thus: how shall persons love justly, intimately, and faithfully, regardless of sexual orientation, in ways that embody the faithfulness, intimacy, and justice of God's love for us? It is not that ethical traditions and teachings (Roman Catholic, for instance) are unimportant or should simply be discounted. Rather, Margaret locates the ethical issue at a more fundamental level than much current discourse.[2]

The question of eucharistic sharing is another perplexing issue that arises again and again in and between churches, in mixed (Christian) marriages, in ecumenical divinity schools, and in other kinds of ecumenical gatherings and endeavors. As the new millennium approached, it too was a question in need of reframing in order to gain greater insight into its significance and to clear a space for the life-giving grace of eucharistic community. Here again Margaret does not let her reflection linger at the level of doctrinal definitions and disputes but searches for the theological and ethical principles embedded in eucharistic relationships and practice that might open a way forward. The fundamental insight she reaches is radically simple and radically faithful: "no one goes away hungry from the table of the Lord." The question, then, is not whether eucharistic sharing is a means to unity or an expression of unity already achieved, or whether churches, sacraments, ministry, and order are real or valid. Rather, the question is how even imperfect community, imperfect unity, and imperfect love can cast out fear and continue to unfold the churches' unity from what is already present in their faith and practice. And, finally, the question is about bread and life for the world, God's mission in Jesus and through the Holy Spirit. No one goes away hungry from the table of the Lord.[3]

By searching out the relational experiences and meanings that ground ethical and theological questions, Margaret is able to suggest ways to move through apparent impasses toward fuller life. She does this with great care and humility, aware of both the truth and the limitations of our moral knowing. The compassionate respect that she extends to persons correlates with another virtue that Margaret herself lives even as she articulates it for our personal and communal consideration—the "grace of self-doubt." The gift and habit of this graced self-doubt is a relational attitude that trusts the inherent power and attractiveness of truth at the same time as it acknowledges the incompleteness of our comprehension. It is a way of being that respects the integrity of the other, so that it seeks to persuade rather than impose, to invite rather than demand. By refusing the temptation to intellectual violence, the grace of self-doubt creates more space rather than less for truthful living.[4]

In this respect, and in regard to each of the examples noted above, the grace of self-doubt is especially an ecclesial virtue. Although at times more notable for its absence than its practice in theological conversation or controversies within the churches, the grace of self-doubt is a loving response to the exigencies of life together in Christian community. It is a corollary, not a contradiction, to faith.

The grace of self-doubt is a fitting place, then, to conclude this reflection on Margaret's ministry of teaching and learning, of encouraging and consoling, of thinking deeply about and acting boldly on the call to make God's merciful love a living and healing presence in the world. For the grace of self-doubt allows us to trust that, in the end, it is not the violent who bear it away, but the gentle who will inherit the earth—and not only the earth, but the home God has prepared for us all.

NOTES

1. Margaret A. Farley, "Moral Imperatives for the Ordination of Women," in *Women and Catholic Priesthood: An Expanded Vision*, ed. Anne Marie Gardiner, 58–61 (New York: Paulist Press, 1976).

2. Margaret A. Farley, "An Ethic for Same-Sex Relations," in *A Challenge to Love*, ed. Robert Nugent, 93–106 (New York: Crossroad Publishing Co., 1983).

3. Margaret A. Farley, "No One Goes Away Hungry from the Table of the Lord: Eucharistic Sharing in Ecumenical Contexts," in *Practice What You Preach: Virtues, Ethics, and Power in the Lives of Pastoral Ministers and Their Congregations*, ed. James F. Keenan and Joseph Kotva (Kansas City: Sheed and Ward, 1999), 186–201. Earlier Margaret had preached on the same topic; the sermon, "No One Goes Away Hungry from the Table of the Lord" was published in Yale Divinity School's *Spectrum* 18 (Fall 1998): 12–13.

4. Margaret A. Farley, "Ethics, Ecclesiology, and the Grace of Self-Doubt," in *A Call to Fidelity: On the Moral Theology of Charles E. Curran*, ed. James J. Walter, Timothy E. O'Connell, and Thomas A. Shannon, 55–75 (Washington, DC: Georgetown University Press, 2002).

Acknowledgments

Poems of Julia de Burgos, cited in chapter six, are found in Jack Agüeros, trans., *Song of the Simple Truth: The Complete Poems of Julia de Burgos* (Willimantic, CT: Curbstone Press, 1997). Used with permission.

Chapter fourteen is based on material earlier published in Charles E. Curran, *The Moral Theology of John Paul II* (Washington, DC: Georgetown University Press, 2005). Used with permission. Copyright 2005 by Georgetown University Press, www.press.georgetown.edu.

The cover image is of an oil painting entitled "Four Women from Four Parts of the Sudan" by Zeinab El Tigani. Used with permission.

The editors are grateful to Charles Camosy and Elizabeth Agnew for research assistance, and to Barbara Hanrahan and her staff at the University of Notre Dame Press.

Introduction

Maura A. Ryan

The presence of women theologians has not only changed the sociology of who is doing theology today, it has fundamentally changed the way of doing theology.[1]

Nowhere is Catherine Mowry LaCugna's observation better illustrated than in the contributions of Margaret A. Farley to contemporary Christian ethics. A feminist pioneer, she has stretched the content of theological ethics, bringing to the center concerns often overlooked or trivialized: the role of equality and mutuality in a theology of sexuality and marriage; the ethical and theological dimensions of commitment; the adequacy of normative accounts of "nature" and "the natural"; domestic violence; the abuse of authority by religious leaders; and the disproportionate vulnerability of women globally to the threat of AIDS. More than thirty years a beloved teacher and mentor at Yale Divinity School, she has helped to change the face of the field through the many people—women and men—she has helped to form and develop as Christian ethicists. However, as the essays in this collection show, the influence of feminist theologians such as Margaret Farley extends not only to what questions are posed to Christian ethics today or who is part of discerning an adequate response, but to the very way Christian ethics is done. Inspired by Vatican II and challenged by the women's movement of the 1960s and 1970s, her generation of women brought to theology not only their distinctive voices and their

1

particular concerns, but a self-conscious and self-critical attention to the relationship of sexuality, knowledge, and power. In other words, they *engendered* theology.

THINKING WITH GENDER

As Susan Parsons so aptly describes, gender is a "disruptive thread of argument—undermining certainties of truth, behaving badly, cutting across normal expectations, troubling what is natural, and turning over our thinking."[2] Gender is also a matter that today we cannot seem to avoid. It has pressed itself upon us as a primary category for understanding human experience and as such has become a foundational issue for Christian ethics. To engage seriously in the enterprise of ethics in this day and age is almost necessarily to "think with gender," to give an account of what it means to exist as men and women within a particular set of human relationships, to have a certain sort of body with its specific capabilities and vulnerabilities, and to act in light of a given description of the world and our place within it.[3] At once revealing our self-understanding and calling it into question, gender implicates us immediately in the deepest concerns of both theology and ethics: "Gender is one of the ways in which we think differences, so that it stands as a marker of what is unique to woman and to man, and it allows us to wonder why and how it is that we are not alike. So, too, it is one of the ways in which we think our common humanity, about what it is that makes us beings who are able to live together, to love one another, and to form relationships."[4]

Gender has been at the heart of what has been called today's "postmodern moment" in ethics, first as feminists have taken up postmodernism's critical attention to language and power as well as its skepticism concerning the objectivity of reason, but also as the feminist critique of the established order has helped to undermine the previously "settled landscape of the moral life."[5] In its many varieties and through its various developments, feminism has contributed to the demise of the "Man of Reason," calling into question inherited forms of universalism; changing the subject of ethics through its insistence on the significance of women's experience as a source for interpreting moral value; "troubling what is natural" in its rejection of divinely sanctioned assumptions about the body and embodiment that shore up patriarchal social relations; and pressing for a description of human agency that accounts not only for the powers of freedom and will but also for the grace and the burden of our inescapable sociality.[6]

Farley has often reminded her readers that feminist theology was born out of women's growing awareness of the disparity between what they had been taught about their identity and role within the human community, the culturally and religiously enshrined images of womanhood that they had received and in some part internalized, and their own experience of themselves and their lives.[7] The counterweight to this deepening sense of dissonance has been to give methodological priority to women's distinctive religious and moral experience, thereby exposing distorted or distorting accounts of women's "nature."

But engendering theology has not meant simply "adding women's perspectives to the mix and stirring." Feminists have insisted that intellectual and religious traditions are deficient (indeed dangerous) to the extent to which they have failed to "think difference," either by rendering difference invisible epistemologically or by casting sexual difference in terms that mask underlying issues of value and of power, such as representing woman as body to man's mind, emotion to his reason, passivity to his activity, dependency to his autonomy, ordained to a domestic role to his public role.[8] Thus, as Eleanor Haney put it, "women's experiences are not mere addenda to theological and ethical reflection, but critiques of all other reflection."[9] It has not been enough simply to "return to biblical or Lutheran or Thomistic sources and seek to 'make them come out right' with respect to women"[10] (or with respect to any other group that has been marginalized or rendered invisible within and by virtue of those sources). Gender is a "disruptive thread" precisely because, taken seriously, it leads to a thoroughgoing critique of the very foundations of truth and issues a challenge to the ability of any normative theory to adequately represent the Good or to generate ideals for just human community.

Farley recognized this early on in a reflection on the significance of feminist consciousness for the interpretation of Scripture: feminists "know that no other tradition or movement has adequately addressed the situation of women."[11] This is not, she argued, just a failure of extension. Rather, it represents the need for a radical reexamination of working conceptions of the human and of prevailing categories of human relation. It makes clear the urgency of incorporating the experience of all persons and all groups. Farley predicted then that when women's experience as a theological and philosophical vantage point came into its own, it would revolutionize theological ethics, not just in the call for new interpretations of human dignity or better theoretical models for talking about the requirements of equality and justice within human relationships, but by transforming moral imagination, as the "old order" (of women's unquestioned inferiority to men) gave way to new possibilities for recognizing the potential of all human beings.[12]

DIFFERENCE AND BEYOND

The weight given to women's experience in feminist method has made feminist ethics acutely sensitive to the destabilizing effects of difference. In the face of criticism by women whose experience (by virtue of race, class, sexual orientation, or geography) remained invisible in claims asserted on behalf of women's rights or needs or desires, feminists have had to face squarely their own universalizing pretensions. As they have developed in response to a chastened and deconstructed understanding of women's experience, contemporary feminist methods have become both self-consciously and irreversibly "bound up with the historical, the particular, the situated, the contingent."[13] As attention to the particular and the situated has joined postmodern doubt about the ability of theory to transcend embedded relationships of power and social constructions of knowledge, feminist theologians have had to struggle along with feminists in general with the question of whether ethics has been brought to some kind of end, if it is not finally impossible to do what ethics requires: to identify common elements of human experience that suggest what is needed for a good life in community, to posit essential features of humanity that are everywhere worthy of protection.[14]

However, despite the importance given to deconstructing Christian sources, to acknowledging the limits and biases that constrain our access to the Good or to the ultimate, engendering theological ethics has not been just about dismantling or de-centering. In general, feminist theology remains committed to the belief that there are "theological truths . . . so fundamental to the life of faith that, while we may recast, reconstruct, and even revolutionize them, we may not finally relativize or dismiss them."[15] Thus, feminist theological ethics has retained a commitment to a realistic epistemology in some form, to the belief that we can experience morality's claim on us in the context of lived relationships, and to the possibility of discovering shared moral convictions across cultural and geographical boundaries. This commitment rests in part on the practical and political consequences for women's lives of a complete and thoroughgoing relativism: "[S]o long as oppression, hierarchies of power, and relative visibility of lives are part of human society, it is not possible to conclude that everyone's voice carries equally adequate 'truth.'"[16] Like other liberation theologies, which emphasize the necessary relationship between theory and praxis, feminist theological ethics shares the conviction that ideas, conclusions, and claims must matter for the lives of women and men. And in order for them to matter, our claims must be, in Serene Jones's words, "bold, normative, and powerful enough for persons to stake their lives on."[17] As Farley and others have always recognized, to abandon the effort to arrive at an adequate or appropriate universalism is at best to collapse moral debate into endless conflict and at worst to surrender the field to the powerful.[18]

But the impetus within feminist ethics for forging a moral language capable of transcending while still respecting difference follows from more than just the need for feminism to articulate a coherent and compelling political vision. In an essay entitled "Feminism and Universal Morality" Farley grounds a feminist case for common morality on the evidence of shared moral convictions across time and cultures. These convictions presuppose some commonality in human experience, as might be glimpsed in experiences of joy and sorrow, in the desire to be understood and the need to be protected.[19]

Farley is not suggesting that the serious questions posed to feminism and thus to theological ethics by postmodernism should or can be ignored. Elsewhere, she acknowledges that in a world in which the discrete self seems to dissolve altogether we may well ask: "How shall we love? What can it mean to love as a human individual? What sort of love is called for by individuals who are 'only' social constructions, whose identity is 'only' a protean self subject to interpersonal dynamics of power, nonpersonal linguistic codes?"[20] Yet, she insists that it is possible in some human experiences, for example, of love and of suffering, to recognize something of ourselves that is truthful and enduring: there are "locations" in human experience, privileged sites for genuine connection with the "real" beyond us and the "real" within us.[21]

One underlying assumption of this feminist argument for a common morality is that human experience is revelatory of the divine. It is not surprising that as women in the church came to acknowledge themselves as coequal "hearers of the Word" they also became convinced of the importance of publicly witnessing to the conviction that all persons are invited to participate in the enacted drama of God's self-communion within history, to realize something of God's capacity for relationship, our inestimable worthiness in God's sight, and God's desires for our wholeness, individually and together. But Farley also means to say something about the transcendent potential in human experience itself. When we are caught up in the activity of loving, when love arises within us as a response to the beloved as worthy, valuable, loveable, just as when our gaze is held by the affliction of another such that both the observer and the sufferer are stripped of pretension and self-deceit, we find ourselves in the presence of what is genuinely human in another. We can, of course, be wrong, both about our experience of love and our response to suffering. Rather than completely undermining a commitment to this sort of moral realism, however, the possibility of shame in the face of an experience of wrong or unjust love, the spontaneous response of rage in the awareness of suffering that need not be, points us in the direction of the "truth" that lies beyond the limits of our language.

In her essay for this volume, Lisa Sowle Cahill suggests the importance of this commitment for contemporary sexual ethics. Feminists have called into question interpretations of sexual difference that provide the foundation for doctrines of gendered complementarity; they have exposed narrow or one-dimensional understandings of the ends of sexual expression such that potential for union, intimacy, pleasure, and mutuality is lost in the elevation of procreativity; and they have insisted that the lens of justice be brought to bear on considerations of the morality of sexual relationships, not only as it concerns the character of sexual union, but also as it extends to the social institutions (religious community as well as marriage and the family) within which sexual relationships are set. At the same time, feminists like Cahill and Farley insist that we can know in our bodily experience something of God's intentions for the goodness of human sexuality. As a result, it is possible to mine the Christian tradition for its wisdom on matters of love, despite its failure in the past to put its best insights concerning the primacy of justice in service of an ethic for sexuality, marriage, and the family.

Yet Cahill argues for the importance of feminist confidence in the intelligibility of human experience in another way as well. It is precisely the belief that "it is possible for human persons to weep over commonly felt tragedies, laugh over commonly perceived incongruities, yearn for common hopes" that makes it not only imaginable but necessary to build networks across national and cultural boundaries in the service of global justice.[22] This implies in part that we can say something about what is morally obligating about human beings as such and by extension what social arrangements and sexual practices will reflect right relation, which will be conducive to human flourishing. Indeed, as we will see below, the meaning of "respect for persons" has been a central concern for Farley as a feminist ethicist, weaving through writings on the nature of commitment, bioethics, marriage and divorce, and same-sex relations. It also implies that experience can be shared, that there is value to the telling of stories, the expression of outrage and of joy, the release of tears, even if experience is not self-interpreting. The process of identifying parameters for interpreting the meaning of justice in personal or social relationships, and of coming to awareness of women's common experience of sexual and social inequality, grounds solidarity among women and impels action on behalf of those subjected most acutely to injustice.

A JUST AND TRUTHFUL LOVE

Two other concerns central to Farley's work illustrate further ways in which gender has "turned over our thinking" in theological ethics. The first has to do with how we understand persons as moral agents and as subjects within moral relationships. The second has to do with our interpretation of the meaning of justice and of its relationship to other moral principles and values.

In a 1993 essay entitled "A Feminist Version of Respect for Persons," Farley captures a fundamental feminist ambivalence about autonomy as enshrined in Enlightenment-inspired notions of the self.[23] Feminists have been deeply committed to affirming women's right to self-determination against demeaning and falsifying restrictions of custom, law, and religion. At the same time, however, they have been increasingly critical of the elevation of autonomy in ethical and political theory insofar as it has presupposed a self-interested, self-legislating, self-generating individual. Farley concedes that feminists have little reason to bemoan the supposed death of modern philosophy's disengaged, disembodied, wholly autonomous self or to regret the disappearance of the subject who stood as "the isolated bearer of signs, the conscious knower of clear and certain ideas, the self-governing and self-responsible agent whose task was to instrumentalize body and world."[24] Although it has taken different forms, feminist method has acknowledged the inescapable embeddedness of human existence and given room to an impulse toward community as both a qualifier of our freedom and its precondition.

In his essay for this volume, "Self and Other in a Theological Framework," Gene Outka describes the care with which Farley has sought to reconcile the capacity for self-determination with the capacity for self-gift, to give an account of moral agency that adequately reflects the rich dimensions of moral experience. At the heart of Farley's long reflection are the questions "Is there anything intrinsic to persons that inspires us to care for them, that claims our respect, that awakens our love? Is there anything inherent in persons that forbids us to reduce them to what they can do for us, that prohibits us from invading their bodies or their lives, that requires us to pay attention to their needs and their beauty?"[25] Farley's answer is that if persons are worthy of respect, they are so as *integral* beings.[26] Thus, our answer to what it means to respect persons will be adequate to the extent that it takes account not only of the individual's inner capacity for self-legislation, but also of the multiple forces and relationships—social, economic, political, and cultural—that shape freedom and direct its ends. It will be adequate to the extent that it appreciates that freedom and autonomy are not developed in spite of our location within the world but because of it. It will be adequate to the extent that it recognizes that persons are ends in themselves not only because they can freely determine themselves but because "they can know and be known, love and be loved, as both embodied and free."[27]

Several things follow from this insistence on autonomy and relationality as equiprimordial. Taking account of the way in which "we are in the world and the world is in us" resists interpretations of moral obligation that abstract normative claims from pastoral consideration of individual capacities and vulnerabilities. Her 1986 book, *Personal Commitments*, displays Farley's acute sensitivity to the intersection of the possibility of a free and authentic choice for commitment and the many human limitations that can render commitments impossible or dangerous for individuals to continue to live. Farley's work joins other currents in contemporary Roman Catholic moral theology in calling for reappraisal of past teachings, for example, on same-sex relations, which derive ethical norms from biological "givens" in isolation from a consideration of the potentialities of human persons adequately and integrally considered. Moreover, awareness of our historicity and therefore the partiality of our knowledge has implications for the way in which we ought to seek the truth together as members of ecclesial community. At very least, it ought to call into question images of a "teaching Church" that is not at the same time a "learning Church."

For Farley, reflection on the meaning of respect for relationality as alongside autonomy is also set within the broader question of love's relationship to justice. In various places, Farley has argued that feminists ought to resist approaches to the moral life that treat reason and emotion, justice and care, principles and persons as dichotomous. Why this is so—and why this resistance ought to extend beyond feminists—should be obvious by now. For Farley, all human choices involve reasons and emotions, and both our reasons and our emotions are subject to evaluation.[28] The problem for our moral lives (and our moral theories) is precisely how, in light of what norms, we are to evaluate love or judge the appropriateness of our care.[29] Farley's proposal is deceptively simple: love (or care, or compassion) is just when it takes account of the concrete reality of the beloved, when it is "formed by respect for what God has made—for human freedom, relationality, embodiment, historical and cultural formation, uniqueness, and the potentiality of fullness of life in an unlimited future."[30]

A recent work on the challenge of HIV/AIDS to contemporary bioethics helps to fill out what Farley means by a "just love." She begins her book *Compassionate Respect* by recounting her experience at a White House Summit Conference held for religious leaders on World AIDS Day, December 1, 2000. One after another, she writes, the imams, rabbis, patriarchs, archbishops, sheikhs, and other religious leaders spoke of the devastation caused by AIDS, the need for compassion, and the efforts to respond already underway in their communities. Yet, the intersection of gender, race, sex, and poverty in the construction of the epidemic of HIV/AIDS was left unmentioned, and expressions of compassion did not include admission of the role of religious teachings on sexuality and gender in contributing to women's disproportionate vulnerability to infection and death.[31]

In the context of the global AIDS pandemic, love of or compassion for those who are suffering entails, in a basic sense, what it entails in any medical encounter: protection against threats to physical and psychic health and respect for one's human dignity. However, a just love goes beyond recognition of the fundamental equality of all persons, and therefore of their equal vulnerability to illness and death, to attend to the morally significant differences among them, in particular the structural and material conditions that result in disproportionate risks for some both of infection and early death.[32] In this sense, love is *"made true by its justice."* Love and compassion are not just sentiments or raw emotions but the disciplined, reasoned commitment to confront whatever does not respect the potential of all persons for free choice, relationship, health and flourishing, in other words, whatever does not respect what God has made. In the context of the HIV/AIDS pandemic, compassion is made *true* only insofar as it attends not just to the physical suffering of individuals but also to the unwillingness of international powers to respond promptly and adequately to the developing crisis; not just to the particular needs of infected women and their children in sub-Saharan Africa but also the intersecting political, economic, and cultural factors that leave many women without resources for exercising moral responsibility on behalf of themselves and their families.

Several assumptions about the relationship of love and justice are in the background of Farley's reflection on the meaning of compassion under the siege of HIV/AIDS, all of which appear as themes in the essays that make up this collection. One is that it is a mistake to abstract claims about justice from the relationships within which people exercise moral agency, the institutions which form them and which provide theological and ethical tools for reflection and action, and the particular roles which they have assumed or have been given. Cathleen Kaveny's essay on the much debated case involving court-enforced separation of conjoined twins makes just this point. We cannot understand what a "just love" of these children entails or make sense of the court's intervention in this case unless we consider the particular responsibilities that attend the vocation of a parent or the role of public guardian.

Another is that once accepted distinctions between the private and the public spheres, the realm of love and the realm of justice, can no longer stand. Norms governing sexual morality, for example, both draw from and legitimate social orders and relations of power; accepted norms become increasingly dangerous to the degree that they "naturalize" gendered inequality or protect as "private" various forms of domestic and sexual violence. Mary Rose D'Angelo's study of early Christian attitudes toward sexual relations with children illustrates well what is at stake in feminists' unwillingness to exempt intimate relationships from the scrutiny of justice. As it exposes underlying issues of status and the construction of sexual desire in judgments about "good" or "bad" love, her analysis has implications for understanding the union of sexuality, power, and violence in the recent clergy sexual abuse scandal within the Roman Catholic Church. To argue for justice in sexual relation and for equality and mutuality as the hallmarks of a "right intimacy" need not lead to a wholesale rejection of traditional conclusions regarding sexual morality. However, it does mean that we must be willing to test those conclusions for adequacy in light of our evolving understanding of the conditions under which women as well as men, children as well as adults, flourish in relationship. As Farley has often argued, most recently in her 2006 book *Just Love,* "the personal is political" runs in both directions: an adequate sexual ethic must recognize not only that political realities mediate, enable, and circumscribe even intimate decisions, but also that the sexual sphere is related to all other spheres. Our sexual lives are not the whole of our human lives. Still, what happens in our sexual lives is intimately connected with our prospects for living a complete human life.[33]

Finally, it is not enough simply to elevate the significance of relationality in accounts of moral agency. As feminists like Farley are well aware, appeals to community and praise of women's capacities for relationship have served (and continue to serve) to hide nonegalitarian and unjust social arrangements and to silence women's call for political and economic equality. Moreover, our experience is that relationships can be oppressive as well as liberating, respectful as well as demeaning, stifling as well as conducive to growth and flourishing. Religious traditions generate—and embody—false and dangerous visions of community, as well as hopeful and transformative visions. Thus, a feminist version of respect for persons is qualified by what Farley calls a "normative theory of community." The test of a moral community is not in its members' expressed commitments but in the extent to which internal and external relationships reflect mutuality, reciprocity, equality, and solidarity.

For this reason, questions of ecclesiology have been at the heart of feminist theology and ethics. Feminist theologians have insisted that action for justice springs from the authentic witness of the Eucharistic community as it seeks to live together with respect for difference as well as a striving for union, honoring the individual as "hearer of the Word" while creating conditions for mutual accountability for the common good. Whether challenging the Vatican's refusal to consider the ordination of women or the suppression of debate over contested issues in the church under Pope John Paul II, Farley and others have underscored the dangers of a romantic or spiritualized understanding of the church as a prophetic community. The moral authority of the church lies not in the forcefulness of its pronouncements or even in the extent of its important charitable works, but in the coherence of the community's public advocacy for justice with the terms of its inner life, the symbols of its worship, and the language through which it expresses its deepest convictions. In the wake of the sex abuse scandal in the U.S., the call of women in the Church for collegiality, transparency, episcopal accountability, and the empowerment of the laity has assumed a new urgency. It seems more obvious than ever before in this moment of public shame that we need to envision new forms for collaboration in ministry and to cultivate a broad sense of the call to holiness and participation in the witness of the church. Essays by William O'Neill and Leslie Griffin show, in different ways, that what is most important for feminist ethics is not who is on the top of the hierarchy or who gets to speak for the Church—although these are not unimportant—but the conditions under which the Church can hope to accomplish its work of justice.

A TRIBUTE AND AN INVITATION

This collection honors Margaret Farley. Although it is impossible to do justice to the extent of her contributions to Christian ethics, we have tried to reflect something of the depth and breadth of her wisdom and the clarity of her mind. Some of the essays, such as Cahill's "Feminist Theology and Sexual Ethics," focus directly on Farley's thought, tracing its role not only in questioning traditional methods and conclusions but also in the development of a contemporary Catholic, ecumenical feminist ethics. Others take inspiration from her work, offering responses to contemporary problems that are faithful to the challenges Farley has posed to theological ethics. Still others take up problems that long have been of concern for her and other feminist theologians, such as contraception and women's ordination. As much as anything else, it is the volume's contributors themselves—men and women, Catholic, Protestant, and Jewish, some avowedly feminist, others who would never describe themselves as feminist—who speak to the range of Farley's influence and the richness of her thought.

We have sought here not only to give tribute to Margaret Farley but also to tell a larger story, to give some insight into how, through the work of feminist theologians such as Farley, our thinking has been troubled, turned over, disrupted, to allow new questions to be asked of our religious and ethical traditions, new forms of relationships to be imagined, and new interpretations to emerge of the contours of justice and the demands of compassion. As such, this work is necessarily unfinished. Although the essays in part 1 take up emerging problems related to globalization, for example, cross-cultural debate over women and human rights, we can offer only a glimpse, or perhaps a promise, of Christian ethics at the edge of the next frontier.

Finally, we have tried to show something of what is ultimately at stake. Farley has taught us that in this work of theological ethics, we are not only pushed into "thinking with gender," we are invited to *speak of love*. To borrow from Parsons, we are invited to "ask after the way in which a tenderness and a generosity might come to be formed among us . . . a gentleness may find a way to live here . . . a joy for love of God [may be known] as we ourselves are turned into ones who love."[34]

NOTES

1. Catherine Mowry LaCugna, "Introduction," in *Freeing Theology: The Essentials of Theology in a Feminist Perspective*, ed. Catherine Mowry LaCugna (New York: HarperCollins Publishers Inc., 1993), 2.

2. Susan Frank Parsons, *The Ethics of Gender* (Oxford: Blackwell Publishers, 2002), ix.

3. Ibid., 17.

4. Ibid., 17–18.

5. Ibid., 16.

6. Susan Frank Parsons, *Feminism and Christian Ethics* (Cambridge: Cambridge University Press, 1996), 188.

7. Margaret A. Farley, "Feminist Theology and Bioethics," in *Women's Consciousness, Women's Conscience: A Reader in Feminist Ethics*, ed. Barbara

Hilkert Andolsen, Christine Gudorf, and Mary D. Pellauer (Minneapolis: Winston Press, 1985), 295.

8. Margaret A. Farley, "Feminist Ethics," in *Feminist Ethics and the Catholic Moral Tradition*, Readings in Moral Theology 9, ed. Charles E. Curran, Margaret A. Farley, and Richard A. McCormick (New York: Paulist Press, 1996), 9.

9. Eleanor Humes Haney, "What is Feminist Ethics? A Proposal for Continuing Discussion," in *Feminist Theological Ethics: A Reader*, ed. Lois K. Daly (Louisville, KY: Westminster John Knox Press, 1994), 4.

10. Haney, "What is Feminist Ethics," 4.

11. Margaret A. Farley, "Feminist Consciousness and the Interpretation of Scripture," in *Feminist Interpretation of the Bible,* ed. L. Russell, 41–51 (Philadelphia: Westminster Press, 1985), 45.

12. Ibid., 43. See also, Margaret A. Farley, "New Patterns of Relationship: Beginnings of a Moral Revolution," *Theological Studies* 36 (December 1975): 627–46.

13. Margaret A. Farley, "Feminism and Universal Morality," in *Prospects for a Common Morality*, ed. Gene Outka and John P. Reeder (Princeton, NJ: Princeton University Press, 1993), 176.

14. See Parsons, *Ethics of Gender,* ix; Farley, "Feminism and Universal Morality," 177.

15. Serene Jones, *Feminist Theory and Christian Theology: Cartographies of Grace* (Minneapolis: Augsburg Fortress, 2000), 54.

16. Farley, "Feminism and Universal Morality," 178.

17. Jones, *Feminist Theory and Christian Theology,* 54.

18. Farley, "Feminism and Universal Morality," 178.

19. Ibid.

20. Margaret A. Farley, "How Shall We Love in a Postmodern World?" *Annual of the Society of Christian Ethics* 14 (1994): 7.

21. Ibid., 9.

22. Farley, "Feminism and Universal Morality," 178.

23. Margaret A. Farley, "A Feminist Version of Respect for Persons," in Curran, Farley, and McCormick, *Feminist Ethics*, 164–83.

24. Farley, "How Shall We Love in a Postmodern World?" 13–14.

25. Farley, "A Feminist Version of Respect for Persons," 167.

26. Ibid.; emphasis added.

27. Ibid., 177.

28. Farley, "Feminism and Universal Morality," 184. Although I have only touched on it here, the question of free choice has been a longstanding interest for Farley and is the subject of current work in progress. See Margaret A. Farley, "Freedom and Desire," in *The Papers of the Henry Luce III Fellows in Theology*, vol. 3, ed. Matthew Zyniewicz (Atlanta: Scholars Press, 1998), 57–73.

29. Farley, "Feminism and Universal Morality," 184.

30. Margaret A. Farley, *Compassionate Respect: A Feminist Approach to Medical Ethics and Other Questions* (New York: Paulist Press, 2002), 79. See also, Margaret A. Farley, *Personal Commitments: Beginning, Keeping, Changing* (San Francisco: Harper and Row, 1986), 81–85.

31. Farley, *Compassionate Respect: A Feminist Approach to Medical Ethics and Other Questions* (New York: Paulist Press, 2002).

32. Farley, *Personal Commitments*, 82.

33. Margaret A. Farley, *Just Love: A Framework for Christian Sexual Ethics* (New York: Continuum, 2006), xi.

34. Parsons, *Ethics of Gender*, 170.

Part 1

Freedom-in-relation:
Autonomy, Relationality, Solidarity

INTRODUCTION

The essays in this first part treat the implications of globalization for contemporary Christian ethics and explore resources in feminist thought for a global Christian ethic. Together, they capture the landscape that Christian and feminist ethics now confront, as massive changes in the flow of people, information, and capital have generated both a growing sense of global interdependence and a heightened awareness of the diversity of moral contexts and languages across cultures and the risks of "moral imperialism." Lisa Sowle Cahill's essay traces the development of Margaret Farley's sexual ethic, showing first how it came to incorporate fundamental "second wave" feminist concerns for autonomy and embodiment (and thereby to challenge traditional religious norms for sexuality, marriage, and the family) but also how new global realities, for example, the AIDS pandemic, are giving rise to new forms of sexual ethics. Cahill shows how a long-standing focus on the social, economic, and political dimensions of sexuality in feminist sexual ethics allows it today to transcend the personal or private in a more radical sense, as it becomes "social-ethical action" across national borders. Essays by Serene Jones and Letty Russell draw on experiences of transnational feminist dialogue to explore the challenges and the promise of efforts to engage in practical feminist solidarity. Jones's reflections on a gathering of North American and Arab scholars in Women's Studies trace a path between the promise of common ground (more "a shared aesthetic and the space of imagination than principled moral claims") that coalesces in a "restless sense that the 'world is not as it should be' with respect to women's lives," and the impotence of theory to generate meaningful dialogue on the imperatives of justice. Russell sets her argument for the importance of developing a "feminist postcolonial practice of hospitality" (incorporating attentiveness to the power quotient within different cultural and racial groups involved, the perspective of the outsider, and the unfolding nature of God's promise of justice) within the experience of the Third Pan African Conference of the Circle of Concerned African Women Theologians. Both essays are realistic about the hard work involved in developing the sort of international partnerships for action against AIDS, poverty, and various forms of gendered violence suggested by a new, global sexual ethic, as well as about the perils of engaging in cross-cultural exchange. At the same time, we find in both essays the certainty that conversation and imagination can bring women (and women and men) together for a shared future in hope.

Also set in the African context, David Hollenbach's essay, "Human Rights and Women's Rights: Initiatives and Interventions in the Name of Universality," takes a feminist-inspired "common sexual morality" as a starting point for exploring the legitimacy of interventions in the name of women's rights. He argues that honoring cultural difference suggests humility in our conclusions about universal goods and harms. At the same time, following Farley's insistence on the possibility of "locations" of shared moral experience, he shows that some injustices "cry out over the borders," calling for careful but courageous alliances.

Chapter One

Feminist Theology and Sexual Ethics

Lisa Sowle Cahill

North American feminist theory originated with a commitment to women's autonomy and rights that emerged within and
employed the vocabulary of Western (North Atlantic) liberal political traditions. This commitment has helped define feminist theology.[1] But over the past decade and a half or so, feminism has shifted
into a postmodern gear in which cultural and experiential differences
among women have moved to the center of attention. The result has
been greater respect for women of cultures in the South, more self-
criticism by liberal feminists, and epistemological agnosticism about
the content of women's "needs" and "rights."[2] Both the liberal interest
in the self-determination of women and the postmodern attention to
social location and pluralism remain important constituents of feminist thought. At the same time, we have now entered a new phase in
which solidarity, dialogue and cooperative action by and for women
are inspiring renewed interest in finding "common ground" (if not
standards that are strictly "universal") in which to root effective transnational critique and advocacy by and for women around the world.[3]

Among theologians, Margaret Farley has been a leader in the development of feminist theology through these phases. From the beginning, she has held together in her own work the feminist "moments"
of liberal freedom, postmodern criticism, and moral commonality.

Setting the feminist motto, "the personal is political," in a theological context, she furthered the integration of the personal and social dimensions of ethics by subjecting specific behavioral norms as well as institutionalized practices to critique from the perspective of gender equality. Nowhere is this more evident than in her treatment of sexual morality. Farley analyzes the way theologically sanctioned institutions of marriage and family affect the personal situations of women. She also analyzes how power relations in and around these institutions affect the personal lives and possibilities of divorced Catholics, of gays and lesbians, and of women at risk for AIDS. She has moved her ethical theory ever more decisively into the realm of political action. The feminist theological connection between theory, solidarity, and practical political action is demonstrated in her commitment to improve the status of women and girls worldwide, a recent focus of which has been African women's vulnerability to HIV/AIDS.

This essay will accentuate the ways in which Farley has utilized resources in the Roman Catholic moral tradition to develop a feminist theological ethics and a sexual ethics that can meet the challenges of globalization. She employs concepts like moral freedom, common good, and social justice, as well as the idea that there are at least some basic dimensions of human experience and morality that are shared across cultures and eras. She reinterprets these elements in a way that is both historically critical and ecumenical, leading the way for many other Catholic, ecumenical feminist ethicists. A list of these would include, but hardly be limited to, Christine Gudorf, Barbara Hilkert Andolsen, Patricia Beattie Jung, Jean Porter, Anne Patrick, Leslie Griffin, Cathleen Kaveny, Cristina Traina, Maura Ryan, Mary Rose D'Angelo, Julie Hanlon Rubio, and myself. First, I shall explicate Farley's basic approach as a feminist theological ethicist, showing how she combines elements such as individual freedom along with the common good, the definition of a clear justice agenda along with nuanced attention to women's plural cultural situations, and postmodern social criticism along with basic shared values. Finally, I will apply this approach with its defining concerns to three issues of sexual ethics that Farley has addressed (marriage and family, homosexuality, AIDS), linking expectations and opportunities for personal behavior to social institutions, politics, and engagement for social change according to the norm of justice.

A FEMINIST THEOLOGICAL APPROACH

In 1996, Margaret Farley joined with fellow Catholic moral theologians Charles Curran and Richard McCormick to edit a book showcasing and advancing the work of Catholic feminist ethicists.[4] The two essays of Farley's own that were selected for this volume may reasonably be taken as paradigmatic of the themes and orientations she considers central to her work. In the volume's opening piece, Farley balances contrasting concepts to achieve a flexible and nuanced framework for feminist theology. For example, she signals a transition in feminist thought from a concern with women's general well-being to a growing recognition of women's diverse contexts.[5] Yet, despite diversity, she sees feminist ethics as reluctant to "altogether rule out universal norms."[6] Similarly, feminist ethics is based on "the principle of equality," and on individual rights and freedom, but it is equally committed to "the participation of all in human solidarity."[7] Christian feminists specifically are concerned with the virtues of agape and self-sacrifice, but, committed to the equality and solidarity of all, they are critical of the fact that historic Christianity has exalted suffering and exhorted it more for women than for men. Thus it is important for Christian feminists to insist on equality, mutuality, and justice in relationships, even though they see love, sacrifice, and care as virtues for both women and men.[8]

In a second essay, Farley responds constructively to the challenge of defining the meaning of just relationships by proposing a feminist reading of Kantian "respect for persons." Her interest in this fundamental, universal moral demand and its feminist application grows out of her perception that "total relativity of moral norms" is "unacceptable," given the need to seek justice for women across "boundaries of time and culture." Leaving open the possibility of multiple concrete fulfillments, she identifies two components of integral human beings that demand "respect"; these are "autonomy" and "relationality."[9] The end result is a normative vision of "freedom in relation,"[10] a move that retains liberal feminism's interest in the autonomy of women, but qualifies it by putting it in social and relational context. The criterion of relationship that is added to freedom reflects Catholic social tradition's premise of the sociality of the person, as well as the postmodern insight that all freedom, as well as all normative thinking and action, are influenced by their settings and guiding interests. The distinctively Christian component is Farley's understanding of freedom in relation as existing for the purpose of interpersonal love and for the building of communities that support liberation of persons for love and commitment.

These two essays outline a paradigm for Christian feminist ethics. At least three elements in this paradigm should be highlighted. These elements are central to advancing feminist theory and overcoming the separation of personal and social ethics. They also establish the basis on which Farley reflects about sexual ethics. These three elements are (1) *personal freedom*, set in the context of (2) the *common good*, and, in relation to both, what Farley terms (3) a *common morality*. This third element is her way of designating the fact that certain parameters of just personal and social relationships can and should serve as a platform for global advocacy for justice for women.

These three elements provide a basis for a Christian feminist sexual ethics in the following way. With contemporary Christian theology in general, Farley sees love, intimacy, and care as central moral meanings of sexuality. She then insists that just sexual relationships be established through (1) *free and responsible choice*, presupposing and enhancing the values of equality, mutuality and respect. Next, to protect and maintain free, loving, and just sexual relationships implies and requires (2) *justice in the social institutions* in which sexual relationships are formed, especially gender justice (for example, in marriage and family). Finally, the "preferential option for the poor" and solidarity with women worldwide implies that (3) *some basic moral values are shared* in different contexts, especially in regard to justice for women and justice in sexual relationships.

PERSONAL FREEDOM

The obvious reason for the prominence of autonomy and choice in the feminist agenda is the context of patriarchy that gave rise to feminism in the first place. Women historically have been defined by their sexual and reproductive roles in marriage and family, but, while these roles are held up as constituting women's essential identity, they are socially institutionalized in ways that bring women under the control of men. Women's right to make their own decisions about entering sexual relationships and about whether to become mothers is seen by feminists as necessary to women's equality with men and to the formation of truly just and mutual relationships between the sexes. One of the first and most influential Christian feminist ethicists, Beverly Harrison, entitled her major work *Our Right to Choose: Toward a New Ethic of Abortion*.[11] According to Harrison, "genuine liberation" for women entails "the integrity of centered self-direction in expressing our power of relationship. Our dignity as persons depends on that."[12]

In an article defining "sexism," Farley maintains that theories that men's and women's natures are complementary but equal has always resulted in the assignment to women of roles that are "subordinate, passive, and/or restricted to the private sphere."[13] This includes sexual roles, in which women's freedom to initiate, accept, or refuse sexual activity or commitments has been unequal to that of men. In an early article, Farley observes that such patterns of relationship are changing, gradually giving way to more equal roles for men and women in marriage, family, and sexuality, as well as in paid work and other public roles. As a theologian, Farley insists that self-sacrificial love or agape is a virtue, but it is equally normative for women and men. That excludes any understanding that would make women subordinate to men in love relationships or demand more self-sacrifice from women. Just personal relationships must be characterized by "equality, mutuality, and reciprocity."[14] All hierarchical models of gender must give way to collaborative models, in which "equality and freedom" structure "every interpersonal relationship."[15]

Farley's stress on the value of freedom aligns her position with the insights of liberal feminists. Yet it also has roots in the Catholic theological tradition of transcendental Thomism, a school that adapts the teleological moral psychology and metaphysics of Thomas Aquinas to explain the human experience of reaching toward an ever more comprehensive and ultimate horizon of love and knowledge. Writing in the middle decades of the twentieth century, around the same time that feminist theology gathered new force, Karl Rahner and Bernard Lonergan emphasized personal freedom as a religious and ethical category. In common with feminist theologians, they broke loose from oppressive theological constructions that distorted the nature of human responsibility.[16] They challenged traditional theologies that either overemphasized the captivity of the human person by sin, or made individual conscience unduly subordinate to ecclesiastical authorities and norms. Both these theologians reappropriate elements in Thomas Aquinas's analysis of human agency, especially his view that human knowledge, desires, and choices have an intrinsic self-transcending dynamic toward God as the origin and completion of all truth and goodness. Like Rahner, Farley uses human freedom as a primary concept to define agency; like Lonergan, she has long been interested in understanding the internal structure of freedom.[17] Like both of them, she utilizes resources in Aquinas to create a contemporary interpretation of freedom as expressed through relationship and commitment.[18] Farley's most important book thus far, *Personal Commitments*, is an exploration of the moral meaning of freedom-in-relationship, most prominently featuring, but certainly not limited to, commitment in sexual relationships.[19]

The focus of this book is on interpersonal commitments such as promises, contracts, covenants, and vows that have been explicitly and expressly undertaken.[20] In essence, Farley understands such commitments as consisting in a decision by one person to yield to another "a claim over my future free actions," a decision that also gives to the other "the power to limit my future freedom." A personal commitment provides "some reliability of expectation regarding the actions of free persons whose wills are shakable. It is to allow us some grounds for counting on one another."[21] The exploration of dimensions of such commitments is propelled by numerous vignettes interspersed through the text. These give Farley's reflections concreteness and texture, and serve as a reminder to the reader that her contentions about the moral power of commitments are experience-based.

The choice to commit oneself to another person (or community) arises out of a desire to orient one's future action in a certain way, a desire that ultimately springs from love. Committed love responds to the being of the other, and unites that person's being with one's own. The choice of commitment is a choice of what and how to love, and of how to shape one's life in the future in faithfulness to the object of one's love. This inevitably poses the moral dilemma of exit or release from commitments, if the object they once served is no longer loved, is loved less or differently, or if love for that object comes into conflict with other loves or duties. A related question is whether a commitment can cease to be binding in its original form and yet retain some sort of a lesser or at least different moral claim on those who originally entered it. Farley makes the point that the claim of a commitment goes beyond a simple calculation of the relative goods and harms that will result from breaking or keeping it. The very fact of having made a commitment creates a certain bias in favor of a relationship. Even a decision to divorce, for example, does not abrogate all obligations to one's former spouse, and certainly not to the children for whom former spouses will together still share the relationship of parent.[22]

For Farley, the question of whether or not a commitment serves a "just love," or in what form it can do so, is fundamental.[23] She believes "a love is right and good insofar as it aims to affirm truthfully the concrete reality of the other."[24] A just love affirms the equality of persons while still attending to the differences in their own needs, capabilities, and other commitments. When the reality of relationship to another person changes, the commitment too can change or even cease. Under three conditions, a person is released from the claim of a commitment: (1) when it becomes impossible to sustain, (2) when it no longer serves the larger purpose which justified it in the first place, or (3) when the obligation of another commitment conflicts with or supersedes the obligation now in question.[25] A distinctive emphasis of Farley's analysis is the inclusion of self-love within the definition of a just commitment to another. Personal commitment inevitably involves self-sacrifice, but sacrifice has moral limits. Obligations to ourselves can and often do set limits on commitments to others and even justify release from the obligations that commitments bring.[26] Theologically, Farley's interpretation of commitment is patterned by God's unconditional covenant of love with human persons. This covenant makes human commitments possible, but also relativizes them. God's commitment makes possible "the breaking of otherwise insurmountable barriers between persons." Yet fidelity in commitment is given us provisionally, and we are not able to fulfill it perfectly within the limits of finite, historical existence.[27]

While the approach of *Personal Commitments* privileges individual decision making, Farley expands on the larger social and institutional context of personal decisions in her reply to a symposium on the book in the journal *Horizons*. She reiterates her "concern for individual free choice," but calls further attention to the communal conditions of possibility for making and keeping commitments that are implied by biblical covenant symbolism. She also develops the point that the Church as an institution can provide either negative or positive communal conditions of sustaining commitments to marriage and religious life.[28] In a recent work (primarily on bioethics), Farley states clearly that autonomy is a necessary ethical principle but not a sufficient one. Many feminist bioethicists have complemented it with a principle of "care." Care ethics also works primarily with relations between individuals. Therefore, it is necessary to move to a concept that highlights the sociality of persons and the place of individual relations within social institutions as part of the meaning of justice.[29]

THE COMMON GOOD

In fact, the common good has always been operative as a theological-ethical criterion in Margaret Farley's work, even when she is focusing on individual freedom. The "common good" provides the meaning of justice for social relations, and in a way that also includes the personal good of every individual member of society.[30] In principle, the notion of the common good complements an idea of justice as fairness to individuals with an idea of justice as rightly ordered social relations. Hence, it overcomes any possible dichotomy between personal and social justice, since the two are interdependent. Early on in her career, Margaret Farley identified sex and gender as areas in need of change, not only because they have been "based on inaccurate understandings of human persons" and "preventive of individual growth," but because they have been "inhibitive of the common good" and "conducive to social injustices."[31] More explicitly,

> From the standpoint of the Roman Catholic ethical tradition, it is a mistake to pit individual good against the good of the community, or the social good, when what is at stake is the fundamental dignity of the individual. If it is the case, then, that the reality of woman is such that a just love of her demands that she be accorded fundamental personal rights, including equality of opportunity in the public world, then to deny her those rights is inevitably to harm the common good.[32]

Farley's 2000 presidential address to the Catholic Theological Society of America treats sex and gender ethics in relation to the common good. This statement is an excellent illustration of the connection of social to personal justice, and also of the importance of taking positions on sex and gender that not only are consistent along the line from personal to social but are well integrated with positions that bear on other aspects of the common good. This address identifies ways in which what ought to be the Catholic Church's "prophetic witness" on social issues is undermined by the incoherence of the way in which these issues are prioritized, and by the unpersuasiveness of the Church's positions on abortion, on women's rights, and on gender roles in the Church. Worse, all of these get more attention as "Catholic" positions than issues like racism, welfare reform, war and peace, or exploitation of the environment. Another obstacle to an effective Catholic social witness is the procedures by which discourse on these topics is repressed within the Church. According to Farley, it is true that "the church has been in some political arenas a major voice for the inclusion of women's rights and needs in considerations of the common good and in programs for the development of peoples." However, "It is also true that the church's worries about contraception and abortion (and, one might add, the church's refusal to allow women full participation in church ministry and governance) have undercut its best efforts in this regard."[33]

Part of the point here is that there can be no "personal" justice for women if norms on abortion (and selected other sexual issues) are promoted absolutely without acknowledging ongoing debates about the historical development of "doctrine," about the status of very early human life, or about the possible ways in which abortions could be seen as "indirect" and hence justified under the principle of double effect. There can be no justice for women on abortion or contraception if individual actions and circumstances are judged in a way that does not view the problems of women, mothers, and children in the larger social context that is still unfortunately marred by sexism. The Catholic Church will not be a convincing advocate for personal justice for women if it brands as "radical feminists" anyone who raises questions about "official" teaching, and fails to put social justice for women and other oppressed groups at the top of its agenda, ahead of conformity to specific teachings on abortion and contraception, Farley insists. Only if women and men can interact in just institutions will they be able to attain justice in their personal relationships. Just social practices are the condition of possibility of achieving justice in ongoing personal commitments; just personal relationships realize and concretize the common good as a social-ethical concept and criterion.

COMMON MORALITY

Precisely because the common good is always made real and specific at the local and personal level, the details of just moral practices cannot be prescribed in any "universal" way. Feminist critiques of patriarchal models of gender, sex, and society have made it clear that these models were motivated by the objective of establishing and keeping in place a gender-unequal set of social institutions. Feminist critiques have made it equally clear that any model of society or justice will reflect the interests and power relations responsible for creating it, and so cannot be entirely "objective." Nevertheless, it is important to feminist social ethics to identify at least in a general way some criteria by which social arrangements can be declared more or less just or unjust. Farley calls her own view "a 'chastened realism,' one that acknowledges the partiality of all knowledge and the influence of social constructions of meaning on all that we know, but that nevertheless keeps looking to understand things as they are, as best as we can."[34] An important insight of feminist theologies and philosophies of liberation is that, although criteria of justice must correspond to the true reality of women,[35] its specifics should be decided dialogically, with the participation of all who will be affected by the results, and with special attention to those who have been excluded from the process in the past. Feminist criteria for just relationships and societies will necessarily be inductive and revisable, but will still aim toward greater inclusiveness and representative validity, across interest groups, classes, races, and cultures.

In an essay on bioethics, Farley develops the category of "embodiment," a category that has figured fairly prominently in recent feminist thinking about sex. It is a category that connotes dimensions of human materiality, of human vulnerability, needs, and goods—like vulnerability to illness and death, needs for shelter and nutrition, and goods like food, clean water, and health care—that are recognized in every culture.[36] At the same time, embodiment is also partly a socially "constructed" concept—how peoples and cultures experience needs and vulnerabilities, and how access to goods is socially arranged, differ widely. Feminist thinking reclaims women's perspectives on the realities of embodiment, and insists that women's articulated experiences of their own bodies provide the primary content of those aspects of female embodiment that are agreed to be shared.[37]

In her presidential address to the Society of Christian Ethics, Farley takes up the way in which postmodernism problematizes the very idea that there are culturally invariant or even recognizably similar experiences of the human body, or even a stable "self" that subsists beyond or beneath the influences of language, culture, and history.[38] Farley takes postmodern concerns seriously, but is not ready to give up on the possibility that there is "something real and enduring" in other beings and ourselves that allows for the possibility of connection and of love.[39] A moral theory that concedes the impossibility of transcending power relations enough to define indispensable moral values would "leave feminism without the tools for a universal critique of structures of domination and subordination."[40]

To the contrary, Farley is convinced that human persons do experience moral claims based on "some commonality in human experience—in the experience of what it means as a human person to rejoice and to be sorrowful, to be protected or violated, nurtured or stifled, understood or misjudged, respected or used." In 1990, Farley traveled to China as part of a group of twenty theologians who aimed to learn more about Christianity in China and about the situation of Chinese women. She begins a brief essay on her experiences there by quoting from the poet Li Ch'ing-chao. She then adds that these words of a twelfth-century Chinese woman provide some evidence that "whatever the distance between peoples, whatever the diversity between our experiences and our histories, there are profound human emotions and understandings that we can share."[41] Despite cultural differences and rifts in the world community, "it is nonetheless possible for human persons to weep over commonly felt tragedies, laugh over commonly perceived incongruities, yearn for common hopes." Though it may not be possible to devise long or detailed specific lists of justice's requirements, "it is possible to condemn commonly recognized injustices and act for commonly desired goals."[42]

One virtually unavoidable locus for human connection, even in a postmodern world, is suffering and its ability to evoke sympathy and compassion. Suffering places moral claims that are not wholly relativized by cultural difference; "responsibility crosses borders that we do not expect."[43] Compassion as a moral unifier is further developed in a monograph on bioethics, in which Farley links compassion to a principle that has always been fundamental in her thought: respect. The affective response of compassion reveals "an assumption of more acute access to knowledge of the concrete reality of others."[44] The ability to suffer with others implies recognition of the reality of their value. Compassion adds to respect an emotional connection, impelling us to take practical action to ensure that the needs of the respected other are concretely met. On the other side, respect helps ensure that compassionate action will correspond to the reality of the other, not violate his or her autonomy, and aid the decision maker to navigate justly among competing obligations.

SEXUAL ETHICS

Margaret Farley's discussions of sexual ethics are not concerned primarily with disputes over old rules or the development of new ones. Most of all, she begins from a stance of compassionate respect for persons and places sexual behavior in the context of social institutions guiding or controlling sexuality. She then discerns whether normative socially mandated practices serve the freedom of human persons and the mutuality, equality, and strength of their relationships. Sexual behavior is integrated into the common good if sexual practices are just both toward individuals and toward the needs of society as a whole.

The link in Farley's thought between a postmodern critique and a reaffirmation of a sexual common morality is in a point that she emphasizes repeatedly in her writings on sex: even though Christian tradition has nurtured a deep suspicion of the body and sex, human sexual embodiment should be accepted and appreciated as good, and as enabling a profound form of personal commitment.[45] Although with a postmodern critical eye Farley "deconstructs" the "normative" Christian vision of sex, her confidence that there are some "truths" of embodied experience still allows her to insist that the body and sexuality are loci of human goodness and moral value. In an overview of sexual ethics in the Christian tradition, Farley comments that the prevalent note has been affirmation of sex as created good, along with wariness due to the fact that, since sexuality is flawed by sin, "the force of sexual passion cannot be controlled by reason." Hence, celibacy has been advocated as the ideal, even though sex in marriage has been justified for the purpose of procreation, a purpose determined primarily with reference to biological function and hemmed in with numerous specific rules. "Overall, the Christian tradition in the first half of its history developed a consistently negative view of sex."[46]

Turning to the "ethical reconstruction" of sexuality, Farley observes that multiple meanings can be recognized, including "pleasure, reproduction, communication, love, conflict, social stability, and so on." She then adds that most theorists recognize that guidance for sexual behavior is necessary to reduce its potential for evil and enhance its capacity for good. "Safety, nonviolence, equality, autonomy, mutuality, and truthfulness are generally acknowledged as required for minimal human justice in sexual relationships. Many think that care, responsibility, commitment, love, and fidelity are also required, or at least included as goals."[47] Clearly these are all general values, and unanimity is not guaranteed for any on the list, especially those on the second half, in Farley's apparent view. One might also observe that the values identified as key by Farley all concern the quality of relationship between sexual partners, and that two other values, perhaps tied even more strongly to human sexual embodiment—pleasure and reproduction—do not appear as "minimums" or as "goals," or even as "enhancements."

Farley herself is well aware that "readings" of sexual meaning and value always arise from a standpoint, which is precisely why discernment and consensus on sexual morality must arise from a dialogical process. In a conference presentation, Farley identified experience as one important source of sexual ethics but situated it among other sources, such as Scripture, tradition, and secular disciplines, including philosophy, sociology, biology, history, and literature. Experience is a dialogical source in another sense as well. It conveys the actual lived reality of events and relationships, as reality emerges from the interplay of events themselves and of the perspectives of different participants. Experience is always mediated and particular to persons and groups; it is shaped by past realities and by the understanding of past and present reality with which present subjects operate. Yet it can be shared, brought into conversation with the experiences of others, and in the process reappropriated, corrected, or expanded.[48]

While Farley extends the concept of common morality to sexual ethics, that concept remains flexible and open enough to admit of different specifications of normative or acceptable behavior. Yet it remains definite enough to rule out offenses to human dignity in sexual relationships, such as dishonesty, coercion, or violence.

MARRIAGE AND FAMILY

Her essays on the family confirm that Farley regards the social contexts of personal behavior as highly important in defining possibilities for behavior and its morality. Recent cultural and religious movements have attempted to reinstate "traditional family values" in response to a supposed "decline" in the status and future of the two-parent nuclear family. Farley has resisted the attempts of the Catholic Church and others to deal with family crisis by reasserting specific norms about family behavior, specifically sexual behavior. This includes absolute prohibitions of divorce, remarriage after divorce, childbearing outside of marriage, same-sex unions, and premarital sex.

A fundamental problem is that Christian attitudes toward both family and marriage have been ambivalent. The New Testament relativizes family in favor of faith commitment and discipleship. Christian tradition, with its strain of negativity toward the body and sex, and its assumption that women are inferior to men, gave family life second-class status and subjected it to rules having mainly to do with control of sexual behavior and women. Thus heterosexual, procreative, and patriarchal marriage was promulgated as the general norm for those who could not remain celibate. While transgressions of this norm were condemned, it was generally assumed that the internal structure of the family (so defined) was just. Catholic social teaching, for example, saw this structure as natural, and saw the family so structured as a basic institution on which society and its welfare are built. On this family model, women are confined to the domestic sphere, with primary responsibility for childrearing, while men go forth from the family to engage in public work. Despite this division of expertise, however, the authority of men has reigned supreme, even within the domestic circle. While this ethical framework for family life has deservedly come under challenge, Farley agrees that the churches can and should speak a message of hope to families confronting difficulty.[49]

Farley herself concurs that families are under pressure, in at least four ways: family violence; "structural" problems of family relationship, involving gender, the elderly, and the role of children; breakdown and divorce; and the dependence of families on economic, social, and political systems that seem increasingly inhospitable.[50] Farley's own response is to correct the traditional Catholic downplaying of the value of the family in comparison to celibacy, learn from the Reformation valuation of family as a holy way of life under God, and to "discern action-guides" for family life "from the vantage point of our call to make the family, as every other institution, a place of justice."[51] Most obviously, this rules out violence in the family. The churches must overcome their tendency to acquiesce in, or even to encourage, domestic abuse in the name of the "subordination" of women, and must instead support healing for those struggling against it.

As far as structure is concerned, Farley also identifies the patriarchal, subordinationist family as a source of problems. Mutual partnership in marriage and parenthood is an obvious value; the church must recognize that its advocacy for mutuality in marriage and family will suffer in effectiveness unless it can model gender equality internally. Beyond this, the churches must move toward the ideal of intact, equal, and mutual families, while accepting and supporting families who do not seem to follow the idealized structure. Farley traces the high rate of divorce to the modern transition to a marriage culture in which partners have unrealistic expectations about their ability to fulfill all of one another's needs. While she supports the ideal of permanent commitment in marriage, she believes the law forbidding divorce should have more a "pedagogical" than "coercive" function. That is, it should "guide to mutuality, communication, accountability, to integrity, and trust and justice." While it can encourage promise-keeping, it cannot require commitment beyond what it is possible to sustain.[52] In its ability to sustain relationship, commitment, and the nurturing of members, the family is highly dependent on surrounding institutions. Lack of meaningful economic and social support for families leads to family friction and dysfunction; "norms of just distribution of goods and services in society must be appealed to if families are to be supported and healed."[53]

While the strengthening and healing of families may be the goal, the dissolution of marriages, if not families, is a reality the churches cannot afford to ignore. And if their response is unrealistically and alienatingly harsh, their opportunity to bring the gospel of reconciliation and renewal to divorced persons will be wasted. Farley's work on divorce has concentrated on Roman Catholic teaching and its pastoral effects, since the absoluteness of this particular ecclesial communion's teaching against divorce is exceeded by no other Christian church. She also notes with many others that actual practice of Catholics and the tide of theological opinion fail to confirm the stringency of the official teaching.[54]

While Farley's approach to family life is highly institutional and social in its orientation, placing families in the context of the common good, her approach to divorce recenters her ongoing analysis of the components of commitment. Her point of departure is the fact that Catholic teaching on marriage associates its formation and also its indissolubility with the human reality and fact of consent, as provided (actually, reasserted) in the 1983 Code of Canon Law. Marriage, like other commitments, initiates a form of new relationship in which the covenanting parties agree to bind themselves to future actions, placing themselves under the claim of their decision, of the relationship it initiates, and of their covenanting partner. In the Christian view of marriage, the parties also commit themselves to God and to the church, as well as to the larger society.[55]

A marriage may be "impossible" if conditions have so deteriorated that reconciliation is indeed out of the question. Although renewal of the commitment, and acceptance of imperfect marriages as part of the tragic aspect of life, may both have a role to play in avoiding divorce, Farley still believes that "a 'threshold' of real impossibility does exist."[56] If marriage ceases to serve its *raison d'etre*, "to serve love for spouses, for family, for society, for God," the very fact of a commitment to love may demand that the marriage must be ended.[57] Finally, some other serious obligation may supersede the obligation of marriage, the most important of which would be obligations to one's children or to one's own psychological or physical survival.[58] Even though remarriage may be warranted in many cases, a shared "bodily" and "spiritual" bonding, as well as a history together, and the ongoing project of parenting children, all continue to exist and to make some moral claims even on divorced and remarried persons.[59]

GAY AND LESBIAN RELATIONSHIPS

While many Christian ethicists have modified theologically traditional teaching on divorce and even on the family, Farley's advocacy
for compassion and respect for gays and lesbians has been unusually
pathbreaking and courageous. These efforts have been both practical and theological. For example, in 1996, she was interviewed by
students at Yale Divinity about her longstanding support for the Gay,
Lesbian, Bisexual Coalition; in 2002, a *Boston Globe* interview noted
her award from New Ways Ministry, and elicited her further support for gay persons in the Catholic Church.[60] One of Farley's most
acclaimed essays is one in which she endeavors to provide "an ethic
for same-sex relations," and in the process—and in the name of consistency—comes up with an ethic for "opposite sex" relations too.[61]
A distinctive aspect of this essay is that it is composed not as an attack on traditional Church teaching but as an endeavor to find support
and encouragement for homosexuals who remain Catholic and turn to
Christianity for moral guidance.

As on the family, Farley relies on multiple sources of insight. She
concludes that neither the Old nor New Testaments provide absolutely
clear and certain direction about whether same-sex sexual activity
can ever be justified. Uncertainty of the meaning of certain terms,
differences in the cultural significance of homosexuality in biblical
times compared to our own, and apparently conflicting texts are all
part of the picture. Moreover, no biblical text could out of context
serve as a clear and final prohibition, without balancing wisdom from
other sources. Turning to tradition, Farley notes two dominant motifs: procreation as the primary justification for sex and the essential
criterion of male-female complementarity. Observing that the procreative norm is gone, and that the complementarity criterion has
been softened by modern ideals of reciprocity in marriage and sex,
Farley moves on to "secular disciplines," such as the social and natural
sciences. Here she draws on evidence that homosexuality has not been
scientifically demonstrated to be harmful to persons, same-sex preference appears "natural" to some persons, sexual orientation exists on
a continuum, and in any event same-sex orientation does not mean

the rejection of maleness and femaleness. More importantly, sexuality in general has come to be understood as a natural drive, important to the dynamic of human personality. Finally, contemporary experience shows that "homosexuality can be a way of embodying responsible human love and sustaining Christian friendship."[62] Therefore, Farley finds no reason to exclude homosexual relationships from the ambit of the Christian moral life; she proceeds to develop norms that can apply consistently to homosexual and to heterosexual unions.

This she approaches in terms of "a justice ethic for the sexual sphere of human life," featuring the twin criteria so central to her work: autonomy and relationality.[63] Her proposals here are coherent with her other work on sexual ethics. The norms of ethically commendable sexual behavior and relationships are freedom, mutuality, equality, and commitment; sexual desire and pleasure do not exist for their own sakes but for the purpose of relationship. Commitment seems the best context for a humanly rewarding, pleasurable, and long-term experience of sexual relationship. While in the past the tendency of sex to escape control was seen as the major moral problem, today apathy and alienation can be equally problematic for the human fulfillment of sex. Justice in sex means not only observation of limits, but nurturing sexual desire and affection through "a shared life and an enduring love."[64] While procreation is not an absolute norm for all sexual relationships, and not a norm that excludes gay relationships, Farley here acknowledges responsible procreation as a moral concern. Sexual relationships that do not produce children can still be fruitful by opening to "a wider community of persons" in forms of service and other social contributions.[65]

Sexual morality, homosexual or heterosexual, is not just a personal matter. Sexual relationships have social effects; the common good must include a just setting for sexual practices. Farley considers a more receptive Christian attitude to the morality of the relationships of gays and lesbians to be essential to social justice, and to the clear condemnation of violence toward homosexuals. Fair domestic partnership legislation is discouraged by negative religious judgments on gay sexual activity, even if churches and theologians do not condemn social protection for gay unions outright. "Teachings of unnatural sex, disordered desire, and threatening love" encourage "gay-bashing," and must be reversed, or the churches will collude in "the hatred, rejection, and stigmatization of gays and lesbians." Laws protecting gay unions and according gays full civil rights are essential to protect "basic human needs—needs for psychic security, economic security, and sometimes physical safety."[66]

HIV/AIDS

Farley opens *Compassionate Respect* with an account of her participation in a White House Summit Conference for World AIDS Day, December 1, 2000, that was focused on the role of religious traditions in addressing the spread of AIDS in economically and politically marginal nations in the southern hemisphere. This event was the impetus for a major venture, under Farley's leadership, to bring together women from North America, Africa, and Europe so that they could collaborate in fighting the causes and effects of AIDS. A major target of this project is cultural and religious silence about sexual attitudes and practices that make women more vulnerable to AIDS. This project is a magnificent case study in the tie of theory to action, and of social to personal ethics. "Compassionate respect" is a phrase that newly renders Farley's norm of "just love," and especially accentuates the theme of suffering as a recognizable human reality evoking emotion, identification with the concrete situation of the other, and action.

In *Compassionate Respect*, social institutions and practices "around" sex are really the starting place for an ethical critique of the specific sexual behavior that causes AIDS. Religion has been complicit in, and even promoted, attitudes and practices that contribute to the rise of AIDS. The silence around sexual behavior, marital fidelity, sexual orientation, and prostitution "represents a deep shame that comes from the breaking of perceived taboos," a silence that persists even when "the taboos are customarily broken." Because of this shame and silence, feelings of self-blame and social stigmatization are displaced, projected onto others, and victimize substitutes or scapegoats who are more vulnerable, with fewer social protections—women and girls.

"Stories abound, for example, of the exile or even stoning of married women infected by their husbands, and of unmarried women raped and infected by men who think that sex with virgins will prevent or cure their own infection by the AIDS virus."[67] Colluding with the cultural and religious sources of silencing shame are those people, nations, and organizations that control resources but that do not want to admit that they too are partly responsible for the causes of AIDS, which include poverty that contributes to AIDS by disrupting traditional families and rural life, longstanding oppression of women that renders them powerless in the face of male sexual demands or social exclusion, and rigidly controlling and condemnatory views of human sexual behavior and failings.

Farley concludes that "an uncritical imposition of traditional rules can ignore the genuine requirements of justice and truth in sexual relationships," and that this "is no longer sufficient."[68] Nor is it acceptable to perpetuate gender patterns that keep women economically dependent on men and subservient to them, patterns that prevent women from making decisions about sexual relations, safe sex, health care, or transmission of the virus to newborns. A compassionate, just, and hopeful exercise of the preferential option for the poor demands that religious traditions in particular take a radically new attitude, committing resources, empowering the economically and politically poor (especially women), and placing sexual morality in the context of much larger conditions of social function and dysfunction.[69]

To proclaim the preferential option for the poor as a theologian is one thing, and to put it into practice is another. The theological claim that this option is central to Christian identity is meaningless unless Christians exercise it; equally important, hope for change cannot take root without some confidence that theological insights come out of and inspire new practices that are actually making a difference. As a result of her observation that religious leaders at the White House spoke about, and even with, compassion but failed to identify a concrete action agenda to confront issues of power, poverty, and sexuality, Farley resolved to take action. The result was an interfaith Consultation for twenty-five women from the U.S., Canada, and Africa, held in 2002 at Yale Divinity School, in partnership with USAID. Another follow-up project is an ongoing research fellowship program for African women theologians, who spend a semester at Yale doing interdisciplinary work on the AIDS crisis.

More importantly, and on a truly massive scale, Farley spearheaded three conferences in Africa (the first in 2003) to bring African women together with supporters from other continents to share perspectives and develop solutions to the exploitation of women in the AIDS crisis. Under the title "All-Africa Conference, Sister to Sister" (AACSS), these conferences are directed primarily at members of Roman Catholic women's religious congregations and their lay co-workers. Support is sought from women's religious orders, especially in the U.S., with the Sisters of Mercy providing a large initial grant. The rationale and prospectus for the conferences include the following.

> African women are powerful in themselves, yet in response to the AIDS pandemic they have been limited by lack of resources to come together. They are thus prevented from sharing experiences, identifying obstacles, and promoting leadership in the planning and implementing of concerted responses. . . . What the Sisters want is a prayerful atmosphere, a building of trust among them, and the opportunity to examine—in the context of AIDS—relevant aspects of religious life, faith, personal dignity, powerlessness, and sexuality. . . . [T]hey hope to enter a process of freeing and empowering one another to confront the external conditions that constrain and burden them. . . . The presumption from the start was that the agenda for the conferences would have to be in the hands of African women religious . . . all who work together on this have achieved and will sustain a collaborative, cross-culture, approach.[70]

Of special interest here is the fact that the project represents a new form of Christian sexual ethics as social-ethical action for an era of globalization. Certainly commonality within difference among these women is clear. Also in evidence is the positive operation of transnational institutions—the Roman Catholic Church and women's religious orders, especially the Sisters of Mercy—to combat a global problem traceable at least in part to the exploits of market capitalism.

Although there is no one "universal" world order or government that can control either economic globalization or the AIDS crisis, some forms of intervention for an alternate order are emerging. Some of these have transnational or global reach, and are beginning to correct at least some of the injustices of globalization. Religious traditions and women's advocacy groups, far from being paralyzed in the face of global injustice, can marshal their own resources, cooperate with other public and private organizations, and begin to change the global picture of human suffering through concrete compassionate action. Having received money from the U.S. government, AACSS began to develop partnerships with Catholic Relief Services: CAFOD in the UK, Tocaire in Ireland, and the Jesuit agency for AIDS in Africa.

This project is the epitome if not yet the culmination of Margaret Farley's feminist theological ethics and of her work in sexual ethics. First, an aim of AACSS is to enhance the *personal freedom* of women in Africa to make decisions about and take responsibility for their own sexual actions and for their maternal and family roles. It also aims to empower African women to discern their own situation and needs and to work collaboratively so that needs can be met, opportunities created, and potential fulfilled. Second, AACSS represents a commitment to the *common good* of all persons in African societies, and to the good of global society, enhanced by the participation of women as contributors and beneficiaries, and by the cooperation of women across borders. Sexuality in the perspective of this project is not just about individual agreements or personal fulfillment; it is about justice in social roles and institutions that endow sex with its cultural meaning, and that organize sex in relation to economics and politics. Third, African women meet and work with women (and men) from other continents who are sympathetic with the African situation and concerns because they recognize the experiences and needs of African women as being analogous to their own. Though situations of women in such different cultural settings are hardly identical, there is enough commonality to ground a *common morality* of equality and justice for women, and of respect and mutuality in sexual relationships. Just as importantly, the sense of shared meaning among North American, European and African women can motivate action and marshal resources to alleviate suffering. Finally, as a Christian theologian, Margaret Farley highlights and exemplifies the virtues of love and compassion extending across the boundaries of culture, taking shape in new patterns of relationship that both reveal the meaning of solidarity in action and provide hope for the future.

NOTES

1. A philosophical example is Susan Moller Okin, *Justice, Gender, and the Family* (New York: HarperCollins, 1989); a theological example is Beverly Harrison, *Our Right to Choose: Toward a New Ethic of Abortion* (Boston: Beacon Press, 1983).

2. A philosophical example is Uma Narayan and Sandra Harding, eds., *Decentering the Center: Philosophy for a Multicultural, Postcolonial, and Feminist World* (Bloomington: Indiana University Press, 2000); a theological example is Mary McClintock Fulkerson, *Changing the Subject: Women's Discourses and Feminist Theology* (Minneapolis: Fortress Press, 1994).

3. A philosophical example is Martha Nussbaum, *Women and Human Development: The Capabilities Approach* (New York: Cambridge University Press, 2000); a theological example is Cristina Traina, *Feminism and Natural Law: The End of the Anathemas* (Washington, DC: Georgetown University Press, 1999).

4. Charles E. Curran, Margaret A. Farley, and Richard A. McCormick, S.J., eds., *Feminist Ethics and the Catholic Moral Tradition*, Readings in Moral Theology 9 (New York: Paulist Press, 1996).

5. "Feminist Ethics," in Curran, Farley, and McCormick, *Feminist Ethics*, 6. This essay was originally published in 1986 in the *Westminster Dictionary of Christian Ethics.*

6. Ibid., 9.

7. Ibid., 8.

8. Ibid., 9–10.

9. Margaret A. Farley, "A Feminist Version of Respect for Persons," in Curran, Farley, and McCormick, *Feminist Ethics,* 166–67. This essay originally appeared in the *Journal of Feminist Studies in Religion* in 1993.

10. Ibid., 178.

11. Beverly Wildung Harrison, *Our Right to Choose: Toward a New Ethic of Abortion* (Boston: Beacon Press, 1983).

12. Ibid., 106.

13. M. Farley and L. Harrington, "Sexism," in *New Catholic Encyclopedia*, 13:51 (New York: Thomson-Gale, 2003). This is a revised version

of Farley's 1979 entry. See also Margaret A. Farley, "Sources of Sexual Inequality in the History of Christian Thought," *Journal of Religion* 56 (April 1976): 164–66, 174.

14.   Margaret A. Farley, "New Patterns of Relationship: Beginnings of a Moral Revolution," in *Woman: New Dimensions*, ed. Walter Burghardt (New York: Paulist Press, 1977), 70. This volume was originally published as an issue of *Theological Studies* in 1975.

15.   Farley, "Sources of Sexual Inequality," 176.

16.   Among their works, Farley calls attention to Karl Rahner, "The Dignity and Freedom of Man," in *Theological Investigations*, vol. 2 (Baltimore: Helicon Press, 1966), 235–64; and Bernard J. F. Lonergan, *Insight: A Study of Human Understanding* (New York: Philosophical Library, 1958). These citations are given in Margaret A. Farley, "Freedom and Desire," in *The Papers of the Henry Luce III Fellows in Theology*, vol. 3, ed. Matthew Zyniewicz (Atlanta: Scholars Press, 1999), 71n1.

17.   "Freedom and Desire" is an example of an analysis of the dynamic structure of freedom. Farley also acknowledges a debt to Jules Toner (*The Experience of Love* [Washington, Corpus Books, 1968]) in analyzing the structure of freedom and choice; see Farley "Freedom and Desire," 73n14.

18.   Margaret A. Farley, "Fragments for an Ethic of Commitment in Thomas Aquinas," *Journal of Religion* 58 (Supplement 1978): 40–45.

19.   Margaret A. Farley, *Personal Commitments: Beginning, Keeping, Changing* (San Francisco: Harper and Row, 1986).

20.   Ibid., 15.

21.   Ibid., 18, 19.

22.   Ibid., 68.

23.   Ibid., 70.

24.   Ibid., 82.

25.   Ibid., 84.

26.   Ibid., 106.

27.   Ibid., 113.

28.   Margaret A. Farley, "Author's Response," *Horizons* 15 (1988): 134, 136, 137–39.

29.   Margaret A. Farley, *Compassionate Respect: A Feminist Approach to Medical Ethics and Other Questions* (New York: Paulist Press, 2002), 24–39.

30.   For a discussion of the meaning of the common good in Catholic social teaching, see David Hollenbach, S.J., *The Common Good and Christian Ethics* (Cambridge: Cambridge University Press, 2002).

31.   Farley, "New Patterns of Relationship," 52.

32.   Ibid., 68.

33.   Margaret A. Farley, "The Church in the Public Forum: Scandal or Prophetic Witness?" *Proceedings of the Catholic Theological Society of America*

55 (2000): 91. On these topics, see also Margaret Farley, "Power and Powerlessness: A Case in Point," *Proceedings of the Catholic Theological Society of America* 37 (1982): 116–19. Here Farley discusses ecclesiastical actions against members of the Religious Sisters of Mercy of the Union, who as sponsors of Catholic hospitals had come into direct conflict with the magisterium on the issue of tubal ligation.

34. Farley, *Compassionate Respect*, 90n28.

35. Ibid., 28–39.

36. The philosopher Martha Nussbaum has developed a similar approach to moral commonality that she calls "the capabilities approach." Farley cites Nussbaum in *Compassionate Respect*, 60–65.

37. Margaret A. Farley, "Feminist Theology and Bioethics," in *Feminist Theological Ethics: A Reader*, ed. Lois K. Daly (Louisville, KY: Westminster John Knox Press, 1994), 198–200. For the critique that feminism has also falsely universalized all women's experience, assimilating actual differences to a white, middle-class Western paradigm, see Margaret A. Farley, "Feminism and Universal Morality," in *Prospects for a Common Morality*, ed. Gene Outka and John P. Reeder, Jr. (Princeton, NJ: Princeton University Press, 1993), 177.

38. Margaret A. Farley, "How Shall We Love in a Postmodern World," *The Annual of the Society of Christian Ethics* 14 (1994): 7.

39. Ibid., 9.

40. Farley, "Feminism and Universal Morality," 177.

41. Margaret A. Farley, "A New Form of Communion: Feminism and the Chinese Church," *America* 164 (1991): 199.

42. Ibid., 178.

43. Ibid., 18.

44. Farley, *Compassionate Respect*, 39.

45. See especially "Sexual Ethics," in *Encyclopedia of Bioethics*, 5:2363–75 (New York: Simon and Schuster Macmillan, 1995), and "Sources of Sexual Inequality."

46. Farley, "Sexual Ethics," 2367.

47. Ibid., 2374.

48. Margaret A. Farley, "Experience as a Source for Sexual Ethics," (unpublished panel presentation, Catholic Theological Society of America, 1992).

49. Margaret A. Farley, "Family," in *New Dictionary of Catholic Social Thought*, ed. Judith A. Dwyer 371–81 (Collegeville, MN: Liturgical Press, 1994).

50. Margaret A. Farley, "The Church and the Family: An Ethical Task," *Horizons* 10 (1983): 52.

51. Ibid., 70.

52. Ibid., 69.

53. Ibid., 70.

54. Margaret A. Farley, "The Concept of Commitment as Applied to Questions of Marriage and Divorce," *Proceedings of the Canon Law, Society of America* 54 (1992): 87.

55. Ibid., 90.

56. Ibid., 93.

57. Ibid., 93.

58. Ibid., 94.

59. Ibid., 96.

60. K. C. Choi and Rick Richardson, "Interview with Margaret Farley: Reflections on Yale Divinity School and the GLSB Coalition," transcript provided by K.C. Choi; Rich Barlow, "Arguing for a Consistent Sexual Ethic," *Boston Globe*, Nov. 23, 2002, B2.

61. Margaret A. Farley, "An Ethic for Same-Sex Relations," in *A Challenge to Love: Gay and Lesbian Catholics in the Church*, ed. Robert Nugent (New York: Crossroad, 1983).

62. Ibid., 100.

63. Ibid., 100–101.

64. Ibid., 103.

65. Ibid., 104–5.

66. Margaret A. Farley, "Response to James Hanigan and Charles Curran," in *Sexual Orientation and Human Rights in American Religious Discourse*, ed. Saul M. Olyan and Martha C. Nussbaum (New York: Oxford University Press), 108.

67. Farley, *Compassionate Respect*, 10–11.

68. Ibid., 12.

69. Ibid., 18–19.

70. This and other information about these projects is taken from materials sent to me by Margaret Farley, including grant applications, project descriptions, and appeals for financial support to other religious congregations. For a broader picture, see the subsequent article by Farley, "Partnership in Hope: Gender, Faith, and Responses to HIV/AIDS in Africa," *Journal of Feminist Studies in Religion* 20 (Spring 2004): 133–48.

Chapter Two

Human Rights and Women's Rights:

Initiatives and Interventions in the Name of Universality

David Hollenbach, S.J.

This essay will explore claims about the universality of human rights in relation to cultural differences. In particular, it will consider some ways that such claims about universality extend to issues specifically concerning women, and whether protecting women's rights might justify taking initiatives to secure change across the boundaries of societies and cultures. It will argue that there are indeed some rights that belong universally to all human beings, that some of these universal rights have special relevance for women and can thus be called women's rights, and that securing these rights can sometimes justify initiatives across cultural boundaries. In making this argument, the essay will distinguish between initiatives that rely on forms of persuasion such as conversation, education, and moral argument on the one hand, and interventions through the use of coercion on the other. Persuasive initiatives to secure women's rights could include, for example, educational programs that aim to improve the condition of women by gradually changing practices linked to culturally defined gender roles. More coercive interventions could include the use of armed force by the military to secure the most fundamental of human rights by preventing the rape of women in war or as a strategy of genocide or ethnic cleansing.

This essay is suitable in a work in honor of Margaret Farley, for she has addressed some of the questions it considers on a number of occasions. Farley has long been concerned with the question of whether a morality that reaches across the boundaries of diverse cultural and religious traditions is a genuine possibility. This has been evident in the way her teaching has often addressed the question of natural law. It has also been an explicit focus of her writings on the topic of a common morality in relation to feminism and the well-being of women in diverse cultures.[1] As Farley has pointed out, claims about a common human nature have frequently been used in ways that have been oppressive and harmful to women. She has also observed, however, that appeals to a common humanity are often at the heart of efforts to advance respect for women through critique of social institutions and cultural standards. Such critiques often implicitly presuppose that there are criteria of the truly human that reach across the boundaries of cultures, especially as these affect gender roles.

Awareness of both the dangers of claims to universalism and the ways such claims can serve the well-being of women will inform what is said here about human rights and women's rights. In fact, my own work on the normative bases of human rights has been significantly influenced by Farley's thought on these matters. For example, through her influence my dissertation on human rights and population policy included a discussion of this topic in light of its impact on women.[2] More recently, Farley has become intellectually and practically engaged with the way African women's responses to the life and death questions of the HIV/AIDS crisis are shaped by moral and religious traditions regarding sex and gender.[3] These concerns overlap with my own engagement with social ethical issues that are particularly acute in the context of Africa, especially those touching human rights issues. Partly through Farley's influence, the questions of women's rights in Africa have come more clearly into focus for me. So though none of the limitations of this essay can be blamed on Margaret Farley, the direction it takes has been shaped by what I have learned from her, both in more formal and less formal ways. For that influence I am most grateful.

TWO EXPERIENCES AS BACKGROUND

In light of the interest in African concerns that Farley and I have come to share in recent years, it will be useful to enter into the question of human rights and women's rights by recounting two different experiences I had during a semester of teaching and doing research in Kenya several years ago.

The first experience explicitly concerned the universality of human rights. I had been invited to give a public lecture in Nairobi on the topic of my research—human rights in contemporary Africa. Four Kenyans were scheduled to respond, so I was concerned to give adequate attention to the influence of the distinctiveness of African cultures on understandings of human rights. Thus my lecture considered at some length the thought of a number of African intellectuals who had been raising objections to the universality of human rights, claiming that they are Western constructs and thus not appropriate standards for social and political life in Africa. These thinkers noted that when the standards set forth in the Universal Declaration of Human Rights were codified in the aftermath of World War II, nearly all peoples on the African continent were under European colonial rule. Africans and their cultures had virtually no voice in the drafting of the Universal Declaration. So some of the African thinkers I considered in my lecture argued that the prevailing conception of human rights expresses the more individualistic understanding of the person held by most contemporary Europeans and North Americans, and that this conception of human rights conflicts with the stronger sense of solidarity common in African cultures. For example, the Nigerian C. C. Mojekwu had written an early article advocating this line. In Mojekwu's words:

> African concepts of human rights are very different from those of Western Europe. Communalism and communal right concepts are fundamental to understanding African culture, politics and society. One should not make the mistake of thinking that the colonial interlude washed away these fundamental cultures in society.[4]

The perceived link between human rights and the individualistic bias of Western liberalism thus led a number of thinkers to be suspicious of "rights talk" in the African discussions of human rights that began in the 1970s.

Mojekwu's stress on communal rather than individual self-determination is also prominent in the African Charter on Human and Peoples' Rights adopted in 1981 by the Organization of African Unity. The African Charter differs from the United Nations Universal Declaration of Human Rights by calling itself a charter of human and peoples' rights. It declares not only that all human beings are equal but that all peoples are as well. This difference is explained in the preamble to the African Charter, which states that "historical tradition and the values of African civilization . . . should inspire and characterize . . . reflection on the concept of human and peoples' rights." Thus the charter affirms that peoples have the right to self-determination, peoples have the right to pursue economic and social development according to the policy they have freely chosen, peoples have the right to freely dispose of their wealth and natural resources, and peoples have the right to economic, social, and cultural development.[5] Accompanying the list of peoples' rights is a list of duties. These include the duty of the individual to contribute to the national community by placing his or her physical and intellectual abilities at its service, and the duty not to compromise the security of the state of which one is a national or a resident.[6]

Though my lecture in Nairobi did not accept the claim of some African intellectuals and politicians that the solidaristic orientation of African cultures invalidates the universality of human rights, it did take their concerns seriously. Thus I was surprised that one of my respondents objected to the attention I had given to these views. Gibson Kamau Kuria, a lawyer active in the political struggles of the Kenyan opposition against the government of Daniel Arap Moi, strongly rejected such hesitations about the appropriateness of human rights standards in the Kenyan context. He saw no conflict between respect for the cultures of the people of Africa and support for human rights. Indeed Kuria argued that the African intellectuals I had discussed, as well as those Western postcolonial theorists holding similar views, were making a fundamental mistake about the key issues facing the people of Africa in the contemporary situation. Kuria acknowledged that their challenge to the appropriateness of human rights standards was motivated by a desire to protect the people of Africa from colonial control and domination by Western powers. But he also maintained that it would be anachronistic to see this as the central challenge facing Africa today.

Kuria argued that a considerably more urgent issue is the protection of African people against the oppression being visited upon them by indigenous African politicians, such as Daniel Arap Moi, who had been ruling Kenya for several decades. One-party states, the desire of the few for uninhibited power over the many, the use of politics to advance the narrow interests of particular ethnic groups, and straightforward corruption driven by greed are serious threats to the well being of many African people today.[7] The defense of human rights is a key element in a strategy that aims at resisting these threats. Critique of human rights norms, therefore, plays into the hands of those who would use political power to advance their own narrowly defined interests. Kuria clearly had in mind the fact that Daniel Arap Moi had regularly defended one-party rule as necessary in light of the cultural traditions of Kenya.[8] Kuria rejected this position forcefully: "The people in power try to say we [Africans] are different from other communities in the world. This is wrong. Human rights are for all."[9] In other words, Kuria shared—with the African thinkers who were suspicious of human rights standards as excessively Western—the moral objective of protecting the well-being of African people against domination and control by elites, but saw the threats coming from a different quarter than they did. This suggests that assessment of claims about the universality of human rights norms should be based not only on how the values human rights seek to defend relate to diverse cultural traditions but also on what threats to these values are most salient.

A second experience I had in Kenya cast a somewhat different light on the question of the universality of human rights than did Kuria's strong defense of transcultural norms. About half the students in a course I was teaching on Christian social ethics were seminarians studying for the Catholic priesthood in the Jesuit order. A recent Jesuit general congregation had taken a strong position calling Jesuits to greater awareness of the injustices faced by women. Among these injustices, the Jesuit congregation mentioned female circumcision, which it described as a form of violence against women, along with dowry deaths and the murder of unwanted infant girls.[10] Since the practice of female circumcision is practiced rather widely in Kenya, I decided to raise this issue as a case in point in discussing the rights of women in my course. I assigned a chapter defending female initiation and circumcision from Jomo Kenyatta's anthropological study of Gikuyu cultural practices, *Facing Mount Kenya*.[11] This was accompanied by an article from a recent issue of the *Hastings Center Report* that gave an overview of the ethical issues and argued that it should be eliminated gradually through efforts that work respectfully with cultural traditions.[12] To my considerable surprise, the students divided about evenly on whether the practice should be supported as essential to the initiation into adult womanhood in the African cultures where it is practiced, or opposed as a violation of women's rights to bodily integrity and to self-determination in their sexual lives. Those supporting the practice viewed the opposition by the others as an indication of their weakened African authenticity due to regrettable Europeanization. Opposition to the practice was a sign that one had begun to think like a *mzungu* ("white man" in Kiswahili).

Further, following the discussion of this topic, I expressed my surprise at the number of students supporting the traditional practice to a Kikuyu woman working in a secretarial position in a Nairobi university. When I did so, she laughed, shook her head in a genial way, and said that I just didn't understand the people I was trying to teach. In a matter of fact way she commented that she herself had undergone the ritual as a teenage girl, that her daughters had also, and that she hoped this practice would continue for generations to come. She was a fairly well educated urban woman, not a girl from the "bush."

AN ARGUMENT ON UNIVERSALITY AND DIFFERENCE

The arguments on female circumcision, genital surgery, or female genital mutilation (the terminology is evaluatively loaded) as a part of female initiation that I encountered in Nairobi are echoed in the literature that continues to address the question. Amnesty International frames the question as a human rights issue. It sees female genital mutilation (FGM) as a form of violence against women. The practice is viewed as closely linked with the enforcement of the inequality of women in political, social, and economic life, and as reinforcing the submissiveness of women. Thus it is a fundamental issue of universal human rights and should be abolished. In the words of an Amnesty International report:

> FGM is a practice that compounds unspeakable violence against women and young girls with discrimination, repression, and inequality. As the issue becomes more visible in the public sphere, states that allow FGM to be perpetuated face increasing criticism and scrutiny by the international community. It must be made clear that no form of violence against women can be justified by any cultural claim.[13]

In other words: FGM is a straightforward human rights issue; human rights are universal; cultures can and should be challenged in the name of these universal norms.

Martha Nussbaum, an American philosopher who has strongly defended the existence of crosscultural moral standards, sees the practice as a violation of just such standards. Nussbaum acknowledges that women in developing countries face other forms of deprivation and oppression that are more serious than those connected with traditional genital surgeries. Among these she includes inadequate and unequal nutrition, health care, and education; inequality before the law; and domestic violence and rape.[14] Nevertheless, the traditional surgeries are serious violations of the physical integrity of women, denials of women's opportunity to experience some forms of sexual pleasure, and enforcement mechanisms for female inequality. Some women in some African cultures are in fact already challenging these practices, and such internal criticism is beginning to change these practices. And there is little doubt that some women within these cultures "wish outside aid" to help them in their efforts to work for change.[15] Opponents of the practices in developed countries, therefore, should not fear the charge of being Westernizers or colonialists when they take initiatives to help African women overcome these practices. Rather, they should work for cultural transformation alongside the women who are seeking change in African societies. Nussbaum concludes that, in the face of the harm done to women by genital mutilation, we in the developed world "should be ashamed of ourselves if we do not use whatever privilege and power has come our way to make it disappear forever."[16]

On the opposite side of the academic argument are two anthropologists—one female African and one male American. In a provocative reflection on rites of genital cutting among her own Kono people in Sierra Leone, Fuambai Ahmadu notes that she has herself undergone an initiation rite involving excision of the clitoris. She considers herself "neutral" about the continuation of the practice but objects to the view that being an educated woman should be identified with being opposed to the traditional practice. In her experience, the rite had some negative aspects to be sure, chiefly excruciating pain. But both for her and among the women she studies as a professional anthropologist, it also has notably positive dimensions. In effect Ahmadu turns the feminist argument against the practice on its head. In Kono culture, these positive dimensions include "the 'acting out' and celebration of women's preeminent roles in history and society." The rite is an initiation into a "fear-inspiring world, controlled and dominated by women" and the scar left by the surgery is a symbol of common female identity and power.[17] Thus Ahmadu argues strongly against the idea that progress for women and the eradication of the traditional practice are identical. She favors developing practices that reduce the medical risks while retaining the cultural significance of the traditional rites for women's identity. And she supports allowing young women to make up their own minds about whether to undergo the surgery.

American anthropologist Richard Shweder cites Ahmadu with strong approval. He also appeals to a recent study that maintains that the medical effects of the traditional practices are much less harmful than opponents often maintain.[18] In addition, he argues that if we consider the practice from the viewpoint of those who actually undergo it, we will learn that it has genuine value in their eyes. They see it as making them "more beautiful, more feminine, more civilized, and more honorable." "The weight of the evidence suggests that the overwhelming majority of youthful female initiates believe that they have been improved (physically, socially, and spiritually) by the ceremonial ordeal and symbolic process (including the pain) associated with initiation."[19]

Shweder does not advocate a cultural relativism that declares anything goes. He holds that there are indeed universal values. These values can be expressed in multiple ways, however, in different forms of life found in different cultures. Appreciation of diverse cultures from the inside will reveal that they are imaginative ways of being human. It is not possible to realize all of these imagined ways of being human in the same lives at the same time. Thus pluralism is inevitable, and having true respect for human beings calls for having genuine respect for the way they have come to imagine human flourishing. When Westerners consider the traditional practices of female genital surgery, therefore, they are challenged to move beyond an initial impulse of rejection and even revulsion at least to consider the value the practice has in the lives of those who perform it. Respect for their worth as persons as well as the value of tolerance demand nothing less. Like Ahmadu, Shweder leaves open the possibility that the practice might be gradually replaced by other modes of initiation, and he holds that no young women should be forced to undergo it involuntarily. His appeal for greater openness to the practice is thus based on arguments that have a lot in common with the discourse of both human rights and women's rights.

KANTIAN AND ARISTOTELIAN MOMENTS
IN RIGHTS DISCOURSE

What do these competing responses to the practices associated with female initiation in some African cultures imply about human rights and women's rights? Some light can be shed on this dispute by distinguishing two aspects of the arguments. These can be called the Kantian and Aristotelian moments in the development of an understanding of rights. The Kantian moment concerns the question of who is the subject of rights, or to whom the requirements of the human rights ethos are owed. The Aristotelian moment, on the other hand, addresses the content of the human rights ethos. It addresses the question of what specific goods people have a legitimate claim to—the goods others are responsible to provide for them. This question can also be put negatively: what are the harms that people have a legitimate claim not to have inflicted upon them and that others are responsible to avoid inflicting?

Each of these questions highlights a different aspect of the issue of whether it is reasonable to assert that there are universal human rights that apply in the diverse cultures of the world today. The Kantian question concerns the beneficiaries of such a purported universal human rights morality. It concerns the scope of the community that a common morality aims to govern. In other words, it asks about the "we" that is constituted as a moral community by holding the same moral standards in common. The Aristotelian question, on the other hand, concerns the content of such a common morality. What kinds of treatment are people entitled to receive from others and what forms of treatment should they always be immune from? Let us consider these questions in turn.

The Universal Declaration of Human Rights is based on the conviction that there is a worldwide community of which all human beings are members and within which human rights are secured. The terms "all" and "everyone," and "no one" are used repeatedly as the first words in the articles of the Universal Declaration that specify the various human rights. The "everyone" who are the subjects of human rights are to be understood without distinctions based on "race, color, sex, language, religion, political or other opinion, national or social origin."[20] Thus to the question of who possesses human rights, the Declaration's answer is unambiguous: all human beings do. The universality of human rights, therefore, aims to relativize all in-group/out-group boundaries when it comes to the protection of the rights it affirms. This is a challenge to all definitions of religious or cultural identity that suggest rights are owed only to the people who possess that identity. Though discrimination on the basis of membership in the identity group may be legitimate regarding some goods, it is not legitimate when those goods are a matter of human rights.

This stress on universality in human rights discourse follows Kant's lead not only in affirming the existence of universal moral obligations but also in closely linking the reality of moral obligation with the requirement of respect for humanity as such. Kant simultaneously affirmed both the universal reach of moral obligation and the duty to treat every human being as an end and never a means only. Human rights discourse has analogies with Kantian moral philosophy to the extent that it associates the universal reach of moral obligation with the intrinsic dignity of persons. There are, of course, well-known problems with Kant's philosophical arguments for this ethical stance. There are ways to reach Kant's conclusions, however, that may have fewer problems than that associated with Kant's systematic moral philosophy. Let me suggest the very general outlines of one such approach.

The reality of human persons—the kind of beings that humans in fact are—is at the origin of many important moral claims persons make upon one another.[21] Human beings are not things; they possess both self-consciousness and a self-transcendent capacity to reach beyond themselves in knowledge, freedom, and love. A person's capacity for self-transcendence gives rise to a moral claim that she be treated in ways that sustain or at least do not destroy that capacity. To respect a person's ability to know, make choices, and form bonds of love is to respect the claim of what she is and to acknowledge what she can become. Similarly, a second person is capable of experiencing that claim precisely because the second person also possesses the capacity for self-transcendence. This other person is not confined within the limits of his self-consciousness but can genuinely encounter the other as a fellow human being. Thus, one human being is a kind of ought in the face of another. Each person's capacity for self-transcendence makes a claim on others' capacity for self-transcendence. One's ability to know and understand calls out for acknowledgement in the understanding and concern of others. One person's freedom places requirements on the freedom of others. One person's capacity to form bonds of relationship with others calls for acknowledgment and support through the concern of others.[22] These affirmations lead to a vision of the human race as a genuine moral community with reciprocal obligations among all its members. This vision of a universal human community is the basis of the cosmopolitan aspects of Kant's political thought. It sets Kant, and the Kantian aspects of a human rights ethic, at odds with approaches that see cultural differences as so basic that it becomes impossible to affirm that there are any moral obligations or rights common to human beings as such.[23]

To assert this is to make a claim about what is practically reasonable—about what "makes sense" with regard to the way we treat each other and about how moral obligation should be understood.[24] It is a practically reasonable principle of morality that arises from the human condition itself. Indeed, one can argue that all persons who wish to act reasonably should act in accord with the basic requirements of these claims of personhood. Such practical reasonableness takes priority over the simple acceptance of the traditions of one's own culture or of the cultures of the other peoples with whom one interacts.[25] Further, it means that if those traditions contain elements that appear to deny some human beings the respect that their capacity for self-transcendence requires, then those traditions should be critically challenged and, if necessary, changed. In other words, the ought that arises in the encounter among persons makes demands both upon all persons and also upon their cultural traditions. Those rights that give expression to the claims that arise from the condition shared by all human beings are thus universal. Insistence that they be respected is not a form of imperialism or colonialism. It serves the same goal as those calling for respect for diverse cultures see at the heart of their commitment, namely, genuine liberation from any form of domination or oppression.

The demand that the self-transcendence of human beings receive respect, however, remains a very general expression of what is required by a universal or common morality. This Kantian moment in rights discourse does not of itself adequately specify what these culture-transcending moral rights or obligations might actually be. It needs to be made more specific and concrete. In fact, the question of whether there are such universal standards will remain largely speculative until more concrete proposals are made concerning what rights or duties are taken to be universal. The effort to spell out the meaning of respect for human dignity in greater detail can be called the Aristotelian moment in the discussion of the relation between cultural differences and the universality claimed for human rights. Aristotle developed his ethics by seeking to identify what the good life is for human beings. A good life has more than one dimension or characteristic. Aristotle suggested that a good life involves a number of diverse kinds of activity, including both intellectual and practical pursuits.[26] In an analogous way, there will be multiple preconditions for the realization of dignity in people's lives. Answering the question of whether there are universal human rights will depend on determining whether some of these activities are conditions for human well-being in all cultures.

Answering this question calls for reflection on historical and social experience. Such reflection can begin from the insight, articulated by Aristotle but surely intelligible in all cultures, that human beings are really different from both beasts and from gods, and should be treated differently from both beasts and gods.[27] Not being a beast is having the capacity to move beyond self-enclosed materiality. This capacity for self-transcendence, which was stressed in Kant's ethics, is unique to beings with consciousness or spirit. It is a key index of the distinctive worth of human personhood and points to a central aspect of how humans can reasonably expect to be treated by each other. We should support one another in undertaking activities of the spirit such as growing in knowledge, exercising freedom, or forming and sustaining personal relationships such as friendship. At a minimum, we should refrain from preventing one another from engaging in these activities of the spirit. At the same time, human beings are not gods, and human self-transcendence is that of a bodily being and it has material conditions. Human dignity can only be realized if these material conditions are present, and it cannot be realized if they are lacking. Human well-being thus requires not only that one's freedom be secured and protected; it also requires food, shelter, bodily integrity, medical care in sickness, and a number of other material supports. Therefore it can be reasonably affirmed that we have some responsibilities to enable one another to share in the material goods and physical, bodily activities that are among the conditions required for living with dignity. Again, at the minimum we have a duty not to deprive one another of these material basics.

Practical reflections on the actual experience of what it is to be human such as these shaped the thinking of those who developed the list of human rights contained in the United Nations' Universal Declaration. Such reflection has minimal metaphysical presuppositions, and a plausible case can be made that they are compatible with the imaginative visions of human well-being found in most of the cultures of the world. Of course, such practical reflection on human experience may not lead to full agreement on the total set of activities that are prerequisites for living well or even living with basic human dignity. It is also true that people from different cultural or religious traditions will often explain the origins and full significance of human dignity and what it requires through different narratives, metaphysical theories, or theologies. Despite these differences in interpretation, however, it does not seem impossible that practically reasonable people can agree that human dignity means not being enslaved, politically oppressed, or starving when alternative conditions are genuine possibilities. The quest for standards of a common morality and for a universal human rights ethic is the effort to identify prerequisites of human dignity like these. The drafters of the Universal Declaration believed they had at least made a good start in such an effort. The challenge today, in light of the debates about the influence of cultural pluralism, is to determine whether we can affirm a set of human and women's rights as practically reasonable for all. To dismiss the idea that there are such rights simply because it claims to reach across the boundaries dividing cultural traditions would be to decide the matter without giving it the practical reflection it deserves.

Lisa Cahill has observed that the most basic standards of a universal or global common morality may be somewhat less difficult to identify than the highly disputed hard cases might lead one to suspect. Cahill points out that, across considerable cultural and religious differences, there are certain basic needs and goods that virtually all people today agree are due to everyone. The U.N. Millennium Declaration, for example, has set development goals that very few people, including those who stress the significance of cultural differences, would be willing to challenge. These include eradicating extreme poverty and hunger, achieving universal primary education, reducing child mortality, improving maternal health, and combating AIDS, malaria, and other infectious diseases.[28] These Millennium Development Goals, like many of those set forth in other consensus documents, indicate that there is agreement on at least some basic values across cultures and religious traditions. In Cahill's words, these documents "demonstrate that there are certain basic human needs and goods that are not that difficult to recognize globally."[29] One could add a number of negative proscriptions to the positive prescriptions on which most traditions can readily achieve consensus. These could include the moral prohibition of murder, genocide, torture, and enslavement, as well as of less extreme abuses such as political oppression and theft of what rightly belongs to another. Agreement on these matters carries us well along the way toward affirming that many of the human rights affirmed in the Universal Declaration are truly becoming part of a universal ethic or common morality.

RELEVANCE TO WOMEN'S RIGHTS: BACK TO CASES

Where does this leave us regarding the claim that there are rights particularly applicable to women that transcend cultures and are thus universal? Before turning again to a disputed issue such as the relation between human rights and female genital surgeries in African cultures, it may be useful to consider another rights issue with special relevance to women on which there appears to considerably more consensus.

The sexual violation of women has long been a commonplace in the midst of warfare. In fact, through most of human history the rape of women seems to have been taken for granted as an aspect of warfare. In very recent decades, however, the sexual abuse of women by men in the midst of war has come to the fore as a central human rights issue. The contemporary human rights ethos emerged in response to the atrocities of the holocaust and the Nazi genocide of the Jewish people. Women suffered these abominations just as did men. But it has taken the vivid awareness of very recent atrocities to bring to the fore in contemporary discourse certain rights that are especially relevant to women during war. For example, feminist legal scholar Catherine MacKinnon illustrates such atrocities by citing a personal communication to her by an American researcher investigating the abuse of women in Croatia and Bosnia during the war unleashed as the former Yugoslavia disintegrated:

> Serbian forces have exterminated over 200,000 Croatians and Muslims thus far in an operation they've coined "ethnic cleansing." In this genocide, in Bosnia-Herzegovina alone over 30,000 Muslim and Croatian girls and women are pregnant from mass rape. Of the 100 Serbian-run concentration camps, about 20 are solely rape/ death camps for Muslim and Croatian women and children.[30]

MacKinnon argues, however, that such violations have rarely or never been seen as violations of the human rights of women as such. If the women undergoing systematic rape survive, the abuse has traditionally been discounted as an inevitable consequence of war. If the women perish, their deaths are seen as the deaths of Muslims or Bosnians, not women. So these gross violations of the rights of women during war have long been masked.[31]

The passionate protests of MacKinnon and many others against this obscuring of the sexual and gendered aspects of these abuses have begun to bear some fruit. There has been a growing consensus that those who harm women this way should be held fully accountable for violating fundamental human rights. The strongest evidence for this has arisen in an African context. In 1998 the international criminal tribunal for Rwanda convicted Jean Paul Akayesu of genocide, incitement to genocide, and crimes against humanity for his participation in the events in the Gitarama district of Rwanda during the massacres that occurred there in 1994. This verdict was a landmark in international and humanitarian law, for it was the first conviction ever handed down for the crime of genocide. In the context of this essay, it was also significant for its findings that the sexual violence committed against women in the midst of the Rwanda conflict was itself both a crime against humanity and part of the crime of genocide. The tribunal found that Akayesu, Hutu *bourgmestre* (mayor) of

Taba commune, knew of, encouraged, and failed to prevent sexual violence and rape against a number of Tutsi women. In particular, the court found that his action of encouraging the rape of these women was directed at systematically degrading them in their own right (a crime against humanity). He also sought to sexually degrade Tutsi women precisely as members of the Tutsi ethnic group and this was as part of his participation in an effort to eliminate the Tutsi ethnic group as such. Thus the rapes Akayesu encouraged fall under the legal definition of genocide. In the words of the International Tribunal, these women "were subjected to sexual violence because they were Tutsi. Sexual violence was a step in the process of destruction of the Tutsi group—destruction of the spirit, of the will to live, and of life itself."[32]

The tribunal's decisions, therefore, concluded that the rape of the Tutsi women in Taba was an assault on their very humanity. It was part of an attempt to deny their dignity and worth as persons, as beings that should be treated with respect for their capacity for self-transcendence. It was a direct violation of the requirement that these women should be treated with the respect due to persons who are ends in themselves. The rapes that took place in the midst of the Rwanda genocide were certainly not due simply to Hutus imagining that sexual or gender roles might be organized differently from the way Europeans or Americans organize them. These rapes were intended, the tribunal held, quite literally to dehumanize Tutsi women. And this effort to dehumanize Tutsi women was a part of the broader effort to destroy the humanity of all Tutsi persons by killing them. Jean Paul Akayesu is not simply a person from another culture, engaging in a way of living out his sexual life that Europeans and Americans find strange or even disturbing but should nonetheless tolerate. Rather, in the Francophone expression that is tragically often heard in Rwanda today, Jean Paul Akayesu is a *genocidaire*. His behavior was not simply a culturally different variation: it was a violation of minimal requirements of humanity and basic human rights that all people in all cultures can be morally required to respect. And for these violations, the international tribunal sentenced him to spend the rest of his life in prison.[33]

PERSUASIVE INITIATIVES AND COERCIVE INTERVENTIONS

The differences between the human rights aspects of female genital surgeries and of the rape of Tutsi women in the midst of the Rwandan genocide highlights several important aspects of the debate about the universality of human rights in general and of women's rights in particular. Sometimes assertions about human rights and women's rights seek to persuade others to abolish practices one sees as harmful to the realization of human dignity. Amnesty International and Martha Nussbaum both believe that genital surgery as part of the initiation of girls into adult womanhood is a serious violation of their dignity. They call for vigorous efforts to eliminate this practice. The means they envision using to bring about change are persuasion and education. They propose moral arguments and make appeals to moral imagination to persuade the members of the cultures that practice these forms of initiation to abandon them. Even as they envision passing laws in African countries that would make these practices illegal, they advocate such legislation by the route of persuasion and reasoned argument. In other words, they do not envision using coercion to change the cultures where these rites are practiced. Their approach to cultural change in the name of the rights of women is nonviolent. The force of Ahmadu and Shweder's argument on the other side of this debate depends in part on their suggestion that approaches like those of Amnesty International and Nussbaum are in fact coercive manipulations of cultures. But the suggestion that Amnesty International and Nussbaum want to "coerce" cultural change seems misdirected. Further, both Ahmadu and Shweder themselves suggest that it would be better to replace genital surgery with other practices that could play a similar role in the initiation of girls into adulthood. So if the suggestion that cultural change requires coercion is dropped, Ahmadu and Shweder might be able to reach consensus with Amnesty International and Nussbaum on the implications of women's rights in this domain.

The difference between seeking to secure women's rights through persuasion and by coercion becomes clearer if we contrast approaches to female genital surgery with the possible response to the rape of Tutsi women in Rwanda. Many human rights advocates have argued that the larger world should have intervened with the use of force to stop the Rwandan genocide, a view I share. The human rights violations in Rwanda were of such a serious nature that the use of coercion—indeed military coercion—was not only justified but morally required. Thus Romeo Dallaire, the Canadian general who had been in command of the United Nations peacekeeping forces in Rwanda at the time of the genocide, has described the inaction of the international community a "loss of innocence" that "disgusted" him as a human being.[34] Indeed Dallaire suffered a serious psychological breakdown in the aftermath of the genocide because of his sense that he had not done enough to persuade international agencies to take more concerted action.[35] J. Bryan Hehir, highly regarded specialist in ethics and international politics, has referred to the world's inaction in Rwanda as an "abject international failure."[36] Hehir argues that avoidance of the use of force should be the starting point for all efforts to secure human rights, but that truly massive human rights violations such as genocide and ethnic cleansing call for departing from the norm of nonintervention. The classic just war criterion of just cause can be understood and developed in a way that can legitimate and sometimes require overriding the presupposition against the use of force. Hehir suggests this should have occurred in the face of the Rwandan genocide and the ethnic cleansing campaign in Bosnia. In both Rwanda and Bosnia, systematic sexual abuse of women was an integral part of actions that have been judged crimes against humanity and genocide. Preventing and stopping such grave and systematic rights violations can be just cause for the coercive use of force.

Thus action to protect the rights of women does not come only in one form. It can take the form of initiatives that seek to persuade people to change their values and behavior. Such persuasive initiative appeals to the practical reason and moral imagination of those one seeks to persuade. Thus it respects the capacity for self-transcendence through practical reason and moral imagination in those being addressed. It shows respect for members of the cultures that practice these rites both by seeking to advance the dignity of their members and in the way cultural changes are advocated. The ability to imagine that life can be different is a key element of the human capacity for self-transcendence and rationality. To maintain that African peoples who practice genital surgery on girls should not even be exposed to alternatives to these practices is really, though perhaps unwittingly, to suggest that they lack the capacity to make judgments about their own human good. On the other hand, working for women's rights through persuasion that avoids manipulation and subtle forms of co-ercion across cultural differences expresses commitment to human dignity understood in its Kantian dimensions.

Such persuasion begins with the presupposition that members of African peoples deserve the respect of being treated as persons who are fully capable of evaluating their existing cultural practices and de-termining whether they should be continued or not. Of course, those who undertake such efforts at persuasion must be similarly ready to revise their understanding of the effects of the initiation rites through intellectual and imaginative engagement with worldviews that initially seem strange or even abhorrent. Such willingness to revise ones views, or at least to tolerate the behavior judged unacceptable until those who practice it conclude that change is called for, is essential if change is to be brought about by persuasion rather than coercion. It requires a mutual exchange among the partners in the cultural interchange, and this mutuality itself requires commitment to the fundamental human equality of those involved. I have elsewhere called such reciprocal en-gagement with those who are different "intellectual solidarity."[37] This kind of respect for the dignity and capacity for self-transcendence of those who are different is a most basic requirement of a Kantian un-derstanding of human rights. At the same time, by calling those who practice genital surgeries to consider altering their understanding of what their human dignity really requires, it proposes that they revise what we have called the Aristotelian aspects of their understanding of the requirements of human dignity. Thus the Kantian requirement of respect of persons as ends in themselves and the Aristotelian concern to discover the genuine human good in an inductive way can meet in a persuasive dialogue about the practice of female circumcision. Pursu-ing human and women's rights this way can be compatible with com-mitment to advance the rights of women and at the same time show real respect for peoples from the diverse cultures of the world.

But there are limits to this persuasive approach to both human and women's rights, as the rapes committed as part of the Rwanda genocide have suggested to many. Some practices are direct attacks on the human person as such. Hutu behavior in Rwanda was not simply the result of a conception of the human good that the Hutu people and their leaders believed they should seek to realize in their life together. Rather, it was based in a conviction, sometimes explicit, sometimes implicit, that Tutsi persons should not count as human beings at all. The genocide that took place in Rwanda, including the rape of many women that was part of it, sought to deny the fundamental dignity of Tutsi people, both by degrading them to a subhuman level and by killing them outright. In the terms we have been using here, it was an effort to deny the Kantian dimension of the dignity of all Tutsi people. In this broad sense, it was a crime against the very humanity of the Tutsi people, both collectively and individually.

Protection against this sort of violation is the precondition for securing all other human rights—both the rights of individual persons and the rights of cultural groups of persons. It is for this reason that Henry Shue has called the rights that protect one against violations of this kind "basic rights." In Shue's words, "Basic rights are the morality of the depths. They specify the line beneath which no one is to be allowed to sink."[38] Basic rights are the prerequisites for the enjoyment of all other rights and goods. Thus basic rights may never be consistently traded off to obtain less basic goods, for the less basic goods cannot themselves be enjoyed when basic rights are being denied. For example, education is a very great good, and one can argue that all persons have a right to at least the rudiments of an adequate education. One could also argue that education is a higher or more fully human good than minimum condition of not being assaulted or killed. But Shue argues persuasively that prevention of assault and murder is more basic than the provision of education, for assault and murder surely prevent education from happening. Thus the right to security from assault or murder is more basic than the right to public provision of education.[39] In a similar way, the human right not to be subjected to genocide or ethnic cleansing, and women's rights not to be raped as a military strategy intended to demoralize and ultimately to eliminate

an ethnic group, are truly basic rights. They are more basic than the
cultural rights that insure that diverse cultural groups interact in a way
marked by mutuality, equality, and reciprocity. Without protection
against genocide, ethnic cleansing, and other crimes against humanity that are directed at the very personhood of group members, no
humane interaction of cultures will be possible at all.

It is for this reason that the use of coercion may sometimes be justifiable to prevent the systematic violation of basic rights, while persuasion
will be the appropriate means to the promotion of rights that are less
basic. This, I take it, is why it makes sense to conclude that preventing
what happened to women in Rwanda and Bosnia may be grounds for
military intervention, while changing the practice of female circumcision should be pursued by educational and persuasive means.

A distinction drawn by John Rawls can help illuminate what is at
stake here. Rawls distinguishes between liberal peoples and those he
calls "decent peoples." Liberal peoples, as Rawls describes them, support the full range of rights we associate with liberal and, perhaps,
social democracy in the West. These include the rights embodied in
constitutional democracy such as institutional protections of full political equality, the rights to vote and to hold office independent of
religion or cultural background, as well as the right to full freedom
to exercise religious beliefs in public. Decent peoples have a less inclusive understanding of rights. As Rawls describes them, such people
will grant all members of their society the right to be consulted and
heard in the political process. They may not, however, understand the
right to be heard as requiring a universal right to suffrage or to hold
office. Thus Rawls can envision what he calls a "decent consultation
hierarchy" that sets some restrictions on suffrage or on holding office,
perhaps based on religion or culture.[40] The primary case Rawls has in
mind here is clearly some form of Islamic republic that seeks to combine both Muslim and democratic values.[41]

It is important to note that Rawls thinks that being a "consultation hierarchy" of this sort is compatible with respect for the most
basic human rights as Shue describes them. In fact, for such a society
to be considered "decent" in Rawls's terms, it must respect a class
of human rights that are particularly urgent. These include freedom
from slavery, liberty of conscience, and security of ethnic groups

from mass murder and genocide.[42] These rights are taken to be at the very core of a common morality on which all reasonable people can agree in practice, both reasonable Western liberals and reasonable people living in decent hierarchical traditions. In relation to the argument advanced here, the right of women not to be abused as they were in Rwanda and Bosnia can be affirmed as an essential expression of respect for the humanity of women, everywhere and independent of the importance of respect for cultural differences. It can be appealed to as a basis for intervention to stop such abuse of women, even military intervention. On the other hand, the Western understanding of what the dignity of women requires is grounds for seeking to persuade some eastern African cultures to replace the use of circumcision in the initiation of girls. This Western understanding of women's dignity, however, is not an adequate ground for resorting to coercion to bring about cultural change.

The distinction between basic rights and the fuller list of rights associated with Western liberalism thus has significant practical relevance, both for human rights in general and for women's rights in particular. This distinction is related to the difference between moral norms that we judge should be enforced by law backed by police or military power, and those we think should be secured through persuasion, education, and moral argument. It is notable that Rawls draws the distinction between liberal societies and decent societies in a book on the law of peoples. The urgent rights that he associates with decency are those that must be respected by peoples who want to avoid the status of outlaw. Peoples who do not respect these truly basic rights are subject to international condemnation and sanctions. If the violations of these rights are grave, peoples that commit the violations may become subject to intervention by the use of force.[43]

Respect for the religious and cultural beliefs of the diverse communities in our world is surely a crucial requirement of our time. It is also an essential element of an ethic committed to human rights and women's rights. But I hope that this essay has shown that commitment to respect for cultural diversity does not settle all the issues that arise in the pursuit of human rights and women's rights in our time. Distinctions need to be drawn between more and less basic rights, and between the means that are proposed to secure them. If a community appeals to its religious or cultural traditions to justify racism (as did some Afrikaner Christians in South Africa in the apartheid era) or to legitimate denying all education to girls (as do the Taliban in their interpretation of Islam), or to support the practice of female circumcision (as do some African cultures), practical reason justifies raising serious objections. These objections should be raised first of all in the mode of persuasion and moral argument. In some circumstances, however, it may be appropriate as a last resort to go beyond persuasion to some form of coercive sanction. Such coercion could be exercised by international courts with genuine enforcement powers, by the use of economic pressure such as the sanctions that were directed against the apartheid regime in South Africa, or, in the extreme, by military intervention to prevent crimes such as ethnic cleansing or genocide. There are limits to what can be done in the name of culture and religion, even in an ethic that strongly supports the right to cultural and religious freedom. These limits are set by what we can reasonably conclude are the most fundamental prerequisites of human dignity.

Thus, discerning the appropriate ways to pursue the rights of women in our time challenges us with a twofold task. First, we need to pay careful attention to the fundamental dignity of women as ends in themselves who possess the capacity for self-transcendence. This is the most basic requirement of any human rights ethic and also of any ethic that promotes the rights of women. Second, we also need to engage in the cross-cultural dialogue that is required to bring us a more adequate understanding of what this dignity concretely requires in our multicultural, multireligious world. Neither of these tasks can be pursued alone; each will help clarify the understanding of rights and duties discovered in the other. Also, the pursuit of both tasks is essential to discerning when what has been discovered should be proposed to others by argument, education, and persuasion, or whether grave abuses are occurring that require more forceful intervention. The promotion of human rights and women's rights will thus require practical wisdom based on experience and prudential choice guided by a spirit of solidarity. It is a task worthy of the intellectual and practical endeavor it will require.

NOTES

1. See, for example, Margaret A. Farley, "Feminism and Universal Morality," in *Prospects for a Common Morality*, ed. Gene Outka and John P. Reeder, Jr., 170–90 (Princeton, NJ: Princeton University Press, 1993).

2. David Hollenbach, "The Right to Procreate and Its Social Limitations: A Systematic Study of Value Conflict in Roman Catholic Ethics" (Ph.D. dissertation, Yale University, 1975), chap. 4, "The Relation of Family and Society."

3. See, for example, Margaret A. Farley, *Compassionate Respect: A Feminist Approach to Medical Ethics and Other Questions* (New York: Paulist Press, 2002), 3–20.

4. Chris C. Mojekwu, "International Human Rights: The African Perspective," in *International Human Rights: Contemporary Issues*, ed. Jack L. Nelson and Vera M. Green (Stanfordville, NY: Human Rights Publishing Group, 1980), 92–93.

5. *African Charter on Human and People's Rights*, arts. 19–22, in *The International Law of Human Rights in Africa: Basic Documents and Annotated Bibliography*, ed. M. Hamalengwa, C. Flinterman, and E. V. O. Dankwa (Dordrecht: Martinus Nijhoff, 1988).

6. Ibid., art. 29.

7. For a survey of such abuses in Kenya see Korwa G. Adar and Isaac M Munyae, "Human Rights Abuse in Kenya under Daniel Arap Moi, 1978–2001," *African Studies Quarterly* 5, no. 1 (2001). *African Studies Quarterly* is an online journal; this article is available at http://web.africa.ufl.edu/asq/v5/v5i1a1.htm (accessed January 2007).

8. For a discussion of how Moi fomented ethnic conflict and then argued that his form of rule was the only way to hold the country together, see Africa Watch, *Divide and Rule: State-Sponsored Ethnic Violence in Kenya* (New York: Human Rights Watch, 1993), and "Multipartyism Betrayed in Kenya: Continuing Rural Violence and Restrictions of Freedom of Speech and Assembly" (New York: Human Rights Watch, 1994).

9. Gibson Kamau Kuria's response to my lecture is cited in Stephen Mburu, "Rights Dodge the Poor," *Daily Nation* (Nairobi), December 17, 1996, 4. My lecture was published as "Human Rights in Development," *The Independent Review* 1, no. 2 (Nairobi: 1997), 154–60, and a revised version appeared as "Solidarity, Development, and Human Rights: The African Challenge," *The Journal of Religious Ethics* 26, no. 2 (1998): 305–17.

10. *Documents of the Thirty-Fourth General Congregation of the Society of Jesus* (St. Louis: Institute of Jesuit Sources, 1995), decree 14, "Jesuits and the Situation of Women in Church and Civil Society," no. 362, p. 172.

11. Jomo Kenyatta, *Facing Mount Kenya: The Traditional Life of the Gikuyu* (Nairobi: Heinemann, 1982; orig. pub. London: Secker and Warburg, 1938), chap. 6.

12. Sandra D. Lane and Robert A. Rubenstein, "Judging the Other: Responding to Traditional Female Genital Surgeries," *Hastings Center Report* 26 (May–June, 1996): 31–40.

13. Amnesty International USA, "Female Genital Mutilation: A Fact Sheet," available online at: http://www.amnestyusa.org/women/violence/female_genital_mutilation.html.

14. Martha C. Nussbaum, "Judging Other Cultures: The Case of Genital Mutilation," in *Sex and Social Justice* (New York: Oxford University Press, 1999), 126.

15. Ibid., 129.

16. Ibid., 129.

17. Fuambai Ahmadu, "Rites and Wrongs: An Insider/Outsider Reflects on Power and Excision," in *Female "Circumcision" in Africa: Culture, Controversy and Change*, ed. Bettina Shell-Duncan and Ylva Hernlund (Boulder, CO: Lynne Rienner, 2000), 305–7.

18. Richard A. Shweder cites Ahmadu throughout his study "'What about Female Genital Mutilation?' and Why Understanding Culture Matters," in his *Why Do Men Barbecue? Recipes for Cultural Psychology* (Cambridge: Harvard University Press, 2003), 168–216. The medical study to which he refers is that of Carla M. Obermeyer, "Female Genital Surgeries: The Known, the Unknown, and the Unknowable," *Medical Anthropology Quarterly* 13 (1999): 79–106.

19. Shweder, "What about Female Genital Mutilation?" 180, 188.

20. United Nations, *Universal Declaration of Human Rights*, article 2, 1948.

21. Margaret Farley proposes a similar approach to the basis of moral obligation. See her *Personal Commitments: Beginning, Keeping, Changing* (San Francisco: Harper and Row, 1986), chap. 7, esp. 80–84.

22. See William Luijpen, *Phenomenology of Natural Law* (Pittsburgh: Duquesne University Press, 1967), chap. 6, "Justice as an Anthropological Form of Co-Existence," esp. 180. For approaches that are both similar and interestingly different from this, see also Jean-François Lyotard, "The Other's Rights," in *On Human Rights: The Oxford Amnesty Lectures 1993*, ed. Stephen Shute and Susan Hurley (New York: Basic Books, 1993), 135–47, and Jacques Derrida, *Of Hospitality* (Stanford, CA: Stanford University Press, 2000).

23. Needless to say, Kant's moral and political thought is only touched on here. See Kant's different but related statements of the categorical imperative in *The Foundations of the Metaphysics of Morals*, trans. Lewis White

Beck (Indianapolis: Bobbs-Merrill, 1959), esp. 39, 47. For the statement of his cosmopolitan political orientation see especially *Idea for a Universal History with a Cosmopolitan Intent*, in *Perpetual Peace and Other Essays*, trans. Ted Humphrey (Indianapolis: Hackett, 1983), 29–40.

24. Here I am influenced by Margaret A. Farley's suggestion that a practically reasonable approach to moral obligation means that it should "make sense" in light of one's best reflection on what human experience reveals about the human condition. See Farley, "Moral Discourse in the Public Arena," in *Vatican Authority and American Catholic Dissent*, ed. William W. May, 168–86 (New York: Crossroad, 1987), at 174–75; and "Response to James Hanigan and Charles Curran," in *Sexual Orientation and Human Rights in American Religious Discourse*, ed. Saul M. Olyan and Martha C. Nussbaum, 101–9 (New York: Oxford University Press, 1998), at 105–6.

25. Here I agree with the conclusion of Amartya Sen's *Reason before Identity: The Romanes Lecture for 1998* (Oxford: Oxford University Press, 1999). I do not, however, agree fully with Sen's linkage of rationality with choice as opposed to discovery. Practical reason, I would maintain, can discover aspects of the genuinely human that take priority over cultural traditions.

26. See esp. Aristotle, *Nicomachean Ethics*, book X, chaps. 4–6. This point is developed succinctly by John Rawls's discussion of what he calls the "Aristotelian principle" in *A Theory of Justice*, revised edition (Cambridge, MA: Harvard University Press, 1999), no. 65, 372–80.

27. That human beings are neither beasts nor gods and should be treated accordingly is a presupposition of ethical politics. See Aristotle, *Politics*, book I, chap. 3, 1253a. Martha Nussbaum takes this as a fundamental presupposition of her "capabilities approach" to ethics in social and economic life. See, for example, Nussbaum, "Human Capabilities, Female Human Beings," in *Women, Culture, and Development: A Study of Human Capabilities*, ed. Martha Nussbaum and Jonathan Glover, 61–104 (Oxford: Oxford University Press, 1995), at 73.

28. "U.N. Millennium Development Goals," available online at http://www.un.org/millenniumgoals (accessed January 2007). For fuller developments of these goals and some ways to work toward achieving them see "The United Nations Development Declaration," September 18, 2000, online at: http://www.un.org/millennium/declaration/ares552e.pdf (accessed January 2007), and "Road Map Towards the Implementation of the United Nations Millennium Declaration, Report of the Secretary-General," September 6, 2001, online at: http://www.un.org/documents/ga/docs/56/a56326.pdf (accessed January 2007).

29. Lisa Sowle Cahill, "Toward Global Ethics," *Theological Studies* 63 (2002): 337. Probably the most ambitious attempt to outline the goods that all people should have access to and should be able to choose to realize in

their lives is that presented by Martha Nussbaum; see, for example, Nussbaum's *Women and Human Development: The Capabilities Approach* (Cambridge: Cambridge University Press, 2000), esp. chap. 1, "In Defense of Universal Values."

30. Personal communication cited in Catherine A. MacKinnon, "Crimes of War, Crimes of Peace," in Shute and Hurley, *On Human Rights*, 86. MacKinnon also cites a number of reports by human rights NGOs that present similar accounts of the sexual violation of women in war and in peace as well.

31. See MacKinnon, "Crimes of War, Crimes of Peace," 88–89.

32. International Criminal Tribunal for Rwanda, Case No. ICTR-96-4-T, "The Prosecutor versus Jean-Paul Akayesu," decision of September 2, 1998, no. 732. Available online from http://www.ictr.org.

33. The verdict and sentence delivered by the Tribunal in the Akayesu case are available at http://www.ictr.org.

34. Romeo Dallaire, "The End of Innocence: Rwanda 1994," in *Hard Choices: Moral Dilemmas in Humanitarian Intervention*, ed. Jonathan Moore, 71–86 (Lanham, MD: Rowman and Littlefield, 1998).

35. See Dallaire's own account of the events during and after his role in Rwanda in his *Shake Hands with the Devil: The Failure of Humanity in Rwanda* (Toronto: Random House of Canada, 2003).

36. J. Bryan Hehir, "Military Intervention and National Sovereignty: Recasting the Relationship," in Moore, *Hard Choices*, 48.

37. See my *The Common Good and Christian Ethics* (Cambridge: Cambridge University Press, 2001), chap. 6.

38. Henry Shue, *Basic Rights: Subsistence, Affluence, and U.S. Foreign Policy* (Princeton, NJ: Princeton University Press, 1980), 18.

39. Ibid., 20.

40. John Rawls, *The Law of Peoples, with "The Idea of Public Reason Revisited"* (Cambridge, MA: Harvard University Press, 1999), nos. 8 and 9.

41. Rawls illustrates what he has in mind through the example of a hypothetical country, Kazanistan. See ibid., no. 9.3.

42. Ibid., 79. This distinction is similar to that drawn by Michael Walzer between minimal or thin rights and fuller or thick ones; see Walzer, *Thick and Thin: Moral Argument at Home and Abroad* (Notre Dame, IN: University of Notre Dame Press, 1994).

43. Rawls, *Law of Peoples*, 81.

Chapter Three

Transnational Feminism and
the Rhetoric of Religion

Serene Jones

NIGHT ARRIVALS

It was after midnight when the three of us walked out of the airport and onto the busy streets of Cairo. I remember how surprised I was by the light and noise and energetic pulse of a city that seemed startlingly wide awake, even at that late hour. I remember, too, how the shock of the city's energy mirrored my own internal state; not only was I far from sleep, but my pulse was jumpy and noisy, driven by an anxiety located somewhere between disorientation, fear, and hopeful expectation. The fear surprised me, but it shouldn't have. It was my first time in the Arab world since 9/11, and I quickly discovered that despite my best instincts and most liberal of intentions, the media fallout from that day made me apprehensive in crowds of jalabiya and headscarves. It was also my first time to step onto soil so close to a war zone of my own country's making. That I would be perceived as the enemy to some did not escape me; what that perception would require from me, however, did.

Excitement was there, too. It was mid-December in 2003, and the three of us had come to Egypt for a conference bringing North

American and Arab women's studies scholars together to talk about the role of gender in the present-day conflicts in the Middle East. The gathering was the first of its kind and, by design, small, its participants all handpicked, with equal representation from the U.S. and the Arab world. It was clear that we had important things to talk about; while it was increasingly evident that political leaders in the U.S. as well as in the Arab world were willing to use the protection of women as a justification for military aggression, it was equally evident that women, particularly those who thought critically about gender, had not been heard from in the midst of it all. In the U.S., we also knew that the Bush administration was continually deploying "feminist" arguments to fuel its demonized caricature of the so-called woman-oppressing "Arab terrorists." That our Arab women's studies colleagues would have a different take on the matter was certain; and we knew, on this score, we had much to learn.

On the plane ride over Europe, the three of us had studiously read the bios and papers of all the conference attendees and thought we had a good picture of the women with whom we would be talking. It was clear that despite our vastly different social locations, everyone shared a certain set of theoretical commitments. The snappy, postmodern title of the conference said it all: "Gendered Bodies and Transnational Politics." Everyone obviously agreed that gender was a social construct, that class, race, ethnicity, and sexuality were significant features in the always particularized articulations of gender, and that analyzing the relation between discourse and power should be a central part of any academic feminist conversation. We all agreed, as well, that the center of our cross-context conversations was an urgent concern about the imperial designs of the U.S. in Iraq and the Middle East and the role played by global capital in the execution of these designs.

What we could not tell from the bios and the conference description, however, was what difference these shared commitments would make when it came to sitting together in a room and trying to have sustained conversations about what our role as women's and gender studies scholars should be in the midst of these conflicts. Would our common training in the field of "feminist theory" allow us to hit the ground running with respect to our assessment of transnational "gender rhetoric"? Would it let us avoid those age-old and frequently tiresome debates about nature and nurture and permit us to move quickly into interesting forms of cultural analysis and historical argument? Would this shared basis in theory allow us to become "friends" more easily, a goal no one was naïve enough to state but everyone shared? Would it help us build productive coalitions by allowing us to better negotiate the differences between us? Would it in this way enhance the work of justice and further our activist commitments to a progressive political movement capable of responding to the international threats we identified? In short, to use a favored phrase of the ethicist whose work this festschrift honors, would our shared theory ease the "work of love"?

As first a student and then a long-time faculty colleague of Margaret Farley, I have learned from her over the years that building just and caring forms of community is hard work. It is hard not just in the negative sense of being a grinding or unyielding task or even in the more obvious sense of a laborious and time-consuming chore. Although both connotations may apply, for Margaret the notion of hard work refers more fully to the reality that building and sustaining just relations with others, be they our most intimate ones or our most broadly political and intellectual ones, is a task enabled by seasoned and practiced dispositions such as openness, respect, attentiveness, compassion, and a sturdy commitment to the embodied integrity of others, dispositions that all require from us as much discipline and struggle as they do delight and joy. It is an honor to be part of a volume devoted to this topic, "A Just and True Love," and to have the chance to reflect on it in the context of my own work on gender, feminist theory, and globalization, another area to which Margaret has devoted much of herself over the past six years.

For this essay on globalization, I turn to the questions asked above and share my reflections on how the "work of love" unfolded during those days in Cairo.[1] One way I could have chosen to trace this work of love would have been to explore the highly specialized discussions we had, in the areas of political philosophy and cultural anthropology, on the topic of "modernity" and its use in the contemporary discourse about gender in "the West" and "the Arab world." However, while these discussions were quite productive, I have chosen another tack, one that is still about modernity, globalization, and gender but approaches the topic from a different angle. I focus not so much on the conceptual substance of our discussion as on its form of speech, its driving ambitions, and its dispositional shape and character—in short, its rhetoric. Instead of discussing our theories of globalization, I explore the discursive shape of our transnational conversations, noting what worked and what did not; and on both scores I suggest possible reasons why, particularly with respect to the theme "a just and true love."

In the first part of this essay, I describe the excitement of the early sessions of the conference and what it reveals about the common ground that brought us together—a grounding I argue is more about a shared aesthetic and the space of imagination than it is about principled moral claims. Here, I relate the character of our shared feminism in a manner that, on the one hand, resists essentialism or an unreflective liberal universalism while, on the other hand, it still remains bold enough (and intellectually courageous enough) to name what seemed to be rather obvious similarities between us. In the next section, I describe the process by which what started out as a vital and lively conversation quickly fell apart. By the second day, the conversations in our formal sessions—where we shared papers and tried to map out a certain conceptual terrain—had begun to deteriorate dramatically; and by the end of the gathering four days later, our public interactions had become so tense that people stopped showing up for sessions and a conflicted silence reigned. While there were no doubt countless reasons for this, I focus on two that pertain specifically to features of North American feminist thought: first, the imperialism of theory with respect to the aims of intellectual inquiry and political activism; and second, our blind-spots with respect to religion. In the final section, I turn away from these core, structured conversations and take a look at their margins, those coffee breaks, bathroom meetings, hallway chats, and mealtime gossip sessions where fascinating and productive—dare I say, just and loving—interactions did emerge. Here, I explore the place of narrative and practice in feminist discourse, two topics that feminist theologians have long discussed but which nonetheless need constant revisiting, especially in the more secular fields of feminist theory.

Let me note from the outset that my purpose in reflecting on this particular gathering is not primarily to give an interesting "conference report," although I certainly hope to do that. More importantly, I offer these critical remarks because what I saw transpiring in Egypt, in both positive and negative ways, was a microcosm of interactions increasingly taking place between women in the Arab world (and elsewhere) and North American academic feminists. Given the threatening reality of U.S. imperialism, the ever increasing reach of global capitalism, and the immediate threats these pose to the concrete, everyday lives of women, gatherings like these must happen. We cannot afford to avoid them, to treat them lightly, or to enter them with a sense of false assurance or arrogance. If they are to be truly "works of love" and not just clamors of theory, we need to pay careful attention to how we do this work. What I offer here are rather old-fashioned but nonetheless important suggestions as to how that work might most creatively develop. Not surprisingly, they are suggestions that have long guided the work of Margaret Farley, a feminist whose own intellectual propensities model the artful skill of breathing brilliant new life into time-honed wisdoms and sustaining traditions.

A VITALITY OF VISION

The first morning of the conference, we met for our opening round of introductions in a grand, colonial-style hall at the American University of Cairo. The room was abuzz with chatter as we greeted one another and began to move our chairs into a circle for introductions. In terms of our commonalities, it wasn't hard to tell that we were a group of academics. All of us had stacks of file folders on our laps and briefcases of some sort by our sides; and perhaps most telling, a steady stream of books was inciting marvel around the room.

Looking around our circle, we could also see that there were differences between us, ones that we read as quickly as the subtitles on the passing books. At the risk of seeming embarrassingly uncritical, here is a quick overview of the ones I noticed first. The most obvious were at the level of appearance—a theme I later return to under the topic of adornment. With respect to the North American women's hair, there were a ponytail or two and a couple of people with dreds, but no hats or wraps of any sort. We had mostly just low-maintenance, short hair. Several of the Arab women, however, wore headscarves made from different fabrics and wrapped in various shapes; and most of those without headscarves had longer hair. The majority of the women from the U.S. wore long pants with practical but fetching shoes, our unspoken feminist uniform. Our Arab sisters wore more diverse apparel, at least it seemed so to me: sandals, spike-heeled boots, well-polished pumps along with skirts, pants, and dresses, all brighter colors, all designed to keep them warm in the sixty-degree frigidity (to them) of their North African winter. There were other differences as well. The faces of the North Americans showed little jewelry and no make-up or at least tried to look make-up free, another part of our women's studies uniform; in contrast, some of the Arab women wore both, along with shoulder scarves.

There were also a handful of women whom, try as I might, I could not fit so easily into these categories, and I knew it. There was the Iranian woman who I thought looked like Lori Anderson, the Ivy League professor from Jamaica who wore a sari, the Egyptian woman with close-cropped hair. What did it mean that I could both read and not read the cues and expectations these adornments signaled? To say that I, as a feminist academic, was so cosmopolitan that these appearances—both the expected and unexpected—were insignificant to my initial read of our group would be dangerously naïve. To say the opposite, however, that I was simply reading to stereotype, would be to miss some of the complex dynamics at play. We were all reading each other, in ways both conscious and not; and in doing so, in the process of forming that opening circle, we were, the whole group, engaging in bodily practices that mirrored and enacted the dynamics of the conference as a whole. We were reading bodies in ways that both did and did not fit our categories and thereby interacting in a manner that both inscribed and contested our cultural training with respect to gender, ethnicity, and race. Our circle of chairs marked the new border of the group we were becoming—transnational feminists—delineating the space of its own in and out. But what kind of border was it? One that was supposedly permeable, open to difference, drawn together by way of e-mail invitations, university travel accounts, NGO funding sources, a string of traveling books, and a wardrobe as perplexing as it was—now—normative.

When we began to go around the room and introduce ourselves, who we were and what we did and did not share became even more obvious. Meena was from the Sudan and worked with children orphaned by AIDS when she wasn't teaching at the local university. Lilly worked on race and gender in the U.S. women's prison system and taught in the University of California. Halla, who taught at our host university, was writing about an eighteenth-century Egyptian woman novelist and, on the side, ran a "women and memory" community workshop. Betsy had just finished a book on freedom and gender in early American literature and was struggling to get her university's maternity and childcare policies improved. Hoda had just started graduate school in Morocco and wanted to study women in Islam; she told us it was the first time she had flown. Irene wrote books about North American "girl culture" and the declining significance of race and class in media configurations of their sexuality; she also told us about her teenage daughter, Melody. Nelpa had just left a university in the U.S. to return to Palestine, where she was teaching women's studies, sometimes in Ramallah, sometimes in Bethlehem, depending on the daily status of Israel's imposed travel restrictions. Lucinda was a Film Studies professor and had just gotten tenure in the U.S.; she also worked with local labor unions. I introduced myself as a feminist theologian and ordained Protestant minister whose most recent activism centered on single-parenting a very active eight-year-old girl and working with churches around issues of sexuality and social justice. And the introductions went on, each person offering the group their own version of the academic, activist, and personal credentials that brought them to the meeting.

THE RHETORIC OF TRANSNATIONAL FEMINISM

Although it was no doubt the case that such introductions offered—as they always do—only the most superficial of insights into all of our richly complex lives, it was telling to me that each person chose to identify herself according to these particular codes and not others. What did these tell us about the shared "identity performances" of those attending the conference? They showed us what has become, in many ways, the "dramatic script" that women like ourselves all inhabit for the space of these transnational conversations (and beyond), scripts we use to depict the central features of our shared work and lives. In other words, what emerged in these opening comments was a rough sketch of our common story about the world and who we are in it—a collectively scripted tale of the self and its obligations to community.[2]

The dramatic tale went something like this. First, all of us worked in arenas where "women" were the central focus of our academic work as well as our activism. That giving special attention to women's lives is a noble and righteous endeavor was assumed, not because women are somehow "essentially special" but because of a long history of their invisibility and silence. In this regard, there was a clear sense that attending to women's lives is a preferential option emerging out of a pragmatic assessment of need. Second, in the dramatic script of the conference, women were not viewed by anyone simply as static creatures bearing an innately feminine nature. It was our strong consensus that cultural context largely generates the tales we tell about who women are and that these tales are multiple and contestable. Interestingly, with respect to questions of essentialism, it seemed unnecessary to press the issue further than this. We had enough sense of the agility of gender to keep us engaged and moving, and that's what seemed to matter most. Third, there was a shared belief that, when it comes to women's lives, something in each of our local contexts is terribly wrong, and these "wrongs" are increasingly global in their reach. Some called these wrongs oppression, some named them harms, and others called them forms of domination or repression or patriarchy or injustice. Whatever words we used and whatever conscious or unconscious theory stood behind our choice of terms, what mattered in this context was a determined, restless sense that the "world is not as it should be" with respect to women's lives and that the harms being perpetrated against them are serious and deepening daily in their scope and power. In this regard, a moment of trenchant social critique stood at the center of our collective tale.

Tied to this was a fourth dimension to our shared story: Everyone there had a passionate sense that we need not only to observe these harms but also to actively intervene to stop them and to change the social order that produced them. Further, we all seemed to agree that this call to participate in political transformation not only fueled our academic work but also expressed our deepest social commitments, our sense of vocation. We were all activists first, scholars second; and if intensity of voice is at least a partial indication of depth of commitment, then there wasn't a cynic or a dilettante among us—at least as far as our dramatic scripts were concerned. It is also significant to note that with respect to this shared commitment to being agents of social change, there was a corollary consensus that transformation has its roots in collective action and that motivating and participating in local social movements is a crucial part of this, a fact that made us all champions of grassroots organizing.

Finally, embedded in this robust activism was an often unspoken but nonetheless strong assumption that one day, somewhere, somehow, someplace, it might be possible to enact forms of community where women flourished. This was quite striking to me. Despite our different disciplinary and cultural backgrounds, we shared a pragmatic optimism about the future, albeit an optimism constrained by our awareness of the unending necessity of critique and the inevitable provisionality of emancipatory projects. Within the terrain of our imaginations, there existed an elusive space marked "possibility," a place where laws, customs, relationships, social expectations, and cultural institutions were all constructed so that the women who lived within them experienced fullness of life.[3] What we actually meant by "fullness of life," or "flourishing," no doubt differed significantly from person to person and context to context; but again, even here were some shared features. In this place, there would be respect for bodily integrity, safety from sexual violence, shared economic responsibility for child-rearing, access to adequate health care, food, and shelter, and mechanisms for political participation.[4] Integral to this list was also the shared sense that the forms of flourishing we desired included women's pleasure, delight, joy, and experiences of beauty, although when our conversations stumbled into these latter areas, our language seemed always to lose its strength and precision at the very moment our capacity to communicate seemed to matter most.

I offer this summary of our performative script—our rhetoric—not as an exhaustive account of each person's motives and commitments; it surely leaves out much and no doubt invokes elements that individual participants might excitedly contest. [5] For the most part, however, I believe it captures, at a very pragmatic level, the assumptions that framed not only our conversations in Cairo but also an emerging, broader, transnational feminist performative identity. It is a script of who we imagined we were as we sat in our chairs and introduced ourselves that first morning, in the rhetorical space we inhabited for the time of our meeting. Put another way, it is this "story" that formed, at least in part, the imaginary of our transnational feminism, a tale—not a theory—whose power rested more in its ability to attract and compel us than in its logical necessity or shape. Perhaps I might better call it the *poetry of our transnational feminism*, a space where the meaning happened because the play of images and possibilities this common story produced was desirable, life giving, and worthy of our deepest personal investment. Despite our different locations, languages, life commitments, religious values, and so on, we found ourselves collectively taken in by and then enacting a lyrical, almost saga-like poem of our yearning for women's flourishing and the struggle we would undertake to get there—an adventure story of sorts, a love tale, in a way, a fable of enduring value. Our circle of chairs ringed its edges, our clothes fleshed out its characters, our differences marked its mystery, and the arch of time that stretched before us—seven days together in Cairo—gave us permission to see if, perhaps this time, the poem would live again.

THE TEMPTATIONS OF THEORY

What does the presence of this script suggest about transnational feminism and the work of love, the question of this essay? Several things. First, let me describe a temptation that needs to be resisted, one to which I often fall prey. As a feminist scholar, I find it easy to look at the script I have just outlined and do one of two things. The first impulse is toward history and context. I have been trained to ask, almost instinctively, the *archaeological* question. When I do this, I put on the hat of either an historian or anthropologist and begin searching for an account of the script's origin. "How is it that we came to hold this view?" I query, and in response, a myriad of possible scenarios emerge. Could it be a byproduct of the fact that most of the conference participants were formed in Western educational systems that implicitly promote this seemingly Enlightenment view of history and hope? Is the script therefore just part of the very imperial, capitalist legacy we claim to be contesting? Or does it say something about the cultural terrains of Christianity, Islam, and Judaism, terrains within which we were all shaped, even though some of us have ostensibly chosen to reject them? Is it part of shared religious, cultural heritage and its insistent orientation toward agency and a future hope? Or is it perhaps the product of the deeply Marxist sensibilities that still haunt the edges of contemporary social movements, a holdover from the age of revolution, or the era of romantic idealism? Or does its legacy lie in the intellectual tradition of women's studies as it is now emerging in a global context, a legacy in which the tales of feminist activism and critical scholarship continue to be intertwined in complex and shifting ways?[6] Is it ludic feminism, at its worst, or perhaps its best?[7] And the questions could go on and on.

The second, almost instinctive habit of mind that comes into play, for me, when faced with a story like the conference script is the *philosophical* or *theoretical* one. I begin searching for a conceptual framework within which to locate it. In my case (and I am confident that it is also the case for many other feminist theorists), the fields of political philosophy, social ethics, and psychoanalysis present the most appealing options. When donning this hat, I try to pull out of the story a set of principled commitments or analytic insights that I then attempt to line up with certain trends in these contemporary frameworks. When I do this, the results take the form of questions such as the following: Is this story an implicit endorsement of classical liberal social theory and its concomitant commitment to "rights discourse"? Is it just another tale of "freedom, equality, and the dignity of man," albeit an updated feminist version? Another version of the social contract? Or is it perhaps a more communitarian model of a shared vision of the good life? Is it a tale made possible by the habits of mind embedded in our shared communal context, a context created by the unifying spread of global capitalism's culture of consumption? Or is it closer to a "communicative theory" of the political, a pragmatic set of regulative ideals that make our conversations possible without simultaneously reducing our differences? Or is it something else altogether? Could it be that, from a postmodern perspective, the tale is, at its best, a momentary coalescence of otherwise disparate interests, and, at worst, an imperial imposition of my own imagining? If the latter, is it yet another colonial attempt to totalize forces that fundamentally resist such reductions to order? Is it a mere fantasy of closure, a thwarted desire, an object whose possession I seek but can never master? And again, the questions could go on.

By labeling these two forms of reflection "temptations," I do not mean to imply that they are somehow inherently problematic or flawed enterprises. They are not. In fact, both kinds of inquiry can be usefully employed in various contexts to promote the kind of agenda that inspired our Cairo discussions. What I want to suggest here, however, is that the urge to historical or theoretical analysis can also be deployed in ways that hinder conversation and, correlatively, the work of love. A version of this is what I saw happening in Egypt, beginning on the second day.

It started when we split into small groups and began taking turns discussing some of the central themes in the distributed conference papers. The papers were interesting and quite diverse in form and focus. Some of them were close readings of particular events or icons: an analysis of "sex clubs" for teenagers in Iran, a reading of the acquisitions list of a museum in Mexico, an account of gender attributions in a women's prison in the U.S. Others were more theoretical: a philosophical reading of "freedom" discourse in Western liberalism, a broad assessment of pedagogical strategies for teaching feminism in transnational classrooms, a look at the place of "group rights" arguments in present-day North American progressive politics. In these sessions, each person would offer a few comments on her own paper, and then we would talk together about it for ten or so minutes.

These conversations were usually very lively; the specific content of each paper concentrated our attention in a productive manner. Given that no one else in the room was an expert on the specific topic at hand, it was all right for us to ask questions that were not well formulated or to confess complete ignorance of the subject matter before we gaily plunged into unknown territory. It was also acceptable, in these conversations, for us to make very ad hoc connections between their work and our own cultural contexts, intellectual projects, and discrete sites of activism. We could talk about teen sex in Texas or teaching feminism in a Moroccan community center or even armed struggle in the Sudan with a looseness that invited many voices to participate. In this respect, our interactions were not framed by an expectation that our research and our political interests had to fit together to tell a single, comprehensive, liberating story about the world and the place of gender in it. That wasn't the point of these discussions. Our play of mind was not formally structured around any shared desire for analytic closure. The productive pleasure of the back and forth—and the imaginative learning and connections it allowed us to experience—seemed end enough in itself, at least for the moment.

The difficulty came when, at the end of these sessions, we opened up the floor to a more general discussion of the material. The purpose here was to begin mapping the space of transnational feminism in its broadest dimensions and to do so by building on our earlier conversations. When we reached this part of the program, without fail, one of the North American feminist theorists would be the first to speak, and her comments would be of the broadly archeological or philosophical variety described above. Immediately, another North American feminist would follow her, strongly agreeing or disagreeing with the first position. Then, almost like clockwork, a full-fledged debate would spring up between three or four people, a debate in which the goal was not only to win your position but also to show how much you knew and how comprehensive your insights were. Added to this was the goal of displaying how politically astute and progressive your leftist commitments were. After about twenty minutes of this, the session would end, and we would break before starting another small group meeting designed to follow the same pattern of conversation: presentations, small group discussions, and then collective mapping.

THE RHETORIC OF THE FEMINIST *THEORY*

The problem was not hard to see. In the collective discussion times, only a small group of North Americans were speaking. Moreover, those with training in theory were the most dominant of them. At one level, this made perfect sense. Their form of discourse was well suited to that particular format—the format of big group discussions aimed at drawing connections between disparate topics and broad territories. It was clear from the conversation that the theorists among us were the ones trained to speak grandly about any and all topics and to do so by making generalizations that sounded quite brilliant in scope and delivery. It was a game they knew well how to play. After all, the point of feminist theory, understood most broadly, is to explore the fundamental habits of thought that structure our daily modes of thinking—the task of thinking critically about critical thinking.[8] Here was a setting in which habits of many different critical minds were unfurling simultaneously, and the task before us was to construct a conceptual framework to hold them all. From the perspective of the theorists among us, it was intellectual heaven.

At another level, however, it was apparent that this mode of engagement was profoundly ill suited to our work given that it succeeded only, time and again, in shutting down the broader conversation. The deeper we went into the land of theory, the more women fell into the role of silent observers. Although it was not just the Arab women who chose not to speak during these times, they made up the majority of those who sat silent; and by the third day, they also made up the majority of the participants who were opting out of these small group events altogether. As one of the quiet listeners put it to me, "They are talking too much about not much of anything." What was most striking to me about this dynamic was located not so much in the content of the theory being espoused—it was, in my mind, often quite smart and illuminating—but rather in the habits of thought the theory carried with it. It was the form of life the theory bespoke. Or put slightly differently, it was the way in which the theory was performed that became so debilitating.

What were the particularly debilitating features of this performance of feminist theory? Here are just four of the most obvious. First, the performance placed a high value on public speech acts; it mattered greatly that one was *speaking* and, in doing so, *being heard*. Interestingly, this particular value has a long history in feminist politics, a history that now appeared to be turning on itself in a context where the space of the "public" was configured in such a radically different manner. Second, the performative purpose of this speaking was to *theorize*, an activity aimed at crafting overarching, conceptual tales that were both comprehensive in scope and analytically exhaustive in depth. Given this aim, it should not be surprising that, when performed, the voracious goals of the enterprise were mirrored in the voracious affect of its performers. It swallowed all voices in its quest for breadth and depth and thereby narrowed the conceptual field rather than expanding it. Third, this aim of theorizing was strangely intertwined with another, a project of *critique*. Over and over again, the women who spoke did so to expose what they considered to be the misguided or false view of the matter at hand (whatever that might be). In this regard, they enacted the rhetoric of negative dialectics at its best. The problem was, however, in this context, the dialectic consistently failed to accomplish the desired end of liberatory dizziness; instead, it repeatedly produced a complete shutdown of conversation. Fourth, as a form of feminist theory, this comprehensive and critical speech performance had yet another goal before it, that of *enabling social justice*. This goal clearly rested in the underlying assumption of all the speakers that if everyone just understood and accepted what they were saying, then progressive political action would be sure to follow. As to what social justice actually looked like, however, there was little if any discussion of its specific content. Why? To be too bold about the normative work of making strong justice claims was to risk disavowing the treasured deconstructive goals I just described. This was particularly true given that many of the normative claims that brought us together in the first place—that vision I described as our common story—were not founded by critical argument but poetically generated by desire. As would become increasingly apparent to all the women gathered, this tension between the analytic critique and aesthetically compelling norms was no small thing; as the week progressed, it threatened to undo our conversations altogether.

I offer this list of what I consider to be four performative features of the feminist theory exhibited in Cairo not to simply dismiss theory as an inherently problematic enterprise. Rather, I list them to make the point that feminist theory, as a rhetorical practice, is as vulnerable to the needs and desires of its practitioners as any form of speaking. What works in one place can fail miserably in another, as it did in Egypt. Until feminist theorists from North America come to grips with this dimension of our enterprise, the conversations we participate in risk falling, time and again, into a silence like the one I describe. Further, we need to be aware that attending to the rhetoric of our speech involves not just paying attention to our tone of voice or how long we speak or even whether we couch our statements in contextualizing gestures like "I think" or "as a North American." It requires attending as well to the form and aims of the arguments we deploy. In this regard, it involves much more pragmatic and strategic assessment of the forms of discursive engagement that mark our transnational conversations.

I also list these performative features because they illustrate a conceptual problem at the center of much present-day academic feminist discourse. In both my account of the conference's transnational feminist rhetoric/poetry outlined earlier in this essay and of this rhetoric of feminist theory, there lies a deep commitment to emancipatory visions and practices. The flagship "justice" sails at the front of both. They differ from one another in a crucial way, however. In the rhetorical world of feminist theory, there is clearly a tension between, on the one hand, *the descriptive and critical ends* of theory and, on the other hand, its *normative goal of justice* (or whatever term one chooses for "flourishing"). In the world of our broader conversation—the one that emerged in the introductions—the descriptive and critical endeavors are also combined with the articulation of an emancipatory vision; but in this case, pragmatic judgments, not the need for conceptual coherence, bind the three together. Seemingly conflicting impulses are woven together under the unifying pull of political, communal desires.

In the final section of this essay, I will return to this last point and explore further what we might learn about transnational feminism from it. For now, however, I want to attend a little more closely to the tension I have identified in the rhetoric of feminist theory. What is one to make of it? Given the comprehensive, analytic goals of feminist theory, this tension seemed to be most often resolved by repressing the need for normative reflection so that the ends of description and critique could be effectively pursued. This sleight of hand whereby the constantly invoked goal of justice and its poetic grounding are rendered invisible is, I believe, not only one of feminist theory's most practiced habits of thought: it is quite possibly one of the most dangerous features of its intellectual practice. Nowhere do we see this more clearly than in the general attitude that academic feminist theory has had toward religion, and nowhere was its shortcoming made more obvious to me than in our Cairo conversations. To this topic, let me now turn.

THE TEMPTATIONS OF RELIGION

In the early sessions of our meeting—those initial hours when we were introducing ourselves and both crafting and enacting the collective story of our gathering—I was the only participant who mentioned that she was religious.[9] I shared with everyone that, among other things, I taught Christian theology and was an ordained Protestant minister. Over the years, I have grown accustomed to the kind of response this identification elicits from my fellow women's and gender studies colleagues in North America, particularly those who have no formal affiliation with religious studies or theological education. As I spoke these words in Cairo, I half expected to get a similar reaction there. After all, it seemed clear, at least from the papers I'd read, that "religion" was not at the top of most people's list of topics appropriate to academic transnational feminism.

What kind of response did I anticipate getting that morning? If past experience was to be my guide, I thought it would go something like this. There would probably be one or two folks who would go out of their way to express an interest in this dimension of my work. However, the vast majority would either choose to ignore it (usually with an embarrassed silence) or to express some form of hostility toward it. This second reaction would not be obvious, however. Some people might be bold enough to inform me that religious practitioners appeared to be invariably reactionary and that religious commitments seemed intellectually untenable; but these voices would be few. It was more likely that the hostility would come in the quieter forms of a personal story about how miserable one's childhood church experiences were or, even worse, a slightly condescending exploration of whether I was pro-choice and, if so, was I capable of higher thought processes. There was also the chance that if the topic were substantively explored, it would consist of critical observations about the relation between fundamentalism and women—how women are victims of it, globally—another broadly favored sport among progressive academics these days, myself included.

Much to my surprise, however, this is not what occurred. Immediately after I spoke, one of the theory-trained women from North America chimed in that she thought we all needed to talk about religion, that it was crucially important at this point in history. But, she added, she did not know how to do it. Several of my U.S. colleagues nodded approvingly, while most of the Arab women looked agreeable if not also slightly puzzled. The woman from Palestine addressed this response. "All of the Arab women here are Muslim," she said quite matter-of-factly. "I guess that means we are all religious. But frankly, when you talk about religion, I am never sure what it is you are referring to. Everything is religious, isn't it? If so, why do we have to make it an isolated topic of discussion, as if it's something that can be abstracted and examined apart from the rest of our reality?" After this, the room broke into a fast-paced, many-voiced conversation, which concluded only when one of the conference hosts announced that, given the obvious excitement around the topic, we should try to keep religion at the center of our discussion for the remainder of our gathering. And so began a conversation about "religion" that would move in a variety of directions over the next several days, sometimes limping along, sometimes soaring, and sometimes just gently drifting into places we didn't know how to travel.[10]

What did the features of this discussion suggest to me about the character of transnational feminist conversations? As with many of the topics treated in this essay, the suggestive possibilities are myriad. Religion, gender, and globalization are all three areas that, in the massive knot of their presence in women's lives, demand our critical attention, both as disparate realities and, even more importantly, as inseparable dimensions of our collective lived experience. For the purpose of this essay, however, I want to reflect on just three features of that knot, as each was manifest in our conversations in Cairo.

RELIGIOUS CONFLICTS

First, it was fascinating to me that, with respect to religion, the North American and Arab conversations were moving in different directions. The U.S. feminists were becoming aware of an absence in their theory and were puzzling over how to bring the topics of faith and religious community back into the scope of its critical enterprise. They wanted to see it, to make it visible. For the Middle Eastern women, "religion" as a category of social analysis was neither absent nor invisible; they knew themselves collectively to be Muslim, a title they had no difficulty attributing to their varied contexts. In this regard, religion was ubiquitous. The challenge for them, in our conversation, was thus to discover how to speak about this dimension of their reality in ways appropriate to its omnipresent visibility—a challenge the North American women found hard to grasp. Until we were able to recognize that our different environments occasioned these two very different problematics with respect to religion, we would find ourselves talking past one another, again and again.

Second, as I spoke about religion with other North American feminists during our meetings, a new story about feminist theory began to emerge, one that I believe has enormously productive possibilities. It's a tale that begins in a very familiar vein, a tale about the Enlightenment's need to create a space called "the sacred" (or "the religious") in order to define and secure the space of "the secular." As the opposite of reasoned, secular thought, religiosity marked forms of life where tradition and superstitious value held sway, a place where irrational motivation funded action and where unruly passions shaped sentiment. In the imaginary of this modern mind, faith occupied the space of the feminine, the hysterical other whose wandering in the lands of the irrational rendered it immune to the stabilizing pressures of progress, freedom, and equality, the space of masculine thought and action. Here, both religion and the feminine were relegated to the space of the private and the domestic, whereas secularity and masculinity occupied the overtly political and economic space of public social actions. Similarly, in terms of discursive form, religious speech was feminized and defined as either formally dogmatic or informally biographical, both rhetorical styles whose practices were confined to church and home. (Patriarchy as the realm of the fathers and hence tradition also became feminized and was subsequently rendered hidden from public view.) In contrast, the discursive practices of science and logic dominated the rhetoric of public conversation, speech enacted in the public square and marketplace. Here, again, "private" and "public" functioned as distinctions whose alternate presence confirmed, by contrast, the existence of the other.[11] It was in this world of conceptual and institutional distinctions that modern feminism arose, as itself an extension of the liberal political project of the Enlightenment. It was also in this world that Western feminist theory learned to secure its liberal credentials through its critical regard for its oppressive, traditional other—*religion*.

What was interesting about our conversations in Egypt was not this older story but rather our insight into its newest chapter: postmodern feminist theory. While it has been clear for some time that feminist theory has much to contribute to contemporary critiques of this Enlightenment construal of social life, these critiques have not included, interestingly enough, a revaluation of religion. At one level this seems peculiar. If the distinctions between public and private, masculine and feminine, reason and emotion, and mind and body are now up for grabs, why not the secular/sacred divide as well? When the philosophical story of the social construction of religion and the story of the feminine are set side by side, the obvious conclusion seems to be that as one falls, so falls the other. In my experience, however, this has not been the case. Why?

Let me offer a twofold response. First, recall my earlier discussion of feminist theory's story, its impulse toward descriptive comprehensiveness, its disposition toward critique, and its strongly poetic but repressed commitment to social justice. As I argued, there is a long-standing tension in feminist theory between its analytical procedures and the emancipatory telos of normative speech acts, a tension that is finally managed by a sleight of hand through which the assumed goals of justice are not rejected but are obscured or made invisible. It seems clear to me that religion, as a discourse within which normative value and poetic appeal holds pride of place (features that prohibit it from behaving in a manner appropriate to an obedient, repressed second term), is often swept off the table along with justice—its pietistic, unruly presence a threat to the project's postmodern form, its unmanageable insistence on valued ends a problem to be denied.

This is not the whole story, however. There is a second chapter in this tale of religion's strange place in feminist theory. At the very moment feminist theory enacted this repression of religion, it simultaneously invested in religion's becoming a very visible, almost exotic presence as the "other" that feminist theory could oppose and, in doing so, use to secure its position as an emancipatory discourse within the framework of liberal democracy. When it comes to religion, we cannot live with it, but alas, we cannot live without it, either. Sound familiar? It's not all that different from the description French feminist Luce Irigaray has given of the dual place of the "feminine" in Western thought: First, as mother, *she* is a ground that must be repressed so that *he* may thrive as a singular, ungenerated presence; second, as lover, she is an other that, as his opposite, mirrors back to him his contrastive identity, a play that reduces her to a function of her master's repetitive desires.[12] Could it be that for feminist theory, religion occupies the dual role of being, on the one hand, the space of hysteria, the cave from which it crawls, the effaced maternal ground of its origin, and on the other hand, the other that assures feminism's progressive political credentials, that functions as lover, as our desire-laden object of disgust, as a mirror image of our own longing for visibility and love?

RESISTING RELIGION

In these theoretical ponderings about the figure of religion in feminist theory, I have admittedly wandered far away from the halls of the Cairo conference and into a land of discourse where the temptations of philosophical analysis (here, in its psychoanalytic form) threaten to undo possibility. It needn't be so, however. Let me turn back to the gathering of women and make a third comment about what I saw unfolding there in relation to the above critique. If there is any vestige of truth or any helpful insight in this account of religion's plight, it might seem at first glance that feminist theory has before it the clear task of reclaiming religion and that it might best do so by resurrecting it from the grave of its unreflective repression. In other words, the temptation of North American feminists who want to work on religion will be to dig up the version of religion that the Enlightenment created and then buried. If Cairo was any indication, this will be strongly appealing in the North American academy. It's a temptation I saw enacted—almost unconsciously—in our Egyptian conversations, a temptation I gave into as well.

When I introduced myself on that first day, I listed my religion among a number of identity markers that "performed me" for the group in a manner that I hoped would be compliant with our emergent script of transnational feminism. I was a Christian theologian and or-dained minister, along with being a mother, a teacher, and an activist. Implied in this rhetorical account of my identity is the assumption that "religion" actually marks a meaningful site of identity formation that can be distinguished from others. Further, although I did not say it directly, the content of this so-called identity site was filled with many of the distinctions that have marked the travels of religion through the land of liberal social theory and feminism—sacredness, value, and so on. My expectations as to how the others would respond to me suggested as much. In this way, my own rhetoric of religiosity enacted the play of mind I sought to disrupt.

Similarly, as the conversations at the conference turned to the topic of religion, my fellow North Americans started responding to my religious interests in a way that suggested that they, too, wanted to enjoy the pleasures of religion's resurrection. As one person put it, speaking in her most open-minded and enthusiastic of voices, "Oh, let's take seriously that part of Serene's identity that she is naming for us, a name that also marks the experience of so many other women—not only all those right-wing women in the U.S. who support the Bush administration, but also the women here and in the Middle East in general, for religion is such an important part of their lives, too." After this, she proudly turned to look at our Arab conference partners.

The difficulty with this was that, for the Arab women, religion did not work that way. It was not one sphere among many others. It wasn't the binary other to the secular. It wasn't the space of either the hysteric or the lover. As they described it, their religion simply was. Muslim. Transcending all gestures toward the dualism. Resisting the splits of the Enlightenment. Thwarting the logic that feminist theory hoped would contain it. This became apparent at several levels during our conversations.

Of the Arab women gathered, all of them self-identified as "Muslim" but only when pressed.[13] Although it was clear that their range of religious practices varied widely, they did not describe themselves as representing variations of Islamic faith, as I have come to expect from groups of Christian feminists who, when gathered, quickly associate themselves with names such as "Presbyterian" or "Roman Catholic." They were simply Muslim. Moreover, many of the women seemed to me to be what in North America we would call "secular Muslims," implying that while they were formed in a cultural environment marked by Islamic religious practices and collective identity, they felt ambivalent about it intellectually but were nonetheless honest enough to claim it as constitutive of their lived experience. None of them, however, accepted this title either. They were Muslim. For them, this split between practicing and nonpracticing seemed peculiarly West-ern, a form of naming appropriate only to religious communities for whom belief and practice were distinguishable categories in the first place or for whom faith was principally a matter of choice, like the clothes one wears to work. For them, these distinctions did not hold. Interestingly, it was also clear that they did not feel that by claiming the common title "Muslim," they were in any way effacing the differ-ences among them. It simply named what they were, in the midst of all their ethnic, national, and racial diversity.

The effect of a religious sensibility that defied the logic of our catego-rization was uncanny. An undifferentiated presence we could neither dissect nor conceptually control, it demanded our attention by virtue of its insistent givenness and yet would not conform to our usual stan-dards of engagement. There was among the North American feminists gathered a sense of collective discomfort with it, the desire to proceed as normal and not discuss religion, or to caricature it by talking about something called "fundamentalism" and then move quickly onto more important matters. But if we had done that in this context, the strategy would not have worked. Our caricatures would have seemed bigoted, our silence, complicitly imperialist. Given these pressures, the ques-tion loomed large: How were we to proceed? How were we to begin to speak about "religion" when we had no shared understanding of the term's reference? For me, the challenge became even more acute when the temptation of theory was added to the list of inappropriate strate-gies for moving forward. How were we to talk about religion when even the pleasures of abstraction and its drive toward analytic con-sumption were prohibited? What forms of speech and thought might we perform to guide us through shared miscommunications?

I wish I could report that after several days of struggling with these questions, we figured out a process and a language that could bear the weight of these pressures and facilitate the conversation we longed to have. The truth is, however, we never did. The formal discussions continued to wane in attendance and energy, and the best we could do by the end of the conference was to agree that, if we organized another gathering the following year, its whole focus should be "re-ligion." There was absolutely no argument about the important place that "religion" should hold in transnational feminist conversations—it was crucial. As to what this actually meant, however, we did not seem to have a clue.

AFTERTHOUGHTS

Or did we?

Given this rather dismal account of our group conversations, it is easy to suppose that the gathering was, finally, a complete failure. What is remarkable is that it wasn't. Signs of the conference's success were everywhere. As just one example of this success, when my two colleagues and I once again boarded a plane, this time to leave, our conversations were far from depressed or frustrated. Instead, we had a vibrant sense that the conference had been wonderfully productive and that our work back at home in women's and gender studies—and in "feminist theory"—would be forever transformed by the time we had spent there. We were excited—really excited—intellectually about the ways in which the gathering had changed our views about gender, the Middle East, Islam, North America, globalization, religion, and so on. The excitement, surprisingly, wasn't just the thrill of a knowledge won on the hind side of loss or the pleasure of learning from mistakes. While there was a little of this, most of what excited us were substantive, positive learnings—lessons such as a new way of thinking about veils, a different understanding of marriage, a shift in our account of liberalism, an emboldened hope for the future of transnational feminism, a humorous version of the Arabian Nights, a deepened sense of both the commonalities and differences that marked the lives of the women involved, a growing love for Egyptian scarves, an expanding appreciation for the ambiguous character of any "read" we might give to gendered performances in a global context, and the even more ambiguous assessment of colonialism's cultural legacies. In all these ways and more, we discovered that the highest aspirations of the feminist "common story" articulated on the first day had been embodied—quite powerfully—in the learnings with which we were now walking away.

How was it that we came to have such positive afterthoughts about the conference? Answering this question requires looking beyond our formal sessions to the margins of the gathering, those places and times when we were able to more easily avoid the temptations of theory and engage in forms of conversation that opened up the possibility of mutually enhancing insights and critical wisdom—places where the common tale that brought us there was enacted and expanded. As a conclusion to this essay, I want to explore briefly two forms or "spaces" of discourse that marked these alternate terrains of engagement, spaces that I believe might usefully guide feminist theorists and theologians as we try to chart the course of future transnational feminist conversations and projects. They provide examples of forms of speech and practice that, if consciously embraced, might open up contexts where theory fails but continued reflection is desired. In this way, they expand the repertoire of the rhetorics appropriate to arenas such as the Cairo conference and, in doing so, provide different (and better!) strategies for talking about topics like "religion" and "globalization" in a manner that is neither reductive nor imperialist. Not incidentally, they are also rhetorical strategies in which I, as a feminist theologian—and not just theorist—have particular interest insofar as constructive theologians deploy them on a daily basis.

A THOUSAND NIGHTS IN ONE

After the close of the second day's session, one of the conference organizers invited several of us to join her and some friends at a restaurant famous for its stuffed pigeon, a local favorite. We piled into two cabs, our books and bags stuffed under foot, and set out on a harrowing ride through the streets of Cairo. Halla, on whose lap I was sitting—we had six women in the car—smiled at my white-knuckled grip on the back of the front seat. She then pointed to a car driving the wrong way down the busy street, and then another. "How far do we have to go?" I asked her, trying to look relaxed. It was about an hour-long trip, she told me, laughing. She rubbed my back with her hand and began braiding the tasseled ends of my scarf.

"Let me tell you a story," she began. "You have heard of the Tales of a Thousand and One Nights? When I go to community centers and villages to talk with mothers and wives about women's issues, I tell them feminist versions of these stories. They are kind of like your Grimm's fairy tales or Bible stories—tales that tell us who we are, deep somewhere. Telling these women a different but believable story works magic." The rest of the car fell silent at the word "magic." I thought of Esther and Goldilocks and Mary and Midrash, exegesis, and preaching.

As we continued through the streets, for an hour Halla held us captive with one of these stories, the tale of the famous Scheherazade, a brave woman who was fed up with the violence of a king who kept murdering women after he married them. Hundreds of them. In Halla's version of the story, Scheherazade was determined to stop him; her plan was to seduce him and, at night while he slept, cut his throat, thus ending her terror with a slash. Her seduction worked and they married. Her first night with him, however, she discovered two amazing things. First, she actually liked him and felt compassion for him, isolated in his lonely castle, desperately tearing stories from the hearts of women to keep his mind alive and his soul breathing. She also discovered his dreaded secret. The king was impotent—a fact that if known would destroy his power in the kingdom and ensure that the land would be plunged into war. He killed the women to keep them silent, an act which troubled him greatly but which he felt helpless to stop.

Confused by these discoveries, Scheherazade needed time to think and listen to her heart. To hold him off, she began to weave a story of mysterious adventure, one rich enough to distract him from his fatal mission. For hundreds of nights she continued, plying him with ever new tales of far-off worlds; and each dawning day, she would fail to finish the story, ensuring that yet one more night he would keep her alive so that he might have his desire for an ending fulfilled. Something amazing happened to the king, though. Slowly, he began to love and respect her. She, too, began to cherish him like a brother. As the thousandth night drew near, Scheherazade finally saw what she had to do. She pledged to him that she would forever keep his secret because her love for him was greater than her desire for sex or children or revenge or even truth. In return for her silence, she asked him to promise that she could be his companion and equal. Relieved that he finally saw a way out of his terrible dilemma, he let her live, and together they ruled the kingdom—now filled with happy women—for a very long time.

When Halla finally finished, a long silence fell in the cab. We were sad it was over—the story had completely captivated us. We were also delighted, thrilled to hear it from her and to imagine how exciting it must be to tell such tales in the village she had conjured up for us; we could hear in our own chuckles the sounds of the village women's laughter upon discovering the king's secret; we could feel their admiration for Scheherazade's wit and courage. And we could easily imagine people—both men and women—from our own world to whom such a story of violence, surprise, and hope might rightfully apply. It was funny, it was warm, it was believable, it was epic, and it mattered. Perhaps most important of all, it gave to those of us who were not Arab or Egyptian a window into a world of gender construal and power negotiations that we would not have been able to find in our postmodern paper sessions. I wondered about the story of Esther seducing and then chopping off her enemy's head. Would telling that story to Halla begin an interreligious dialogue of a different feminist sort—a conversation whose poetics resist the closures of theory and avoid the critical-normative impasse of so much of our talk? I then thought about *Monster's Ball*. I felt jealous of Scheherazade's gift for story-telling and worried that I couldn't keep myself alive that long. Would I ever rule a kingdom? Where women flourished? Would I ever even live in one? Were empires and kingdoms the same? Did murderous tales of capital's frantic fear of impotence drive markets? What would Jesus do? What was Scheherazade wearing?

VEILED ADORATIONS

The café serving pigeon was in a small house whose walls were carpeted in colors rich and tasseled. Once again, we squeezed into a small space, our bodies scooting closer and closer to make room for the second cab of women. This time Meena was practically sitting on my lap. I began fingering the braids Halla had woven into my woolen scarf strings while telling her story. Meena's headscarf had no fringe; its lightweight polyester gave sheen to its pattern of soft blue, muted roses. I was close enough to see the bobby pins holding it in place, and I was sure she could see the grey roots in my hair that I had been trying to cover for years.

We started talking about clothes, a cliché for sure, but an inevitable one. Where did she buy her scarves? What kind of perfume was that? Was it true that in the U.S. we rarely used sugar for waxing? Don't you hate the facial hairs of menopause? Lifting up my own scarf, I asked if it would be okay to put this over my head when I go into a mosque—I tried to act like I understood it all, but I didn't. Meena said not to worry; no one would probably care one way or the other. What did I wear when I went to church?

I told her when I was growing up in a place called Oklahoma, every Sunday we had to put on our fanciest clothes and shiniest shoes, and wash our hair the night before. Why? she asked. The hair washing and the nice dresses? A million responses flashed through my head— because my mother said so, because it was a big social event and my parents wanted to look like they were raising decent children, because it was convention and we were Calvinists, because we had nowhere to go all dressed up, because we could. The answer that came out surprised me, though.

"Because we are supposed to look beautiful for God, to show God how much we appreciate what God does for us. It's a way of honoring through beauty."

I then asked about her veil. Why?

"The same, I think. There is no better way to honor Allah than by looking beautiful. I wear it for God, I guess. It's an act of praise."

Not to protect you from the gaze of men? I thought. It's not just an act of hiding but of appearing?[14] A practice of being seen, divinely? It's not just about imprisonment but also thanksgiving.[15] All my unarticulated and articulated views of veils came crashing down around me. First, she did not think of her scarf as simply oppressive; she also thought of it as elegant and attractive, the same way I might think about a new pair of earrings as I shove them through the holes punched in my ears. Second, the gazing eye that she performed before, the adoring look she sought, was radically transcendent, belonging to an unspoken, unknowable knower. Not her father nor brothers nor even the guys down the street. It was a gaze without a viewer. What kind of theological aesthetic was this?

"Doesn't it sometimes feel heavy or itchy?" I asked in a less than erudite fashion.

Meena smiled as she reached over and started braiding a different section of my scarf. "Yes, but I don't have to wash my hair every Sunday, now do I?"

A transnational feminist conversation about clothes? Retrogressive? Pandering to patriarchal culture? What would it look like if these kinds of interactions were the material of our meetings and our writings? What if describing daily activities like getting dressed—the practices of adornment—served as the starting point for our exploration of religion? And global capitalism? And gender? For where do the mechanisms of consumerism intrude more intimately into our lives than in the market's ability to inform our dressing and our care for our bodies? And how does the market work its way in? Through its ability to construct desire, through its formation of aesthetic sensibility, through the invocation of pleasures and excess. If this is the case, then I believe if we are committed to a transnational feminism that seeks the flourishing of women, it is going to be here, in the nitty gritty play of our everyday practices—not just of adornment but of other things like cooking, resting, caring for children, going to work—that we'll get the best read of "gender" and "religion" and, in doing so, garner insight into new forms of resistance and common action.

A JUST AND TRUE LOVE

There is, indeed, much more to be said about these matters, particularly about the place of narrative and practices in transnational feminist discourse. After the Cairo conference, I enjoyed imagining what it would look like to have the same gathering of women, even those who specialize in theory, spend time telling the stories that matter most to them: scriptural stories, movie lines, favorite novels, fairy tales, a treasured memory, a painful recollection—stories in which the dramatic scripts that deeply motivate and form us begin to surface and can serve as the material of our critical reflections. What patterns might we see emerging between stories; what forms of coalition might they engender; what impasses might they expose; what kind of "religion" would they render; what kind of selves would they perform? All these questions, it seems to me, take on different meaning when asked in the context of narrative and gender.[16]

Similarly, imagine conference papers describing, in detail, the logic and materiality of certain identified "women's practices." They need not be limited to adornment; we could look at how we practice hospitality, for example—a practice that reveals how we construct and patrol the borders defining our homes, our nations, and our bodies. It is also a practice that suggests how we decide who the "other" is and how she should be treated. It touches as well on the question of how we determine what we give and receive from the community around us, how we negotiate exchanges between parties. When "religion" is approached from this angle, there needn't be an overarching definition of the sacred to hold it; it has the freedom to emerge in a manner consistent with the particular habits of life and imaginative forms of thoughts within which the practice is embedded. As with practices of adornment, the interconnections between practices of hospitality and the logic of U.S. imperialism and global capital would not be that hard to discern. The topics of borders, others, the economy of exchange—all these themes are crucial to our understanding of political and economic forces shaping women's lives today. What better way to engage them than to explore them in the messy lived reality of our daily activities?

I should add, as well, that these conversations around narrative and practice need not exist in walled isolation from the discourses of feminist theory. Theory could live well in their midst, I believe, particularly if the pattern-identifying work of theory remained central. What would be different about the labor of theory in these conversations is that the material theorized would be substantive and immediate and, in this regard, readily available to respond to theory's excesses. In this context, feminist theory's appropriate role as *tool*, not *master*, might be better assured. As such, it would allow, at its best, the Muslim women room to describe what it means to be Muslim without the restrictive frame of "religion" hovering above their every comment. It might allow, as well, a more honest conversation about the relation of Christian theology and Jewish thought to feminist theory, a conversation that by focusing on practices and attending to narratives might avoid the all-too-familiar responses of secular feminists to religion.

Such conversations, I also believe, have the potential to generate insights conducive to nourishing "compassionate respect" for others—a term often used by Margaret Farley.[17] In the intricate tissue of stories and in the awkward and often eccentric motions of practices, people appear before us in ways demanding compassion—their particularity and their vulnerability as well as their flaws elicit from us a response of understanding, if only partially. They also open up the space of our desires and allow our imaginations to be enticed and excited, just as our minds are being educated and sharpened. It seems to me that in the future of transnational feminist dialogue, much will rest on this. For love to be "just"—for its balances to be conducive to human flourishing—I believe it must be so moved. And for it to be "true"—for its form to embody the deepest wisdom of soul—it must be so desired.

NOTES

1. For recent feminist theoretical discussions of globalization, see Saskia Sassen, *Globalization and Its Discontents* (New York: New Press, 1998); Cindi Katz, *Growing Up Global: Economic Restructuring and Children's Everyday Lives* (Minneapolis: University of Minnesota Press, 2004); and Barbara Ehrenreich and Arlie Hochschild, eds., *Global Woman* (New York: Henry Holt, 2004). For a discussion of theory and globalization, see Frederic Jameson, "Notes on Globalization as a Philosophical Issue," in *The Cultures of Globalization*, ed. Frederic Jameson and Masao Miyoshi (Durham, NC: Duke University Press, 1998), 54–77.

2. Chandra Mohanty addresses issues similar to these in her essay "'Under Western Eyes' Revisited: Feminist Solidarity through Anticapitalist Struggles," *Signs* 28, no. 2 (2002): 499–535.

3. I realize that in my telling of this common story, I imply a teleological form of emancipatory discourse that has been heavily criticized by many North American feminist theorists who prefer a more distopic account of its ends. My interest is in exploring whether one can be utopic at the aesthetic level without committing to it on a philosophical level. I think this happens all the time in feminist discourse, and that rather than treating it as a critical problem, we need to engage it more as part of an understandably ambivalent relation to hope.

4. It was telling how our shared assumptions converged with those outlined, with respect to women, in *Convention on the Elimination of All Forms of Discrimination Against Women*, United Nations Document A/34/46 (Sept. 3, 1981).

5. This formulation has been helped by an early work of Seyla Benhabib, *Critique, Norm, and Utopia: A Study of the Foundations of Critical Theory* (New York: Columbia University Press, 1986), as well as by her more recent work, *The Claims of Culture: Equality and Diversity in the Global Era* (Princeton, NJ: Princeton University Press, 2002).

6. For an excellent account of the tales generative of women's studies over the past several decades, see Robin Wiegman, *Women's Studies on Its Own: A Next Wave Reader in Institutional Change* (Durham, NC: Duke University Press, 2002).

7. Teresa L. Ebert, *Ludic Feminism and After* (Ann Arbor: University of Michigan Press, 1996).

8. For an excellent discussion of globalization and theory, see Anthony Appiah, *Thinking It Through : An Introduction to Contemporary Philosophy* (New York: Oxford University Press, 2003).

9. The other person for whom religious faith was a significant part of her life was Jewish, an identity that in this context was publicly unacknowledged and yet loudly noted in its silent presence.

10. See Tomoko Masuzawa, *In Search of Dreamtime: The Quest for the Origin of Religion* (Chicago: University of Chicago Press, 1993), and *The Invention of World Religions: Or, How European Universalism Was Preserved in the Language of Pluralism* (2004); Otto Maduro, "'Religion' Under Imperial Duress: Postcolonial Reflections and Proposals," The 2003 H. Paul Douglass Lecture at Drew University, *Review of Religious Research* 45, no. 3 (2004): 221–34.

11. Carla Freeman, "Is Local: Global as Feminine: Masculine," *Signs* 26, no. 4 (2001): 1007–37.

12. Luce Irigaray, *Speculum of the Other Woman*, trans. Gillian Gill (Ithaca, NY: Cornell University Press, 1985).

13. I realize that in these comments, I risk oversimplifying what was surely a much more complex response to the question about religion and the status of "religious identity" for Muslim women. For a much more detailed account, see Fatema Mernissi, *Women and Islam: An Historical and Theological Inquiry*, trans. Mary Jo Lakeland (Oxford: Basil Blackwell, 1991), and *Women in Moslem Paradise* (New Delhi: Kali for Women, 1988).

14. In recent feminist work on "the veil," the politics of its adornment are far more complicated than this short story suggests. In my account, I do not mean to downplay either its restrictive uses or its more explicitly political uses. See Meyda Yegenoglu, *Colonial Fantasies* (New York: Cambridge University Press, 1998), and Nilüfer Golë, "Veiling: The Symbol of Islamization," in *The Forbidden Modern*, 83–130 (Ann Arbor, University of Michigan Press, 1996). See as well Fatema Mernissi, *Beyond the Veil: Male-Female Dynamics in Modern Muslim Society* (Bloomington: Indiana University Press, 1987).

15. See Fatema Mernissi, *Dreams of Trespass: Tales of a Harem Girlhood* (Reading, MA: Addison Wesley Pub. Co., 1994).

16. Sidonie Smith and Kay Schaffer, *Human Rights and Narrated Lives: The Ethics of Recognition* (New York: Palgrave Macmillan, 2004).

17. Margaret Farley, *Compassionate Respect: A Feminist Approach to Medical Ethics and Other Questions* (New York: Paulist Press, 2002).

Chapter Four

Postcolonial Challenges and the Practice of Hospitality

Letty M. Russell

The Circle of Concerned African Women Theologians held its third Pan African Conference in Addis Ababa, Ethiopia, in August 2002 on "Sex, Stigmas and HIV/AIDS: African Women Theologians Challenging Religion, Culture and Social Practices." There were 140 women theologians from 25 African nations present along with a few observers from partner groups.[1] Among the observers was a delegation from the Yale Divinity School YDS Women's Initiative: Gender, Faith, and Responses to HIV/AIDS in Africa. The delegation included Shannon Clarkson, Margaret Farley, Letty Russell, and Yolanda Smith. The Circle was inaugurated in 1989 and now has 500 members on the African continent and abroad who are committed to research, write, and publish on issues affecting African women and women of African descent. It is a space for women from Africa to do communal theology based on their religious, cultural, and social experiences and draws membership from diverse backgrounds, nationalities, cultures, and religions.

It was no accident that Margaret Farley was part of the group attending the Circle meeting. She had been the one to respond to the call of the HIV/AIDS pandemic in Africa by organizing a group of women theologians at Yale in cooperation with Core Values Initiative of the United States Agency for International Development (USAID) and the Yale Center for Interdisciplinary Research on AIDS (CIRA). When she participated in the White House Summit Conference for World AIDS Day in 2000, Margaret had pointed out the need for a critical look at the impact of religious teachings regarding human sexuality, the status of women, and poverty.[2] Nearly thirty million persons in Africa were living with HIV/AIDS by the end of 2001 with five million being newly infected in that year alone, according to the World Health Organization. This represented almost three fourths of all cases in the world. As the AIDS pandemic continued to burn its way across Africa, women were at increasing—and disproportionate—risk of infection and death.[3] In 2002, Kofi A. Annan declared that 58% of those infected were women and "a combination of famine and AIDS is threatening the backbone of Africa—the women who keep African societies going and whose work makes up the economic foundation of rural communities."[4]

The beliefs and practices of many religious institutions contribute to women's risk of infection, and yet faith practices can often inspire and sustain women as they face illness, suffering, and loss. As a result of Farley's speech she was invited to form a group from Yale to cooperate with USAID in following up the challenges that she had made at the summit conference. The YDS Initiative was created as just one small way of responding as theologians to the pandemic by forming partnerships with women theologians in Africa to examine the intersection of gender, faith, poverty, and AIDS. Its purpose was to support the African women who were using every effort to confront those cultural and religious traditions that have become death dealing to women and their families.

Through this Initiative we seek to do our part by raising funds with USAID and other agencies in the U.S. to support the African women in a journey of *compassionate respect*, but also forming educational and publishing partnerships and developing a widening international network of women in solidarity in the struggle against AIDS, poverty, and gender oppression.[5] In this work we are constantly struggling with our own colonial past and present, as well as our implication as those benefitting from U.S. imperialism. Together we face many postcolonial challenges and seek to find ways to develop a feminist postcolonial practice of hospitality. What follows in this essay is an attempt to reflect on this process by discussing both the challenges and the possibilities of developing partnerships in which we practice hospitality and discover ways women can join together across many different barriers as postcolonial subjects.

POSTCOLONIAL FEMINISM

In 2001, I participated in a panel at the American Academy of Religion honoring Gustavo Gutiérrez on the thirtieth anniversary of the publication of his book, *A Theology of Liberation*.[6] In his response to the panel Professor Gutierrez pointed out that theologies are always changing because they cannot be separated from historical process. Our new situation, he said, is that we are *post everything;* we love to be *post,* but we do not live in a post racist, sexist, classist, imperialist world. It is this dilemma that we all face as we seek a future to live in! We seek to be postmodern but the legacy of modernity and the enlightenment is all around us. We seek to be postcolonial but various forms of colonialism and imperialism surround us.

Understanding the challenges

To discuss postcolonial feminism is to begin a dialogue with those who are writing postcolonial political theory and literary interpretation. Building on postmodern critical analysis and especially the writings of Edward Said, such as *Culture and Imperialism* and *Orientalism*, scholars have been writing about postcolonial biblical interpretation as well as postcolonialism, feminism, and religious discourse.[7] To understand the challenges as well as the invitations to dialogue we must first look at the language used to describe this perspective and then at the invitation to be postcolonial subjects together.

   An important resource for my exploration in this essay is the writing of Musa Dube, a Circle member, senior lecturer of New Testament at the University of Botswana, and consultant to the World Council of Churches on HIV/AIDS in Africa. Her interest in postcolonial feminist interpretation of the Bible challenges us to look at imperialist perspectives in the biblical tradition and particularly in the New Testament. Dube distinguishes between postcolonialism and postcolonial subjects. She says,

> The word *postcolonial* has been coined to describe the modern history of imperialism, beginning with the process of colonialism, through the struggles for political independence, the attainment of independence, and to the contemporary neocolonialist realities.[8]

In this view colonialism has not ended, it has only changed form and become *post*colonialism. Those who write this theory are committed to the same agenda as Gutiérrez: to work for a time when we could be, in reality, *postcolonial*!

One way of working for this is to claim an identity as a *postcolonial subject*. To be a postcolonial subject is to recognize that we all share in this groaning and unjust world together, and that often we are both "former colonizer" and "formerly colonized" at the same time. For this reason it is necessary to work together, critically analyzing the sources and practices of privilege, but also looking for liberating spaces in which we can share our commitment to work against both international oppression and gendered oppression.[9]

For Dube postcolonial feminists are to join in resisting all forms of *imperialism*, understood as a "structural imposition of a few standards on a universal scale" that assumes that the "other" is a blank slate to be inscribed with this universal culture in disregard of their own particular culture and to be rendered dependent on those who maintain these standards.[10] Such linguistic, cultural, political, and economic forms of domination include the hierarchical structures and thought patterns of *patriarchy*, but focus more on the international political and cultural structures of domination used against what Dube calls the "two-thirds world," the majority of the world who are oppressed.

Issues of difference

In her article, "Go Therefore and Make Disciples of All Nations," Musa Dube proposes

a strategy of postcolonial subjects, which calls upon both the domi-
nator and the dominated to examine the matrix of past and present
imperialism and to map ways in which they can speak as equal subjects who meet to exchange words of wisdom and life.[11]

This is no easy task. Yet it is a task with which white feminists should
be very familiar. A critique of gender, race, and class differences has
long led us to seek out ways of cooperating to construct the differences in a more egalitarian pattern, while also recognizing that all of
us, from countries of the north or of the south, are still caught in a
web of contradictions in this regard.

Postcolonial feminists use the term *hybridity* for this contradictory
mixture of our socially constructed lives. Women from colonized societies often have educations and social status that gives them access to
colonial culture, while at the same time are in touch with their own
cultural roots and religion. Women from colonizing societies also
vary greatly in this mixture of privilege and power and lack thereof.
In acknowledging the push and pull and the constant interplay of the
cultures in their lives, women can use the concept of hybridity to
resist dualistic thinking that puts them into essentialized categories of
"oppressor" or "oppressed."[12] Analyzing this hybridity calls for the use
of what Musimbi Kanyoro has called, "engendering cultural hermeneutics."[13] Such analysis shows how a particular culture functions and
helps us understand how people interpret and live out their faith, and
is as important as understanding the culture of biblical and church
tradition and those who have shaped that tradition. As cultures and
peoples intersect and create ever new patterns of relationship, the
ways of honoring differences and interpreting our ever changing reality are crucial.

The concept of *difference* can be used as a tool for both negative
and positive ways of understanding one another. It is negative when
difference is an excuse to downgrade, exclude, silence, or oppress.
Thus the "other" becomes an object of scorn as an inferior person
simply because of biological characteristics that don't meet the universal norm of whiteness, maleness, health, or affluence. According to
Iris Marion Young this form of *essentializing difference* is practiced by

dominant groups and used as a way to mark a group as having no common nature with the "normal or neutral ones."[14] The dominant groups reinforce the negative use of difference to exclude other groups out of fear of loss of privilege, as well as loss of an identity that finds its value over against the "other."

In our competitive and capitalistic societies it is difficult to resist a way of life in which certain persons are excluded as surplus, unneeded, and inferior. Audrey Lorde reminds us:

> Certainly there are very real differences between us of race, age, and sex. But it is not those differences between us that are separating us. It is rather our refusal to recognize those differences, and to examine the distortions which result from our misnaming them and their effects upon human behavior and expectation.[15]

From a feminist postcolonial perspective, however, those declared to be less than full persons because of their race, gender, orientation, or nationality can also claim difference as a positive indication of their own distinct identity, culture, language, and history. This claiming of *relational difference* allows members of a group to relate to one another and to value their social identity without expecting everyone to be the same or needing to mark other groups as inferior. In a postmodern world in which peoples have begun to assert this relational difference, unity can no longer be imposed as uniformity, and difference calls out for new forms of respect, relationality, and interdependence. In *Justice and the Politics of Difference* Iris Young says:

> The assertion of a positive sense of group difference by these groups is emancipatory because it reclaims the definition of the group by the group, as a creative construction, rather than a given essence.[16]

Such an emancipatory understanding of difference is built on an understanding of social justice that attends not only to distribution but also "to the institutional conditions necessary for the exercise of individual capacities and collective communication and cooperation."[17] Injustice refers to constraints of oppression and domination that prevent groups from participating fully in the life and decisions of their society. In this view justice includes the absence of oppression, a "putting things right" in people's lives, and not just the presence of distributive rights.

This postcolonial analysis of difference raises questions of the Christian tradition. What are the ways it honors the rainbow diversity of God's creation, and what are the ways it is part of the imperialism of essentializing difference. In what ways does it connect the intention of God to put things right with the need to establish social structures of relational and emancipatory difference?

CHALLENGING CHRISTIAN TRADITION

If we are to find our way to new structures of interdependence as postcolonial feminist Christians, we need to join our sister theologians from around the world to work critically with our Christian theological and biblical traditions. Clearly there is a deep ambiguity in the foundational stories of divine liberation in the Jewish and Christian traditions. It would seem that, in our time of intolerance and fundamentalism in many religions, people forget the insight of Judith Plaskow:

> It is not in the chosenness that cuts off, but in the distinctiveness that opens itself to difference that we find the God of Israel and of each and every people.[18]

Election as a problem

As soon as we begin to take the question of difference seriously in our theological investigation, we discover that the doctrine of divine election is in many ways ambiguous if not contradictory in its teaching of divine choice for service to the nations. Often the chosenness of the community manages to swallow up the mandate for outreach to others. In fact, the doctrine of divine election and its subsequent use in nation building and colonialism have often become a screen for imperialism and racial domination.

The covenant story of deliverance in Exodus goes with the story of conquest in Joshua. The land of Canaan is promised both to Abraham and his descendants and to Moses although that land is already occupied by other groups of people (Gn 15:18–21; Ex 3:17).[19] Christians, claiming superior revelation of God's redemption, carried this story forward as a universal messianic mandate from Christ [Is 16:6–8; Mt 24:14; Mt 28:16–20]. According to Rosemary Radford Ruether these Christian claims to universalism "were shaped culturally within the Greco-Roman Empire, which believed itself to be a universal empire containing the one true humanistic culture."[20]

This combination of messianic universalism and Greco-Roman imperialist universalism gave Christians a mandate for mission that provided inspiration for its combination with European imperialism in the nineteenth century. Following Edward Said, Musa Dube says that imperialism teaches us "to think about distant places to colonize them, to depopulate them."[21] The legacy of this imperialism is still with us today as seen by the actions of the United States in Afghanistan and in the Middle East.

The doctrine of election has become problematic in a world in which the dominant few justify their chosenness on the basis of essentializing difference. As Renita Weems has pointed out, a womanist analysis of sexism and racism must criticize theological and cultural assumptions and biases of the Bible by beginning with the analysis of election. She asserts:

> the Bible's renown, I believe, is grounded in large part in the claim of Israel's (and later the Church's) election. Therefore, to identify the biblical world as patriarchal . . . is to talk about symptoms. Those who have been excluded from Judeo-Christian theological discourse and structures must begin their work with an analysis of "election."[22]

The understanding of election in the Bible is frequently ambiguous and contradictory. For instance, to be chosen by God is to be chosen as a *partner* in the care of the earth and of all God's creatures. Yet to be chosen as a king or as a special people is to exercise *dominion* over those not so favored by God. In the Bible we discover over and over a cycle of deformation of election as the idea of election for survival and service turns into election for security and superiority. The idea of Israel as a unique people chosen by God is critiqued by the prophets such as Amos (9:7), and in later writings such as Ruth and Jonah (4:9–11).[23] Nevertheless, the persistent criticism of the exploitation of election for personal or national gain did not change the belief that the people of Israel were a special part of God's plan for the whole world.[24]

It is not surprising that this pattern continues in the New Testament. Both the Gospels and Paul struggle with whether the teaching of Jesus about welcome into God's household is only for the Jews or for all people. For instance, Mark's version of the Syrophoenican woman, portrays Jesus himself as needing to be taught by the woman that it is possible for him to heal those who are not God's children (7:24–30).

Postcolonial feminism and the doctrine of election

The recent critiques of this biblical message along with its contemporary forms of messianic and imperialistic universalism by postcolonial scholars challenge us all to search out ways the patriarchal and imperial paradigms are constantly at work in biblical and church tradition and in cultures. In my opinion postcolonial feminism can help us with this project for a number of reasons. First, as Mary Ann Tolbert has said, we need "to recognize the legitimacy of self-consciously adopting different perspectives on a text at different times."[25] There is no one universal meaning of a text or tradition. They are all subject to continuing discussion of our many local readings that vary with time, space, and culture. Second, postcolonial feminist interpretations are a critical tool for the transformation of Christian traditions in ways that may be life giving to those who share in the struggles of colonialized and oppressed peoples. Third, we have been invited into a discussion of how to move toward interdependence in our traditions as well as our actions by acknowledging ourselves to be postcolonial subjects who are caught in the web of global destruction.

In response to God's invitation to be partners in the mending of creation we can do no less than to search for ways that the traditions that make sense of our lives and faith can do so without being destructive of other peoples and of the creation itself. Election as a word of hope in the situation of an oppressed group should not become a word of exclusion and privilege in the situation of a dominant group. It has provided a source of identity in a particular social-historical reality, but has become contradictory when it is abstracted as a doctrine that is universally applicable. Without a grounding in the reality of oppression and in an emancipatory understanding of difference, election as a gift of God's grace quickly becomes deformed into a justification of privilege and injustice.

Using a Christian feminist postcolonial interpretation I would like to propose three possible ways to begin resisting deformation in the doctrine of election so that we are open to the practice of hospitality and justice. Our analysis of difference and hermeneutic of the "other" can pay attention to the *power quotient* involved in what is said and who is saying it. It can give priority to the *perspective of the outsider*, and can also rejoice in *God's unfolding promise*.[26]

Power Quotient. The doctrine of election, like other interpretations of Christian tradition, is socially constructed. Its meaning changes over time and in different social, political, and economic contexts. One important factor in how we read and interpret the meaning of God's calling in person's lives is the power quotient in the relationships of the groups involved. In the history of the church this understanding of God's special care has fulfilled a need for identity as human beings for those who were powerless. Those who were nobody could affirm their own self-worth and *inclusion* as children of God granted full human dignity and worth as a gift of God's love. No wonder not only the tribes of Israel and the nobodies of the early church, but also those in every culture who have been considered less than human, have found strength to resist many different forms of oppression. However, when a people who consider themselves special in the eyes of God have the power and privilege to dominate others this understanding of election is deformed and turns into a hierarchy of orthodoxy and exclusion.

A postcolonial interpretation would make it clear that this deformed understanding of election helped provide divine reinforcement of racism and imperialist expansion in the United States, South Africa, and elsewhere. It would also lead us to ask about the power quotient when reading texts such as Luke 14:7–14. In this parable of the wedding banquet, persons are asked to take the lower seat in humility, and to invite the poor to their banquets, and not just friends who can repay. According to Sharon Ringe, writing in *The Postcolonial Bible*, even a white woman writing from the U.S., can use a postcolonial reading to look at the text and see that the elite groups, like the leader of the Pharisees who invited Jesus for a meal, are being enjoined to humility and generosity.[27] She could check the guest list for those who are missing. Where are the women in the story? Would they count as "poor, crippled, lame, and blind?" What if those who are excluded decided to have a meal instead of being brought in? In the parable, as in our churches today, the guest list and seating of the chairs is still arranged by those in power. Surely the table that we long for would find a way to include all who would share the power.

An example of this need to be sensitive to the power quotient in seeking relational difference was the meeting of the Circle in Addis Ababa mentioned at the beginning of the paper. The four of us from Yale were guests who were given voice because we had formed a partnership with the Circle leaders in mobilizing African women theologians to work on transformation of theology and practice in faith communities of which they were a part. We had much to learn about how they approached the problems of gender, power, and stigma and worked to break the silence around the issues of HIV/AIDS.

We were postcolonial subjects, working together on a giant problem to create hope in the midst of a pandemic of death. Yet there was no way we could provide leadership in such a venture even though a person like Margaret Farley had a wealth of experience and knowledge of medical ethics. Our participation was a result of the African women theologians' decision to use the Circle meeting to address issues of HIV/AIDS. Our participation and search for ways to join the struggle was also dependent on the "Plan of Action" of the Circle conference and that of our funding partners, and not just on our own plan. Clearly attention to the power quotient was crucial to the recognition that God has elected all of humankind and the creation itself for mending and healing so that we could search for ways of being part of that healing grace.

Perspective of the outsider.   Resisting the deformation of election also requires us to be attentive to the perspective of the outsider. In the history of the church, election has also pointed to the church's calling to witness and service. Here the emphasis in biblical and church tradition has been on the task for which the community has been chosen. This witness and service has also been deformed by an assumption that those who share the gospel are the ones who bring Christ and that their role of service makes them superior to others. A postcolonial feminist reconstruction of election would ask what our calling to service means by *listening* to those on the margin who define their need and teach us the meaning of God's welcome and hospitality. "A preferential option for the outsider" is the same as what Latin American liberation theologians call God's "preferential option for the poor." It is not an exclusive option but is a starting point for attention and work to overcome injustice.[28]

A postcolonial feminist reading of Matthew 28:1–20 would be another way of resisting a deformed understanding of election. One such reading is that of Musa Dube in her article "Go Therefore and Make Disciples of All Nations."[29] For Dube, Matthew's text shows both messianic and imperialist universalism, possibly leading to the deformation of the calling of all people to discipleship. Nevertheless, it represents those who were outsiders to the Jewish synagogues and to the dominant Greco-Roman society. In emulating the oppressors of his time by speaking of the universal mandate of Christ, Matthew shows us the mixture or hybridity that is part of the lives of most postcolonial subjects. He speaks from an oppressed community but uses the terms of power in his own political and cultural context.

Careful attention to various forms of deformation and misreading has long been part of the interpretation of Matthew 28 and the meaning of the Trinitarian formula, God's mission and the authority to go evangelize those who may not want to be evangelized, the women as missing persons on the mountain of commandment, and so on. It would seem that just about the only word that is uncontested is "behold" in Christ's assurance "behold I am with you always (28:20, KJV).[30] Perhaps we can say, however, that the promise of Christ's spirit in our midst is also a promise to open up our hearts and lives so that we can truly *listen* to the perspective of the many outsiders who keep telling us that they want to live out their own life-giving story.

At the Circle Conference the women were very careful to recognize their own privilege in being able to meet and write about HIV/AIDS when others of their own friends and families were in the middle of struggles with sickness and death. A way of doing this was to listen to the perspective of the outsider and invite women living with HIV/AIDS to share their story. One such woman was Brigitte Syamalevwe from Zambia. She told her story of working with her husband to take their lives and make them count for others no matter what. For ten years they had been running an orphanage for children and working to break the silence about their sickness.[31] Brigitte made it clear to all the women, including ourselves, that listening is both *hearing* and *heeding* a call to work for the well-being of those who speak from the perspective of an outsider.[32]

Unfolding promise.   Like other social critiques and theological insights, postcolonial feminist interpretation leads us to realize that the stories and teachings of the Bible and of Christian tradition are often harmful to our health or to the health of others who become the objects of our interpretations. One other safeguard to the deformation of election by those who think they know the only answer to the meaning of God's calling is to recognize that God's promise is a promise and not a guarantee. It is *a promise that keeps unfolding* in new ways in our lives and in lives which are so very different than our own. The unfolding nature of God's promise of justice and love serves as a safeguard against misuse of religious practices to "guarantee" that we are chosen, and changes our understanding of election as new challenges to the meaning of God's promises become clear to us.

A postcolonial feminist interpretation that brings this home is Musa Dube's interpretation of Matthew 15:21–28, the story of the nameless Syrophoenician woman in Mark 7:24–30, who is turned into a nameless Canaanite woman in Matthew's version.[33] This text has had many feminist interpretations because it goes beyond the emphasis on Gentile mission and is focused on a woman who talks Jesus into expanding his mission beyond the people of Israel.[34] Mark presents the Syrophoenican or Greek woman as assertive, articulate, and willing to find Jesus and confront him in order to heal her daughter. Matthew's version, however, seems to present more of a deformation of the idea of election. Here all people are to be welcomed, but *not all are to be of equal worth*. In Dube's postcolonial interpretation the woman is demoted by Matthew to the status of Canaanite, with a daughter "tormented by a demon," evoking memories of the first conquest of the Canaanites and their demonic worship of "false gods." The woman is so clearly *other* that Jesus even calls her a "dog" rather than a child of God.[35] This form of election leaves the "other" out. At the very least it has to be challenged as the woman challenged Jesus to open up the promise to all people without requiring them to become people of God.

Certainly the journey to become postcolonial subjects with our African women theologian sisters has been an unfolding process in which we have not known what we could or should do. We only knew the promise of God's concern for all people and worked in expectation that we would discover our part in this partnership. Although we began with a conference at Yale with African women from faith-based communities, and listened to their desire to support the work of the Circle on HIV/AIDS, we did not know that this would also lead Farley to expand this support by creating a program called "Sister to Sister: Women in Ministry Responding to HIV/AIDS" so that Roman Catholic Sisters and laywomen could reflect on their struggles to address the issues of prevention and care in Africa.[36] Nor did we know that a way would be opened up through Farley's contacts with the Yale Medical School to sponsor three African women theologians as research scholars to be trained to evaluate ways that changes in faith and cultural values affect the sexual and gender practices in faith communities. Each step calls forth another, for the promise of God is not a blueprint but a journey of faithful service. As the promise unfolds we may be helped to move beyond old patterns of essentializing difference toward a pattern of relational difference in which God's hospitality and welcome is lived out in ever changing ways.

Practicing Hospitality

Election is not the only Christian tradition that describes ways that people of the covenant should relate to their neighbors. Another important tradition in this respect is that of hospitality. In facing the challenge of a world of abundant difference and abundant experience of exclusion and suffering, it would seem that a feminist hermeneutic of hospitality could make it clear that in God's sight no one is "other."[37]

Partnership with strangers. In this interpretation *hospitality is partnership with strangers*: those who are different because of gender, orientation, ability, race, class, or nationality, and not just a form of "terminal niceness" with our friends. The practice of hospitality by welcoming strangers is not optional for those in the Christian tradition (Mt 25:31–46; Rom 12:13).[38] In his book, *New Testament Hospitality,* John Koenig writes that

> *philoxenia*, the term for hospitality used in the New Testament, refers literally not to a love of strangers *per se* but to a delight in the whole guest-host relationship, in the mysterious reversals and gains for all parties which may take place. For believers, this delight is fueled by the expectation that God or Christ or the Holy Spirit will play a role in every hospitable transaction [Heb 13:2; Rom 1:11–12].[39]

Hebrews 13:1–2 reminds us to practice "mutual love" and to show "hospitality to strangers, for by doing that some have entertained angels without knowing it." This reference to Genesis 18:1–15 points us back to the many stories in the Hebrew Scriptures of hospitality. Here Abraham and Sarah entertain three strangers who turn out to be God and two angels. They bring the news that makes Sarah laugh! She is to conceive and have a child in her old age. Such stories of hospitality and the surprise of discovering God in our midst abound in the Bible, and echo clearly in the Matthew 25 account of the last judgment, as well as the resurrection stories of Christ's appearance such as the road to Emmaus in Luke 24 (Mt 25:31–46; Lk 24:13–35).

Another key aspect of the theology of hospitality as understood in biblical perspective is that of responding to God's hospitality toward us. In telling the Exodus story, the Hebrew people remembered that they had been strangers and exiles and were now called to do justice toward all people and care for the orphans and widows and all who needed special care (Ex 23:9; 22:21–27; Dt 10:17–20; 24:14–15).[40] This understanding of hospitality is closely connected to the view of difference as relational instead of an occasion for fear and hatred.

Hospitality is not just serving our family and friends, or even those we see as "other." It is about the joy of sharing love for others and the unexpected gifts that come in that encounter with those who are different from us. It is also about the hospitality of a God who continually lives in relationship, sharing love among all three members of the Trinity and reaching out to us in love and inviting us to share that welcome with others.[41]

Practicing hospitality as postcolonial subjects. The practice of hospitality as postcolonial subjects is also fraught with dangers of deformation. Some might prefer to develop the biblical understanding of partnership or *koinonia* as an expression of relational difference, but the situation of power inequality with multiple and shifting differences calls for a theological concept that emphasizes the stranger, the one who is different.[42] It focuses on honoring the guest-host relationship as we work to make that relationship a mutual one of giving and receiving, of being both host and guest to one another so that neither of us are any longer strangers to one another.

In our world of essentializing difference, imperialism, patriarchy, and many other forms of domination and hatred, the practice of hospitality toward others is a crucial step in finding those who are willing to be partners. At the same time hospitality calls us to take people's messages and actions seriously, resisting those that perpetuate injustice or are not life-giving. The *hybridity* of our familial, cultural, political,

and economic contexts in which we are interconnected and simultaneously living out roles as part of colonizer and colonized groups
challenges us to listen with new ears to the cries of pain and hope that
are offered by our brothers and sisters, and to join them in imagining
a different way of relationship that points to God's intention to mend
the whole of creation, beginning with ourselves.

Musa Dube closes her article on "Postcoloniality, Feminist Spaces,
and Religion" with a discussion of "two-thirds world feminist spaces
and strategies." The "spaces" she describes are those spaces of international and gendered oppression which the women of the two-thirds
world inhabit. The strategies for resisting this oppression and creating
new space to breathe in are many. Her first strategy is

> decolonization of inherited colonial education systems, languages,
> literary canons, reading methods, and the Christian religion, in
> order to arrest the colonizing ideology packed in claims of religious
> conversion, Western civilization, modernization, development, de-
> mocratization, and globalization.

The other postcolonial strategies of resistance include:

2) Willingness to embrace and confront indigenous religious and cultural views;
3) Reasserting diversity in cultural, economic, and political systems;
4) Confronting oppressive aspects in one's own indigenous systems
   of gender;
5) Adopting a hybrid means of resistance and liberation;
6) Using whatever traditions are a help in the struggle.[43]

This list is a "tall order," but it is by no means unique to Dube and postcolonial feminists. Many of our sisters from the southern hemisphere
share in this struggle of resistance that calls for hybrid strategies.[44] For
instance, Nyambura Njoroge describes the courage to struggle against
death as "a spirituality of resistance and transformation," urging us to
follow the example of Rizpah in her resistance to the senseless killing of
her sons when King Saul, their father, dies (2 Sm 21:9–14).[45]

The question for us is how to join these sisters and their brothers in such struggles against imperial and gendered oppression. What is our role as we join Margaret Farley in the search for "right relationship and just love"? This question can only be answered by each of us in our writing, teaching, and ministries as we work out ways of celebrating the emancipatory power of relational difference as a crucial part of justice and the overcoming of oppression and domination. This is also a "tall order" for those of us from former colonizing nations who seek to practice hospitality as postcolonial subjects. Perhaps the three ways of resisting deformation in our theology of election and hospitality can be helpful in looking briefly at examples from a global context.

The first way was paying attention to the *power quotient*. My partner, Shannon Clarkson, and I recently returned from teaching with Mercy Oduyoye, Elizabeth Amoah, and Rabiatu Ammah at the Institute of Women in Religion and Culture, in Accra, Ghana. Together we worked on issues of gospel and culture in a group of fifteen women from eight different countries as part of an international feminist Doctor of the Ministry program sponsored by San Francisco Theological Seminary and the World Council of Churches.[46] In this course the issue of power quotient was always at the center of the dialogue because a major purpose of this doctoral program is the empowerment of women from countries of the South as they become subjects of their own theology and history as leaders in their communities. We are working to provide resources and educational tools for writing theology in English as part of this empowerment. This means, however, that we are also perpetuating the imperialism of the English language and western educational standards. The practice of hospitality looked more like a balancing act of power and empowerment as we worked through our differences day by day.

I have described the importance of resisting deformation in our theology of election by beginning from the *perspective of the outsider*. This is equally important for the practice of hospitality as we listen to the pain of others and respond to their initiatives. According to Iris Marion Young, listening is hearing and heeding the call to be just in our concrete social and political practices.[47] This practice of hospitality is important for persons in all walks of life, including those who work in academic institutions. One such person is Ofelia Ortega, who practices hospitality as the president of the Evangelical Theological Seminary in Matanzas, Cuba.[48] Her ministry there in Matanzas has helped transform it from a struggling institution into a welcoming community. New dormitories were built so students and their families could live together in community. Gardens were planted so that the seminary could grow its own food. Enough was planted so that if the people from the surrounding city stole the produce for their families there would still be enough to go around. The faculty and staff now include a number of new women who have joined the men in creating a partnership of learning. Listening to the perspective of the outsiders such as student wives, the poor, and women theologians enabled Ofelia Ortega to create a community of hospitality that respected difference.

The third way of resisting deformation in our theology of election and practicing hospitality was to recognize that *God's promise is always unfolding.* This is highlighted by the project of women from Brazil, Chile, and the United States who came together to create an opportunity for ecofeminist encounter and dialogue in what they called *A Shared Garden* project. Mary Hunt and Diann Neu from Women's Alliance for Theology, Ethics, and Ritual, Silver Spring, MD, joined Ivone Gebara from Recife, Brazil, and the collective of *Con-Spirando* in Santiago, Chile, to hold three encounters during 1997–98 in the three locations.

This traveling workshop for women in South, Central, and North America was an attempt to create a network throughout the Americas among women theologians, pastors, and community workers to do theology. Using their imagination they transformed their experience of what is into what could be.[49] Describing the event in Chile, Ivone Gebara said:

> We must go beyond the separations that come from economics. . . . We know we must keep our own cultures, our specific problems, the taste of our own food. Not everything has to be McDonald and Coca Cola. But we have [begun] to share an experience together of something very rich and good.[50]

Such an interpretation of hospitality is yet another invitation to us all to join together in imagining a different world, one like a shared garden where all are welcome. This is our invitation to work together as postcolonial subjects finding the many ways to keep faith with our sisters and brothers as well as with a God who knows no partiality. None of this can claim to be very effective in the face of overwhelming global challenges, but we can "keep on keeping on," hoping that Gustavo Gutiérrez was right in his final remark at the Denver meeting, as well as at the beginning. He said that we need an additional beatitude in the Sermon on the Mount (Mt 5:1–12). We need to add, *blessed are the obstinate and stubborn*, those who refuse to stop trying to make the world postracist, postcolonial, and more like the one for which God longs. May such a blessing be with Margaret Farley and with us all!

NOTES

1. "Sex, Stigma, and HIV/AIDS: African Women Challenging Religion, Culture and Social Practices," report of the third Pan African Conference of the Circle of Concerned African Women Theologians, Addis Ababa, Ethiopia, August 4 to August 8, 2002, provided by Dr. Musimbi Kanyoro, Coordinator of the Circle 1996–2002.

2. Margaret A. Farley, *Compassionate Respect: A Feminist Approach to Medical Ethics and Other Questions* (New York: Paulist Press, 2002), 6–20.

3. "Join Us: Gender, Faith, and Responses to HIV/AIDS in Africa," pamphlet of the YDS Women's Initiative, 2002.

4. Kofi A. Annan, "In Africa, AIDS Has a Woman's Face," *New York Times*, December 29, 2002.

5. Farley, *Compassionate Respect*.

6. Gustavo Gutiérrez, *Teologia de la liberacion, Perspectivas* (Lima: CEP, 1971). The panel was entitled, "Liberation Theology and the 21st Century: Celebrating, Past, Present and Future," Denver, CO, November 19, 2001.

7. Edward W. Said, *Orientalism* (New York: Vintage Books, 1979), and *Culture and Imperialism* (New York: Alfred A. Knopf, 1993); Laura E. Donaldson and Kwok Pui-Lan, eds., *Postcolonialism, Feminism and Religious Discourse* (London: Routledge, 2002).

8. Musa W. Dube, *Postcolonial Feminist Interpretation of the Bible* (St. Louis, Missouri: Chalice Press, 2000), 15.

9. Musa W. Dube, "Postcoloniality, Feminist Spaces, and Religion," in Donaldson and Kwok, *Postcolonialism, Feminism and Religious Discourse*, 115. Cf. Iris Marion Young, *Justice and the Politics of Difference* (Princeton, NJ: Princeton University Press, 1990), 39–65.

10. Musa W. Dube, "Go Therefore and Make Disciples of All Nations," in *Teaching the Bible: The Discourses and Politics of Biblical Pedagogy*, ed. Fernando F. Segovia and Mary Ann Tolbert (Maryknoll, NY: Orbis Books, 1998), 233.

11. Dube, "Go Therefore," 234.

12. Dube, "Postcoloniality," 117.

13. Musimbi R. A. Kanyoro, *Introducing Feminist Cultural Hermeneutics: An African Perspective* (Cleveland: Pilgrim Press, 2002), 26.

14. Young, *Justice*, 170.

15. Audrey Lorde, "Age, Race, Class, and Sex: Women Redefining Difference," in her *Sister Outsider: Essays and Speeches* (Trumansburg, NY: Crossing Press, 1984), 115.

16. Young, *Justice*, 172.

17. Ibid., 39.

18. Judith Plaskow, *Standing Again at Sinai: Judaism from a Feminist Perspective* (San Francisco: Harper and Row Publishers, 1990), 107.

19. Robert Allen Warrior, "A Native American Perspective: Canaanites, Cowboys, and Indians," in *Voices from the Margin: Interpreting the Bible in the Third World*, ed. R. S. Sugirtharajah, 287–95 (Maryknoll, NY: Orbis Books, 1991). Also quoted in Dube, *Postcolonial*, 18.

20. Rosemary Radford Ruether, "Feminism and Jewish-Christian Dialogue," in *The Myth of Christian Uniqueness: Toward a Pluralistic Theology of Religions*, ed. John Hick and Paul F. Knitter (Maryknoll, NY: Orbis Books, 1998).

21. Dube, *Postcolonial*, 17; Edward Said, *Culture and Imperialism*, 78.

22. Renita Weems, "The State of Biblical Interpretation," 31–33, lecture from a conference on "Gender, Race, Class: Implications for Interpreting Religions"; tapes available from Princeton Theological Seminary, Princeton, NJ.

23. Letty M. Russell, *Church in the Round: Feminist Interpretation of the Church* (Louisville, KY: Westminster John Knox, 1993), 162–67.

24. Elsa Tamez, "God's Election, Exclusion and Mercy: A Biblical Study of Romans 9–11," *International Review of Mission* 82 (January 1993): 29–37.

25. Mary Ann Tolbert, "When Resistance Becomes Repression: Mark 13:9–27 and the Poetics of Location," in *Reading from This Place: Social Location and Biblical Interpretation in Global Perspective*, ed. Fernando F. Segovia and Mary Ann Tolbert (Minneapolis, MN: Fortress Press, 1995), 332.

26. These three clues were developed through my interpretation of the story of the Syrophoenician woman in Mark 24–30 with parallels in Matthew 15:21–28; see Russell, *Church in the Round*, 162–64. A fascinating analysis of this text from many different perspectives is found in Hisako Kinukawa, "De-colonizing Ourselves as Readers and The Story of the Syro-Phoenician Woman as a Text," in *Distant Voices Drawing Near: In Honor of Anne Wire*, ed. Holly Hearon (Collegeville, MN: Liturgical Press, 2004).

27. Sharon H. Ringe, "Places at the Table: Feminist Postcolonial Biblical Interpretation," in *The Postcolonial Bible*, ed. R.S. Sugirtharajah (Sheffield: Sheffield Academic Press, 1998), 143.

28. Robert McAfee Brown, "Reflections of a North American," *The Future of Liberation Theology: Essays in Honor of Gustavo Gutierrez*, ed. by Marc H. Ellis and Otto Maduro (Orbis Books, 1988), 493. Cf. Gustavo Gutierrez, *The Power of the Poor in History* (Orbis Books, 1983), 128.

29. Dube, "Go Therefore."

30. The idea that only "behold" is uncontested was suggested to me by Shannon Clarkson when discussing Matthew 28. Unless otherwise marked, scripture quotations are from the *New Revised Standard Version of the Bible*.

31. "Sex, Stigma, and HIV/AIDS," Circle report.

32. Young, *Justice*, 5.

33. Dube, *Postcolonial,* chap. 9, "Decolonizing White Western Readings of Matthew 15:21–28," 157–95.

34. See, for instance: Elaine M. Wainwright, *Shall We Look for Another? A Feminist Rereading of the Matthean Jesus* (Maryknoll, NY: Orbis Books, 1998), 89–92; Sharon H. Ringe, "A Gentile Woman's Story," in *Feminist Interpretation of the Bible*, ed. Letty M. Russell (Philadelphia: Westminster Press, 1985), 65–72.

35. Dube, *Postcolonial*, 148–50.

36. "Women's Initiative Consultation: Project on Gender, Faith, and Responses to HIV/AIDS in Africa," February 28–March 3, 2002. Sponsored by Yale University Divinity School and the United States Agency for International Development with the help of the POLICY Project."

37. Letty M. Russell, "Postkoloniale Subjekte und eine Feministische Hermeneutik der Gastfreundschaft," in *Als hätten sie uns neu erfunden*, ed. Heike Walz, Christine Lienemann-Perrin, and Doris Strahm (Luzern: Beobachtungen zu Fremdheit und Geschlecht, 2003).

38. Christine D. Pohl, *Making Room: Recovering Hospitality as a Christian Tradition* (Cambridge, UK: Eerdmans, 1999), 31.

39. John Koenig, *New Testament Hospitality: Partnership with Strangers as Promise and Mission* (Philadelphia: Fortress Press, 1985), 8.

40. Christine D. Pohl, *Making Room: Recovering Hospitality as a Christian Tradition* (Grand Rapids, MI: Eerdmans, 1999), 20–35.

41. Margaret A. Farley, "New Patterns of Relationships: Beginnings of a Moral Revolution," *Theological Studies*, 36, no. 4 (1975): 627–46, especially at 645–46.

42. See Letty M. Russell, *The Future of Partnership* (Philadelphia: The Westminster Press, 1979).

43. Dube, "Postcoloniality," 115–17.

44. Elsa Tamez, "Cultural Violence against Women in Latin America," in *Women Resisting Violence: Spirituality for Life*, ed. Mary John Mananzan et al., 11–19 (Maryknoll, NY: Orbis Books, 1996); Musimbi Kanyoro, "Cultural Hermeneutics," in *Women's Visions: Theological Reflection, Celebration, Action*, ed. Ofelia Ortega, 18–28 (Geneva: WCC Publications, 1995); Mercy Oduyoye, *Daughters of Anowa* (Maryknoll, NY: Orbis Books, 1995); Kwok Pui-lan, *Discovering the Bible in the Non-Biblical World* (Maryknoll, NY: Orbis Books, 1995).

45. Nyambura J. Njoroge, "A Spirituality of Resistance and Transformation," in *Talitha Cum! Theologies of African Women,* ed. Nyambura J. Njoroge and Muse Dube, 66–82 (Pietermaritzburg: Cluster Publications, 2001).

46. Advanced Pastoral Studies, San Francisco Theological Seminary, San Anselmo, CA; Institute of Women in Religion, Trinity Theological College, Legon, Ghana.

47. Young, *Justice*, 5.

48. Ortega, *Women's Voices*, and "Will Development Imply Changes?" *Ministerial Formation*, 88 (January 2000): 10–22.

49. Young, *Justice*, 6.

50. Imogen Mark, "Women of Americas gather in Santiago," *National Catholic Reporter*, March 14, 1997, 12.

Part 2

A Just and True Love

INTRODUCTION

Part 2 continues an exploration of fundamental themes for feminist theological ethics: the nature of the self and the sources of morality, the role of emotion in the work of justice, and the possibilities for retrieving a covenantal framework for an ethic of mutuality. Gene Outka's essay, "Self and Other in a Theological Framework," traces Farley's interests in the relationship of autonomy and relationality in the experience of moral obligation. Outka's distinctive concern, however, is with the way in which convictions about God inform and sometimes moderate how we understand that relationship. It is both our capacity for union with God and with others and the potential for estrangement this side of the eschaton that teach us the possibilities for human love. A right love of God and neighbor considered theologically compels us at the same time to realize that we are not God and to endeavor to love, however imperfectly, "who and what God loves." Along with Outka's essay, essays by Ronald Garet and Ada Maria Isasi-Diaz suggest the implications of an integral account of agency for imagining and participating in human-divine relationship. Our human relationships, however fragile and incomplete, can nonetheless be nourished by models of Trinitarian love, in the mutual self-gift of distinct persons. As Garet tests the implications of Farley's attention to covenant relations as a model for a "life of active receptivity and receptive activity," we are led far into the paradox of our relationships with God and others, relationships marked by intimacy as well as distance, union and holy otherness. Ada Maria Isasi-Diaz draws from the work of Puerto Rican poet Julia de Burgos to argue for the place of the emotions in our understanding of moral knowledge and moral agency. It is not only reason that judges emotion, argues Isasi-Diaz, but emotion that tests and tutors reason. "Justice and love kiss," when the passions, ignited and nurtured, lead to principled action on behalf of the most marginalized.

Chapter Five

Self and Other in a Theological Framework

Gene Outka

It is true, as Sartre suggests, that some of our experiences of others are experiences of being threatened; that we seek self-justification whether by mastery or by submission. . . . But these are not the only possibilities for relating to others. . . . An obligation to respect persons requires that we honor their freedom and respond to their needs, that we value difference as well as sameness, that we attend to the concrete realities of our own and others' lives.[1]

FARLEY ON AUTONOMY AND RELATIONALITY

Margaret Farley addresses in instructive ways the inexhaustible subject of human self and human other. Two central topics that occupy her are autonomy and relationality. She incorporates feminist and Roman Catholic contributions, and also Kantian, Sartrean, and postmodernist ones. I consider initially two of her essays. In one, she takes as her point of departure the strand of moral thought called "respect for persons"; in the second, she canvasses postmodern writings. In both, she articulates and nuances claims about self and other resident elsewhere in her corpus.[2]

After I sketch her claims about self and other, I ask how a possible theological framework may amplify rather than conflict with these. And I suggest further influences that theological vantage points exert. My interest lies generally in how traditional Christian convictions about God and God's relation to the world may guide our reckonings and inform our judgments about human autonomy and relationality, and so throw distinctive light on debates about self and other. This inquiry is, obviously, palpably vast. I offer here selected proposals. Nor do I presume to speak for Farley once I turn to this offering. I continue, however, to wrestle with the claims themselves, and I start with her citation of a sentence from Basil Mitchell that grounds respect in our capacity to love God and one another rather than in our powers of self-legislation.

Respect for Persons

This phrase refers to a tradition in moral thought we associate quintessentially with Kant's second formulation of the categorical imperative: "Act in such a way that you always treat humanity, whether in your own person or in the person of any other, never simply as a means, but always at the same time as an end."[3] Farley thinks the notion of respecting persons as ends in themselves warrants ongoing defense. She has endeavored, year in and year out, with eyes open to myriad difficulties, "to keep trying to articulate the unconditional value of persons."[4] Her efforts include locating features or aspects *about* persons that evoke our respect. She calls these obligating-features. They are aspects that obtain for all of us, whether we are male or female, and however greatly we differ in our particular histories and experiences. These features constitute intrinsic grounds for our respect and serve to specify its meaning. Two candidates for this status recur in her writings: autonomy and relationality. One, she holds, is as "primordial" as the other.[5]

Autonomy is itself influentially vindicated by Kant. Farley claims that feminists should partly affirm and partly correct his case for autonomy. Kant is right that autonomy is, as Farley puts it, "that feature of persons whereby they are not solely determined in their actions by causes external to their own reason and will, not even by their own desires and inclinations."[6] Part of the cogency of the injunction to respect persons as ends in themselves depends on this feature. I return later to the question of how best to construe such dependence. Farley also claims that Kant is wrong to suppose that the "not solely determined" feature requires us to affirm certain other things frequently attributed to him. That is, *pace* such attributions, feminists may affirm autonomy, but need not thereby oppose freedom and affectivity, nor downplay human vulnerability, nor neglect individual histories of desire, social-historical situatedness, and communal formation.

These further references to affectivity, vulnerability, and formation deserve their own space. Relationality presents itself accordingly as the second candidate. It fixes attention on the person as inescapably social and dialogical. Feminists press its significance, though in this instance they hardly do so alone. In the West, Aristotle, Augustine (Farley quotes his statement that "there is nothing so social by nature" as human beings[7]), Hegel, Feuerbach, and Marx variously construe such inescapability; and in the twentieth century George Herbert Mead, Martin Buber, and communitarians of several stripes do so too. Farley summarizes: "No one today would argue that persons are as autonomous as either Kant or Sartre thought they were. . . . Persons are in the world, and the world is in them. They are in society, and society is in them. They are in biological, psychological, cultural history, and their history is in them like the rings of a tree."[8]

Such massive indications compel us to include on the ground floor of ethical theorizing interpersonal and social realities. Farley posits relationality as an obligating-feature of persons. However, she issues two important cautionary notes. First, she thinks that feminists should beware of undiscriminating alliances. Her example is communitarian philosophy. Appeals to relationality prove to accommodate thick communities of heterogeneous kinds. "Community" is an umbrella term, under which inegalitarian and exclusionary social relations no less than egalitarian and inclusive ones may lodge. To struggle against traditional communal roles that perpetuate arrangements of domination and subservience, for example, requires a complex diagnosis; we say too little when we simply announce that we affirm relationality and reject atomistic individualism. She concludes that "feminist ethics needs an understanding of relationality that will yield a *normative* theory of community."[9] Second, Farley thinks that feminists should heed the vicissitudes of autonomy in its post-Kantian history, for these complicate and may jeopardize the prospects for relationality from another angle. She finds Sartre to represent a powerful warning sign. To be sure, Sartre claims that autonomy begins in, and only in, a concrete encounter with another. In this, he is "relational." But he is also melancholy. As Farley reads him, "autonomy needs relationships in order to be actualized; yet in relationships freedom must either crush the autonomy of the other or surrender the autonomy of the self."[10] Ontologically, it seems that we either fight all the time or submit all the time. And historically, even when we prefer Kant's account of persons as ends in themselves, we must admit that it fails to block a subsequent development where autonomy grows more isolated and competitive. Farley's judgment in the latter case is this: "Kant's concern for respect for persons was not sufficient to counter the stronger drift of the whole Enlightenment toward the self-defining agent."[11]

Postmodern Developments

Postmodern critical philosophy adds its own currents to an already swirling sea. Farley welcomes the urgency of the challenges it brings to the subject of self and other. She acknowledges that so-called postmodern thinkers differ widely among themselves, and that one must select. Here she commends a frankly eclectic approach to such thinkers, and finally to commonplace historical lines of division themselves. Rather than dwell on tensions and incompatibilities, she seeks to garner helpful insights from premodern, modern, and postmodern epochs, and not confine herself to one of these alone.[12]

On issues that pertain to autonomy, she faces nonetheless the contention that postmodernism brings about "the death of the self, the end of subjectivity." And she distinguishes two readings of this contention. The first includes claims she embraces. "The self that is dead is a certain version of the self; it is the self which modern philosophy characterized as disengaged, disembodied, wholly autonomous, and self-transparent. And the subject that has disappeared is the isolated bearer of signs, the conscious knower of clear and certain ideas, the self-governing and self-responsible agent whose task was to instrumentalize body and world."[13] The second reading, however, erases more than her account of love can accommodate. "If the 'self' is really dead; if there is only process and relation without agency; if there is indiscriminate desire and no real choice of affective response issuing in action. . .; then there is not much point in asking how we shall love in a postmodern world. Either we will not love in any recognizable sense at all, or we will not be responsible for our socially constructed loves."[14]

Against this second reading, she extols three proposals that reckon with postmodern critique, but sustain both agential freedom and receptivity to the other. Charles Taylor endorses a "strong sense" of the self, which engages and "can be affected by what is not itself," and yet that is not "wholly lost as a self."[15] Seyla Benhabib maintains that a viable feminism modifies the Enlightenment construal of autonomy by allowing subjectivity to be "contextually situated, socially structured (by language, narrative, culture)," yet "does not (against reason and experience) relinquish freedom, intentionality, and accountability."[16] Edith Wyschograd discovers in the stories of the saints a depiction of the self that preserves the language of desire but attains selfhood only as it meets and relates to the other.[17]

Appeals to reason (though again, not reason opposed to affectivity) and experience continue to count for her as she considers issues pertaining to relationality. The three proposals above elaborate relational engagements of self and other that accord with her account of love. That account appeals to experiential locations where we recognize "something real and enduring" in others and in ourselves. We cannot construe experience here as self-standing, yet we also cannot reduce it, exhaustively and without remainder, to cultural location or projection. She considers two such locations: where we experience love itself and where we experience others' suffering. We respond to what is lovable ("as beautiful or valuable in some way") and we see in suffering a power that elicits "sympathy, solicitude, and compassion."[18] Both locations show a reality that allows us to conclude, in the midst of all challenges, old and new, "that we should love in a postmodern world in the same way that we should love in any world."[19]

This last note recalls the features or aspects *about* persons that obtain for all of us, whether we are male or female, and that warrant our respect. Finally, she claims, "the capacity of persons to love one another and the world, and (as theologians and philosophers of religion must surely add) their capacity to love and to love freely what is sacredly transcendent and immanent, makes them worthy of respect."[20] Here she cites in support Basil Mitchell's insistence "that it is human persons' 'capacity to love one another and to love God, rather than their powers of self-legislation' that makes them 'proper objects of respect.'"[21] While she focuses on ethical obligation in the essays I consider, she keeps open the prospect of loving "what is sacredly transcendent and immanent."

Here we reach a transition point. So far I have sketched claims Farley makes that seem right to me, for example, that we may affirm autonomy and also affectivity, vulnerability, situatedness, and formation, and that we need an understanding of relationality that yields a normative theory of community. About autonomy and relationality generally, I find two questions to be always with us: What sense of each should we elaborate? What combination of both should we offer? In posing them, I assume as Farley does that a self is primarily social, but not merely the result of social forces. And in addressing them, I assume that these questions persist within various frameworks. We address them in terms of our own framework, but we neither address them alone nor prevent possible convergences. Still I now ask how we address these questions within a framework where God and a relation to God stands explicitly at the center.

The point of transition then is love of what is sacredly transcendent and immanent. That we are capable of loving God—as well as one another and the world—introduces considerations whose bearing on how we think of human self and other repays our attempts to ascertain. I concern myself especially here with what this may imply for human autonomy and relationality.

I approach these implications as follows. I accept the perspicacity of the Bible in that I believe we are commanded to love God with all of our hearts, souls, and minds, and our neighbors as ourselves (Matthew 22:37–39; Jesus brings together Deuteronomy 6:5 and Leviticus 19:18). Both are *commandments*, but they are *not* (barring strained exegesis) *one* commandment. To be sure, in crucial respects they are "like" each other. Still I affirm their mutual irreducibility as well as their mutual inherence. And I connect Mitchell's insistence with certain strands in the Christian tradition, and so integrate the respect he locates with more particularist convictions. The connections I draw require me initially to locate overlaying convictions about God and God's relation to the world. I do not see how we may trace the implications above unless we have before us some rudimentary outline. But I must limit this inquiry. I make three schematic proposals and comment on each, and leave specification for another time.[22]

THREE PROPOSALS

Proposal One: *God's Actions* Ad Extra *Establish a Basic Framework for Love of God and Neighbor*

Let us say something explicit about our sense of God's identity, of *who* God is whom we are to love with all our heart. I do not pronounce on answers that persons "at large" or in other religious traditions give. My aim is confessional inquiry, not apologetics. I identify with that part of the Christian tradition that proclaims no God who is somehow *above* the Trinity. A stress on God-relatedness should be trinitarian here from beginning to end. And I place this inquiry within the second half of a distinction Christian theologians traditionally draw between the Godhead in itself (the immanent Trinity) and God's actions *ad extra* (the economic Trinity, which is first in order of knowledge), where we specify thematically the shape of God's self-disclosure and governance in our existential and historical reality.

An Inclusive Framework.   Such thematic specification constitutes an inclusive framework that is, straightforwardly, the structure of creedal belief. This structure is composed of a narrative, the basic elements of which are found in the Bible, and also in Christian creeds, forms of worship, preaching, and teaching. In the course of time, theologians attached technical names to the basic units of this narrative. I continue to work with a traditional scheme: creation, fall, the covenant with Israel, incarnation, the church, salvation, and last things.

Briefly, *creation* refers to the divine origin and preservation of the world, and whatever order and coherence we find there. *Fall* refers to the appearance of sin and evil, and the distortions and derangements they bring into the world. *The covenant with Israel* refers to God's particular relation to a people God chooses, a people in whom the history of redemption is rooted and by whom all of the nations will bless themselves. *Incarnation* refers to the life, death, and resurrection of Jesus Christ, and the gift of the Holy Spirit. The *church* refers to the Christian community in its corporate life and in the lives of persons who identify with it, and in its relations to surrounding social worlds. *Salvation* refers both to justification, as God's utterly free love that rescues human beings and the consequent freedom and love they are to show in human interaction; and to sanctification, as God's action in and through the Holy Spirit that works to regenerate and transform human beings, both in the characters they develop and the quality of community they realize. *Last things* refers to the final state of the world when God's purposes are fulfilled, the promise of which warrants a manner of life in the present dominated by hope.

Our sense of God's identity derives from such *ad extra* actions that God undertakes and to which the narrative attests. In this narrative, God relates to human beings as creator, reconciler, and redeemer. God remains the center of value and human beings are depicted in their relations to God as the center. We may enjoy a relation to God that is for its own sake. *This* relation is an end in itself, and is *sui generis*. A relation to God is the greatest of all goods. God is the alpha and omega of our existence. Our relation to God takes its rise from God's side, not ours. God's gracious initiatives are unilateral in that they presuppose nothing other than God's love.

The narrative further conveys a sense of ourselves and our situation. Taken cumulatively, it locates us in "the time between the times." It indicates that part of the drama of our lives unfolds in the interaction of divine and human freedom, where we move between God's grace and covenant love and "particular providences," and actively correspond on our own level, and with our own capacities, or fail to correspond. We follow God at a distance, a distance that God's alterity and our creatureliness—including our finitude and the corruption under which we now labor—combine to effect. Yet we may genuinely follow, in the pattern our own attachments, actions, and virtues assume. And in light of the narrative, I take Christian theological ethics to focus on the normative aspects of our lives in the time between the times, and thus to features that contribute distinctively to an account of the character, possibilities, and limits of the Christian community and of humankind in the time we now have.

We may accordingly ascribe a certain status to the basic units of this narrative. The narrative is judged to be true, to stand in need of promulgation, and to be comprehensive. It summarizes a way of seeing the world, the panorama of human history and the meaning of creaturely life in the present, that purports to be true. No part of this seeing is thought to stand outside a biblical world, though the creedal elements are theologically conceived. The Bible and the tradition thus remain indispensable for the comprehensive convictions that the creed registers. Without these sources, the convictions lack determinateness. Of course we know huge numbers of things from other sources. But we do not thereby cease to need to return to these particularist points of departure. Furthermore, actions *ad extra* tell us things that we cannot simply tell ourselves, and the narrative about them has to be promulgated. This extends to the first love commandment. I do not originally tell myself that I should focus my love first and irreducibly on God, and should enlist my various powers as I do. Finally, all of the convictions serve as necessary points of reference. It is a mistake to seize upon one and heed it exclusively. Taken together they furnish parameters that test the adequacy of more detailed proposals put forward.

Although this narrative is something on which we rely, we should beware of getting things too pat. Those whose love for God is based on God's *ad extra* actions are called upon to interpret each of the convictions so far noted and to estimate how the convictions relate to each other. Each of the elements affords interpretive leeway, and an interpretation of one element may have implications elsewhere. Disputes arise when certain convictions, though they do not logically entail each other, nonetheless cohere as a determinate constellation. Some constellations fail to harmonize sufficiently with others to foreclose debate. In addition to intramural disputes, extramural disagreements arise that reflect more radical departures that jettison certain elements, or at least alter them so thoroughly that they are more discontinuous than continuous with anything recognizably traditional. Assumptions about inherited sin, for example, under interpretations of the fall, are sometimes rejected *tout court* on extramural scientific or moral grounds. Even here, however, we may assess more clearly questions posed from outside the structure when we expressly identify what is being criticized and in some instances left behind. In any event, those who work within the comprehensive structure delineating God's actions *ad extra* face an intramural amalgam of more specific possibilities to sift and weigh.

An Augustinian Constellation.   The constellation of specific possibilities that I find most perspicuous I associate with an Augustinian legacy. This legacy offers a particular explication of a scripturally based theistic view. The view is more inclusive than Augustine himself; it is a mobile line rather than *the* line from him. Still, the legacy represents one development with certain characteristic emphases. Regarding human selves, Oliver O'Donovan describes how, for Augustine, "the loving subject stands in a complex and variable relation to the reality his love confronts. . . . Thus we do well to speak of . . . the complex order of reality that is love's object."[23] This pluriform character of reality means that a relation to God has both the highest status and its own integrity and exigencies. And it means that our love for one another has its own integrity and exigencies. Yet the reality stands also under mysterious siege: one that confounds not only our yearning for total harmonies in this life but our more complacent assumptions that we can be good solely by self-exertion and self-repair. Grace is glorious and sin is terrible; although we have to do with God in everything, we remain continually in danger.

Proposal Two: Between the Times, Our Love for God and Neighbor
Displays Our Real But Relative Independence as Creatures

These overlaying convictions affect claims about autonomy and relationality in myriad ways. I inquire now about the place of creaturely
agency in our love for God and neighbor ("creaturely agency" seems
a more theologically apt locution than autonomy, though I sometimes
refer to the latter as well as simply to freedom and will). We may
regard such agency as constitutive of the sort of creatures we are. Yet
in its operations it reaches higher and sinks lower than contemporary
debates about autonomy usually acknowledge. Let me attempt to sift
claims, again some of them new and some previously introduced.

On creaturely agency as internal to an account of the image of God,
and of sin and moral evil.   Our agency is traditionally implicated in
both constructive and destructive possibilities. On the constructive
side, human creatures are made, to employ biblical language, in the
image of God. This is often taken to include a capacity for intentional
activity, moral accountability, and friendship, in relation to God and
with one another. To believe that we resemble God in part by virtue
of this multidimensional capacity prompts us to set our "being able
to carry on intentional activity," for example, "our ability to envisage
and work toward the achievement of goals . . . in the context of divine
activity."[24] On the destructive side, Augustine's insistence that "I had
a will, as certainly as I knew I had life"[25] is often taken to mean that
our distinctiveness includes our having wills that may withdraw from
the will and plan of God. Our relative but real independence extends
so far that there "is something intrinsic about creatures, their contin-
gency and nonnecessity of obedience, that makes them able to depart
from God's rule."[26] Here I accept Margaret Farley's claim noted above
that persons "are not solely determined in their actions by causes external to their own reason and will, not even by their own desires and
inclinations." But in its *de facto* operations, we find creaturely agency
to be volatile, set within "a good world gone wrong."[27] Our agency is
again a constituent in our resembling God, and part of a good world
that is real, not a fiction, positive, not negative. Yet our agency also

operates in our perverse imitation of God, our unfairness to others, our self-destructive habits and self-aggrandizing pursuits. Its dynamics can include surd-like disordering in various directions. Each of us is, as Augustine professes, a "great deep."[28] "Autonomy" may refer to this, indispensably, but as we thicken and dramatize our portraiture we catch more fully our agency's place in delineating both our created dignity and post-fallen twistedness.

On love for God and our creaturely agency.   We may enjoy a relation to God that is for its own sake: our created dignity, of which our agency forms part, means nothing less than that such enjoyment comes as a remarkable prospect. It is to be seen as a gift of God's love rather than as a claim we make. And it is emphatically never a mere means to something else. We are not to appraise our relation to God by virtue of how well it promotes other genuine but finite goods, such as our physical well-being. And a relation to God is the greatest of all goods. God is the alpha and omega of our existence, and the one with whom we have decisively to do in this life.

Love for God between the times leads us to view our creaturely agency in two more determinate ways (among others we might cite). We find that such love orders and accentuates our agency, but that our agency remains liable once more to wantonness.

First, love for God allows us to trace a normative sequence from dependence on God to personal integration, a sequence that tracks a constituted order. Peter Brown writes of a profound change that Augustine inaugurates: "In substituting for the classical ideal of an available self-perfection, the idea of a man, placed as a stranger in an uncomprehending land, a man whose virtue lies in a tension towards something else in hope, in faith, in an ardent yearning for a country that is always distant, but made ever-present by the quality of his love, that 'groans' for it, Augustine could well be called the first Romantic."[29] This is right, provided that we focus on communion with God as that "country." Augustine insists that he depends on God for the quality of his love, indeed for whatever integrated personal identity he has. "If I do not remain in" God, he states in the *Confessions*, "neither shall I abide in myself."[30] Thus he goes *from* his relation to God *to* his relation to himself. That this dependence proves at the end of the day to heighten *his* individuality as well differs from "romantic" programs that either reverse the sequence, or finish and not only start with ourselves. In the latter case, we are to plumb our own depths to discover and subsequently cherish an incomparable originality that we *possess* immanentally.[31] In short, the tension Brown describes in Augustine occurs in a theocentric rather than an anthropocentric framework.

Second, heightened individuality and attention to the interior life flow from remaining in God. Augustine confesses to God in a fashion that posits the singularity of one's own relation to God. Singularity correlates with the possibility that God addresses me as someone who stands distinctively, irreducibly in God's presence. To be thus addressed leads me to view my life, and to infer that each of us should view his or her own life, as possessing a meaning and significance that remains non-interchangeable. Singularity thereby points to matters of consuming importance. That God addresses me indicates that God does not subsist in deistic aloofness and that I am more than the indifferently substitutable plaything of historical forces. Awareness of this address is beyond price. I take the claim to form part of the exigencies of a personal relation to God. Augustine's confession also assumes that God knows the entirety of his loves, that God's providence reaches this far. Augustine's own attachments should accordingly matter to him even when, on given occasions, events he cannot control defeat what he intends to do, or when his neighbors stay ignorant of what he does or forbears.

Still, we may reverse this sequence and violate this order. We need not do so when we extol, for example, "self-direction" as such, since our love for God may take up some of its features. Rather, we do so when we effectively deny that our creaturely agency itself *suffices* for us. At some point I may transmute love for God into inordinate imitation of God. When this happens may remain opaque to me. But I give evidence that transmutation has likely occurred when it is not enough for me to honor my agency. I seek power instead to determine the value of things solely by my own will; I hold that I alone determine the limits of my actions.[32] My desire to be sovereign progressively sets the terms for my relating to everything else. I cease to care whether pluriform reality confers any order of loves. Above all, I answer no longer to God but only to myself.

On love of neighbor and self and our creaturely agency.   The love commandments link normatively together love for God and love of neighbor. What status our real but relative agency has as we try ourselves to forge the links is complicated to plot. I visit briefly here three sites of inquiry where our creaturely agencies operate: in attesting to God's love for our neighbors and ourselves, in our own love for God and neighbors and ourselves, and in our own love for neighbors and ourselves.

First, we attest to God's love for us by witnessing to God's actions *ad extra* and seeking to adhere to the terms of the narrative identifying these actions. So we worship God as Creator and revere creation and our place in it. We confess that we are sinners to whom grace has come and take due measure of living continually in danger; for example, we acknowledge that no one of us is good enough to govern another without the other's consent. We abide by the particularities of God's covenant love and heed always the significance of God's election of Israel and the subsequent mission of the church. We follow Jesus as savior and as model; we do not simply duplicate his saving work, but we may correspond significantly to his manner of life, as the Holy Spirit enables us. We devote ourselves to the well-being of neighbors inside and outside the church, to the church's communal transmission of the narrative, to its "testing of the spirits," and to community discipline. We honor salvation, both as justification and sanctification, which are inseparable and contemporaneous, yet where sanctification admits of varying degrees, and we commit ourselves to the theological virtues of faith, hope, and love. We yearn for eschatological transformation and last things, where human history is fulfilled rather than annulled, and we savor foretastes in the time between the times. These various attestations—where we witness, adhere, worship, revere, confess, abide, heed, follow, honor, yearn, commit, and savor—make sense only as we affirm our agential powers.

To attest to God's love for us as we know it in God's actions *ad extra* links the two love commandments in the following generalized way. If we attest to God's love, we want what God wants, and love whom and what God loves. God loves our neighbors as well as ourselves. So our agential fidelity and loyalty to God's love lead inexorably to love of our neighbors and to the complexities of proper self-love. Put differently, we miss a key ingredient in what we believe *God* wants, in light of *ad extra* actions, when we fail to embrace our neighbors as we love God.

Second, in our own love for God and neighbors we face again the importance of affirming the mutual irreducibility of these loves as well as their mutual inherence. As agents, we are capable of affirming both *qua* discrete loves. We worship and glorify God, but not our neighbor. We help our neighbor in distress and exhort him or her to repent, but not God. The key recognition for me is this. Not everything that God does to us and for us, and not everything that our love for God encompasses, can or should be reproduced in our love for one another, just as, once more, our love for one another has its own integrity and exigencies. Thus I submit that we should attend to the specific nature of the links rather than separate their features entirely or blend their features wholly together.

Yet some defenders of human autonomy claim that these loves conflict unavoidably. They assume that between God's action and ours there is competitiveness in principle. That is, they assume that strictly zero-sum relations obtain. In modernity and postmodernity the assumption of zero-sum relations typically manifests itself in claims that God's power, either as domination or benevolence, must collide with human liberation. For they presume that God's action and ours are commensurable enough that they may directly compete, that they belong on a continuum of degrees, and that we may treat them as rivalrous and adjudicate their respective legitimacies. They contend that we should alter and harness God's action in order to enhance and empower our own. I cannot assess this influential contention now (though I do so elsewhere).[33] Disputes about it increase the volatility surrounding creaturely agency. But I believe that it is a mistake to assume there must be competitiveness in principle. We avoid it by refusing to exempt human agency from total dependence on God and by articulating "a metaphysics capable of formulating that dependence in ways that respect all of the modalities of creatures, including freedom."[34] On this understanding, God's transcendence is not antithetical to, or necessarily contrastive with, either God's immanence or our created exigencies. "If it makes sense to say that God can call forth a nondivine being with an integrity of existence of its own, then it makes sense to say that God can call forth nondivine beings with real powers of their own to influence other creatures."[35] A central part of such understanding is that our creaturely agency *owes itself* to God's creating action.[36]

Third, in depicting our own love for our neighbors and ourselves, we may appropriate the language of respecting neighbors as ends in themselves. This language is not the last word in our depicting, nor must we, in appropriating it, defend major parts of the ethical theory in which Kant himself embeds it.[37] Still, we may annex such language into the narrative so far identified. In the immediate context, for example, we may draw on an account of persons as ends in themselves to suggest how creaturely agency occupies an indispensable place in specifying what love or respect of the other includes. We may say that the love enjoined requires that we view no neighbor *either* as a totally passive recipient of one's generosity *or* as a "mere means" to one's purposes. Creaturely agency guards against each deformation. We do not respect persons as ends in themselves when we regard them only as our patient beneficiaries, sheerly determined by causes external to their own reason and will. For then we deny them not only room for maneuver but finally any independent center of consciousness that retains even limited efficacy, which persists as an agent-relative standpoint. Creaturely agency confounds this denial, disclosing something irreducibly first personal that recoils from our attempts to dispense with it. We *also* do not respect persons as ends in themselves when nothing about them counts in our eyes unless and until it promotes our own acquisitive designs. Creaturely agency confounds this movement as well. It authorizes resistance to being other people's instruments. It helps us fathom why we disdain and what we miss in strictly manipulative social relations. In brief, unless we make creaturely agency integral to the injunction to love neighbors as ends, we are unable to specify sufficiently how both self and other should remain terminal points for our attitudes and actions.

The allusion to resistance anticipates however more destructive conflictual possibilities. Theologically viewed, the Sartrean turn mentioned earlier suggests one recurrent way in which our creaturely agencies operate under post-fallen conditions. To deny one another more than instrumental significance leaves us wary and lonely. A combative "relational" dynamic ensues, where again it seems that unless we fight all the time, we submit all the time. Sartre's own insights here are valuable some of the way. Yet we should take pains over how far we generalize from such a combative dynamic. To say on its basis, for example, that ontological hostility governs all encounters between self and other levels unacceptably the constructive as well as destructive possibilities intimated earlier. Here is another point at which we address the question of what combination of autonomy and relationality we should offer.

I think Augustine offers a more adequate generalization than ontological hostility in his sentence (part of which Farley cites as I note previously): "For there is nothing so social by nature, so unsocial by its corruption, as this race."[38] That we are social by nature suggests that constructive dimensions of autonomy and reciprocity stand as our normative created lot. As the fall is parasitic on creation, so twistedness depends perversely on goodness. Thus we link our capacity for love, for respect, for justice, to a good creation. This limits the reach of strictly combative dynamics. They are not so deep that we posit for example a single egoistic spring of human motivation. Since we never efface completely our status as morally capable creatures, or do without free and caring relations that mark our interdependence, we reject with Augustine a picture of human beings as "essentially" antisocial, aggressive, and competitive. Miikka Ruokanen remarks incisively that Augustine is "an ontological or natural optimist," and at the same time, "a moral or voluntary pessimist."[39] I take the optimism to assume, for example, that reality retains a normative dimension (there are real values and disvalues in a good world gone wrong), that once more we do not cease to be accountable creatures, and that the intelligibility of appeals to justice survives, doubtless imperfectly, but ineradicably nevertheless. I take the pessimism to assume, for instance, that lasting temptations assail us and that our "arrogantly looking to domination" corrupts *how* we often appeal to justice in fact (such as when we often select only those arguments that vindicate us and our causes, and hold opponents responsible for all that goes wrong in given clashes).

When we keep clear this relation between creation and fall, we may go on to say that part of what post-fallen conditions require from us is to recognize that diminished prospects can afflict various self and other encounters, and that we should make provision for prospects we neither welcome nor laud. Not to make provision exacts a heavy eventual price in naiveté and sentimentality. And the provision we make includes accepting prohibitions and injunctions that promote the constructive dimensions of self and other encounters here and now even as they are tied to matters that threaten these dimensions. The second table of the Decalogue for instance forbids certain actions and exchanges that typically do harm, but in forbidding them it acknowledges them, and has its force in relation to what it acknowledges. Similarly, forgiveness makes sense only when a *bona fide* wrong has occurred. In sum, it seems that there are some prohibitions and injunctions we need only after the fall. The provision we make still permits ample liberty to search for reconciling strategies beyond fighting or submitting. Prohibitions and injunctions also help us to discern what is diminished. And yet we may do this from the vantage point of a (personal, agential) love that would still prefer in any given case that there be no diminution to discern and with which to cope.

Proposal Three: Between the Times, Our Love for God and Neighbor Displays Our Relational Bonds as Creatures

The relations *between* us—between God and ourselves, and between our neighbors and ourselves—are ineliminable. Yet they too range from the sublime and compassionate, to the prudent and cooperative, to the mean and unjust. Let us trace more concertedly how a constellation of overlaying convictions guide among possibilities.

Between God and Ourselves: Communion and Friendship. What God's actions *ad extra* disclose lead us to a qualitative difference pointing to God's transcendence, to a portent of communion pointing to God's immanence, and to a friendship that remains *sui generis*. Joe R. Jones writes: "The basic ontological distinction in Christian theology is that between the Creator and the creature: this is radical and incommensurate."[40] An account of pluriform reality, of differences and points of correspondence, should abide by this distinction. It attests to one hierarchy we cannot and should not seek to dismantle. As creatures, we depend on God, basically, in a qualitatively distinct way. God's actions also disclose more than this founding difference. They warrant Augustine's confession that God is "utterly good, utterly powerful, most omnipotent, most merciful and most just, deeply hidden yet most intimately present."[41] These attributes have been elucidated and debated through the centuries, and I must content myself to say only this. Predicated of God, "good" and "powerful" combine to point to something like utterly *good and right power*. To ascertain the sense of good and right power, we associate God's goodness with God's love and God's power with God's freedom. So Barth depicts God as "the being of . . . the one who loves in freedom."[42] God's love and God's freedom, always distinct, always connected, to be interpreted together, without one being more basic than the other, are the attributes that shape our understanding of all others. And for Christians, the final warrant for concluding that God's relation to the world is that of "loving dominion"[43] is the Christological paradigm. We construe the actions of Jesus to be the enacted intentions of God.

This understanding of *ad extra* actions cuts against an influential charge that God's relation to the world on traditional reckonings encompasses distant, apathetic, nonengaged, separative transcendence. Biblical metaphors themselves collide with allegations of noninvolvement. Eugene Borowitz locates these: "God weeps, pants, suffers, roars, regrets, rages, threatens, punishes, and much else, in response to humankind's freely chosen sinfulness."[44] Such metaphors may raise other difficulties, but they disconfirm the charge. References to distant noninvolvement also collide with repeated affirmations of God's immanence no less than God's transcendence, and the *sui generis* dependence this immanence brings. Sarah Coakley confesses: "for me, the *right* sort of dependence on God is not only empowering but freeing. For God is no rapist, but the source of my very being; God is *closer* than kissing (I am happy to put it thus, metaphorically); indeed God, being God, is closer to me even than I am to myself."[45] Augustine would concur.

A relation to God can then be deeply personal and interactional. I want to appropriate Aquinas's claim that "Charity signifies not only the love of God, but also a certain friendship with Him; which implies, besides love, a certain mutual return of love, together with mutual communion."[46] We can say that God desires fellowship for its own sake and that this desire involves God no less than ourselves. God actively wills to commune. Indeed, the traditional concern to keep human love responsive means that even when no positive human response takes place, God's love perdures. From God's side, the will to communion is irrevocable, and the grace it reveals is prevenient. The friendship between God and ourselves precludes undifferentiated union and includes genuine interaction.

This relation to God that is beyond price may yet evoke a corresponding view of our relations to one another. I remarked earlier that to be aware that God addresses me forms part of the exigencies of a personal relation to God, and that this address leads me to view my life, and to infer that each of us view his or her life, as possessing noninterchangeable meaning and significance. That is, noninterchangeable meaning and significance may obtain for all of us. For if God may address me as a human being in this way, God may address neighbors similarly. And this makes sense of the claim that if we are to correspond to what God grants, we should regard each of us as irreducibly valuable, and we should treat one another as such. I think we travel no great distance from this to appropriate the language once more of persons as ends in themselves. We may elaborate to say that each person is (1) incommensurable with the value of contingent desires satisfied or profits secured; (2) noninterchangeable, both in the sense that he or she is unquantifiable and so can never be measured or traded, and irreplaceable in that his or her loss cannot be compensated (the presence of one person cannot make good the loss of another); (3) permanent in that in no circumstances can someone cease to matter.[47]

To appropriate in this way leaves us open still to recognize that our relation to God is not an equal relation. Here a passage from Buber articulates for me part of what need not and should not be lost: "God and man, being consubstantial, are actually and forever Two, the two partners of the primal relationship that, from God to man, is called mission and commandment; from man to God, seeing and hearing; between both, knowledge and love."[48] Although much more may be said, and "man" must refer to human beings, this passage locates basic movements that shape the interplay between honoring differences and likenesses between God and ourselves. I gloss them as follows. God does things that we do not, including things that found us and are directed toward us. We acknowledge, attest, and correspond, on our own level and with our own capacities, and are permitted to enjoy real but relative independence, and real relations with others. And between God and ourselves, both may know and both may love, without blurring or separation.

Between Our Neighbors and Ourselves: Unqualified Regard and Friendship as Fruition.   The real relations we enjoy with others have, as I said, their own integrity and exigencies. They are extraordinarily complex. I have also said that Farley is right: we need a normative theory of community. In addition to claims she makes in this regard with which I agree—for example, that we remain responsible for our socially constructed loves, that we allow subjectivity to be contextually situated, that we attain selfhood only as we relate to and are affected by others—I continue to ask how matters stand when we view our relations within an explicitly theological framework.

How matters stand most obviously is that we no longer think only of a relation of love with one another and the world. We think now as well of a relation between God and ourselves. And when we think of the latter, I submit that we then should always conduct a twofold inquiry: how the discreteness in these loves, and more vastly the differences between God and ourselves, affect an account of human self and other; and how likenesses in these loves, and more vastly points of correspondence between God and ourselves, affect an account of human self and other. Some conclusions send us back to our limits (we realize that we are not God and should not "play God"). Others dispose us to imitate or at any rate correspond (we too should love who and what

God loves, and in a measure, as God loves). The search for the right interplay may exceed our powers and remain incomplete between the times, but it matters now nevertheless for the illumination it brings. Let me give two extended examples beyond the claims already made.

First, we may attend to differences between God and ourselves that are salutary, that clarify and inform who we are and what we may fittingly envisage for ourselves. Such attention can yield inferences that *resist* transferring sovereignty from God to ourselves. We claim that we *should* direct unlimited obedience to God alone, and infer that we *should not* direct it to any creature. We then see human governance as failing to gain sacral legitimacy. No institutional arrangement mirrors or extends God and God's relation to the world *sufficiently* to constitute a sphere that warrants unlimited obedience to *it*. Such obedience is perforce misdirected. A question that requires its own space is how far this inference gives trouble for theocratic arrangements, whether Christian, Jewish, or Muslim.

Some feminists likewise affirm that accenting differences can have salutary effects in our own relations. Yet they also insist that we have a perpetual fight on our hands. I think both the affirmation and the insistence get matters roughly right.

On the one side, Rosemary Radford Ruether refers to a "liberating sovereign." "Because God is our king, we need obey no human kings. Because God is our parent, we are liberated from dependence on patriarchal authority."[49] She recognizes that the language may work "to establish a new liberated relationship to a new community of equals for those in revolt against established authorities. This is true not only in the formation of Israel and in the rise of the Jesus movement; again and again throughout Christian history this antipatriarchal use of God-language has been rediscovered by dissenting groups. The call to 'obey God rather than men' has perhaps been the most continuous theological basis for dissent in the Christian tradition. Throughout Christian history women discovered this concept of direct relation to God as a way to affirm their own authority and autonomy against patriarchal authority."[50]

On the other side, Ruether adds that the pattern of a liberating sovereign coexists with an oppressive one that she also repeatedly accents, namely, that established communities reassimilate images of God as father and king to traditional authorities where "human lordship and patriarchy" once more gain ascendancy.[51] I think we may say that we should struggle always to see how differences between God and ourselves impel us to look with a permanently critical eye at our myriad human entanglements. They warn us against complacent assumptions that it is a simple, short-lived matter to extrude societal stereotypes and status quo power arrangements when we refer to God and to what God ordains. They also warn us against the damage that crude metaphorical associations may inflict, where for instance the male represents God to humanity and the female represents humankind in relation to God. A protest against gross sexual essentialisms is one I heartily join.

Second, we may attend to points of correspondence between God and ourselves that are salutary, that show congruities between the loves testifying to our pluriform reality. Our love for our neighbors and ourselves must make its way between dimensions that resemble the genuine interactions that marks friendship with God, and yet differ in the mutual benefit and mutual vulnerability they demonstrate. Thus our love engages positive and negative dimensions of ordinary human interaction, with myriad encounters where each side is able to help and harm each other, where we can mutually meet needs, render assistance, and enrich one another, and we can abuse, manipulate, and do or suffer a host of other injuries. These circumstances show that we are deeply social and antisocial creatures.

When our loves correspond, we may influence and sometimes transform our ordinary interactions, but not in a way prior to the eschaton that removes mutual benefit and mutual vulnerability as features of the distinctively human world we share. Possible points of correspondence are perhaps most intelligible in an ecclesial context, yet I hardly do justice to the rich possibilities this context provides (for example, the special bonds within the church, the significance of washing one another's feet in John 13:3–17, the stress on self-giving, the challenge to the friend-foe distinction). I simply suggest here one of the ways in which a point of correspondence forges the links between the two love commands. It consists in wanting the best for the other. (Let us agree that "the best" avoids problematic meddlesome-ness and paternalism, and permissive antiauthoritarianism.) I think we may elaborate by saying that a mark of love that corresponds to God's love is its *unqualified* character. One regards the other's good for the other's own sake, or, more emphatically, one wants the best for the other and is ready to protect and promote what is best, independently of any assurances that a response in kind will occur. Moreover, such wanting never ends, whether or not a response occurs.[52] Still, we may compatibly *not require* a response in kind and still *want* it.[53] If I am right that this mark of love suggests a *bona fide* point of correspondence to grace, unqualified regard or something akin to it should form part of a comprehensive depiction of neighbor-love.

Let me discuss one transformative possibility in the traditional lan-guage of agape and philia. Agape refers to the unqualified wanting the best for the other. Philia refers to a positive dimension of relationality, to the bond of communication, understanding, and delight *between* people, where we are with one another and not simply *for* another or receiving *from* another.[54] The possibility is this: *agape promotes the realization of philia without guaranteeing it, and without ceasing to be love when philia is unrealized.* We can compatibly join unqualified re-gard for the neighbor with a desire and a hope for a response in kind. We can view actual attainment as the fruition we seek. Between the times, to want the best for the other does not, however, assure a re-sponse in kind. Sometimes the delights of sustained philia will ensue; sometimes we must be content to stand fast. Unqualified regard pro-motes philia, however, by liberating us, for example, from certain self-referential anxieties that tend to block the realization of philia. As a consequence of such anxieties, our concern for others is held hos-tage to our concern that others confirm us. We care *about* them but not in the first instance *for* them. We start by caring about the effect their approvals and disapprovals have on our own self-esteem, not by revering their own lives in their otherness. Two elements coexist in these anxieties. Others matter too little: their approval of us proves to be a condition for whether we care or continue to care about them at all. Others matter too much: in seeking to secure their approval, we are problematically liable to do their bidding, to be controlled by their appraisals of us. Agape gives us independence from these anxieties: from not caring unless they care and from caring unduly what others think of us and thus allowing them to set the terms for the confirmation of ourselves we want, above all, to obtain. I suspect that in the deepest relations between people *both* parties display an ingredient of unqualified regard.[55]

These last remarks are fragmentary. It cannot be otherwise here. I offer them to endorse and join Farley's commitment year in and year out to keep trying to articulate the unconditional value of persons.[56]

NOTES

1. Margaret A. Farley, "A Feminist Version of Respect for Persons," in *Feminist Ethics and the Catholic Moral Tradition*, ed. Charles E. Curran, Margaret A. Farley, and Richard A. McCormick, S.J. (New York: Paulist Press, 1996), 177.

2. The corpus includes theological explorations to which I am indebted in the constructive proposals I later offer here. See, e.g., her searching discussion in chapter 8, "Commitment, Covenant, and Faith," in *Personal Commitments: Making, Keeping, Breaking* (San Francisco: Harper and Row, 1986), 110–35.

3. Immanuel Kant, *Groundwork of the Metaphysic of Morals*, trans. H. J. Paton (New York: Harper Torchbook, 1964), 96.

4. Farley, "A Feminist Version of Respect for Persons," 176.

5. Ibid., 170.

6. Ibid., 168.

7. Ibid., 170.

8. Ibid., 176–77.

9. Ibid., 171.

10. Ibid., 174.

11. Ibid., 175.

12. Margaret Farley, "How Shall We Love in a Postmodern World?" *The Annual of the Society of Christian Ethics* (1994): 8.

13. Ibid., 13–14.

14. Ibid., 14–15.

15. Ibid., 15.

16. Ibid., 16.

17. Ibid.

18. Ibid., 11, 17.

19. Ibid., 19.

20. Farley, "A Feminist Version of Respect for Persons," 177.

21. Ibid., 183; Basil Mitchell, *Morality: Religious and Secular* (Oxford: Clarendon Press, 1980), 134.

22. The specification occurs chiefly in my volume, *God and the Moral Life: Conversations in the Augustinian Tradition* (Oxford: Oxford University Press, forthcoming). Two of my recent essays contribute as well to such specification; I reiterate here some of these convictions, though in an altered context: "Theocentric Love and the Augustinian Legacy: Honoring Differences and Likenesses between God and Ourselves," *Journal of the Society of Christian Ethics* 22 (Fall, 2002): 97–114; and "Faith," in *Oxford Handbook of Theological Ethics*, ed. Gilbert Meilaender and William Werpehowski, 273–90 (Oxford: Oxford University Press, 2005).

23. Oliver O'Donovan, *The Problem of Self-Love in St. Augustine* (New Haven, CT: Yale University Press, 1972), 12–13.

24. Alvin Plantinga, "Augustinian Christian Philosophy," in *The Augustinian Tradition*, ed. Gareth B. Matthews (Berkeley: University of California Press, 1999), 19.

25. Augustine, *Confessions*, trans. Albert C. Outler (Philadelphia: Westminster Press, 1955), VII.7.5, p. 137.

26. Edward Farley, *Divine Empathy: A Theology of God* (Minneapolis: Fortress Press, 1996), 38.

27. This phrase I take from C. S. Lewis, *Mere Christianity* (New York: Macmillan, 1960), 48; it is cited by Graham Walker, *Moral Foundations of Constitutional Thought: Current Problems, Augustinian Prospects* (Princeton, NJ: Princeton University Press, 1990), 114.

28. Augustine, *Confessions*, trans. Outler, IV.14.22, p. 89.

29. Peter Brown, "Political Society," in *Augustine: A Collection of Critical Essays*, ed. R. A. Markus (Garden City: Doubleday Anchor, 1972), 323.

30. Augustine, *Confessions*, trans. Outler, VII.11.17, 148.

31. Gene Outka, "Self-Realization," in *The Westminster Dictionary of Christian Ethics*, ed. James F. Childress and John Macquarrie (Philadelphia: Westminster Press, 1986), 572–75.

32. Scott MacDonald, "Petit Larceny, the Beginning of All Sin: Augustine's Theft of the Pears," *Faith and Philosophy*, 20, no. 4 (2003): 393–414.

33. See Outka, *God and the Moral Life*, chap. 8.

34. David Burrell, "Divine Action and Human Freedom in the Context of Creation," in *The God Who Acts: Philosophical and Theological Explorations*, ed. Thomas F. Tracy (University Park: Pennsylvania State University Press, 1994), 109.

35. Kathryn Tanner, "Human Freedom, Human Sin, and God the Creator," in Tracy, *The God Who Acts*, 117.

36. See the arresting statement of this in Søren Kierkegaard, *The Journals of Kierkegaard: 1834–1854*, trans. Alexander Dru (London: Oxford University Press, 1959), 180–81. For one elaboration, see William P. Alston, "Hartshorne and Aquinas: A *Via Media*," in his *Divine Nature and Human Language* 121–43 (Ithaca, NY: Cornell University Press, 1989).

37. Margaret Farley claims for example that autonomy is not the only reason for regarding persons as ends in themselves when she reviews Alan Donagan's *The Theory of Morality* (Chicago: University of Chicago Press, 1979) in *Religious Studies Review* 7, no. 3 (1981): 233–37.

38. Augustine, *The City of God*, trans. Marcus Dods (New York: Modern Library, 1950), XII.27, p. 410. R. A. Markus translates discordiosum as "anti-social" in his *Saeculum: History and Society in the Theology of St. Augustine* (Cambridge: Cambridge University Press, 1989), 95. I attend in more detail to Augustine's sentence in my "Augustinianism and Common Morality," in *Prospects for a Common Morality*, ed. Gene Outka and John P. Reeder, Jr. 114–48 (Princeton, NJ: Princeton University Press, 1993).

39. Miikka Ruokanen, *Theology of Social Life in Augustine's De civitate Dei* (Göttingen: Vandenhoeck & Ruprecht, 1993), e.g., 157.

40. Joe R. Jones, *A Grammar of Christian Faith: Systematic Explorations in Christian Faith and Doctrine* (Lanham, MD: Rowman and Littlefield, 2002), 252–53.

41. Augustine, *Confessions*, trans. Henry Chadwick (Oxford: Oxford University Press, 1998), I.4.4, 4–5.

42. Karl Barth, *Church Dogmatics*, II/1, trans. T. H. L. Parker et. al. (Edinburgh: T. & T. Clark, 1957), 257–321.

43. Christopher Morse, *Not Every Spirit: A Dogmatics of Christian Disbelief* (Valley Forge, PA: Trinity Press International, 1994), 127.

44. Eugene B. Borowitz, *Exploring Jewish Ethics* (Detroit: Wayne State University Press, 1980), 9.

45. Sarah Coakely, "Afterward," in *Swallowing a Fishbone? Feminist Theologians Debate Christianity*, ed. Daphne Hampson (London: SPCK, 1996), 170.

46. Thomas Aquinas, *Summa Theologica*, I-II, q. 65, a. 5; from *Summa Theologica of St. Thomas Aquinas*, I, trans. Fathers of the English Dominican Province (New York: Benziger, 1947), 865.

47. See Gene Outka, "Respect for Persons," in *The Westminster Dictionary of Christian Ethics*, 541–45.

48. Martin Buber, *I and Thou*, trans. Walter Kaufmann (New York: Scribners, 1970), 133.

49. Rosemary Radford Ruether, *Sexism and God-Talk: Toward a Feminist Theology* (Boston: Beacon Press, 1993), 65. For feminist assessments that dwell on differences between God and ourselves as susceptible to an alienating mode of domination and control, see, e.g., Sallie McFague, *Models of*

God: Theology for an Ecological, Nuclear Age (Philadelphia: Fortress Press, 1987); Anna Case-Winters, *God's Power: Traditional Understandings and Contemporary Challenges* (Louisville, KY: Westminster/John Knox Press, 1990); Daphne Hampson, *After Christianity* (Valley Forge, PA: Trinity Press International, 1996).

50. Ruether, *Sexism and God-Talk*, 65.

51. Ibid., 66.

52. For remarks on the relation of unqualified regard and equal regard, see Gene Outka, "Letters, Notes, and Comments," *Journal of Religious Ethics*, 26, no. 2 (1998): 435–40.

53. In addition to what I claimed along these lines in Gene Outka, *Agape: An Ethical Analysis* (New Haven, CT: Yale University Press, 1972), see Outka, "Theocentric Agape and the Self: An Asymmetrical Afffirmation in Response to Colin Grant's Either/Or," *Journal of Religious Ethics*, 24, no. 1 (1996): 35–41; John P. Reeder, Jr., "Extensive Benevolence," *Journal of Religious Ethics*, 26, no. 1 (1998): 59; and Timothy Jackson, *Love Disconsoled: Meditations on Christian Charity* (Cambridge: Cambridge University Press, 1999), 82.

54. See the engaging depiction of philia in Edward Collins Vacek, S.J., *Love, Human and Divine: The Heart of Christian Ethics* (Washington, DC: Georgetown University Press, 1994), esp. 280–330.

55. See again Outka, "Theocentric Agape and the Self," 35–41.

56. Brian Sorrells assessed an earlier draft of this chapter, and made improving suggestions for which I am grateful.

Chapter Six

Justice and Love Shall Kiss

Ada María Isasi-Díaz

There I was, marching in one more demonstration. Another attempt to convince public opinion that justice has to prevail. Volunteers, many of them elderly, had greeted me cheerfully when I arrived at the march's staging area. Their enthusiasm gave me the strength I needed to get my feet going, to begin waving my homemade sign, and to start chanting those catchy phrases that in a few words capture the urgency of our cause. A sense of despondency, a sense that what we did made absolutely no difference, had been taking over my spirit. Some of my friends soon arrived and I was happy to participate with them in the demonstration, discussing as we went along many issues in which we were involved. After about five hours the event was over and the now tired but no less cheerful elderly volunteers thanked us for coming as we made our way to the subway station.

That evening as I watched the skimpy media coverage the demonstration received, I thought about the lack of passion I had felt in the morning. I was not any less committed to justice, but I was lacking the passion—the intense emotional charge—that had sustained me during the many years I had been engaged in different struggles for justice. The excitement, the aliveness I used to experience about being involved in justice issues seemed to have diminished. Of course I continued to consider the struggle for justice essential to my sense of vocation in life, believing it to be an intrinsic element of who I know myself to be. For me, to struggle for justice has always been a way of being self-determining and making sure that the poor and the oppressed could likewise determine for themselves how to live their lives. However, reflecting on how I had felt when I arrived at the march that morning, I grew concerned about how I was going to motivate myself to continue my involvement if it stopped being deeply satisfying, if it became less life-giving. I knew that, at least for me, intellectual understanding and willful belief in justice would not be enough.

It was not until a few months later that I was able to take time to be by myself and go back to the questions and concerns that my lack of enthusiasm about marching in a demonstration had signaled. I am not the kind of person who can simply "turn the page" and keep on going without paying attention to unresolved issues. Though I do not need to have all the answers, I do need to be clear about the questions, to reflect on them so they do not turn problematic and weaken my resolve. I knew that what was unsettling me was how to be faithful to my commitment to justice if I was not passionate about it. In an attempt to recapture the driving conviction I had about justice I started by meditating on some of the biblical texts that had originally sparked and for years had sustained my concern for justice. I reread a couple of books and several articles that had been helpful in providing me with the reasons for my participation in struggles for justice. I took time to carefully recall my time in Perú thirty-some years ago when the poor of Lima had taught me a lasting lesson: without justice, religious beliefs and practices could indeed become "the opium of the people." Justice had been for a long time one of my "most fundamental convictions and . . . most fundamental loves,"[1] and I wanted this to continue to be. My commitment to justice not only intersects with my moral convictions and is intrinsic to my loves, it is not only an expression of them,[2] it is a constitutive element of them. To continue to have justice as central in my life I had to bring back the intense drive—the passion—that has had moved me for so long. It was the only way to hold back "the gradual flattening of emotional bonds into sheer obligation or duty."[3] I had to resist at all costs the lack of passion that was gnawing at my determination and was eroding my worldview—the programmatic vision that holds and enlivens who I am and what I do—for to live ruled by obligation would destroy me.

Following Margaret Farley's advice in her book *Personal Commitments,* I fanned the flames of memory and hope so I could grow once again into a love of justice—a passion for justice—that had been so life-giving. A review of my participation in justice struggles made me aware that I was not stuck in the same "old" vision of justice. As a matter of fact, I had come to see justice itself as a process. Without much effort, out of the ever-evolving meaning that justice has had in my life, new expectations about justice and for justice in society have emerged during the years. Yet these new expectations did not seem to bring back my passion, my emotional involvement in the struggles for justice. Besides the need for memory and hope, Farley also talks about the need for "relaxation of the heart." I had every reason to believe I was not fanatic about justice but rather that a "steady zeal" has given me staying power. What else was "relaxation of the heart" calling me to do? I had to remain clear-sighted about what the struggle for justice means for me. I had to be patient with myself and, instead of worrying about "failing in fidelity," I had to remain "present in hope" by not evading but rather embracing the struggle to light up the fire of passion for justice once again.[4]

Since life does not stop while we are going through a crisis, no matter what kind of crisis, I continued teaching, giving public lectures, writing, working with grassroots Latinas. One morning, in Cuba, where I go every year to teach in a Protestant seminary and work in a Catholic parish, I woke up with a verse from the Bible running through my head: "Justice and love shall kiss." I repeated the verse to myself all day long believing that it was important for some reason I could not see right away. I was surprised when I looked up the verse to find out that I had it wrong. Psalm 85, verse 10, talks about justice and peace, not about justice and love. But the strong and persistent thought that had come into my mind and into my heart had been about justice and love, not justice and peace. I decided that instead of correcting myself I would allow "justice and love shall kiss" to stay with me, to nestle in me. I wanted to see where this thought would lead me. In the days that followed I began to understand little by little that I had indeed not paid enough attention to love as an important element in my commitment to justice. I came to realize that recapturing my passion for justice had to go hand in hand with bringing about a much closer relationship in my life between love and justice. I understood more and more that the passion—the intense emotion that compels me to be committed to justice—if it is to have staying power, has to come from love and be sustained by love.

I went back to Farley's *Personal Commitments,* reread it carefully, and spent time meditating on several of its passages. Farley clearly indicates that commitment to justice is indeed commitment to persons and that "we need a way to keep us connected with, present to, the *object* of our commitments—what we love and have promised to love."[5] She talks about Susan whose commitment to the poor and homeless was not a matter of willful determination but rather the "result of her seeing, again and again, the reality of the persons, lovable and homeless and poor."[6] Farley insists that "every commitment to persons involves some form of mutuality."[7] She explains that even when we are committed to others who do not know about our commitment or do not accept our commitment to them, even then, mutuality is present. "Something in the other binds me to her or him, calls to me, makes it easier or more difficult for me to be faithful, places in sharp relief the painfulness of the forms of mutuality that are missing."[8] In her assertion about the need for mutuality in every commitment, it seems to me that Farley makes love central to any commitment, and, given the issue I was wrestling with, this meant that love had to play a central role in my commitment to justice. Had I stopped loving the poor? Had I stopped loving oppressed and marginalized women whose life-struggles have been a source of strength and creativity for me for so long? Did I not care any longer about this earth of ours, so mistreated and disfigured by our greediness and destructive self-centeredness?

Thinking about love of neighbor in my life I remembered the first time my concept about what it means to love had been challenged. I was 17 years old when I came from Cuba to live in the U.S. As I began to have friends and became part of different groups in college, church, and neighborhood, I began to learn about cultural differences and the role they play in the way we love and in the way we express our love. I come from a culture that is very public about its emotions. We Cubans wear our emotions on our sleeves, we say laughing loudly.[9] It is very clear for us that we need to show our love not just in words. For us, demonstrating our love is part of the love itself: showing love helps to bring it about. This is the sacramental nature of the expressions of love, of what Farley calls "the deeds of love."[10] Such expressions are part of the love itself and without them love suffers, is diminished. With time, as I had adapted myself to life in the U.S., I had become much more guarded about expressing my emotions. In this society public expressions of emotions embarrass people. Expressing emotions makes us vulnerable for it reveals what is deep in our hearts, what moves us, and in the U.S. vulnerability unfortunately is often seen as weakness. I remembered how in those first years living in the U.S. I was pained by what I considered the coldness of friends, by what I believed were barriers they put up to keep relationships at this or that level instead of allowing relationships to flourish to the fullest. And now that I was faced with the task of rekindling passion for justice I realized that maybe I had killed that passion by not expressing it or by expressing it only in the quiet and private ways accepted by this society.[11]

Decades after arriving in the U.S. I became a social ethicist. One of the main reasons for this choice was because it was for me a way of being involved in the struggle for liberation of Latinas, of grassroot women whom society marginalizes, rendering them invisible and ignoring what they have to contribute to society. I have helped to formulate a theo-ethical discourse, *mujerista* theology, as a way of taking seriously the lived experience of grassroot Latinas, their struggles to be self-determining persons with an important contribution to make to society. In elaborating *mujerista* theology, therefore, I have always worked extensively with the ethical understandings of the moral subject. I understand the moral person as being both an agent who takes decisions and acts on them, and a subject who perfects herself through those decisions and actions—all of this in the middle of and through the multiplicity of one's relationships.[12] Decisions are a taking hold of understandings and desires and translating them into action. At the core of any action is a decision, and at the heart of any decision is desire, for we never choose what we do not desire. Desires, in turn, are informed and formed by God's grace, reason, emotion, and one's intuitions. Decisions and choices are a taking hold of one's desire and understandings, identifying with them freely, and translating them into action.[13]

As I analyzed my commitment to justice and worked to elaborate a *mujerista* understanding of justice, I realized that I still have very good reasons for the decision I took to make justice a priority in my life—I have very good reasons for my commitment to justice. Without the struggle for justice my life would be empty or at least much less fulfilling than it has been. I knew that this struggle played an important role in the sense I have of God's presence, of God's grace, in my life. The only element that had informed my commitment and now seemed to be absent or to have decreased was the emotional component. As I meditated on this, I realized that my dwindling emotional attachment for justice indicated somehow a weakened sense of self, for "there is an emotional bedrock of self-consciousness that constitutes the self, the person who makes moral decisions."[14] There was no option. I had to reimmerse myself in my culture and allow my emotional self to come forth and express openly what I felt so deeply.

To do this was no small task for, even in this first decade of the twenty-first century, not many think of emotions as a positive element of morality. Until recently emotions have been thought to be at odds with reason. The psychological model of human functioning most prevalent even today insists "first, that reasoning *can* be thoroughly detached from emotion; second, that only detached reasoning will be reliably objective; and third, that emotions will only bias, cloud, and impede moral decision-making."[15] But I was not to be deterred. My own personal needs plus my commitment to make present in U.S. society through *mujerista* theology the valuable elements of Latina culture—as I believe expressing one's emotions is—spurred me on. I set out to recapture expressing my emotions not only as an element of my commitment to justice but of my whole life. I decided to examine the role of expressing emotions in morality and ethics. I knew, however, that it was not only a matter of stirring up any emotion. Indeed, although negative emotions like anger, resentment, shame, disgust may also move one to action, still none of these have been strong motivational factors in my life. I knew that what I had to stir in myself was love, an "emotional love," a felt and expressed love, a passionate love. I knew that it was not only a matter of being committed to justice with my intellect and will, but of loving justice intensely. Love is the only emotion that has had staying-power in my life, that has really inspired me, encouraged me, stimulated me time and time again. To stay committed to justice I had to once again love justice passionately.

THE POETRY OF JULIA DE BURGOS

I wanted to recapture love and, because emotions are a different state of consciousness from the rational one, I knew that I could not reason my way into emotions. Where was I to turn, given that I live in a culture where reason and intellect reign supreme, where insights, imagination and emotions are not considered important? One night I surprised myself by wanting to write poetry. It was a first for me. In the poem I wrote my "justice-self" speaks to my "love-self." Recently I had been introduced to the poetry of Julia de Burgos, the Puerto Rican poet, and I was undoubtedly influenced by one of her poems in which two "sides" of herself talk to each other.[16] The poem I wrote has my love-self, my emotional self, telling my justice-self, my rational self, that she has remained in the background long enough, that for years she has carried my justice-self and that now she wonders whether the justice-self has sacrificed her or instead provided her with a future by giving meaning to her life. Julia de Burgos's poetry was a godsend for me. Reading her poetry in Spanish took me back to my cultural matrix where emotions are nurtured and celebrated. The force and beauty of her poetry immersed me in Julia's world of emotions, particularly in her world of love and loving. Soon I was not only reading her poetry but studying it and learning about this poet who, for Puerto Ricans and for the rest of us who know her work, is "more than a writer, more than a national poet; she is a legend."[17] Julia's poetry has given me fresh insights into emotions and their role both in my self-understanding and in the way I conceptualize my mission in life. Julia's poetry has validated my need to express my emotions, corroborating my belief that the expression of emotions is an integral element of the emotion itself. Julia's poetry has allowed me once again to embrace my need to express my emotions as part and parcel of communicating my ideas, of making who I am and what I do intelligible to myself and others. Her goal as a poet was precisely that, "to communicate her emotions, not to relate private anecdotes. . . . In her poetry one finds a woman who goes through an intimate process of dramatic highs and lows in the way she thinks as well as in her way of feeling."[18]

What made me turn to the poetry of Julia de Burgos when I needed to rekindle passion for justice in my life and to weave love into its understanding was that "love was a constant passion and goal of Julia's conscience."[19] Though many want to reduce her life to her failed relationship with a man, which they claim led her to become an alcoholic and to an early death when she was thirty-nine years old, there is evidence of precisely the contrary. There is proof of the "courage with which the writer struggled with hostile social conditions for each minute of her life and artistic potential. Looked at from this perspective, the work of Julia de Burgos is not a symbol of her defeat but of her struggle to create."[20] Her willingness to struggle, to be faithful to her need to communicate her emotions, became an integral part of Julia's moral horizon, of the person she believed she was called to be. And that was precisely what I felt I needed to focus on in order to rekindle my passion for justice.

Before an analysis of Julia's poetry, a short biographical sketch is in order. Julia de Burgos was born in 1917, in Carolina, Puerto Rico. She was from a very poor family, the oldest of thirteen children, of whom six died as infants of malnutrition. She was a good student and her parents asked for financial help so Julia could attend high school and go to the university. When she was only nineteen, Julia received from the University of Puerto Rico a grade-school teacher diploma. She married when she was twenty but the marriage lasted only three years. Julia joined the nationalist party, which struggled for Puerto Rico's independence from the U.S. In 1937 she was fired from her job as a teacher, perhaps because of her political activities, and she began to earn a living from her writings, publishing articles and poems in newspapers and magazines. That year she privately printed her first book of poetry but later decided that her work was not good enough and took back the copies she had sold or given away. The poems in this first book have been lost.

In 1935 her mother had been diagnosed with cancer, so in 1938 Julia paid to have her second book of poetry printed and went from town to town by bus selling the book in order to pay for her mother's medical care. This book of her poetry "offers the voice of a woman who rebels against her circumstances, who feels the socio-economic, political and cultural injustices as humiliating constraints that impede her free self-realization and that of her people."[21] Her mother died shortly thereafter.

In 1939 Julia met and fell in love with Juan Isidro Jiménez Grullón, a leftist politician from a well-to-do Dominican Republic family. Also in that year one of San Juan's leading cultural centers sponsored a recital in honor of Julia. At the beginning of 1940 she traveled to New York, probably following Jiménez Grullón, and later that year she followed him to Cuba. Jiménez Grullón never married Julia for he already was married and his family had threatened to disinherit him if he divorced. After the couple lived together in Cuba for a while, the relationship ended and Julia moved back to New York in June of 1942. While in Cuba she wrote her third book of poetry, published posthumously, and sketched the outline for a fourth one that she never finished.

When she moved to New York she married a second time and lived for a while in Washington, DC. During this time she earned a living as publisher of a weekly Hispanic newspaper and by doing office work. In 1946 she was back in New York where she survived working at all kinds of odd jobs: office work, translator, salesperson, sewing in a factory. By then she was drinking heavily, and by 1951 she had been hospitalized six times. She collapsed on West 105 Street in New York on July 6, 1953, dying at Harlem Hospital. She was carrying no identification so her body was buried in the paupers' common grave. Eventually some friends found out about her death, her family was notified, and two months later her remains were taken to Puerto Rico where she is buried in Carolina, near San Juan, where she had been born.[22]

Julia's poetry has been studied from many different points of view. Perhaps the biggest controversy among scholars has to do with how much her poetry is autobiographical, how much her poetry reflects not only her socio-historical setting but also her personal life. As a neophyte when it comes to the work of Julia de Burgos and because of my interest in the role of emotions in her work, I tend to follow the proposal of a well-known expert on her poetry, María M. Solá, who insists that one cannot tie the poems of Julia directly to events in her life. However, Solá also indicates that "even though emotions are the main message of the lyrical text, poetry always includes meanings related to the historical circumstances in which it is written." [23] There is a certain distance between Julia, the woman, and the voice one hears in her poems, referred to by some scholars as a "lyrical speaker." I believe, however, that there is also a certain continuity between the two. Whether it was so or not for Julia, the lyrical speaker in her poetry suffers great sorrow and pain at being rejected by the beloved and having to leave him. Yet "to have lost trust in the fact that love can bring harmony, save the person from her struggles—that is even worse. . . . [W]hat disappears is the belief that love can save. . . . For the lyrical speaker, her main defining quality, what defines her, is her own ability to move with her word. To be able to create is the path she has to follow. The road that starts in herself and heads towards the future, beyond her death—that is the poetry her voice creates."[24]

I have chosen three poems written during different periods of Julia's life because of their personal appeal. As an admirer of her poetry, I will stay as close as possible to the text, noting how emotions, readily and passionately expressed, are never absent. I hope to show that emotions more than reasons are the vehicle she uses to communicate.[25] For Julia, emotions are a way of knowing and of expressing her being.

Her first extant book of poetry opens with a poem she dedicates to herself, "*A Julia de Burgos.*"

To Julia de Burgos

v. 1   Already the people murmur that I am your enemy
         because they say that in verse I give your I to the world.

v. 2   They lie, Julia de Burgos. They lie, Julia de Burgos.
        Who rises in my verses is not your voice. It is my voice
        because you are the dressing and the essence is I;
        and the most profound abyss is spread between us.

v. 3   You are the cold doll of social lies,
        and I, the virile starburst of the human truth.

v. 4   You, honey of courtesan hypocrisies; not I;
        in all my poems I strip my heart.

v. 5   You are like your world, selfish; not I
        who gambles everything betting on what I am.

v. 6   You are only the ponderous lady very lady;
        not I; I am life, strength, woman.

v. 7   You belong to your husband, your master; not I;
        I belong to nobody, or all, because to all, to all
        I give myself in my clean feeling and in my thought.

v. 8   You curl your hair and paint yourself; not I;
        the wind curls my hair, the sun paints me.

v. 9   You are a housewife, resigned, submissive,
        tied to the prejudices of men; not I;
        unbridled, I am a runaway Rocinante
        snorting the horizons of God's justice.

v. 10   You in yourself have no say; everyone governs you;
        your husband, your parents, your family,
        the priest, the dressmaker, the theatre, the dance hall,
        the auto, the fine furnishings, the feast, champagne,
        heaven and hell, and the social, "what will they say."

v. 11   Not in me, in me only my heart governs,
        only my thought; who governs me is I.

> You, flower of aristocracy; and I, flower of the people.
> You in you have everything and you owe it to everyone,
> while I, my nothing I owe to nobody.

v. 12   You, nailed to the static ancestral dividend,
        and I, a one in the numerical social divider,
        we are the duel to death that fatally approaches.

v. 13   When the multitudes run rioting
        leaving behind ashes of burned injustices,
        and with the torch of the seven virtues,
        the multitudes run after the seven sins,
        against you and against everything unjust and inhuman,
        I will be their midst with the torch in my hand. [26]

In the beginning of this poem, social protest is presented by the lyrical speaker as a struggle to fulfill herself fully as a human being. The lyrical speaker seeks to express how she breaks with the social mores that keep women in bondage. Emotions for Julia de Burgos were not something pertinent only in the personal or private sphere, as we see in the last part of the poem where the lyrical speaker "inserts her personal awareness in the situation of the people, delineating the rebellion of the masses as a revolutionary response to prejudices and class injustices."[27] She will struggle to find God's justice (v. 9)—"*horizontes de justicia de Dios*"—burning down anything that is unjust, as the poem ends, "*con la tea en la mano.*"[28] For Julia behind the personal struggles of the lyrical speaker there is a social space, and "emotions have their origin in the social practice and in a system of evaluations."[29]

Very early in the poem there is an explosion of emotions when the lyrical speaker accuses of lying (v. 2) those who identify her with a woman ruled by social conventions. It is impossible to think of reading this one line in any other way but as an emotional outburst.

Mienten, Julia de Burgos. Mienten, Julia de Burgos.

The verse consists of the two shortest sentences in the poem, the repetition portraying vehemence. "This emphasis underlines a drastic opinion . . . and perhaps points to the attempt to call herself to conscience."[30] These two short sentences are like sharp arrows aimed at the thick cloak of social traditions and customs that limit who women are and how they can live their lives. The same sense of strong demand and great urgency will be expressed by the longest sentence in the poem, the last one, where a barrage of words leaves the reader breathless, conveying the passion of the lyrical speaker as she makes certain she communicates clearly that nothing will stop her from destroying the barriers society imposes on women.

> *Cuando las multitudes corran alborotadas*
> *dejando atrás cenizas de injusticias quemadas,*
> *y cuando con la tea de las siete virtudes,*
> *tras los siete pecados, corran las multitudes,*
> *contra ti, y contra todo lo injusto y lo inhumano,*
> *yo iré en medio de ellas con la tea en la mano.*

The body of the poem consists of a series of statements in which the lyrical speaker and the woman who abides by the social mores of her time—both of them are in Julia, are part of Julia—are set against each other. In all of the points/counterpoints the lyrical speaker never allows the other to speak, accusing her throughout the poem with sarcasm and derision of being nothing but a pretense while she herself is the essence of woman (v. 2). The first of the points/counterpoints describes the feel of each of the two women in the poem. The one who abides by social rules is "cold"; the one who struggles to be faithful to the essence of what it is to be a woman is a "virile starburst" (v. 3).

> *Tú eres fría muñeca de mentira social,*
> *y yo, viril destello de la humana verdad.*

"A starburst is a vivid but ephemeral light. By modifying it with the adjective 'virile' the semantic charge is augmented, giving the spark greater ability to illumine."[31] This adjective indicates a strong affective emotion.[32] The use of the adjective "virile" can be interpreted "as a linguistic betrayal since virility represents strength and control, qualities attributed to males. . . . The woman cannot be virile because

society does not allow it. To be virile is the prerogative of the males
. . . but the lyrical speaker can be virile because she is breaking with
the established schemas for women."[33]

The lyrical speaker talks about how through her poems one can see
her naked heart. She uses her emotions to fight rather than using logical argument or pointing to reasons (v. 4).

> Tú, miel de cortesanas hipocresías; yo no;
> que en todos mis poemas desnudo el corazón.

The lyrical speaker places feeling[34]—*sentir*—before thinking—
pensar—(v. 7).

> Yo de nadie [soy], o de todos, porque a todos, a todos,
> en mi limpio sentir y en mi pensar me doy.

She refers to her heart—*corazón*—before talking about her thoughts—
pensamiento—(v. 11). In this verse, in identifying herself as the one who
decides for herself who she is instead of letting society order her around,
her heart—emotions—come before her thoughts—her head.

> En mí no, que en mí manda mi solo corazón
> mi solo pensamiento; quien manda en mí soy yo.

In this poem, Julia de Burgos shows that to be able to understand
she has to feel. She moves away from considering reason and emotion
in a linear or in a dualistic fashion and instead sees them as intertwined. The poem shows how she constructed her subjectivity using a
paradigm different from the one prescribed by society. In it she breaks
the false unity of the "bourgeois Cartesian subject," indicating not a
binary possibility for different "kinds" of women but signaling a dialectic reality that does not stop with the private but is also part of the
public sphere.[35] Her poetry inserted in the social imagination a valid
sense of resistance on the part of women that does not leave behind
the struggle against sexism but understands it as part and parcel of
the struggle for the liberation of her people. Part of struggling for

liberation from a woman's perspective is made clear by her unabashed reference to emotions as a positive element. Towards the end of this poem Julia chooses to identify with her people instead of with the aristocracy (v. 11).[36]

Tú, flor de aristocracia; y yo, la flor del pueblo.

Julia's poetry "deconstructs the paradigms that organize the ethical and social fantasies of a common life at the same time that it offers a cartography of a freer community."[37] This is why scholars can claim that for Julia writing poetry was a morally subversive revolutionary activity.[38]

The second poem I have chosen is called *"Canción de mi sombra minúscula."*

Song of My Miniscule Shadow

v. 1   Sometimes my life wants to explode in songs
        of unexpected anguish!

v. 2   I would like to stay in the secret of my pains
        pricking like stars,
        but my soul can't reach the silence
        of the poem without words,
        and leaps through my lips made dust by intimate vibrations.

v. 3   There is only one door open in the path where my life
            passes
        unknown to smiles.
        I start to find its trail,
        as if the cosmos had concentrated its energy
        and my entire emotion would go there,
        like pieces of destroyed butterflies.

v. 4   My emotion wheels through one of those savage islands of
            pain.

> I have let myself arrive where
> happy songs die,
> and pain makes a date with the transparent paint of the sky.

v. 5   The premature rose that fell in my eyes wounded by
> rosy petals hurts me;
> and the last look of a bride of the air
> who died of chasteness upon feeling she was flesh
> for the kiss of man.

v. 6   The pain of the twilight that won't woo again
> the pale daisy of the woods
> bleeds in the pain of the evening fallen on my back.

v. 7   Taken by a sprout of spray
> a teardrop that rose to space
> cries from mystery in my cloud flight

v. 8   The pain that wheels in the abandoned instant
> comes to dance its rhythm in my flesh tormented
> by cosmic anxiety.

v. 9   And the emotion explodes in useless songs,
> inside this mirage of greatness
> from which my shadow,
> minuscule,
> departs . . .[39]

Scholars seem not to pay too much attention to this poem, but I have found it to be the only one in which she speaks directly about her emotions and, through the use of metaphors, identifies with them. In this poem the lyrical speaker and the object to which she is referring—her emotions—are one and the same thing. It is as if no words existed that could express what she wants to say; as if the lyrical speaker identifies with what she is talking about through her emotions instead of through ideas. Her emotions are the object of her contemplation and she does not simply talk about them but participates in them by identifying with them. This poem, then, makes it possible for Julia the woman-poet to satisfy her ontological need to express her emotions. Expressing her emotions, which is the same as having or feeling emotions, is an experience for her as real as the experiences constituted by events.[40] Writing this poem, then, is a liberative praxis for her, allowing her to be what she seemingly was not able to be in her day-to-day life.[41]

The poem starts with an emotional explosion similar to the one in the previous poems we have analyzed, *"estallar,"* made to stand out by making it the verb of an exclamatory sentence. The lyrical speaker then expresses her desire to stay inside herself with her emotions, but they are throbbing in such a way that they jump out of her mouth. Sorrow is the focus of this poem. The lyrical speaker talks about her emotion being shattered into pieces, and the pieces are of something—love—as beautiful as butterflies, the beauty making the destruction all the more painful (v. 3). She again refers directly to her emotions and acknowledges that they have led her to her death (v. 4). She speaks about sorrow, an emotion that causes pain, using various metaphors in an attempt to communicate not only the depth of the sorrow but also the fact that nothing will be able to take the pain away (vv. 4–7). In the last verse, faced with the finality of her painful emotions, the lyrical speaker cannot but feel "cosmic anxiety" and experience great futility. Having started with an explosion of emotions, she returns to that same theme. It is important to notice that even in the midst of the pain, anxiety, and futility that she experiences, the lyrical speaker acknowledges that through her emotions she has touched greatness. But the failure expressed in "useless songs" only allows a minuscule part of her, her shadow, to escape.

In the book that Julia worked on mostly when she was in Cuba, published posthumously, there is a poem called *"Canción hacia dentro."*

Inward Song

v. 1   Don't remember me! Feel me!
        There is only a warble between your love and my soul.

v. 2   Both my eyes navigate
        the same endless blue where you dance.

v. 3   Your rainbow of dreams always has in me
        an open meadow among mountains.

v. 4   Once my sobs were lost
        and I found them sheltered in your tears.

v. 5   Don't remember me! Feel me!
        A nightingale has us in his throat.

v. 6   The rivers I brought from my cliffs
        empty only on your beaches.

v. 7   There is confusion of flight in the air . . .
        The wind carries us in its sandals!

v. 8   Don't remember me! Feel me!
        The less you think me, the more you love me.[42]

This poem addresses someone who is only important in so far as the person is the object of the lyrical speaker's love. The readers of Julia's poem presume the beloved to be Jiménez Grullón, but despite the fact that most of Julia's poetry consists of love poems, little is known from them about the beloved. Her poems are really not about the beloved but about love, about the emotion of love that she feels and with which she identifies. References to the beloved in Julia's poems are rare. He appears mostly as an object of reproaches, reproaches that at times are sarcastic.[43] In this poem she tries to make the beloved understand that the important thing is not to remember the loved one but to feel her, that the less the beloved thinks about her, allowing feelings and emotions to be dominant instead, the more love will flourish. The tone of the whole poem is one of instruction, of trying to convince the beloved to do what is best for love: to feel, to have deep emotions on which the poem tries to capitalize.[44]

At the beginning, in the middle, and at the end of the poem the lyrical speaker repeats the leitmotif of the poem,

¡No me recuerdes! ¡Siénteme!

These two sentences are not exclamations but commands with exclamation points used for emphasis. The first sentence, in the negative, does away with the regular manner in which one deals with the beloved. It is as if the lyrical speaker were telling the beloved to throw away all her pictures, all the mementos that might feed the memory. Instead the beloved is ordered to feel the loved one. It is as if the lyrical speaker were commanding the beloved to embrace himself, to hold his arms tight around himself so he can feel her, so he can embrace the deep emotion that he feels for her. Such an insistence on not thinking might well have to do with the fact that for the lyrical speaker it is in her emotions that her love can take flight. It is what is born within her—the emotions—that fulfills her. Only as a second step does she seek to "shape in the external world the emotion that is consuming her inside."[45] In these short imperative sentences repeated throughout the poem the lyrical speaker clearly indicates that "the act of sensual love is superior to remembering. She prefers an alienating amnesia to the absence of compenetration between the flesh and the spirit generated by a shared embrace. Love for Julia is passion; for her the falling in love of courtly love is equivalent to lack of willpower and indifference."[46] In these repeated verses remembering is an abstraction from which the lyrical speaker wants to flee while seeking the immediacy of the emotion of her love, which for her is life-giving.

This insistence of Julia in writing about the emotions is an element one finds in mystical writings. Though for some the mystical experience consists of union with the divine born of an intuitive sense of God, I believe that the mystical experience is "the experiential knowledge of the presence of God that has as its goal a sense of contact with God."[47] As experiential knowledge, then, the mystical experience involves the whole person, and that can only happen if the senses are involved. In the mystical experience one is in the midst of God, experiences God in a way that far surpasses thinking about God. The

mystical experience is not about understanding God but about appre-
hending God, and this is what the lyrical speaker is asking for in this
poem: to be apprehended by the beloved, not just to be remembered.
The lyrical speaker has the same difficulty as the mystics, that is, not
being able to put into words what she has experienced. It is impossible to find words to express the intensity of love she has and that
is why she calls for sensing and feeling, for emotions.[48] Words might
indicate or teach, but they fail when it comes to expressing what is
inside her.[49]

Another mystical element in this poem comes in the second verse.

> *Mis dos ojos navegan*
> *el mismo azul sin fin donde tú danzas.*

The color blue, linked in this verse to infinitude, is a reference to
heaven. Heaven, not the sky, communicates a religious sentiment.[50]
Perhaps here it points to the immensity of the love or to the divinization of the beloved, divinization brought about by the love of the lyrical speaker. This is reminiscent of a verse by Delmira Agustini, the
Uruguayan poet, a contemporary Julia never met, who speaks of love
"as if I had the head of God in my hands."[51]

The interconnection and compenetration between the lovers are
made explicit in the poem. The second line of this repeated verse
holds the lyrical speaker and the beloved together. The first time, only
the smallest possible distance, the wispy song of a bird, separates their
souls. When the verse is repeated in the middle of the poem, the lovers are in the tiniest of spaces, the throat of a bird. These images try
to convey the closeness desired. The last time the verse appears to end
the poem, the insistence is on love that is not found in merely thinking
about the one loved.

The poem struggles to communicate the oneness of the lyrical
speaker and the beloved. Mostly it is the lyrical speaker—Julia—the
one who moves to be in/with the beloved.

> v. 2   *Mis dos ojos navegan*
> *el mismo azul sin fin donde tú danzas.*

v. 4   *Una vez se perdieron mis sollozos,*
          y los hallé, abrigados, en tus lágrimas.

v. 6   *Los ríos que me traje de mis riscos,*
          desembocan tan solo por tus playas.

Only once is the beloved the one who moves to be in/with the lyrical speaker (v.3).

Tu arco iris de sueños en mí tiene
siempre pradera abierta entre montañas.

This leads to a verse that speaks about confusion, as if the lack of movement on the part of the beloved created a storm. The winds will only grow calm when they hold together the lover and the beloved. But, in the end, ideas expressed in words are not enough to communicate the compenetration that the lyrical speaker seeks with the beloved. Metaphors also fail her. All that she has left is to turn to emotions, to beg the beloved, for the third time, to affirm the emotions he has, to give himself over to the passion that the love between them has birthed.

For Julia de Burgos writing poetry was a way of being, which was not apart from the need she had to communicate. What she sought to communicate were her emotions, which in turn constituted her primary way of knowing and relating to reality. When I read Julia's poetry, I often picture her with her emotions in her arms, embracing them, caressing them, receiving from them affirmation and affection. I spend time contemplating this picture Julia paints trying to grasp my own emotions, allowing them to come into consciousness, affirming them and feeding them by expressing them. I repeat time and again to myself the injunction the poet addresses to the beloved in the last poem I have analyzed, *"Siénteme."* I do so convinced that to love I have to feel deeply, I have to allow my emotions to break through to the surface of who I am and to let them be part of my decisions, of my way of acting and being with myself and with others. I have to express my emotions, making public what motivates me, what is most alive in me. In embracing my emotions I come to know, to live and to be more fully—that is why I am willing to risk being vulnerable. This is the key lesson I have learned from Julia de Burgos, and this learning was what allowed me to turn my attention to the role of love in my work on behalf of justice. This learning has given me back my love for justice, the passion for justice that was birthed in me by the poor of Peru four decades ago. This whole journey into validating my emotional self and expressing it has led me to understand the importance emotions in general and those connected to love in particular play in morality and ethics.

EMOTIONS, EXPRESSING EMOTIONS, AND ETHICS

Margaret Farley argues that love has to be at the heart of commitment. For Farley love is an emotion and it is something we do.[52] Emotions are a state of consciousness, a way of knowing and of being. Yet emotions command little attention (or respect!) particularly in weighty matters for they are volatile and voluble. Their less-concrete-than-we-would-like feel, however, should not lead to giving them less importance and to thinking of them as less relevant when dealing with reality. Their fluidity has to do with the fact that emotions attribute great importance to objects and persons outside ourselves, objects and persons that that we do not control, which makes us vulnerable. This makes us think that we cannot trust emotions: our lack of control over what is valuable and significant for us. At play in the lack of valuation of emotions is also the confusion in common parlance between "feeling" and "emotion." In this case "feeling" refers to generalized, nonintentional consciousness or sensation with little cognitive content. However, feeling also refers to sensations, perceptions, or thoughts "with a rich intentional content . . . [that] may enter into the identity conditions for some emotions."[53] When used in this latter sense, whether we use "feelings" or "emotions," they are weighty matters and we risk cutting ourselves off from a way of being and a way of knowing that can enrich us, that can provide us with resources for the struggle to enable fullness of life for ourselves and others.

Emotions are a type of cognition, a way of knowing, for they are linked to the receiving and processing of information. That "elaborate calculation, . . . computation, or even reflexive self-awareness" are not part of emotions does not mean that they should be "demoted" from the category of intellectual function ("demoted" in quotes because I do not agree with the diminished value given to what is not purely intellectual).[54] This understanding of emotions rejects the more common view that they are "'non-reasoning movements,' unthinking energies that simply push the person around, without being hooked up to the ways in which she perceives or thinks about the world."[55] The fact that emotions "take place in a living body does not give us reason to reduce their intentional/cognitive components to nonintentional bodily movements."[56]

As cognitive functions emotions are about something, they are not unspecific or difused but have an object in sight. Furthermore, the object of one's emotions is intentional, that is to say, "it figures in the emotion as it is seen or interpreted by the person whose emotions it is. Emotions are not *about* their objects merely in the sense of being pointed at them. . . . Their aboutness is more internal, and embodies a way of seeing."[57] This aboutness is part of the emotion's identity, the way the object is seen, what differentiates fear from hope, for example. Emotions have to do with what one believes about an object. This means that beliefs are not a simple way of seeing something but a complex and serious way of seeing a situation, an object, a person. When one connects thought to emotion one does so not simply as "a heuristic device" that reveals feelings, feelings being considered apart from thinking. If one sees thought as a mere heuristic device instead of inserting thought into the definition of the emotions itself, how could one discriminate among different types of emotions?[58]

The understanding that emotions have to do with what one believes places us already in the realm of morality and ethics. But the relevance of emotions for our moral life also has to do with the role value plays in them. "The intentional perceptions and the beliefs characteristic of the emotions . . . are concerned with *value*, they see their objects as invested with value and importance."[59] Moreover, "the value perceived in the object appears to be of a particular sort. It appears to make reference to the person's own flourishing. The object of the emotion is seen as *important for* some role it plays in the person's own life."[60] The object of the emotion has importance in and of itself and it also has importance for the person's ends and goals, for "the person's flourishing."[61] This means that emotions, as relevant judgments of value that have to do with assenting to the way we see things and with acknowledging it as true, are sufficiently internal to emotions to be "at least a part of the identity conditions of the emotion."[62]

Emotions, then, include judgments not as external causes but as constituent parts, and these judgments have to do with the goal of one's life, with fullness of life. Emotions are part of our way of knowing and, therefore, the information emotions provide must be taken into consideration in the process of evaluating and deciding. The value judgment component of emotions that is linked to one's interests, to one's fullness of life, indicates how things are with this important aspect of our moral considerations. Emotions, therefore, undoubtedly are elements that morality and ethics need to take into account.

In short, emotions are

> intelligent responses to the perception of value. If emotions are suffused with intelligence and discernment, and if they contain in themselves an awareness of value or importance, they cannot . . . be sidelined in accounts of ethical judgment. Instead of viewing morality as a system of principles to be grasped by the detached intellect, and emotions as motivations that either support or subvert our choice to act according to principle, we will have to consider emotions as part and parcel of the system of ethical reasoning. We cannot plausibly omit them, once we acknowledge that emotions include in their content judgments that can be true or false, and good or bad guides to ethical choice.[63]

This is why it is important to school our emotions, to shape them in a moral way, in a way that will serve our process of decision making. Indeed we are clear about the fact that we need to assess our emotions; that we need to evaluate them in reference to a situation or to a possible course of action. But we also need to ascertain whether our choices are

consistent with our moral self, a self in which we are invested emotionally as well as rationally. The lack of attention to emotions—and not
expressing them plays a big role in ignoring them—allows us to become callous, not to empathize with others, to rationalize choices that
ignore the negative consequences that our actions can have on others,
not to care for the good. It also allows our emotions to be much more
easily manipulated. Those in power use enormous amounts of money to
manipulate our emotions through the media and advertisement. Unless
we are consciously aware of our emotions, unless we realize that to act
contrary to our emotions is as much a violation of ourselves as acting
contrary to our reason, we will continue to be manipulated and used.

EMOTIONS AND EMOTING: A LATINA PERSPECTIVE

Emotions, then, are part of the workings of the mind. Emotions are
"vital signs or signals from myself to myself" that contain information,
shape how I process that information, contribute to shape what I think,
and contribute to how I will respond in the future.[64] I know what I think
by putting thoughts into words. But more than that, there is ample evidence that without words the process of thinking is severely impaired
or simply impossible. I want to claim the same for emotions. Without
emoting, emotions are severely impaired or simply impossible. How
we show our emotions is very much determined by culture. The issue
here is not the "how" but the very fact that expressing emotions is an
intrinsic element of emotions, just as are the other elements discussed
above. Emotions are harshly limited if they are not expressed, limited
not only as to their effects on cognition, beliefs, values, motivations,
actions. Their very existence is severely limited. It is a fact that unless
we emote, unless our behavior is what we believe is appropriate given
the emotions we are experiencing, we question if we are feeling the
emotion or just thinking about it. An example here is helpful.

My oldest brother died quite suddenly when my father was eighty-
nine years old and beginning to be senile. At my brother's funeral my
father was extremely concerned about not being able to cry. I tried to
comfort him by telling him we all knew how much he loved my brother,

that we all were aware of how sad he was that his oldest son had died. But he knew, and so did I, that something was amiss. In reality I believe that his senility did not allow him to grasp fully the tragedy of his son's early death. His lack of tears was in direct proportion to his lack of emotion about the event, lack of emotion related to the fact that his mind could not comprehend fully what was going on. What a difference in my father from the way he was forty years ago! In 1961 I watched him help fragile old nuns who had to abandon Cuba against their will. My father did not know the elderly nuns. We just happened to be at the airport when they got off the plane. I remember tears streaming down his face as he helped carry them down the stairs of the plane.

Lack of emotional response certainly can lead—does lead—persons to be morally impaired. Persons without emotional response "cannot really feel the moral imperative or oughtness of the rules as part of their own reactions. They do not feel the emotional 'mustness' or demand of conscience, nor do they feel anxiety or fear over possible transgressions."[65] It is important to point out here that, when I am talking about emotional response and reaction, I am referring to showing emotions, to outwardly expressing what we know inside in other ways than through reason, for the outward expression is part of the emotional way of knowing and the emotional way of being. Again, how the emotions are expressed is culturally bound. But we cannot claim that emoting, in and of itself, is socially constructed for emoting is an intrinsic element of the emotion. Not to show emotions is to deny the emotions—and this means cutting ourselves off from a way of knowing, from a form of cognition.

Expressing emotions and the emotions themselves are two sides of the same coin. Emotions are not like ideas that one can have even if one does not express them. To have emotions is to express them. How are we friends with someone who is profoundly in love, or with someone who has suffered a great loss? With the person in love, well, we have to listen to the many stories about the beloved that she never tires of telling. The fact is that expressing how much she loves the beloved is part of the loving. That is why the person in love delights in talking about her beloved. And the friends that listen often feel the love—they understand it in ways they would not be able to do if, let's say, they would just observe it. The emoting present in the telling is part of the loving and therefore the friends can apprehend the love present in the emoting. The same thing is true about being friends with someone who is sad. Her expressions of sadness make the sadness concrete, they communicate the sadness because it is part of the sadness. We know that we have to allow ourselves and others to express sadness. It certainly is not good to wallow in sadness—to continue to cry endlessly. But to be sad is to talk about the sadness, about the reason for the sadness. When we talk about sadness or hear others talk about their sadness, we experience the sadness, because the expression of the sadness in words, tears, quietness, or some other culturally bound way, is part of the sadness itself. These two examples clarify what we know well: the expression of emotions is intrinsic to the emotion; emotions do not exist unless they are somehow expressed.

Why do some people simply not allow themselves to express their emotions? Why are there circumstances in which people who usually emote freely will not do so? I believe the repression of expressing emotions is tied to the fact that the objects of our emotions, what is valuable and important to us in such a way that we have tied it to our personal fulfillment—to the fullness of our lives—are beyond our control and this makes us vulnerable. This is why, at least in many of the Western cultures, little boys are taught not to cry. As future men they must learn they have to be in control of themselves and the situations in which they are involved; they cannot allow emotions to control them. Therefore, they are taught not to emote. The same is true of persons with power, who have the means to impose decisions. Often they seem so calm, so "cool," the ones in control of themselves and the situation, showing no emotions, which is the same as having no emotions. The powerful cannot allow themselves to emote for that would show lack of control and vulnerability.

EMOTIONS AND JUSTICE

What can we say about the relationship between emotions and justice? The old portrait of justice, a blindfolded woman holding a scale, says it all. Justice has been made to depend on objectivity, on being apart from any individual point of view, from any particular way of understanding, from any specific situation. Justice has been conceptualized as applying the same rule to all precisely because it is beyond any given situation. It is commonly thought that justice needs to be impartial if it is to be universal—in the sense of being above or beyond any specific circumstance. Objectivity, impartiality, and universality have been married to rationality—rationality depending on the use of the intellect apart from any affective function of reason. "The impartial reasoner is detached: reason abstracts from the particular experiences and histories that constitute a situation. The impartial reasoner must also be dispassionate, abstracting from feelings, desires, interests, and commitments that he or she may have regarding the situation, or that others may have."[66] Following this way of thinking, those who seek justice are called to set aside passions, feelings, desires, and personal interests. Those who theorize about justice have insisted on reasoning apart from any particular consideration precisely so that moral subjects can come to know the universal principles and be guided by them. "This requires abstracting from the particularity of bodily being, its needs and inclinations, and from the feelings that attach to the experienced particularity of things and events. Normative reason is defined as impartial, and reason defines the unity of the moral subject, both in the sense that it knows the universal principles of morality and in the sense that it is what all moral subjects have in common in the same way. This of reason thus stands opposed to desire and affectivity as to what differentiates and particularizes persons."[67]

This understanding of objectivity, impartiality, and normative reason in reality masks issues of power, control, and domination. In *mujerista* theology we have repeatedly pointed out how so-called objectivity is nothing but the subjectivity of those who have the power to impose their own point of view on others. The understanding of objectivity that is commonly used makes it impossible to pay attention and value the experiences—the subjectivity—of those who are marginal in society, who have little or no power. In *mujerista* theology we understand objectivity as the need to disclose our subjectivity, to make known our motives, our prejudices, the worldview that colors our way of acting. In *mujerista* theology we have insisted on partiality instead of impartiality and, together with other liberation theologies, we have privileged the poor and the oppressed, valuing their way of dealing with reality as important for all those who seek justice. In our work, we have questioned normativity time and again for it is the apparatus that maintains the status quo in which Latinas and other marginalized people are kept oppressed. We recognize that groups, families, communities, societies all need norms, but we contend that we need to keep in mind at all times that norms are socially constructed and that they need to be flexible. Norms have to be always under revision, balancing the wisdom we receive from the past with the challenges that those who are excluded present to us.

In reworking these understandings we have had to pay attention to emotions, to how we feel when our point of view is considered subjective and the one of the dominant group is the one proclaimed objective. It is precisely the experience of being ignored and not valued that makes us rebel against this way of thinking. It is the sense of commitment to and love for the poor and the oppressed that leads us to privilege their viewpoint. We do so not because they are morally better but because being excluded they have little or nothing to protect in the present situation and can see options for a just future that those who need to protect privileges and riches cannot see. Finally, to allow—desire—flexibility when it comes to norms, we have had to be aware of how frightening changes are, of how we prefer what we know—because we think we have some control over it—than what we do not know. To see norms as changing and evolving we have to take hold of our fears, including the fear of risking the unknown, so justice may flourish, instead of continuing to claim that change is not reasonable.

For Latinas the way we express our emotions almost always works against us in the U.S. As mentioned earlier, our passionate way of communicating is considered irrational because what is reasonable is considered to be "cool"—emotionless. This ignores the fact that though there is a difference "between what a discourse says, its substantive content or message, and how it says it . . . no discourse lacks emotional tone; 'dispassionate' discourses carry an emotional tone of calm and distance."[68] Furthermore, the substantive content or message does not remain the same regardless of how it is said. At times we have to "translate" for grassroot Latinas what they hear not because they do not know the meaning of the words used to communicate the message but because the way it has been said is foreign to them or, from their point of view, does not go hand in hand with the content being expressed. The meaning of a discourse, "its pragmatic operation in a situation of communicative interaction, depends as much on its rhetorical as its assertoric aspects."[69] This is why we struggle to elaborate our own ethical-theological discourse and to express in our own way who God is and how we relate to the divine. To include emotions in the way we explain ourselves and our beliefs about the divine, is not irrelevant to the content we wish to communicate in *mujerista* theology.

"BEING EMOTIONAL"

Our emotions play a leading role in our moral lives, attaching us to what is good and causing aversion for what is wrong. If it is true that reason judges and tutors emotions, it is also true that emotions need to test and tutor reason. This leads to a moral life in which emotions, thoughts and decisions are integrated into a whole. We have paid little attention to the role of emotions in ethics and morality to the detriment of our integration as full human beings. Many times our struggles for justice have fallen short precisely because we have not paid attention to the emotions that can motivate and maintain them despite obstacles. We have not paid enough attention to the emotional attachments that can help us on a daily basis chose once again to carry on in spite of so many obstacles. We have to understand the need we have to "be emotional" in order to be able to imagine changes and to proceed to bring them about. It is much more comfortable to stay with what is known, to allow ourselves to fear the unknown, than to stir ourselves to risk change. Without expressed emotions—and there are no other kind—we will not be able to move ahead beyond what is. Emotions are very necessary "to spark moral indignation . . . [and] new moral visions of liberation."[70]

Those of us who risk expressed emotions in order to have them play a greater role in our lives will be rewarded with a rich life, not free of difficulties and dangers, but at least, I believe, with greater possibility of contributing to the struggle for justice. Miguel de Unamuno, the Spanish philosopher, pointed out that "one has to live in the midst of a continuous vertigo of passions because only those who are passionate accomplish truly lasting and life-giving deeds."[71] It is important, therefore, to give ourselves over to loving, to living in the most passionate way possible, without setting up frontiers to hold passion at bay. As Julia de Burgos says in her poem *Momentos,*

Yo, universal,	*Me, universal,*
bebiéndome la vida	*drinking life*
en cada estrella desorbitada,	*in each out of orbit star,*
en cada grito estéril,	*in each sterile scream,*
en cada sentimiento sin orillas.	*in each sentiment without shores.*

NOTES

1. Margaret Farley, *Personal Commitments: Beginning, Keeping, Changing* (San Francisco: Harper and Row, 1986), 9.
2. Ibid.
3. Ibid., 6.
4. Ibid., 58–60.
5. Ibid., 54.
6. Ibid.
7. Ibid., 61.
8. Ibid.
9. I remember years ago at a presentation I made, a very quiet, almost somber, woman sitting in the first row, who smiled when I said this. After the presentation, she waited until the end of the line and then came to tell me she was Cuban and she was quiet and reserved and timid. "But I always tell them that I am the exception that proves the rule, that Cubans are loud and flamboyant about showing their emotions."
10. Farley, *Personal Commitments,* 30.
11. I am sure that those who know me will laugh when they read this. I continue to be loud and quite expressive by the standards of this society. I laugh to myself thinking, if only I would really let loose!
12. Charles Curran, *Directions in Fundamental Moral Theology* (Notre Dame, IN: University of Notre Dame Press, 1985), 63–97.
13. Farley, *Personal Commitments,* 26–27.

14. Sidney Callahan, *In Good Conscience: Reason and Emotion in Moral Decision Making* (San Francisco: Harper Collins Publishers, 1991), 95.

15. Ibid., 99.

16. I thank my dearest friend, Nina Torres-Vidal, professor of literature at the Universidad del Sagrado Corazón in Puerto Rico, for introducing me to Julia's poetry.

17. María M. Solá, "La Poesía de Julia de Burgos: Mujer de Humana Lucha," in *Julia de Burgos, Yo Misma Fui Mi Ruta*, ed. María M. Solá (Río Piedras, Puerto Rico, 1986), 9. This and all the other translations from Spanish texts, except Julia's poems, are my own.

18. Ibid., 10–11.

19. Ibid., 11.

20. Ibid., 12.

21. Ibid., 19.

22. This short biographical sketch is based on the chronology found in Solá's book. I also gathered some details from Ana L. Duran, "Julia de Burgos existencial," in *Actas del Congreso Internacional Julia de Burgos*, ed. Edgard Martínez Masdeu (San Juan: Ateneo Puertorriqueño, 1993), 165–94.

23. Solá, "La Poesía," 7.

24. Ibid., 20.

25. I am confident that though some scholars of Julia's poetry might disagree with my emphasis on the role of emotions in her work, none would deny that emotions do play a very important role in it.

26. Jack Agüeros, trans., *Song of the Simple Truth: The Complete Poems of Julia de Burgos* (Willimantic, CT: Curbstone Press, 1997), 3–5. Throughout this paper I have changed some of the translation provided by Agüeros.

27. Mercedes S. Julián, "La que se alza en mis versos," in Solá, *Julia de Burgos*, cited in Silvia Sauter, "Julia de Burgos, poeta consciente de su auto-fragmentación," in Masdeu, *Actas*, 339.

28. All of the verses in Spanish from Julia's poems are taken from Agüeros's book.

29. Sauter, "Julia de Burgos," 382.

30. María Monserrate Matos, "Notas de un trabajo inconcluso de José Emilio González (A Julia de Burgos)," in Masdeu, *Actas*, 37.

31. Belén Román Morales, *La Poesía de Julia de Burgos: Ícono de la Nueva Mujer Puertorriqueña* (privately printed, 1999), 12.

32. Matos, "Notes," 39.

33. Román Morales, *La Poesía*, 12.

34. In the next section of this paper I explain that "to feel" and "feelings" are often used as a synonym of experiencing an emotion or an emotion itself.

35. Sauter, "Julia de Burgos," 388–89.

36. María Arrillaga, "La ruta de Julia de Burgos," in Masdeu, *Actas*, 411.

37. Sauter, "Julia de Burgos," 386–87.

38. Ibid., 391.

39. Agüeros, *Song*, 289–91.

40. See below, the section of the article titled "Emotions and Emoting: A Latina Perspective."

41. Iris Zavala Martínez, "Aspectos psicohistóricos en la subjetividad de Julia de Burgos: La poesía como praxis," in Masdeu, *Actas*, 293–95.

42. Agüeros, *Song*, 151.

43. Román Morales, *La Poesía*, 53–54.

44. Ibid., 72.

45. Doel López Velásquez, "El erotismo en la poesía de Julia de Burgos," in Masdeu, *Actas*, 50.

46. Ibid., 51.

47. Helmut Hazfeld, *Estudios sobre la mística española*, cited in Reynaldo Marcos Padua, "Misticismo y panteísmo en la poesía de Julia de Burgos, in Masdeu, *Actas*, 250.

48. Mayuli Morales Faedo, "Julia de Burgos: la poesía como autoreflexión," in Masdeu, *Actas*, 219.

49. Emilio Orozco, *Poesía y mística: Introducción a la lírica de San Juan de la Cruz*, cited in Padua, "Misticismo y panteísmo," 256.

50. Román Morales, *La Poesía*, 43.

51. Delmira Agustini, "Lo Inefable," in *Literatura Hispanoamericana: Antología e introducción histórica*, ed. Enrique Anderson Imbert and Eugenio Florit (New York: Holt, Rinehart and Winston, Inc., 1960), 578.

52. Farley, *Personal Commitments*, 30–32.

53. Martha C. Nussbaum, *Upheavals of Thought: The Intelligence of Emotions* (Cambridge: Cambridge University Press, 2001), 60. Here I follow the study of emotions by Nussbaum because of its completeness, and because it weaves philosophical and psychological views of emotions with ethical and moral perspectives.

54. Ibid., 23.

55. Ibid., 24–25.

56. Ibid., 25.

57. Ibid., 27.

58. Ibid., 29–30.

59. Ibid., 30.

60. Ibid., 30–31.

61. Ibid., 31. Nussbaum makes an important distinction about the role emotions play in one's goals and ends. She uses the Greek word *eudaimonistic* instead of its English spelling "eudaemonistic" for the Greek word is not limited to happiness or pleasure as the supreme good. This conception of

human flourishing, of fullness of life, is inclusive of all to which the person imparts intrinsic value in her life and which are "not all valued simply on account of some instrumental relation they bear to the agent's satisfaction. This is a mistake commonly made about such theories, under the influence of Utilitarianism and the misleading use of 'happiness'" as the only supreme good. See ibid., 31 n23 and 32.

62. Ibid., 48.

63. Ibid., 1.

64. Callahan, *In Good Conscience,* 103–5. The work of Sydney Callahan here cited provides the basis for much of what follows.

65. Ibid., 107.

66. Iris Marion Young, *Justice and the Politics of Difference* (Princeton, NJ: Princeton University Press, 1990), 100.

67. Ibid.

68. Iris Marion Young, *Inclusion and Democracy* (Oxford: Oxford University Press, 2000), 64–65.

69. Ibid., 67–68.

70. Callahan, *In Good Conscience,* 132.

71. Miguel de Unamuno, *Historia de la Literatura Española*, cited in López Velásquez, in Masdeu, *Actas,* 51–52.

Chapter Seven

Mouth to Mouth, Person to Person

Ronald R. Garet

When the Holy One came to give the Torah to Israel, he uttered it to Moses in its order, Scripture and Mishnah, Talmud and *Aggadah*, as is said, "The Lord spoke all these words" (Exod. 20:1). Even what a faithful student was someday to ask his teacher, the Holy One uttered to Moses at that time.[1]

PERHAPS THERE ARE ANGELS

In my first weeks of graduate school, I often heard my teacher, Sister Margaret Farley, speak of "the human person." Believing (quite wrongly, as it turned out) that I knew what a "person" is, and thinking the expression "human person" redundant, I asked Margaret after class one day: "Why do you say 'the human person'? Aren't persons and humans the same thing?" My teacher smiled at me and said, most gently, "Perhaps there are angels. Perhaps angels are persons."

Not only what Margaret said, but how she said it, revealed to me that there was more to this topic than I had perceived. Her answer insisted on nothing, foreclosed nothing, accepted me without reproof, but opened a horizon I was free to grow into if I wished, and if I could. In the quiet of her answer I heard my question return to me. A young man, twenty-two years old at the time, and not thinking of angels—why is he so confident in his own personhood? Will the angels be kinder to him than he to them?

I understood little about persons—this was the bad news. The good news was that these elusive beings might make up in abundance what they lacked in self-evidence. The world might be filled with unlooked-for persons! Could the newly opened possibility of angelic persons somehow speak to my human personhood, rest my personal being on firmer ground? As the persons of God surely speak—those persons of whom, in my confidence (about language, the human situation, and myself), I was not thinking—those persons whom Margaret named in her answer carefully by not naming them at all explicitly. "If you and I are persons, Ron," so Margaret seemed to say to me, "then perhaps this is because we are being addressed by the most real and true persons, person to person. The ground of our own personal being may consist in how these persons relate themselves to us, and to one another: for their life is in relationship. As we are in relationship now, in our small way." (But not so small, perhaps.)

In the classroom, in my studies, in friendship and young love, in tentative vocational choices, I was moved by the promise of the personal in Margaret's teaching. The ideas so central to her teaching and writing—of the person as a relational being, mutuality as a real possibility for personal relations, active receptivity and receptive activity as dispositions deeply interfused with one another and essential to mutual love, commitment as a maturing and fostering (not a disabling) of the freedom of persons in relation to one another—have stayed with me through the passing years. They influence me still, and I am thankful for their guidance in my everyday life as a teacher of law students and as a scholar writing about constitutional law, jurisprudence, and hermeneutics. In our marriage, Susan and I remember what we learned from Margaret when we were her students, and rely on her now much as we did many years ago when we lived at the Yale Divinity School. The only difference is that instead of knocking at her office door when we need her guidance, we come hand-in-hand to gates of insight that she opened to us.

Readers familiar with her work will know that Margaret Farley has developed the central ideas mentioned above, about personhood and mutuality, in her writing about covenant relations, the communal life of the Trinity, sexual ethics, feminist theology, and Scriptural interpretation. Of course, this is not a complete description of her interests, or an adequate summary of her subtle and suggestive writing. I have named these topics, however, because I will explore them here, following Farley's lead. But my point of departure, the text that best expresses the ideas with which I will be in conversation here, is the concluding chapter of *Personal Commitments*, in which Farley offers an interpretation of the Biblical theme of covenant.[2]

Farley sees in covenant relations a model of the life of active receptivity and receptive activity. In the bestowal of the Torah at Sinai, for example, the people are not wholly passive and God is not entirely active. In receiving the law, the people are active: they make promises to abide by it, and undertake the hard work of filling out its meaning as new problems arise and as community life is challenged in new historical circumstances. And God's activity includes an important element of receptivity: a readiness to accept sacrifices offered by the people, and an acknowledgment that in their custody of the Torah the people will need to work out for themselves its meaning and instruction. Here, Farley points out the need to improve upon certain traditional Christian understandings of the law in covenant relations, and of the relation between law and love.[3]

Needless to say, the fact there is active receptivity and receptive activity on both sides of covenant relations does not render God and human persons equal to one another. Nonetheless, the promises undertaken and the relationship deepened at Sinai truly foster (exemplify and motivate) mutual love between and among human persons. Farley goes on to suggest that the mystery of the communal life of God as understood in the doctrines and images of the Trinity likewise enables human persons to grow in capacity to give and receive love in relations of equality. Finally, Farley insists that covenant relations and the Trinitarian life of infinite personal self-giving and receptivity are relevant not only to our love of God, and to our most intimate (and in that sense "personal") life relationships, but also to the content of justice and the right ordering of society for the common good.[4]

To explore these powerful ideas, and their connections with Farley's contributions to feminist theology, Scriptural interpretation, and sexual ethics, I will offer an interpretation of covenant relations in terms of the striking Biblical image of "mouth to mouth" communication and communion. God says of Moses, in Numbers 12:8, "With him I speak mouth to mouth in a clear appearance and not in enigmas." I will suggest that this mouth-to-mouth relationality is both a kiss (a personal intimacy) and an institutional legal reality (including law's authority and transmission, its application to new and hard cases, and its meaning and worth). In the union of these two dimensions of intimacy and legality, a union essential to covenant and commitment, speaking mouth-to-mouth realizes and exemplifies the relational being of human persons. This mouth-to-mouth relationality is oral Torah, which is central to rabbinic Judaism[5] but not always well-understood in Christian accounts of law. Accordingly, I will draw upon oral Torah, including *aggadah* and *midrash*, to work out the covenant-relational meaning of mouth-to-mouth in its twin aspects of intimacy and legal ordering.

Oral Torah, which is at once the topic and the text and the method of this essay, does not figure so prominently as an explicit theme in Farley's writings. But her work, her writing and teaching, nonetheless seems to me to evince a vivid appreciation of the Shekhinah, who is oral Torah and the presence of God-dwelling-with-us (Shekhinah, from *shakhan*, to dwell). The Shekhinah's abiding with us in the circumstances of our suffering and exile shows God's fidelity to us in our covenant relations, including in the authority of law and its overall accessibility to our jurisprudential imagination, even as unresolved halakhic problems persist. So when Farley speaks of Rachel weeping for her children,[6] she names God's nearness to us, a nearness that is both compassion and jurisprudence—the reality that is the Shekhinah in exile. And when Farley affirms that the covenant presence preserves the memory and hope of a deeper love,[7] we once again associate Rachel with the Shekhinah, and recall Jacob and Rachel kissing at the well, with tears of joy at what is both a restoration and a betrothal. And we anticipate in their mouth-to-mouth a return of Shekhinah from her exile.[8]

Similarly, in concluding *Personal Commitments*, when Farley refers to God's words (through Moses) to the people, "You have seen . . . how I bore you on eagle's wings and brought you to myself" (Ex 19:4)[9]— words that express God's maturing of our freedom for covenant—she also calls to mind the death of Moses (by God's holy kiss). The Talmud remembers that "Moses was laid upon the wings of the Shekhinah, and the Ministering Angels kept proclaiming, 'He executed the justice of the Lord, and His judgments with Israel.'"[10] I cite these texts to illustrate how traditions in oral Torah might express, or translate, or interpret, Farley's vivid sense of the divine presence as God's fidelity to us even within the circumstances of our suffering; of covenant relations as enabling for us our personhood with and for one another; and of a law that matures and honors our highest possibilities for love and for justice.

As the boards that frame God's dwelling-with-us ("tabernacle," *mishkan*, from the same root as Shekhinah) are joined to one another, so the angels (the Zohar teaches) join wing enfolding wing, closely united. Students of Torah, it is said, are similarly joined to one another in the give and take of study.[11] They are faithful to their teachers and to their students, always learning with them and from them.[12] They remember them and honor them. And in their studying together, they almost feel as if they have come to know and be known by the angelic persons, enfolded in their presence, wing touching wing.

SPEAKING MOUTH TO MOUTH AS NEARNESS

Hear now my words: if there be a prophet among you, in a vision I the Lord make myself known to him. In a dream I speak with him. My servant Moses is not so; in all my house he is trusted. With him I speak mouth to mouth in a clear appearance and not in enigmas; and the representation of the Lord does he behold.[13]

In this passage, Numbers 12:6–8, "mouth to mouth" describes a central feature of a particularly prized form of prophecy. The wider scene of action at Sinai illuminates this feature and its special worth. The mouth-to-mouth encounter is distinctive not only in the clarity and directness of the communication (it is not enigmatic) but also in constituting a communion in which Moses as prophet is both receptive and active. He receives God's words, but he also speaks with God and undertakes to speak God's words to the people. By contrast, Aaron and Miriam, to whom God speaks in this passage, simply hear God's words—the words of God are in their ears, not in their mouths, unless Moses puts them there.[14] So we may say that "mouth to mouth" is a mode of communication and communion in which the word of God, Torah as law and as instruction, is fully transmitted.

"Mouth to mouth" not only names this transmission but also suggests that it has the spiritual quality of intimacy. Though respect for the mystery of this intimacy might argue against pursuing the suggestion, writers within Jewish and Christian traditions have not been too shy to describe the intimacy as a kiss. In both traditions, the principal move has been to bring the encounter of God and Moses at Sinai, and the new covenant between God and Israel, into the orbit of the text, "Let him kiss me with the kisses of his mouth," which opens Song of Songs.[15] But I will be particularly concerned to relate that text, and its attendant associations between intimacy and covenant, to the action surrounding Moses and Miriam as presented in Numbers and in related rabbinic traditions.

After drawing attention to certain ethically and jurisprudentially salient features of the Biblical association between covenant and kiss, and to specifically Christian scriptural texts that perhaps assume such an association, I will return to the narrative context in Numbers—to Miriam, whom God chastises and segregates from her people. Next, I draw upon the Zohar to develop further the idea of a mouth-to-mouth communication and communion that is both intimate and legal-normative: a kiss of commitment. Following that, I ask how far this idea stands up under, or takes on new meaning within, the argument and the action of Numbers—especially when the written Biblical narrative is understood within traditions of oral Torah. In conclusion, I tentatively point to some respects in which Trinitarian conceptions of divine personhood might be understood to remember and celebrate these traditions.

Ethical and jurisprudential features of mouth-to-mouth relationality

We have reason to be wary when erotic images of physical intimacy are made to convey ideas about what is essential to personal relationships or to norms of social justice. Too often, motivations and meanings that render the erotic idiom appealing or familiar turn out to depend upon and reinforce demeaning stereotypes about male and female natures. The agency of women is reduced by analogy to an outdated image of the female role in procreation as essentially passive. Or, fault and stain are associated more fundamentally with women than with men.[16] But in kissing, women and men are engaged reciprocally in the same physical activity; both partners are active and receptive in relation to one another. Perhaps even the ancients, who read the physiology of intercourse as a manifesto of distinct and hierarchically ordered gender roles, saw in kissing a more equal and mutual relation. And it could not have escaped notice that two women kissing, or two men, were engaged with one another in just the same physical way as a man and a woman. The same words could be used to describe the mouth-to-mouth contact in same-sex and different-sex kissing.[17]

In associating covenant with the erotics of the kiss in Song of Songs, Biblical traditions use an idiom that suggests a partnership of giving and receiving continuously on both sides. But it is equally significant that though the kiss is a consummation and communion, it does not signify (as procreative intercourse could signify for the ancients, and also for us) merger or synthesis, or the transcendence of the partners in a *tertium quid*. This retaining of distinction even within joyful communion makes the symbolism of the kiss especially well-suited to express elusive ethical concepts. So the Psalmist says that "Lovingkindness (*ḥesed*) and truth will meet; justice and peace will kiss."[18] These goods retain their distinct and defining worth even as they are reconciled to one another through God's decisive action in history. God does not reveal that somehow these goods were just the same as one another all along, that their distinctiveness was just an illusion or an artifact of an inferior grade of existence. Justice is not the same as peace. Nor does the ideal of the rule of law permit right judgment to be moderated to avert conflict or ill will. When justice kisses peace, it is not in any way abated, but to the contrary it is fully realized in the law in accordance with God's goodness.

In addition to suggesting these ideas of reciprocity and distinctness, the symbolism of kissing—at least as a Biblical symbolism—implicates character and moral agency. The mouth that kisses has already been poised countless times in daily life between purity and impurity in eating and in speaking.[19] It brings to the kiss a similar possibility for good and evil, fidelity and betrayal.[20] The kiss concentrates the already acute moral significance of orality in a fateful contact of two mouths, two freedoms, two organs for the giving and receiving that is love's life.[21]

But Biblical traditions also associate God's kiss with the withdrawal of life. If the Shulamite's words of longing have colored our understanding of the "mouth-to-mouth" relation between God and Moses, so too have accounts of Moses's death. Rabbinic tradition remembers that God took Moses's soul by a kiss. "Then the Holy One, blessed be He, took the soul of Moses and put it in safekeeping under the throne of glory. And when He took it, He took it only by means of a kiss, as it is said, *By the mouth of the Lord*, Deuteronomy 34:5."[22] Mouth to mouth God spoke with Moses, performing covenant, sustaining life with law; mouth to mouth God took the soul of Moses with a kiss. The ambiguity here is not moral. It casts no doubt on the goodness of the covenant. But the traditional understanding of the covenant and of the death of Moses as mouth-to-mouth kisses colors both events, both what is given and what is taken away, in a single shade, making each sacred act share in the awe and mystery of the other. We will need to keep in mind this spiritual or mystical meaning, along with the symbolic features (reciprocity, distinctness, and the fateful meeting of two freedoms) that give the kiss such striking moral meaning.

Steven Fraade reminds us that "Israel desires, and is privileged with, the 'mouth to mouth' intimacy of God's revelatory kiss, yet also, in fear of the potency of such unmediated divine contact, prefers to receive revelation via an intermediary agent. . . . 'You [Moses] speak with us, and we will hear, but let not God speak with us, lest we die' (Exod. 20:16, as well as Deut. 5:22–24)."[23] Fraade goes on to explain how rabbinic tradition, articulately and brilliantly ambivalent about immediacy, relocates mouth-to-mouth intimacy to the *bet midrash*, the house of study, where the oral encounter with the law (transmission, inquiry, application) is performed in collegial dialogue. Through this relocation, the revelation that was made at Sinai and the revelation that is not yet fully actualized are substituted from past and future into the present. The taking of Moses's soul with a divine kiss, a mouth-to-mouth culmination that already captures or remembers the pedagogical sequence that links God to Moses and Moses to the *paideia* of Israel, is repeated in the final chapter of every sage's life story, in each devoted student's oral acclamation of each beloved teacher.[24]

But oral Torah is not only a pedagogy but a jurisprudence. It is both a body of substantive legal norms (the Mishnah) and a set of secondary norms governing how the primary, action-governing norms are to be interpreted and applied. But as jurisprudence it is also an account of the nature or status of a legal system and of the legal propositions within it. In this account, not only legal rules or principles stated at a high level of generality (such as those given in the Ten Words or Decalogue), but also legal propositions that are much more particular, such as those given in holdings and dispositions in cases, count as authoritative—they are all law sources when viewed *ex ante*, that is, from the standpoint of a new (real or hypothetical) case to be decided. Moreover, the corpus of legal propositions is held to be complete. Together, the primary and secondary norms, coming from written Torah as well as from the work of the sages and from subsequent rabbinic practice, supply all that is needed to bring a fact-situation under the law. Legal reasoning, therefore, always has the potential to bring out otherwise hidden dimensions of meaning in the manifold facts and particulars of the universe. For "halakhic man," as R. Joseph Soloveitchik said, actual and potential empirical reality always can be brought within the action directives (whether obligations, prohibitions, permissions, and so forth) and narrative contexts of the normative universe embodied in the Sinai covenant.[25]

Have we arrived at a paradox? Mouth-to-mouth relationality, which at first presents itself as intimacy—as a kind of kiss—now shows itself to be a fully institutionalized legal reality. This duality seems hard to reconcile, especially if the kiss of orality is regarded as romantic or expressive (personal in the sense of spontaneous, or private, or highly individualized) and if legality is understood to be impersonal (in the sense of highly ordered, public, and collective). But intimacy (as in the kiss) is a kind of nearness. And the completeness that is central to the jurisprudence of oral Torah is also a kind of nearness.

> For this obligation [good work, precept: *mitzvah*] with which I charge you this day is not too baffling for you, nor is it too distant. It is not in heaven, that you should say, "Who among us can go up to heaven and get it for us and cause us to hear it, that we may do it?" Neither is it beyond the sea, that you should say, "Who among us can cross to the other side of the sea and get it for us and cause us to hear it, that we may do it?" No, the word is very close to you, in your mouth and in your heart, to do it.[26]

The word of instruction and obligation is "not in heaven" but "very close to you, in your mouth." The kiss of intimacy and the jurisprudence of halakhah are not in tension with one another because they are both species of closeness, of nearness. Oral Torah is the presence of God (the Shekhinah) realized in our active embrace of and being embraced by the completeness of God's *nomos*.

The holy kiss and a Christian ideal of the personal

Thus far I have made some reference to the Hebrew Bible and to its reception in Jewish traditions. But Christian writings also affirm a communication and communion that is mouth to mouth. Paul concludes four of his letters by commending the faithful to greet one another with a "holy kiss" (*philēma hagion*).[27] The "holy kiss" to which Paul refers has been interpreted as a ritual sharing of the *pneuma* among believers, a breathing of the Holy Spirit into one another, recalling Christ's breathing of the Holy Spirit upon or into the apostles.[28] Though kissing lips may touch cheek (or foot, Luke 7:38), mutual communication of the breath/spirit would involve a kiss that is mouth to mouth. Chrysostom ("golden mouth"), for example, describes Paul's "holy kiss" as a kiss on the mouth.[29] Augustine, commenting on

John 20:21–22, describes the Spirit of Christ as "the same Spirit that the Lord gave his disciples when he breathed on them and said 'Receive the Holy Spirit.' For he in some way placed his mouth to their mouth when he gave them the Spirit by breathing on them."[30] Moreover, to be effective as a mutual "drink of one Spirit" (1 Cor 12:13), to unite the faithful in mutually drinking the spirit that dwells within, such a kiss would be given and received with open mouth.[31] Such kissing is made explicit in Song of Songs: "How beautiful is your love, my sister-bride! how much better is your love than wine! . . . honey and milk are under your tongue . . ." (4:10–11).[32]

The "holy kiss" is presented in Paul's letters as a concluding greeting (or commendation of such a greeting). The first letter of Peter ends similarly with a "kiss of love," *philēma agapēs*.[33] Concluding his very brief second letter, having urged the church (his audience) "to live a life of love," John says: "Having many things to write unto you, I would not write with paper and ink: but I trust to come unto you, and speak face to face, that our joy may be full."[34] The King James version chooses "face to face" to translate a phrase, *stoma pros stoma*, literally "mouth to mouth," whose range of associations corresponds closely to the Hebrew of Numbers 12.[35] It is clear that John prizes oral communication and communion.[36] He associates it closely with the life of love, and sees in it a promise of joy in all its fullness. He trusts in the possibility of oral relationality—as God trusted Moses, and so engaged him mouth to mouth. Did John and his audience, with the emergent rabbinic tradition, also associate this relationality with a holy kiss? And today, how might we understand as kiss the divine-human encounter? Is it part of our personal reality?

The Jerusalem Bible translates John this way: "I hope instead to visit you and talk to you personally, so that our joy may be complete." This nice phrasing brings out the very "personal" nature of speaking mouth to mouth (whether this speaking is between John and the church, or between God and Moses). In concluding this essay, I will say a bit more about mouth to mouth as a personal relation, an encounter that is "person to person." Here it need only be noted that the idea of "person to person" would seem to be on a different plane from "mouth to mouth" or "face to face." We think of ourselves as being persons; traditional creeds of the Christian churches affirm God's unity in three persons; but we would not say that we or God are mouths or faces. But the oral encounter with God can lay claim to an epistemic primacy. "For the Lord gives wisdom; out of his mouth comes knowledge and wisdom" (Prv 2:6; though the Hebrew means "his mouth," the Septuagint translates "his *prosōpon*"—his face—using the same word that will sometimes designate "person" in Greek trinitarian and Christological formulations). What we know, we know in and through the word of God as spoken, preached, and passed down in teachings (mouth to mouth), as well as in and through the written word that is scripture. John's epistemic claim might be stronger: that the knowledge which brings full joy is fostered better in mouth-to-mouth encounter than in "paper and ink." If this claim has merit, then what we know of ourselves as persons, of God as person or persons, of love as our calling, and of our personal relationships with neighbors and with God, must emerge from (or at least be consistent with) the revelation that is mouth to mouth.

Miriam: nearness and distance

How, if at all, are we to understand or reconcile this theme of nearness, in its pedagogical, ethical, and jurisprudential meanings and aspirations, with the narrative frame in Numbers? We recall, and are stung by the recollection, that God pronounces mouth-to-mouth relationality as the perfection of prophecy in answer to Miriam's and Aaron's criticisms of Moses, and as the immediate preface to Miriam's punishment.[37] Miriam does not share in Moses's unique mouth-to-mouth relation with God, but is afflicted with leprosy and segregated for a time from her people. In a way, this narrative compels us to experience the kiss of commitment not only from the internal perspective of those included in relations of intimacy but also from its social correlative, the external viewpoint of those excluded. What lovers specially share together they necessarily withhold from others.

Often the traditions that make possible such special (but exclusive) pledges share this very feature. Strong legal commitments and the hermeneutic norms that enable a community to understand and undertake them typically define an unwelcomed "outside," as if someone must be made to experience distance as the price to be paid for another's nearness. A stranger looking in on a traditional wedding ceremony, for example, might feel herself distanced twice over—once by her status as outside the marital union, and again by her status as outside the community whose memories and hopes supply to that union its frames of meaning.

We might see Miriam—excluded not only from the mouth-to-mouth communion between God and Moses, but also (for a time) from the community itself—in this stranger. But Miriam is no stranger; she is a prophet in her own right, as the argument in Numbers assumes (by distinguishing her prophetic status from that of Moses). More fundamentally, any impression of Miriam as on the outside, looking with longing but not much understanding upon a mouth-to-mouth intimacy from which she is excluded, is precisely backward. The scripture text first articulates mouth-to-mouth intimacy as an element of the divine rebuke: as an answer to Miriam, and not as ingredient in her question or as object of her longing. Mouth-to-mouth is not what Miriam first wants but then is told that she cannot share. Instead, mouth-to-mouth is first disclosed to her—as account of God's communication and communion with Moses—in God's reply to her. (I will take up below the question of what Miriam said or did to evoke this answer—a question which again leads back to her own prophetic stature.)

We will have to take a fresh look, then, at how the Sinaitic "mouth to mouth" belongs to, or is associated with, or is colored by, the words of longing, "Let him kiss me with the kisses of his mouth." It will not do to think of Miriam as being rebuked for such a longing, for inappropriately wanting kisses that God offers only to Moses. I would almost rather say that God in answering Miriam teaches her, and us through her, the truest longing for the sweetest kisses; and because she is our teacher our very learning from her about the desire for kisses is itself a kiss, a mouth-to-mouth with her.

But an interpretation of the texts along these lines must come to terms with the punitive and violent nature of a response that inflicts leprosy upon Miriam and segregates her from her community. How, if at all, does such a response, or such a biblical narrative, stir in us or encourage within us any recognition of God's love for us? We might feel instead that if the precious kiss of mouth-to-mouth communication and communion is disclosed within a punitive response, within affliction seemingly intended as a badge of degradation and within a segregative sanction, then such a kiss cannot really be intimate, any more than the physical contacts and the desires aroused in an abusive domestic relationship are true intimacies.

Our own possibilities of recognition and response are enabled or disabled in part by our self-understanding as either inside or outside an interpretive community. When he rebukes the Emperor Theodosius for ordering a bishop to rebuild a synagogue burnt down by Christians acting with the bishop's encouragement, Ambrose asks rhetorically: Why should a Jew receive a kiss of peace? Why should a synagogue receive a kiss that is meant for the church, when the church (not the synagogue) believes in Christ and expresses its faith and love by saying, "Let him kiss me with the kisses of his mouth"?[38] Here the intimate bonds of those in communion with one another in and through the church are the obverse face of violence inflicted on Jews represented as unbelievers. Those excluded from the kiss are excluded also from justice and from peace.

Miriam's fate foreshadows that of her descendants. Denied the kiss, they are excluded and afflicted. But the texts (the narrative in Numbers and the arguments in Ambrose's epistles) are quite different from one another, and belong to us (or we to them) in different ways. Ambrose has already determined that he has nothing to learn from Jews as such; though their written Torah has been expropriated in his Bible, he has nothing to do with their oral Torah; their committed nomic practice he scorns as unbelief. His refusal to the Jews of any apostolic kiss or kiss of peace is the reflex of a dismissive hermeneutic. Ambrose reads their written scripture, their "Let him kiss me with the kisses of his mouth," even as he turns his mouth aside from any communion with the oral tradition that receives and understands the story of Sinai within the interpretive community of the people Israel. By contrast, there is no fixed exclusionary standpoint in Numbers, no single author decisively reading Miriam out of the tradition. A story is told; but how do we relate ourselves to it, and how do we establish the text? Should we receive the story-as-written within the bigger Bible, the coherent compendium of oral tradition about Sinai, about covenant, about Miriam?

Posing such questions turns attention to who "we" are—Christians? Jews? Jewish women who have been excluded from the house of study? Jewish women who have made the house of study their home? "We" define ourselves in part, and are defined in part, by the texts that have standing to teach us. To the extent that I allow myself, or am allowed, to be one of Paul's readers, invited into a community of the "holy kiss;" to the extent that I am not only a reader of John, of what he wrote in paper and ink, but one to whom he comes "face to face (mouth to mouth), that our joy may be full"—to this extent I understand myself as heir not only to Scripture but to "*all these words*" (Ex 20:1), including the oral traditions. So I will read the story of Miriam accordingly, honoring her prophetic stature as the *aggadic* (oral narrative) traditions insist. I will find a seat in the house of study, and open my mouth there in acclamation of my teacher; and perhaps Miriam too will be there, as much "inside" as "outside" the joyous marital kiss. Perhaps, without Miriam, without the traditions that continue to articulate her strong prophetic voice, I would be the stranger double-distanced from mouth-to-mouth communion.

COVENANT AS KISS

"And the Lord spoke to Moses face to face" (Ex 33:11). We can suppose that this "speaking face to face" is a radical copresence, in which Moses is completely engaged with God's word of Torah. This engagement encompasses everything that any sage, student, rabbi will ever study and come to understand; every application of the law to a new dilemma; every insight into the ultimate integrity of God's self-communication in itself and for us; every joy in the divine presence.

The Zohar relates this copresence (in its two dimensions of intimacy and jurisprudence) to a union or reunion of the male and female aspects of God. As the destruction of the primordial world was due to "the lack of a face-to-face embrace for the male and female countenances,"[39] so "the process of divine evolution is complete" when "[f]ace gazes upon face" and the male and female aspects of God are united in peace and joy.[40] This supernal communion has its analog and its stimulus in Torah study—in the devoted student's "face to face" encounter with the beloved text.[41]

Even within this erotics of joinder, the communion remains specifically a conversation because what is learned has propositional content, and also because there is an undertaking, an exchange of promises. "Face," like "mouth," expresses the undertaking (the right ordering of the life of the community according to God's righteousness) as presence; the labor of study, the demanding work of bringing the law to bear in ever more integrated and coherent ways, is not a deficit or distance but a nearness of God. But as Maimonides suggests, "face" also specifically signifies the moral element in the divine-human communication and communion.

Maimonides traces the Hebrew noun *panim*, face, to the verb *panoh*, to turn, thus associating "face" with the exercise of agency or of practical reasoning (as in: turning toward an objective, accomplishing an end).[42] This derivation illuminates the relation between intimacy and legal normativity in the bestowal of the law. For in Maimonides' view, Moses's "turning" toward God, that is the "face" he presents to God's face, is not a seeking of intimacy but a seeking of right government. If it had been intimacy Moses sought, his relation to God at Sinai would not have been intimacy; but because he did not seek intimacy for its own sake, he was welcomed into intimacy.

Moses's intercession (Ex 33) after his people worship the golden calf illustrates this paradox. Though God proposes to send an angel in the vanguard of the people, Moses pleads to be shown God's way and God's glory. In response, God speaks to Moses as a friend, face to face, and promises that the divine face (presence, countenance) will go with him. God says, "I will make all my goodness pass before your face," but also tells Moses that "You cannot see my face, for humankind does not see me, and live."[43] Thus Moses does not see the divine face; instead, the face-to-face encounter consists in the dialogue and in the revelation of the divine goodness (so that Moses will know the way, the law by which to govern). Maimonides stresses that Moses is motivated not by voyeurism or a personal desire for union, but by his responsibility to the people—"a people for the government of which I need to perform actions that I must seek to make similar to Thy actions in governing them."[44]

The Zohar does not contradict this view of Moses's union with the Shekhinah. The tenth *sefirah*, oral Torah (Shekhinah) as Malkhut (Kingdom), is "the wisdom of practical affairs and government."[45] This practical wisdom for government is Moses's "bride," who fully reveals herself to him. But in commenting on Exodus 33, the Zohar stresses the longing for intimacy and the joy in experiencing it. It associates the Exodus text with Song of Songs (1:2): "Let him kiss me with the kisses of his mouth; for your love is better than wine."[46] The Zohar explains that "kissing expresses the cleaving of spirit to spirit; therefore the mouth is the medium of kissing, for it is the organ of the spirit (breath)."[47] The kiss unites Moses (and the people) with the Shekhinah (oral Torah—also called "the Community of Israel"), but it also unites her with Tiferit (a higher *sefirah*).[48] "Therefore the Community of Israel prays: 'Let Him kiss me with the kisses of His mouth, that His Spirit may be united with mine and never separate from it.'"[49]

The loving kiss is better than wine (Song of Songs 1:2, 4:10–11), the Zohar explains, because it brightens the face/countenance with a more spiritual radiance. "Let him kiss me with the kisses of his mouth" expresses "a more burning desire, in which affection issues from the mouth."

> For when mouth is joined with mouth to kiss, fire issues from the strength of affection, accompanied by radiance of the countenance, by rejoicing on both sides and by gladsome union. "For thy love is better than wine," to wit, than that wine which exhilarates and brightens the countenance, which makes the eyes sparkle and induces good feeling [i.e., the wine libation offered on the altar].[50]

So "mouth to mouth" is not unrelated to "face to face"—the loving kiss is fiery and makes a glowing countenance, as the face of Moses glowed when he descended Sinai.[51]

The kiss is ultimately a clearinghouse for all of the senses and modes of apprehension. In the kiss, intimacy and spiritual awakening or empowerment can be described experientially as synaesthesia—hearing voice expands into seeing voice and tasting it, seeing light expands into radiant voice and warm joy. Such vocabularies are necessary to describe a full encounter between the divine and human realms, or the exchange of what the Zohar calls "words of love between the Upper and Lower world."[52]

> We have been told that at the revelation on Mount Sinai, when the Torah was given to Israel in ten Words, each Word became a voice, and every voice was divided into seventy voices, all of which shone and sparkled before the eyes of Israel, so that they saw eye to eye the splendour of His Glory, as it is written, "And all the people *saw* the voices," Exodus 20:18. Yea, verily, they *saw.* The voice so formed warned each individual Israelite, saying: "Wilt thou accept me with all the commandments implicit in me?" To which the reply came: "Yes." Then the voice circled round his head once more, asking: "Wilt thou accept me with all the penalties attached to me in the Law?" And again he answered "Yes." Then the voice turned and kissed him on the mouth, as it is written, "Let him kiss me with the kisses of his mouth."[53]

I have quoted this extraordinary passage at length because it so vividly celebrates both a reality of legal authority and a reality of intimacy, associating both with dazzling multisensory apprehension culminating in the mouth's kiss. Notably, the voice asks the people to accept not only the penalties of the law but also the obligations that will need to be worked out—"the commandments implicit in me." The people are asked to embrace not only certain rules or principles, but also everything that fills the space within or between them. In other words, the passage describes the affirmation not only of legal authority but also of the hermeneutic practices and norms of argument by which that authority becomes concrete in the course of deciding new and difficult cases.[54] All of this—the intensity of apprehension in the relationship with God, and the institutions of law—is consummated with the mouth's kiss. Within this understanding, orality is one of the doors of perception, but it is also and equally one of the gates of righteousness.[55]

MIRIAM AND MUTUALITY

Though only Moses spoke with God mouth to mouth, the sages of Israel maintain that not only Moses but also Miriam and Aaron died by means of God's kiss.

> [T]he Sages have indicated with reference to the deaths of Moses, Aaron, and Miriam that the three of them died by a kiss. They said that the dictum [of scripture], "And Moses the servant of the Lord died there in the land of Moab by the mouth of the Lord," indicates that he died by a kiss. Similarly it is said of Aaron: "By the mouth of the Lord, and died there." And they said of Miriam in the same way: "She also died by a kiss."[56]

This tradition seems to suggest a relaxing of the rigorous insistence on the exclusivity of Moses's mouth-to-mouth encounter with God. After all, if death by kiss and covenant bestowal are bound together in their mysterious depths, and if Aaron and Miriam share in the death by kiss, do they not also share in the covenant bestowal? (Recall that as God's words were in Moses's mouth, so were Moses's words in Aaron's mouth.) If Miriam too dies by divine kiss, does she not also participate in the divine mouth-to-mouth? But Maimonides offers this qualification: "But with regard to her it is not said, *by the mouth of the Lord*; because she was a woman, the use of the figurative expression was not suitable with regard to her."[57] This little note of distinction might sound merely fastidious, prudish about metaphor, were it not for the drama of Numbers 12. The action there elevates Maimonides' scruples into a dramatic lesson. Though a wedge is to be driven between Moses and *all* others (Miriam and Aaron included), the story in Numbers 12 has the effect of specifically disabling Miriam, disqualifying her from mouth-to-mouth divine/human relationality.

It is not difficult to discern the outlines of the moral or lesson of the story, just as an account in the written Torah. Miriam uses her mouth to slander Moses, while Moses (slow of speech, modest in his ways) uses his mouth to engage and be engaged by God. Moses encounters God face to face, receiving and transmitting the law, descending Sinai with radiant face; while Miriam, in punishment for slander, wears the law upon her face (her punishment, which afflicts her with leprosy). But the lesson is enriched and complexified in oral Torah accounts. These are just the accounts to which we must attend if we are to understand mouth-to-mouth internally. Here is what is written in Numbers, along with some significant elements of the story that have been preserved in *midrash* and rabbinic commentaries. (These elements are given in italics.)

> And Miriam and Aaron spoke against Moses because of the Cushite woman whom he had married; for he had married a Cushite woman. *Now whence did Miriam know that Moses had separated himself from his wife? Rabbi Nathan says: Miriam was at the side of Zipporah at the time when it was told to Moses (Numbers 11:27), "Eldad and Medad are prophesying in the camp." When Zipporah heard (this), she said: "Woe unto the wives of these men, if they (the husbands) are required to prophesy, for they will separate themselves from their wives just as my husband separated himself from me.* . . . And they said: "Has the Lord indeed spoken only with Moses? Has he not spoken also with us?" *Yet we have not abstained from marital relations.* And the Lord heard. . . . And the Lord. . . called Aaron and Miriam; and they both came forth. And he said: "Hear now my words:. . . With [Moses] I speak mouth to mouth. . . . Wherefore were you not afraid to speak against my servant, against Moses?" And the anger of the Lord was kindled against them; and he departed. And . . . behold, Miriam was leprous, as white as snow.[58]

The Miriam who acts in this ampler recounting of the story (a reduction of still richer rabbinic accounts) is not motivated primarily or exclusively by envy. She is not lashing out just because she feels excluded from intimacy with God. She is championing conjugal rights and obligations.[59] But her defense of these conjugal relations is nonetheless problematic, since Moses has been directed by God to separate from his wife.

> Rabbi Judah ben Bathyra says: Moses kept away from his wife only because he was so told by the mouth of the Almighty, as it is said, "With him do I speak mouth to mouth" (Numbers 12:8): mouth to mouth I told him "Keep away from thy wife," and he kept away.[60]

This is intimacy against intimacy—"mouth to mouth I told him 'keep away from thy wife.'" Miriam rejects the terms of the paradox. She defends Zipporah (Moses's wife or former wife), sympathizes with her, takes her side in what looks like a legal argument against Moses and even against God. Moses is breaching his marital obligations in withdrawing from Zipporah. Miriam and Aaron are also prophets, yet they do not abstain from marital relations.

Remembering the story in this way, the traditions of oral Torah not only place Miriam squarely within the main stream of Jewish family law and sexual ethics, but also recall her specific credentials and contributions as a prophet of Israel. As she is presented in these traditions, Miriam's heroism and prophecy are manifested in her defense of conjugal life under the harsh and oppressive regime of slavery. She defied Pharaoh's order that the newborn Israelite boys be killed, and served as midwife to the worthy women of Israel for whose sake God delivered the people from bondage in Egypt. This association between Miriam and subversive midwifery is so firm that it is called upon to explain one of her many names. "Miriam was called *Puah* (Ex 1:15) because she defied [*hophiah*] Pharaoh, all but thumbing her nose at him, saying, 'Woe to this man when God comes to settle with him.'"[61] "*Puah* is Miriam; and why was her name called *Puah*? Because she cried out [*po'ah*] to the [unborn] child, and brought it forth. Another explanation of *Puah* is that she used to cry out through the Holy Spirit and say, 'My mother will bear a son who will be the saviour of Israel.'"[62]

Another oral tradition about Miriam celebrates in her youthful heroism the very character and commitments she will later express in her defense of conjugal relations against Moses's abstention. In his despair at Pharaoh's decree about the newborn Israelite boys, Amram, Miriam's father, divorced Jochebed (Miriam's mother and lead midwife), causing all of the other men to divorce their wives. But Miriam argued forcefully against her father:

> Father, thy decree is more severe than Pharaoh's; because Pharaoh decreed only against the males whereas thou hast decreed against the males and females. Pharaoh only decreed concerning this world whereas thou hast decreed concerning this world and the World to Come. In the case of the wicked Pharaoh there is a doubt whether his decree will be fulfilled or not [witness subversive women like Miriam!], whereas in thy case, though thou art righteous, it is certain that thy decree will be fulfilled.[63]

Persuaded by his daughter's cogent arguments, Amram took back his wife; the other men followed his example; and thus Moses could be conceived and born, and could deliver an intact people, and bring them Torah.

There are many more stories about Miriam, all of which contribute to the oral tradition about orality itself and illuminate the complex ways in which Miriam both does and does not participate in mouth-to-mouth communication and communion. On the one hand, she is punished for speaking out against Moses and is told explicitly that only Moses encounters God mouth to mouth. On the other hand, her defiant character is not a deficiency but is integral to her own prophetic career. Moreover, when she speaks out on behalf of Zipporah's conjugal claims, she is not simply defending her own (and Aaron's) credentials (as prophets who are married and continue to have marital relations), but holding firmly to the same conjugal ethic on which she insisted against Pharaoh and Amram. So the biblical narrative, as received by a community committed to the oral traditions, includes a countercurrent that preserves the worth of Miriam's protest even as it approves her harsh punishment. Complexly and rather unexpectedly, Miriam safeguards—even against Moses and God—the very mutuality that the mouth-to-mouth relation between God and Moses also expresses and symbolizes. Accordingly, she does not simply wear the law upon her face, as an object; it is in her mouth too, even before Sinai, when as articulate subject of the law she makes her stunning and decisive case against the men's unilateral separation from the women. So it is not surprising that Miriam, like her brothers, whose mouths spoke God's words, should die by God's kiss. Given what we know of her through the stories, we sense that her piety would not have been offended, whatever the men may have thought, if the mouth of God in receiving her soul had met her own mouth, in a kiss sweeter than wine and tasting of milk and honey.

PERSON TO PERSON

Paul's hymn to love in 1 Corinthians (the text to which Farley turns in the last pages of *Personal Commitments*)[64] draws the image and concept of "face to face" into a Christian account of the virtues and of the unfolding of revelation.

> Now we are seeing a dim reflection in a mirror; but then we shall be seeing face to face [*prosōpon pros prosopon*]. The knowledge that I have now is imperfect; but then I shall know as fully as I am known. In short, there are three things that last: faith, hope, and love; and the greatest of these is love. (1 Cor 13:11–13)

Paul's idiom echoes the LXX renditions of the Hebrew Biblical idiom *panim el-panim* (much as John echoes the LXX renditions of *peh el-peh*, mouth to mouth).[65] I will close with a tentative reading of the hymn to love (within the overall argument of 1 Corinthians) as a contribution to Miriam's argument. This is just a way of inviting further thought about how the conception of covenant relations as face-to-face and mouth-to-mouth figures within Christian understandings of love.

Paul takes positions on the whole range of issues raised in Miriam's complaint, and in that sense participates more or less "internally" (as Rabbi Gamaliel's student) in an ongoing debate. Is celibacy necessary to (the highest form of) prophecy? The argument of 1 Corinthians takes a step toward Miriam. Conjugal relations are not, or do not create, an impurity that must be cleansed before prophetic communication and communion can proceed. But Paul is less convinced than Miriam that such relations are an unmixed blessing for God's people. Marital life may prove a distraction from love's highest and most urgent occupations. Yet Paul defends the mutuality of marriage. If partners are to be celibate in marriage, they should accomplish this by mutual consent, not by unilateral withdrawal.[66] Just here, Paul goes further perhaps than Miriam. He agrees with her, and with rabbinic tradition, that conjugal intimacy is governed by correlative rights and obligations. But Paul further stresses the mutuality of spousal undertakings. Where the rabbinic Miriam takes men to task for abandoning the marriage bed, Paul's concern is that the choice be a mutual decision, taken realistically and for the right reasons.

But Paul's wider message to the church at Corinth is also quite consistent with the face value of Numbers 12, its apparent lesson. Don't be jealous over spiritual gifts, Paul admonishes the Corinthians, in words he might also apply to Miriam. The main point of spiritual gifts, he stresses, is the good of the community, not individual distinction.[67] Paul says this to a factionalized church, but his view has much in common with Maimonides' interpretation of Moses at Sinai.

Like Numbers 12, the hymn to love contrasts modes of prophecy. A direct or immediate apprehension is distinguished from a lesser, enigmatic apprehension.[68] Paul defers the higher or more direct knowing—it obtains "then," not "now." In Numbers, the immediate apprehension is already enjoyed by Moses. In fact, the words that God has put in the mouth of Moses are bestowed also upon the people of Israel forever.[69] But these differences do not mean that our texts are inconsistent with one another. God's communication and communion are with us now mouth to mouth, though we do not see God's face—the beatific vision is "then," not "now." The kiss of covenant is near to us—so near that John trusts to come to us and speak with us mouth to mouth, that our joy may be full. From this harmonizing perspective, we can assume that the love that is Paul's theme and John's already constitutes our metaphysical and moral reality and our expectation, and that this love, both in its divine-human and in its neighbor-neighbor forms, is a direct, immediate—"personal"—bestowal.

Speaking mouth to mouth is the present reality of person to person, as its deferred reality is seeing face to face.

In this light, Paul's idiom (face to face, person to person) both recalls (echoes, but also participates in) the covenant relations established at Sinai and points toward the relational conception of personhood that belongs so centrally to trinitarian Christianity. The *prosopon* of whom Paul speaks is at once the *panim* of Genesis and Exodus and the "person" affirmed in trinitarianism and in Christology—for example, in the formula "one Person (*prosopon*) and one Subsistence (*hupostasis*), not parted or divided into two persons (*prosopa*)."[70] The face-to-face or person-to-person relationship, whether understood as immanent in God's own being or "economically" as disclosed in God's deeds of salvation *pro nobis*, is importantly (though elusively) mouth to mouth. What eludes crisp conceptualization, though, may yet be imaged: as in a depiction of the trinity in which "the dove [symbol of the Holy Spirit] unites the Father and Son by having the tips of its wings touching, indeed, actually issuing from or entering into the mouths of the first two divine Persons."[71] It is not too difficult to see in this picture an account of the source and the warrant of the "holy kiss" here below[72]—the divine communion that is mouth to mouth enabling and inspiring our own.

Surely there are important limits to the use of creaturely images, or analogies to the functions of creaturely organs, as theological representation devices. But the image of the oral procession of the Spirit may aid us, in prayer and worship, to express joy and wonder, and thankfulness, that the divine mouth-to-mouth should in some way bring the whole creation to voice, praise, and song. A kiss that is inclusive and sufficient unto itself nonetheless invites me; a teaching that far exceeds my understanding nonetheless is near to me, in my mouth; defying the passage of years and the sequence of generations, a tradition makes a sacred time and sacred space, the house of study, in which I am always with my beloved teachers and students.

In that house, I will always ask my teacher why she speaks of "human persons," and her answer will always be humane and humanizing, personal and person-making. My asking and her answering will always enfold me. In that moment, repeated and extended, I become aware always of personhood in God's inner relationality, and personhood again in God's relationality to and with us. Though the sacred time of seeing "face to face" is futurity, the possibility of speaking person to person is forever present and need not be deferred. All such speech participates or is modeled in the giving and receiving at Sinai—where everything was asked and answered, mouth to mouth, person to person. That bestowal forever binds possibilities of intimacy and possibilities of actual human governance in a common grace.

I read Paul's moving and motivating words in a Bible made special because it was given to Susan, my wife, by the church that first called her—the inscription says, "To the Rev. Susan Hazard Garet on the occasion of your ordination to the Christian ministry." As I read, I remember that in the traditions of oral Torah, "face to face" describes the communion of bride and groom, their faces illuminating one another, at their wedding.[73] I remember that John, trusting to speak mouth to mouth "that our joy may be full," associates the fullness of joy with the wedding day—agreeing here with the *Sheva Berakhot*, the seven blessings that belong to the Jewish marriage liturgy.[74] And I recall that Paul's words, of the greatness of love and the possibility of growth and the hope for face-to-face encounter, belong liturgically to the Christian order of marriage.

Susan and I remember well our wedding day, when Margaret and our friend Hillel Levine cocelebrated our marriage. That is to say, we remember well that they did, though we are a little hazy on what they said. One of them told a Hasidic story—I think it must have been Hillel. One of them smiled on Susan and me, and said, "The two of you may kiss." I think it must have been Margaret. I don't know for sure; I was a little distracted, and once again the angels were not on my mind. But I will testify that the words of the Lord are sweet; oh they are sweet in the mouths of the daughters of Miriam.[75]

NOTES

I am grateful to Rachel Adler, Mordecai Finley, Steven Fraade, Daniel Gordis, Leslie Griffin, Dan Klerman, Susan Laemmle, Hillel Levine, David

Nirenberg, and Nomi Stolzenberg; to participants in a U.S.C. Law School faculty workshop on an earlier draft; to my Hebrew teachers, Karina Sterman and Rivka Dori; to my research assistants, David Margolis, Bill D'Angelo, and Brian Fodera; and to Shawn Zambrows and the U.S.C. Graduate Christian Fellowship.

1. Hayim Nahman Bialik and Yehoshua Hana Ravnitzky, eds. *The Book of Legends (Sefer Ha-Aggadah): Legends from the Talmud and Midrash*, trans. William G. Braude (New York: Schocken Books, 1992), 441, excerpt §375. For each excerpt Bialik and Ravnitzky provide citations, which I omit.

2. Margaret A. Farley, *Personal Commitments: Beginning, Keeping, Changing* (San Francisco: Harper & Row, 1986), chap. 8, "Commitment, Covenant, and Faith," 110–35.

3. Ibid., 124–32.

4. Ibid., 127–35.

5. Rabbinic Judaism receives as canonical and authoritative not only the written Torah (Scripture) but also the oral Torah—all that God said to Moses at Sinai and that Moses passed down, from generation to generation to the sages of Israel. "The Lord spoke *all* these words" (Ex 20:1); see the extract at note 1, supra. The Hebrew Bible reports that upon Sinai, having delivered the law to Moses, the Lord instructed him: "Write you these words: for according to these words [literally, 'by the mouth of' these words, *'al-pi hadvarim*] I have made a covenant with you and with Israel" (Ex 34:27). "R. Yohanan maintained: The greater part [of the Torah] was given orally, and only the smaller part is in the written text, for Scripture says, 'By the mouth of these words' (Ex 34:27)"; Bialik and Ravnitzky, *Book of Legends*, 440 §374. (Cf. Dt 17:10–11: "Act by the mouth of the word which they declare to you . . . by the mouth of the Torah which they direct you, and according to the judgment [*mishpat*] which they speak to you." The specifically oral referent is identical in the case of testimony by witnesses at trial; see Dt 17:6.) The same idiom in Dt 34:5, *'al-pi Adonai*, "by the mouth of the Lord," provides the basis for the traditional view that God took Moses with a kiss. See text at note 22, infra.

6. Margaret A. Farley, "Weep for Yourselves and for Your Children," *Criterion* 21 (Winter 1982): 19–21, at 20–21.

7. Farley recalls God's words of assurance to Rachel, "There is hope for your descendents" (Jer 31:15–17). "Weep For Yourselves," 20–21.

8. On the doctrine of the divine kisses, see Zohar II, 97a (Mishpatim), quoting and commenting on Genesis 29:11 (Jacob kissing Rachel); Harry Sperling and Maurice Simon, trans., *The Zohar* (1984), 3:293. See also Pinchas Giller, *Reading the Zohar: The Sacred Text of the Kabbalah* (Oxford: Oxford University Press, 2001), 50–51.

9. Farley, *Personal Commitments*, 126, 131.

10. B. Talmud Soṭah 13b (quoting Dt 33:21).

11. Zohar II, 171a (Terumah); Sperling and Simon, *The Zohar*, 4:91. The reference is to Exodus 26:17 (design of the dwelling-with-us of God).

12. I am grateful for what I have been taught by my students Mordecai Finley, Rachel Adler, and Daniel Gordis—gifted rabbis and interpreters of Judaism. This essay is much indebted to them, though errors remain my own.

13. Nm 12:6—8. Translations from the Hebrew Bible are my own, unless otherwise stated; but in most cases my renditions conform closely to standard editions. However, when quoted sources contain internal quotations from the Bible, I retain the Bible translation given in the source.

14. Ex 4:15; cf. Dt 18:8.

15. For an example within the Christian tradition, see Gregory the Great, *Expositiones in Canticum Canticorum*, quoted in Nicolas James Perella, *The Kiss Sacred and Profane: An Interpretive History of Kiss Symbolism and Related Religio-Erotic Themes* (Berkeley: University of California Press, 1969), 290n14.

16. Margaret A. Farley, "New Patterns of Relationship Between Women and Men: The Beginnings of a Moral Revolution," *Theological Studies* 36 (1975): 627—46, at 635—38 (traditional gendered conceptions of female passivity and male agency, embedded in historical understandings of sexuality and procreation, have hindered development of a more adequate understanding of the complex interplay of activity and receptivity in fully Christian love). See also Margaret A. Farley, "Feminist Consciousness and the Interpretation of Scripture," in *Feminist Interpretation of the Bible*, ed. Letty M. Russell, 41—51 (Philadelphia: Westminster Press, 1985); Margaret A. Farley, "Sources of Sexual Inequality in the History of Christian Thought," *The Journal of Religion* 56, no. 2 (1976): 162—76.

17. Xenophon, in his playful banter between Socrates and Critobulus about finding a gentleman friend, uses much the same description of the kiss (*pros to stoma prosoiseis; to stoma pros to stoma prosoisō*) as John in his epistles (*stoma pros stoma*; see notes 34—35, infra).

18. Psalm 85:11 (BHS; 85:10 KJV, RSV).

19. The mouth is an organ for eating life-giving foods that are pure and sweet; but it may also eat impure foods, abominations, and the fruit that brings death (Gn 2:16—17). We "taste and see that the Lord is good" (Ps 34:9), but without the Lord we "taste death" (e.g., Mt 16:28). The mouth may ornament the law by recitation, prayer, and studious dialogue, or provoke its judgment by speaking slander. To the humble Moses, the mouth of God brings self-communication and communion; but God warns his stubborn people that "I will not go up with you . . . lest I consume you on the way" (Gn 33:3).

20. Kisses that promise love may bring deceit and betrayal (Prv 27:6, Lk 22:47–48). We who in our highest realization embrace and are embraced by the Lord in a loving kiss, in our sinfulness instead may kiss the golden calf (Hos 13:2).

21. Farley's teaching and writing are in conversation with Sartre, who understood personal intimacy within the categories of sadism and masochism, of fixing the other as object or being fixed as object. Farley agrees with Sartre that intimacy can participate in this dynamic of objectification, but does not agree that it must so participate, or that mutuality is not possible when two freedoms encounter one another. So she would reject a Sartrean interpretation of the kiss as enabling personhood only in and through a conflict of freedoms; cf. Margaret Farley, "A Feminist Version of Respect for Persons," *Journal of Feminist Studies in Religion* 9 (1993), 191–93. Leslie Griffin informs me that Farley has taught these lines from Delmore Schwartz, which hold out the possibility of a more mutual kissing: "Kiss me there where pride is glittering. . . . I'll kiss you wherever you think you are poor, / Wherever you shudder, feeling striped or barred": Robert Phillips, ed., *Last and Lost Poems of Delmore Schwartz* (New York: Vanguard Press, 1979), "Two Lyrics from Kilroy's Carnival: A Masque; I. Aria," 7.

22. *The Fathers According to Rabbi Nathan*, trans. Judah Goldin (New Haven, CT: Yale University Press, 1974), 65. See also Bialik and Ravnitzky, *Book of Legends*, 104 §137: "In that instant, the Holy One kissed Moses, and took his soul with that kiss."

23. Steven D. Fraade, "'The Kisses of His Mouth': Intimacy and Intermediacy as Performative Aspects of a Midrash Commentary," in *Textual Reasonings: Jewish Philosophy and Text Study at the End of the Twentieth Century*, ed. Peter Ochs and Nancy Levene, 52–56 (Grand Rapids, MI: Eerdmans, 2002), at 53.

24. Ibid., 55.

25. Joseph B. Soloveitchik, *Halakhic Man* (Philadelphia: Jewish Publication Society of America, 1991), 20–24. See also Robert Cover, "Foreword: Nomos and Narrative," *Harvard Law Review* 4 (1983): 97 (in the Jewish legal tradition, narratives that articulate the meaning of conduct and character—*aggadah*—are integral to rules that govern conduct—*halakhah*; both are necessary to Torah or *nomos*).

26. Dt 30:11–14 (cf. Rom 10:8).

27. Rom 16:16, 1 Cor 16:20, 2 Cor 13:12, 1 Thes 5:26. For discussion of these texts, see L. Edwards Phillips, *The Ritual Kiss in Early Christian Worship* (Cambridge: Grove Books, 1996), 7–13.

28. Perella, *Kiss Sacred and Profane*, 13–19.

29. Phillips, *Ritual Kiss*, 32.

30. Augustine, sermon 42, quoted in Perella, *Kiss Sacred and Profane*, 18.

31. Psalm 118:131, "I opened my mouth and drew in the Spirit," and discussion of patristic uses of this text, in Perella, *Kiss Sacred and Profane*, 45. By the kiss "the breath-spirit of him who kisses is transfused into it [the soul]; just as those who kiss one another are not content with the tasting of their lips but seem to pour their spirits into one another"; Ambrose, *Liber de Isaac et anima*, quoted in Perella, *Kiss Sacred and Profane*, 44.

32. But a brief touching of the lips might have sufficed for purposes of ritual symbolism, while reducing (not eliminating) erotic dangers. "The apostle called the kiss holy. When the kingdom is worthily tested, we dispense the affection of the soul by a chaste and closed mouth," Clement of Alexandria, quoted in Phillips, *Ritual Kiss*, 24.

33. 1 Pt 5:14.

34. 2 Jn 1:6, 1:12; cf. 3 Jn 1:13–14.

35. Like Hebrew *peh*, Greek *stoma* means mouth. John's idiom is close to the LXX of Numbers 12:8.

36. Perhaps John prizes mouth-to-mouth speech because it is more likely than writing to preserve mysteries or conserve a tradition against distorting influence, or because some words of love are so intimate that they are best spoken rather than written, or because it honors the way of Christ (who spoke and preached).

37. Rachel Adler suggests that when a story such as this is read aloud, we can use special techniques of vocalization to express how the story disturbs us and challenges us to engage it with our full critical capacities; see her *Engendering Judaism: An Inclusive Theology and Ethics* (Philadelphia: Jewish Publication Society, 1998), 72.

38. Ambrose, letter 41, in *Select Library of the Nicene and Post-Nicene Fathers of the Christian Church*, ed. Philip Schaff and Henry Wace (2nd series; repr. Edinburgh: T. & T. Clark, 1989), vol. 10, *St. Ambrose: Select Works and Letters*, 448. See also letter 40, ibid., 440–45.

39. Giller, *Reading the Zohar*, 97; Zohar III, 292a–292b (Idra Zuta); Roy A. Rosenberg, *The Anatomy of God* (New York: Ktav Publishing House, 1973), 157.

40. Rosenberg, *Anatomy of God*, 8. Margaret Farley warns that "to use the images of masculinity and femininity to represent the Godhead runs the risk of sealing yet more irrevocably the archetypes of the eternal masculine and the eternal feminine"; Farley, "New Patterns of Relationship," 643. Though yearnings expressed in mysticism for a reunion of the male and the female in God are in one sense aspirations to wholeness, in another sense they are reifications of the very vocabulary of gender difference.

41. Zohar II, 99a (Mishpatim); Isaiah Tishby, ed. and trans., *The Wisdom of the Zohar: An Anthology of Texts* (Oxford: Oxford University Press, 1989), 1:197 (text) and 1:284 (discussion).

42. Moses Maimonides, *The Guide of the Perplexed*, trans. and ed. Shlomo Pines (Chicago: University of Chicago Press, 1963), 1:26.

43. Ex 33:19–20.

44. Maimonides, *Guide,* 1:124–25.

45. Tishby, *Wisdom of the Zohar,* 1:372. As David signifies Malkhut/governance on the male side, so Rachel, Miriam, and Esther on the female side. Id., 288.

46. Cf. William of Saint-Thierry, who desires revelation of the Father "face to face, eye to eye, kiss to kiss: 'Let him kiss me with the kisses of his mouth'"; *Exposition on the Song of Songs,* quoted in Perella, *Kiss Sacred and Profane,* 290n14.

47. Zohar II, 124b (Mishpatim); Sperling and Simon, *Zohar,* 3:348. I am grateful to my student, Mordecai Finley, for teaching me the texts at notes 47–53.

48. Tiferit is Jacob to Shekhinah's Rachel; see notes 8–9, supra.

49. Sperling and Simon, *Zohar,* 3:348.

50. Zohar I, 70a (Noah); Sperling and Simon, *Zohar,* 1:235.

51. Ex 34:29–33 (descending Sinai with the second set of tablets, his face made terrifyingly resplendent by his discourse with God, Moses must veil himself before he can hold discourse with a people who have sinned in idolatry).

52. Zohar II, 146a (Terumah); Sperling and Simon, *Zohar,* 4:14.

53. Ibid., 13–14. "Ten Words": Ten commandments, but also ten words by which the world was created, and ten *sefirot* (divine emanations). "The people *saw* the voices": Maimonides explains that "the Hebrew language substitutes the apprehension made by one sense for that made by the other"; *Guide,* 1:99.

54. "Implicit commandments" can be interpreted in different ways. "Let him kiss me with the kisses of his mouth" might mean that God made the whole universe of legal norms explicit at Sinai (but only to Israel; the other nations would have to work out the details on their own). Bialik and Ravnitzky, *Book of Legends,* 434, §488. Or it may mean that the sages would elaborate the Torah's precepts in a way that would surprise Moses—even though the law developed by the sages was already given to him at Sinai. Ibid., 232, §140.

55. William Blake, "The Marriage of Heaven and Hell," plate 14, in *The Complete Writings of William Blake,* ed. Geoffrey Keynes (London: Oxford University Press, 1966), 154; Psalm 118:9.

56. Maimonides, *Guide,* 2:627–28 (emphasis omitted). "By the mouth of the Lord" is *'al-pi Adonai*; see note 5, supra.

57. Ibid., 628 (emphasis in original). Rabbi Eleazar argued that although Miriam too died by a kiss, the phrase "by the mouth of the Lord" is not

used, "because such an expression would be disrespectful to her, as a pious woman." Michael Fishbane, *The Kiss of God: Spiritual and Mystical Death in Judaism* (Seattle: University of Washington Press, 1994), 18.

58. Rashi's commentary to Numbers 12:1–2, in R. Abraham ben Isaiah and R. Benjamin Sharfman, *The Pentateuch and Rashi's Commentary: A Linear Translation into English (Numbers)* (Brooklyn: S. S. G. R. Publishing Co., 1949), 119–20.

59. Ellen Frankel, *The Five Books of Miriam: A Woman's Commentary on the Torah* (New York: G. P. Putnam's 1996), xx. On a spouse's "right to sexual satisfaction in marriage," see Daniel H. Gordis, "Marriage: Judaism's 'Other' Covenantal Relationship," in Rela M. Geffen, ed. *Celebration and Renewal: Rites of Passage in Judaism*, ed. Rela M. Geffen, 90–131 (Philadelphia: Jewish Publication Society, 1993), at 116–17.

60. *The Fathers According to Rabbi Nathan*, 19. See Exodus 18:2, 19:15; the interpretation of Exodus 3:5 at Zohar III, 180a (Hukkath), Sperling and Simon, *Zohar*, 5:243–44; Rashi's commentary to Numbers 12:4, in *The Pentateuch and Rashi's Commentary*, 120; Maimonides, *Guide*, 2:533.

61. Bialik and Ravnitzky, *Book of Legends*, 59, §12.

62. B. Talmud Soṭah 11b.

63. B. Talmud Soṭah 12a.

64. Farley, *Personal Commitments*, 134–35.

65. Deuteronomy 34:10: the Lord knew Moses face to face (*panim el-panim*; LXX *prosōpon kata prosōpon*). In Genesis 32:30, Jacob says "I have seen (*ra'iti*) God (*elohim*, not the Lord) face to face (*panim el-panim*; LXX *prosōpon pros prosōpon*). The LXX rendition of *peh el-peh* (mouth to mouth) in Numbers 12:8 is *stoma kata stoma*, while the letters of John (2 Jn 1:12, 3 Jn 1:14; see notes 34–36, supra) have *stoma pros stoma*. I am grateful to Bill D'Angelo for annotating the Greek texts.

66. 1 Cor 7:1–7, 10–11.

67. 1 Cor 14.

68. Compare *en ainigmati*, 1 Corinthians 13:12, with *di ainigmatōn*, Numbers 12:8 (LXX).

69. Is 59:21.

70. "The Symbol of Chalcedon," in *The Creeds of Christendom*, ed. Philip Schaff, 6th ed. (Grand Rapids, MI: Baker Book House, 1931), 2:62–63. See also Jaroslav Pelikan, *Christianity and Classical Culture: The Metamorphosis of Natural Theology in the Christian Encounter with Hellenism* (New Haven: Yale University Press, 1993), 239–44. The KJV translates 2 Corinthians 2:10, *en prosōpō Christou*, "in the person of Christ."

71. Perella, *Kiss Sacred and Profane*, 254, 259.

72. See text at notes 27–31, supra.

73. Zohar III, 44b (Ki Tazria'); Moshe Miller, *Zohar: Bereishit I* (Morristown, NJ: Fiftieth Gate Publications, 2000), 177; cf. Sperling and Simon,

Zohar, 5:8. The faces of Moses and Miriam were radiant with knowledge—indeed, Miriam was named Zohar (splendor, radiance) because her face so radiated light. Zohar III, 163a (Shelaḥ Lecha); Sperling and Simon, *Zohar*, 5:235–36; B. Talmud Soṭah 12a. "[A]ll the virtuous women of that generation came to Miriam. Then they all ascend like pillars of smoke in this wilderness. That day is called the day of the marriage celebration. The women on the eves of Sabbaths and festivals all come to Miriam to gain knowledge of the Sovereign of the Universe"; Zohar III, 163a (Shelaḥ Lecha); Sperling and Simon, *Zohar*, 5:236.

74.   2 Jn 1:12, Jn 3:29. Gordis, "Marriage," 112 (sixth and seventh blessings); cf. Jer 33:11.

75.   "From your judgments [your *mishpatim*] I have not turned aside; for you have taught me [*horeitani*, from the root *y-r-h*—the root also of *moreh* (teacher) and of *Torah*]. How sweet to my palate has been your utterance, above honey to my mouth." Ps 119:102–3. Cf. Ex 4:15, Dt 18:18, Is 59:21; and cf. text at notes 31–32, supra.

Part 3

The Meaning and Practice of Love

INTRODUCTION

The essays in this section illustrate how the principles and methods of feminist ethics developed in earlier chapters enrich, modify, and sometimes overturn conventional theological and ethical analyses in particular cases. New Testament scholar Mary Rose D'Angelo examines early Christian treatments of sexual relations between adults and children, asking what can be learned about the impact of such practices on children. D'Angelo shows how relations of social power function to determine the circumstances under which children might become subject to adult sexual advances as well as to maintain patterns of silence and denial which mask victims' suffering. Drawing parallels to the contemporary sex abuse crisis in the American Catholic Church, she argues that reordering the moral power of the tradition requires "a form of distributive justice, an understanding of chastity as a right to physical integrity and autonomy owed by all to every human being, including children." Brian Linnane also addresses the problems of credibility that face Catholic sexual ethics in the aftermath of the clerical abuse crisis. Drawing from feminist criticism of "act" or "form" centered approaches to sexual ethics, he questions interpretations of chastity that characterize moral responsibility solely in terms of abstinence. Rather, he argues, an ethic capable of promoting the successful integration of sexuality will incorporate norms of relational justice, such as consent, mutuality, commitment, equality, and fruitfulness.

Essays by Anne Patrick and Cathleen Kaveny suggest, in different ways, the implications of feminist commitments for reinterpreting traditional concepts such as "vocation," "virtue" and "character." Patrick reflects on public standoffs in the 1980s between Farley's religious community, the Sisters of Mercy, and the Catholic hierarchy over contested issues such as sterilization and abortion. Although there proves no single way to honor mission and identity under crucible conditions, Patrick shows how these religious women refused to individualize or spiritualize their vocations. Their sense of God's call is given expression not in a false or "blind" obedience but in the very act of accepting responsibility to oppose evil and to form structures that respect human dignity.

Kaveny's analysis of a celebrated case in medical ethics involving court-ordered separation of conjoined twins takes seriously feminists' insistence on the moral salience of human experience. Compassion for individuals as moral agents involves, among other things, attending to the way in which the particular roles and relationships that constitute their lives, as well as the institutions within which those roles and relationships are embedded, define the contours of moral obligation. Roles, practices, and institutions that undermine human flourishing, and hence compromise the development and exercise of genuine moral virtue, should be called into question. Not all of the ways we have described the obligations of parents to their children, for example, are conducive to the well-being either of families or children within families. At the same time, our commitments within communities are constitutive of our understanding of human flourishing, even when the choices we are forced to make for their sake are difficult and imperfect.

Chapter Eight

Feminist Ethics and the Sexual Abuse of Children

Reading Christian Origins

Mary Rose D'Angelo

> Contemporary wisdom, such as it is, continues to
> depend on both past wisdom and the exposure of past
> mistakes. . . . [A] focus on human suffering is part of what
> is essential if the interaction between history and ethics is
> to be fruitful for Christian ethics today.[1]

In one of our discussions of the revelations about the sexual use of minors by priests that have played a prominent role in the lives of Roman Catholic communities in the U.S., Canada and Europe, Margaret Farley raised the question of sex with children in the context of Christian origins. Did sex with children play a role in Roman practice? How did it interact with imperial "family values"? Did early Christians reject Roman mores, and value and protect children more consistently than their contemporaries? Do the violations of children that have recently preoccupied the church emerge from ancient practice? Do they contradict the moral insights of early Christianity?

This essay responds with an attempt to reread some aspects of ancient views and practices of sex with children and adolescents. In turning to the past, I am, of course, not attempting to relativize the damage done by sexual abuse of children by contextualizing it in a long history. On the contrary, I seek to examine the use of children in the history of sexuality in the light of the central hermeneutical privilege that Farley awards to human suffering, in particular to:

> the kind of suffering that has the power to uproot life, that can be in itself the equivalent of death, that almost always includes some form of humiliation, some social degradation, that has the potential to attack the self, chaining down thoughts—to become a "state of mind" that persons can live in sometimes 20, 30, 50 years, a lifetime, and in which one's very soul threatens to become its accomplice, pulling to inertia and despair.[2]

The victims who have voiced their pain ten, twenty, and thirty years after being abused by priests whom they and their families trusted confirm that sexual abuse constitutes the kind of suffering Farley describes. They have repeatedly attested to suffering that perdures over, indeed preoccupies, long periods of time, and that attacks the self. Many have voiced the emotional disempowerment and the inability to form mature relationships that resulted from this early exploitation.

Attempting to bring together the current crisis with the moral framework of ancient Christianity is fraught with difficulties on many levels. Not least is the complexity of defining "the problem" in the abuse crisis. For most Catholics, the issue has been at least twofold: the sexual abuse of minors on the part of priests and the abuse of office on the part of the bishops who protected abusers. Further complications have been raised by the distinction between pedophilia and ephebophilia that was a focus of the National Review Board Report.[3] The John Jay Study, using numbers submitted by the dioceses, concluded that 80.9 percent of those reporting abuse were male.[4] This led the National Review Board to the conclusion that it is essential to consider homosexuality in addressing the issue.[5] For some bishops, these aspects of the reports have been a means of redefining "the problem" into two different problems—a very small minority of priests who were technical pedophiles and a much larger group (still, of course, a minority) who are to be explained as homosexuals who prefer young boys. From this perspective, all that is necessary is to eliminate the "bad apples" and to enforce the Church's repudiation of homosexuality. In contrast, for the victims, victim advocates, and a substantial portion of lay Catholics the same issue lies behind the abuse of children under eleven and of adolescents and indeed behind the sexual harassment or rape of non-minors—college students, employees, parishioners. That issue is priests' use of their ecclesiastical status and of the church's moral authority to solicit and coerce sex.

Other difficulties arise when one turns to the ancient texts of Roman, Jewish, and early Christian literature and the remains of imperial art and material culture. Some arise from the limitations of the sources themselves. Voices from antiquity survive sporadically, and those that do survive give evidence about a relatively narrow male elite (even among the rather less elite Jews and Christians), with an egregious lack of interest in the experience of women, slaves, and social subordinates. The visual imagery that survives is also limited in scope. None of this material can be taken to communicate voices of the ancient victims directly; all must be read to some extent against the grain.

Recent scholarly literature has attempted a more sophisticated reading of ancient sexual practice, but presents problems of its own. Its major contribution has been the observation that in antiquity sexual experience was constructed not in terms of a fixed sexual identity based on a preference for one sex or another, but in terms of polarities of activity and passivity in the act of penetration, and of relations of social power. Passivity was always and only suitable for the socially subordinate: women, children, and some subordinate males.[6] Thus the terms "heterosexuality" and "homosexuality" do not apply to but rather obfuscate ancient sexual practice. Yet even studies that fully recognize the problematic character of these concepts still find it nearly impossible to avoid them.[7]

This work has largely been driven by the laudable desire of scholars to reduce "the vehemence of the negative judgment that continues to be made regarding homosexual activity and relationships."[8] Much evidence about same-sex *eros* from antiquity that treats the traditions and practices of pederasty, and the ancient description of the objects of desire as "women and boys," has obscured the age of many of those "women." Combined with the scholarly tendency to refrain from moral condemnation in studying one's sources, these factors have led most scholars to avoid directly engaging the topic of the sexual use of children in Roman antiquity.[9] Rather, texts about pederasty or the "girls" and "boys" who are pleasure or *delicium* to one or another poet are invoked to demonstrate the degree to which ancient sexual desire was not bound by "heterosexual" or "homosexual" preference. While the goal is to undermine the "naturalness" of a heterosexual norm, the pleasure of the text can sometimes seem to justify or even celebrate the ancient model. Thus Cantarella even suggests that the parallel between the approved age at which boys became candidates for erotic pursuit and the legal age of first marriage for girls (twelve) suggests that children of this age were "less childish."[10]

The goal, then, is to reread this material so as to put the children in the center of the investigation, without either ignoring the moral questions about the ancient texts or accommodating the "vehemence of the negative judgment" against contemporary gays and lesbians. I begin with resources from Farley's work. First, as a hermeneutical tool, suffering points to the absence of justice in social arrangements. Justice was also a major concern in antiquity, and then, as now, required attention to what is due to persons. In antiquity, the obligations of justice were defined in accordance with the location of persons on a multilayered and hierarchical continuum. For contemporary ethics, feminist ethics in particular, justice demands a minimal level of equity in the treatment of persons. As the basis of just loves, Farley has proposed two features of persons that create an obligation of respect. The first is autonomy, that is, the capacity to be and to be valued as an end in oneself and not as an instrument of another person, a community, or the human race.[11] Respect for "the autonomy of persons sets a minimum but absolute requirement for the free consent of sexual partners."[12] The second is relationality, that is, the capacity of persons to interact with their world through understanding and desire, to be centered beyond themselves in love. Thus:

Respect for persons together in sexual activity requires mutuality
of participation. . . . A condition for real freedom and a necessary
qualification of mutuality is equality. The equality which is at stake
here is equality of power.[13]

Secondly, in addressing the intersection of history, ethics, and spirituality, Farley juxtaposed Foucault's reading of the theorizations of
sexuality in the ancient world with Catherine McKinnon's critique of
his work.[14] Foucault's influential study delineated sexual desire as produced (rather than repressed) by the sites of social power and so under
constant change and revision.[15] McKinnon charged that by regarding
only the male desiring subject, Foucault elides a substratum of sameness that the "history of sexuality" includes (or perhaps I should say
excludes): the repetition from generation to generation of the abuse
of women.[16] Foucault explicitly acknowledged that the Greek texts
on which he focused gave access only to the subjectivity of elite adult
men.[17] He further remarked upon the ancient division of sexuality
into the alternatives of the (good and bad) love of boys and marriage,
but organized his investigation on that divide rather than calling it into
question. My reading of the ancient materials will attempt to find the
chiaroscuro of suffering on the part of women and children in antiquity. Thus I aim at making women and girls visible, making suffering
visible, and making power visible.

EARLY CHRISTIAN COUNSELS AND
THE CORRUPTION OF CHILDREN

The canonical New Testament makes no explicit references to the
sexual exploitation of children. But two texts of the early second century, contemporary with the later New Testatment texts, prohibit an
apparently sexual vice designated "child-corrupting" (*Didache* 2.2,
Barnabas 19.4, cf. *Barnabas* 10:6–8).[18] The Greek word *pais* can be
translated either "child" or "boy." For this essay I have chosen to use the
generic "child." But the verb "child-corrupt" (*paidophthoreō*) seems to
have been formed as a pejorative revision of *paiderasteuō* or *paiderasteō*,

both of which mean "practice the love of boys, be a lover of boys."[19] The compound word appears almost entirely in Christian texts, and may have originated with early Christians or ancient Jews. The *Testament of Levi*, probably of Jewish origin, uses the noun "child-corrupters" (*paidophthoroi*) in a list of the vices of a wayward generation of priests (17.11). Slightly later Christian apologetic writers also identify the corruption of children as a particularly pagan vice, one that is laid aside in Christianity. Justin accuses the pagans of child-corrupting in the *Dialogue with Trypho* (95.1), and both Tatian (*Ad Graecos* 8.1) and Theophilus (*Ad Autolycum* 1.9) decry Zeus as a child-corrupter for his rape of Ganymede.[20] These Christian texts are explicitly apologetic; Tatian and Theophilus especially seek to convince their readers that Christianity is more consonant with their true ethical values than are the traditional pantheon and practice of the Greek world and the Roman empire.

Examining the context of this neologism offers an avenue into early Christian construal of ancient sexual use of children. In what follows I will briefly describe the conventions of pederasty and the meaning of "corrupt," then look at sexual practice in the immediate context of Christian origins, the Roman imperial period. Turning to the ancient Jewish and early Christian texts that use the word *paidophthoros*, I will argue that ancient Jews and Christians, rather than producing a new and superior morality in their rejection of this pagan practice, read the biblical laws as enshrining and exceeding the moral practices that their Greek-speaking imperial audiences revered. And I will raise the question of whether references to child-corrupting envisage only the sexual exploitation of boys or also are concerned with the sexual exploitation of girls.

PEDERASTY AND CORRUPTION

In pairing pederasty and adultery, and in coining or promoting the parodic neologism *paidophthor-*, the ancient Jewish and Christian writers reflect a change in the valuation of ancient pederasty that can only be understood against its traditions. Pederasty designates a specifically male social arrangement, to some extent a civil institution for citizen men, in classical and fourth-century-BCE Greek cultures. The relative merits of marriage and the love of boys were conventionally debated, but the question was which was the higher or more satisfactory practice of love rather than whether the young man should choose between "homosexuality" and "heterosexuality."

As Foucault points out, the love of boys was a site of moral reflection on the meaning and practice of love.[21] Its roles were fixed—a lover (*erastēs*) pursues a boy (*pais*) as his beloved (*erōmenos*), offering him little gifts, education, military training, and social contacts, seeking in return his friendship and sexual favors. The good lover was thus a teacher of the young, one who engendered his beloved's growth in nobility and manliness, and did not expose him to shame. The boy's role was even more morally freighted. To allow himself to be the passive object of another's pleasure was to forgo dominance for submission, to be unmanned, to take the female role; yielding could threaten his future status in the city. To protect his honor (and therefore the honor of his present and future family), he was required to deny his lover satisfaction, to be impervious to or to dissimulate pleasure in sex, and to yield (if at all) only after long pursuit and to the right love, the noble lover who seeks his good and also will ennoble him in a stable bond of friendship (*philia*).[22] Xenophon and Plato each offer a theory of the good love of boys through the voice of Socrates. Xenophon's Socrates argues that love must be for the soul rather than the body, idealizing the (supposedly) Spartan view that the one who desires the body will never attain the truly good.[23] Plato's innovation, Foucault suggests, was to remove the moral weight from the reciprocal good behavior of the boy and his suitor, laying it instead upon inquiry into the nature of love, the love of truth, and self-mastery in erotic asceticism.[24] In Plato's vision, the lover of boys who goes or is led rightly moves from loving one beautiful body to all beautiful bodies to beautiful customs (in other words, ethics) to beautiful ideas to the knowledge and love of beauty itself—so that the individual beloved becomes, in a sense, a means to be transcended. Plato further complicates the pattern by making the elder Socrates the pursued rather than the pursuer.[25]

In describing the pederastic tradition as morally coded and socially sanctioned, I do not concede that it was benign. The pattern that required pursuit on the part of the older partner and resistance on the part of the beloved, even in the rather idealized version that emerges in the texts, places a heavy onus on the boy's behavior, in a fashion that differs little from the long-standing (and not yet expired) demand that girls and women provide the restraint in sexual pursuit. It created a passage into civic life in which young boys were divided into winners and losers based on their response to the desires of adult men in positions of power. As they grew older, they were schooled into becoming the lover/pursuer.[26]

The pederastic traditions excluded women and contributed to the maintenance of women's inferior status. There is no evidence from the period that a similar pattern of combined pedagogy and courtship existed between girls and women.[27] Rather, for citizen girls the years of adolescence that boys spent in exploring and achieving a civic life were the years of (first) marriage. Young girls were understood to pass under the tutelage of their husbands in order to learn from them how to run their households.[28] In addition, pederastic traditions excluded noncitizens and slaves, both male and female, whose bodies were available to the masters from an early age.

The formulation "child-corrupting" (*paidophthor-*) transforms and parodies the words for pederasty by substituting for *erast-* (loving, desiring) a form of the root *phtheir-*, which means destroy or corrupt, and has multiple referents. In this context "corrupt" refers to the loss of virginity. The Greek verb is frequently used of the rape or seduction of young girls; the first meaning of the noun *phthoreus* is seducer.[29] Similarly it was once common in English to speak of girls who had been raped or seduced as "ruined." "Child-corrupting" is likely to have a double reference to a physical loss of virginity and to mental perversion. This double meaning is suggested already in Plato's *Apology of Socrates*. Socrates repeats Meletus's accusation: "He says that Socrates injures the youth, corrupting them, and that he does not acknowledge the gods whom the city acknowledges, but other new spiritual powers."[30] His defense makes clear that the privileged youths who are Socrates' adherents follow him of their own free will (23c–d), insists that Socrates never claimed to be or was a teacher (33a–b), and points out that neither the men who as youths were his followers nor their families have complained against him (33d–34b). The last point underlines that "corruption" of the sexual integrity and moral allegiance of citizen boys was understood as an injury to their families.

THE ROMAN PERIOD

The classical pederastic traditions reflected in the texts of fifth- and fourth-century Athens belonged largely to the past by the time that the Jewish and Christian texts addressed pederasty. Scholarship on early Christianity had tended to focus upon Judaism and the Greek world as its context, and rightly so. But the Roman domination and conquest of the Mediterranean was well under way by the second century BCE, and was increasingly justified by claims of Roman moral superiority. By the first century CE, Greeks and Jews alike had long been subjects of the empire. The first real emperor, Augustus, who ruled from 31 BCE to 14 CE, conducted a sort of "family values" campaign that focused anxieties upon adultery, lowered birthrates, the mixing of the social orders, and the neglect of the gods. Marginal subjects of the empire, like Jews and Christians, were especially vulnerable to the need to show that their own moral standards met and indeed exceeded the ethical rigor of the Roman law and custom.[31]

The pederastic traditions of Greece are echoed in some Latin literature of the Augustan period. Plutarch and Achilles Tatius, Greek writers of the second century CE, continue the tradition of staging a debate over the relative erotic merits of "boys" on the one hand and marriage on the other.[32] These two writers ultimately opt for the love of women and marriage, but allow love for boys a substantial defense.[33] But, in Foucault's view, the love of boys was no longer a site of serious moral discourse.[34] In part this must be because Roman social mores and legal stipulations prohibited the sexual use of citizen boys. Thus the Roman evidence produces two apparently contradictory pictures: a celebration of a carefree and nearly omnivorous erotic quest on the one hand, and on the other a combination of stringent legislation protecting citizen dependents and moralizing that condemned sexual profligacy.

Roman literature, art, and inscriptions celebrate an erotic quest summarized in the sentiments of this prayer to Priapus, the god of fertility:

Grant me a flowering youth; grant me that I may please good boys and girls with my naughty prick, and that with frequent fun and games I may chase away the worries that harm the soul, and that I may not fear death too much.[35]

Latin love poetry echoes the sentiments of this inscription; the pursuit of "girls" and "boys" figures as a consistent theme. In the Augustan period, Horace's *Odes* and *Satires* fluctuate between moralizing pleas for the emperor to enforce the most stringent of family values and the celebration of his own "passions for a thousand girls, a thousand boys" (*mille puellarum, puerorum mille furores*; *Satires* 2.3.325). In the *Odes,* moralizing laments over the decline of Roman mores are artfully juxtaposed with poem after poem celebrating the pursuit of one girl or boy, then another. In addition, Catullus, Tibullus, Propertius, Virgil, and Lucretius (among others) all wrote poetry that envisage both "boys" and "girls" as the object of love for men; Ovid feels obligated to explain his preference for girls and women.[36] Graffiti and the *Carmina Priapea* likewise assume the sexual availability of both "girls" and "boys."[37] The gap between literature and life is always substantial, and writers of satire are particularly difficult to interpret as witnesses to social mores. But Petronius's *Satyricon* turns on plot of competition between two youths, Encolpius and Ascyltos, over a young boy named Giton. Their names suggest that they are freedpersons. Particularly notable is a scene in which Giton is "married" to a little girl of "not more than seven years" (25) by one Quartilla, who claims not to be able to remember having been a virgin (26).[38] Martial and Juvenal likewise assume that boys as well as girls and women are suitable (or at least widespread) objects of sexual pursuit. Finally erotic art provides representations of sex with boys as well as girls/women, not only on items of extraordinary luxe, like the Warren cup, but also on the more widely produced and used red pottery.[39]

As in English usage, the words for girl and boy in Greek and Latin do not apply to age alone. They could refer to any love object, regardless of age (as "boyfriend" and "girlfriend" often do in English).[40] They were frequently used for slaves and other subordinates, as "boy" and "girl" have been used in American English to refer first to slaves, then to African-Americans, servants, and women employees of any age.[41] In theory then, the love objects described and addressed in lyric and satiric poetry need not have been "boys" or "girls" according to age. But the early age of marriage, the distaste for adult men who continue to submit to sexual penetration, and the often expressed physical loathing for the signs of age in women combine with the legal prohibitions against sex with citizen women and children to suggest that age and subordinate status were very frequently joined markers for objects of erotic quest. Conversely, "boy" or "girl" can be used to relegate the beloved to the appropriately subordinate status of a child.

The age of desirability for boys seems to have been from the very earliest onset of puberty to the coming of a full beard. Williams identifies this period with the beginning and end of adolescence: from the first signs of puberty, which he places at between twelve and fourteen years, to the early twenties.[42] The Warren cup offers two representations of male-male coupling; one of the youths being penetrated appears to represent the beginning, the other the end of this period.[43] One platform of the debates over whether boys or girls/women offer better scope for love was the observation that girls/women remain desirable after boys turn into hairy competitors.[44]

The age at which girls were (first) married was parallel to the age at which boys were desirable. Twelve was the legal age for marriage of girls and ten for betrothal.[45] In elite circles girls tended to be married quite early, sometimes even earlier than the legal age.[46] Augustus's wife Livia had been married for the first time at fourteen; his sister Octavia was married at about the age of fifteen; his daughter Julia was betrothed in her early childhood and finally married at fourteen.[47] In less elevated circles, however, girls seem to have begun to marry in their middle to later teens, with a majority married by the age of twenty.[48] Even so, first marriage seems to have served as the end of childhood for girls, who dedicated their toys to the household gods at the wedding ceremony.[49] Men on the other hand tended to marry after the age of twenty-five, and boys were afforded a long period of social growth and sexual exploration.[50] In the same years, girls were learning to take their (often much older) husbands as their teachers, ideally in modesty and prudent household management.[51]

Williams's estimate places the boundaries of Roman taste for boys well outside the years that current social science identifies as the province of pedophilia (obsession with children under the age of eleven). The texts and plastic representations of erotic scenes with boys seem to me to be rather more ambiguous. The texts do not name specific ages at which a male child is too young to be desirable; they emphasize rather "smoothness" (hairlessness). A number of the plastic representations of young boys could well be younger than twelve, just as there is evidence that some girls were married before the age of twelve. For the Roman period, however, it is the upper boundary that must not be infringed in the love of boys: adulthood, rather than childhood, renders a boy off limits. Seneca the Younger, in a letter propounding the Stoic principles of living according to nature, rails against those who unnaturally prolong the youth of boys to maintain their sexual attraction, asking, "When his sex ought to have rescued him from indignity (*contumeliae*), will not even his age rescue him?"[52]

PROTECTING (SOME OF) THE CHILDREN?

Reading the love poets alone might give the impression that the pursuit of *eros* was without limits or penalties in the late republic and early empire. In fact, both social mores and legal measure sought to draw very clear limits on those who might be pursued. Freeborn Roman citizens, at least those with social power, were off limits.[53]

These limits were grounded in the antithetical concepts *pudicitia* and *stuprum*. *Pudicitia* designated the state of physical integrity and the virtue exercised to maintain and protect it.[54] *Pudicitia* was essential to the status of freeborn Romans: Valerius Maximus's exempla of *pudicitia* from the Roman past are examples of the extreme penalties paid by those who perpetrated or suffered *impudicitia* (*Memorable Words and*

Deeds, 6.1). Conversely, *pudicitia* was denied to slaves, whose persons were at the disposal of their masters, and who had neither status nor *pudicitia* to lose; for freedmen and women, both status and *pudicitia* were compromised. These realities are enshrined in an epigram attributed by the elder Seneca to Haterius in the context of a defense of a freedman charged with being the *concubinus* of his patron: "*in-pudicitia* is a crime in the freeborn, a necessity in a slave, and a duty in a freedman" (*inpudicitia in ingenuo crimen est, in servo necessitas, in liberto officium*). According to Seneca, this *bon mot* became the origin of double meaning for the words duty and dutiful (*officium, officiosus*) inspiring jokes like "you do me no duty" and "he returns a lot of duty to him."[55]

Craig Williams's study of the concept of *stuprum* defines it as "violating of the sexual integrity of freeborn Romans of either sex."[56] His description of its function is helpful: "the concept of *stuprum* served to idealize the inviolability of the Roman bloodline, to maintain the distinction between free and slave and to support the proprietary claims of the paterfamilias or the head of the household."[57]

The laws that criminalized certain forms of sexual behavior cannot be perfectly recovered. The first of them was the *Lex Scantinia,* whose exact date and provisions are disputed. It seems to have been a product of the republic, in force by the earlier part of the second century BCE. The contexts in which this law is invoked suggest that it at least criminalized *stuprum cum puero,* sex with a freeborn boy, and submission to penetration on the part of a freeborn male.[58] Allied with the *Lex Scantinia* and apparently also originating in the second century, was a praetorian edict called *de pudicitia ademptata* that protected freeborn women, girls, and boys not merely from violation but from pursuit in the public street.[59]

Moral legislation was part of the campaign for public and marital morality launched by Augustus, and it was seen by his supporters as a central justification for the title *pater patriae,* a title he finally accepted in 2 BCE.[60] The *Lex Iulia de adulteriis coercendiis* in 18 BCE produced Augustus as the defender of marriage and of husbands against adultery. But it also penalized *stuprum,* certainly *stuprum* with an unmarried girl or a woman, perhaps also with a boy.[61] A second Julian law penalized the unmarried and childless and rewarded childbearing, but with careful attention to the maintenance of social rank. These laws were constantly reinvoked and adjusted by later emperors, who like Augustus were probably more concerned to reassert and display their devotion to Roman values than to remedy specific ills. In the same vein, the emperor Domitian seems to have prohibited the castration of freeborn boys and the prostitution of freeborn boys in brothels. The poems of Martial that praise Domitian for these laws offer pathetic images of the prostituted child and his miserable mother (*Epigrams* 9.5, 7) and refer to the emperor as *Ausonius pater* (9.7.6) and "father of the world, chaste prince" *(parens orbis, pudice princeps;* 9.5.1).

What was at stake in these laws was status. As has frequently been remarked, the axis on which sexual experience was understood was that of activity to passivity, and the determinant was penetration. The loss of status that came from "corruption" or the suspicion of corruption were differently constructed for freeborn boys on the one hand and freeborn girls and women on the other. For girls, the rights of both their *paterfamilias* and of their husbands or future husbands were infringed when they were subjected to sex. For boys, what was threatened was their future status as rulers of other men. Dio Chrysostom, a philosophical preacher of the later first and early second century, explains the desire for pederasty as resulting from getting away with adulterous desire for other men's wives and daughters. If adultery and seduction become too easy, he warns, the perpetrators will "cross over into the men's quarters, lusting to humiliate those who will soon be rulers, judges and generals, so as to find there some difficult and recherché form of pleasure."[62] Sexual use was seen as reducing boys or men to female status, and charges of boyhood sexual compliance constituted an important resource for political invective.[63]

One might argue that Dio Chrysostom's complaint that those who want sex with males seek "to humiliate those who will soon be rulers, judges and generals" manifests a concern for the ability of children to develop autonomy. Indeed, a form of autonomy for the moral subject might be said to have been the absolute goal of Stoicism. Philosophers of the first two centuries of the common era were increasingly focused upon what Foucault calls the "care of the self." The influence of Stoicism in the Roman period increased both suspicions of emotions and pleasure and the importance of nature as a criterion, or perhaps an arbiter, of morality. Musonius Rufus (middle to late first century), limits sexual expression to procreative sex within marriage (*Diatribes,* 12.64.1–4), excluding both adultery and sex with males as against nature (12.64.6–10). Musonius goes so far as to declare that sex with his unmarried woman slave is as shameful in a man as sex with her male slave is generally considered shameful to a woman owner (12.66.6–10). The idea of limiting sex in this way was not entirely new: the Athenian participant proposes similar mores for the ideal city in Plato's *Laws.* Plato derives his proposals from the dictates of nature, which tell against "sowing" in ground that cannot bear fruit or will bear fruit to another (*Laws,* 838d–842b). For Musonius, these strictures guard against the softening, weakening demands of pleasure and luxury (12.63–64).[64] In the same period, medical opinion became suspicious of sex as a toll on health; doctors advised the limitation of sex and provided prophylactic regimens to prevent and remedy the expenditure it was understood to entail.[65]

The laws, social mores, and most philosophical reflections envisaged the goal of autonomy for a limited few—elite, freeborn boys. Girls, women, slaves both male and female, and all lesser orders were to learn submission rather than autonomy. Moral autonomy was possible for them, but it was to be achieved and practiced within the social boundaries allotted to them.[66]

TEXTS OF TERROR

The ancient texts rarely if ever give the reader any idea how the ancient child/adolescent victim experienced sex. The voice of lyric poetry is that of the pursuing lover; the beloved, whether girl or boy, talks back only in his imagination or memory.[67] Perhaps there is a clue in Ovid's claim that he prefers women because, unlike boys, women also get pleasure from sex.[68] But it is not clear that this comment reflects the actual experience of young boys (or, for that matter, of women, including twelve- and fourteen-year-old brides). It is at least partially formed by the literary conventions of pederasty, which required that the lover pursue and the beloved withdraw and deny.[69]

Perhaps a better—or rather worse—insight into the experience of the victims emerges in the following brief and equally literary excerpt. Tibullus depicts Priapus giving advice to the pursuer of boys that is no doubt shaped by this convention:

> The boy will be gentle with you—then you will be able to steal some lovely kisses. He will fight back, but he will give them to you when you seize them. At first he will give them to you when you seize them, but then he will on his own offer them to you when you ask, and finally he might even want to cling to your neck.[70]

The "kisses" to be stolen are probably euphemistic, suggesting further thefts.[71] Considered from the perspective of a resistant child, Priapus's counsel constitutes a kind of text of terror, advising its addressee to dismiss the boy's fear, repulsion, and pain with an assumption that "no" means "yes." Boys and girls subjected to this level of aggression were likely to have been slaves and other social subordinates, and to have been pressed into sexual service from a very young age. For a young slave boy or girl or the prostituted child, food, shelter and survival depended upon the willingness to comply, indeed to please the molester.[72]

The fearsome and painful aspects of early sex must also have been a feature of marriage for young girls, even the freeborn and elite. Plutarch's *Marital Maxims* opens with a subtle reference to this problem of early marriage, counseling that the groom should be patient with the bride's first quarrels, and that the wife not be put off by the pain of first intercourse, lest "having submitted to the sting she miss the sweetness that follows."[73]

Sexual violence emerges also in the pleasure of the sexual threat. Graffiti record a wide range of phallic boasting.[74] So do the *Carmina Priapea,* a set of diverse and anonymous poems celebrating Priapus, the Roman god of fertility. Always depicted with an oversized and erect penis, Priapus guarded gardens by threatening potential thieves with his bared weapon. Many of the poems are written in his voice: "I warn you, boy, you will be screwed; girl, you will be fucked; a third penalty awaits the bearded thief."[75] Sexual threats against both men and women also play a major role in the *Epigrams* of Martial, and they celebrate the pleasures of violence in the erotic quest:

> Kisses I reject save those I have ravished from reluctance, and your anger pleases me more than your face: so I often beat you, Diadumenus, to make myself solicit you often. I achieve this: you neither fear nor love me.[76]

Alongside these traces of erotic violence, Martial's verses manifest a favored trope of erotic poetry: the reversal in which the male adult freeborn lover complains of the cruelty and arbitrary domination of the beloved boy or girl and of his own abjection.[77] Both the reversal of dominance and erotic violence are also characteristic of poetry that celebrates the pursuit of girls. Evidence of violence against wives is less explicit but does exist, though it is accompanied by evidence of moral disapprobation.[78]

In sum then, the sexual use of children and adolescents in the Roman empire exhibited some conspicuous ambiguities. Celebration of the erotic quest and a kind of phallic jousting were central motifs of literature, art, and graffiti, while legal measures and social censure drew a line around the children and wives of the freeborn, at least the elite. Slaves, freedpersons, clients, and the declassé were more or less free game. The voices of the philosophical moralists focused on the self-control and cultivation of the elite, whose moral excellence guaranteed the Roman right to rule.

An inscription of the first century BCE articulates the purity stipulations given by Zeus for those who wished to enter a domestic sanctuary in Philadelphia. Among them were sexual requirements that also characterized the Judaism of the period (see below) and would be formative for Christianity:

> A man [is not to take] another woman in addition to his own wife, either a free woman or a slave who has a husband, nor is he to corrupt (*phtherein*) either a child [boy] or a virgin, nor is he to counsel

another [to do so], but if he should witness anyone [doing this] he must not hide it or keep silent about it. . . . A free woman is to be pure and is not to know bed or intercourse with any other man save her own [husband]. If she does know, she shall not be pure [as before] but is defiled and full of corruption within her family [i.e., she has corrupted her family line] and is unworthy to worship.[79]

Can it be said that ancient emphasis on marital morality acknowledged the debt of respect for the autonomy and relationality that Farley marks as constitutive of human persons? In fact, the Stoic ethical goals of self-rule and freedom from passion (*apatheia*) might be read as a concern for autonomy, and even slaves and women were credited with the ability to attain them within the constrictions of their social roles. And the concern to protect the prerogative of the patriarchal family might be seen as a form of concern for relationality. But a social debt of respect for autonomy was owed only to those whose right and obligation to rule the world required that they become self-ruling. Women, slaves, and other inferiors were obligated rather to learn the limits of their autonomy and relationality within the complex web of submission and domination that structured their world.

ANCIENT JEWISH STRICTURES ON THE SEXUAL EXPLOITATION OF CHILDREN

The early Christian condemnation of "child-corrupting" in part builds on earlier Jewish apologetic and polemic against or appeal to the Roman imperial order. Ancient Jewish texts seem to treat sex with boys/children as a pagan vice. On the whole, modern interpreters have read these texts as demonstrating that rejection of homosexuality or of sex between men was particularly the concern of Jewish and then Christian writers.[80] But a more careful examination of the texts suggests a different picture. First, ancient Jewish apologists actually claim that Jews practice (though more stringently) the same sexual morality that Roman mores acknowledge, and that the Roman rulers violate.[81] Second, although the texts do condemn male to male intercourse, they are frequently concerned with the exploitation of boys or children.

The most overt hostility to the Roman order appears in the *Sibylline Oracles*. In the second century BCE, the *Third Sibylline Oracle* depicted male-male intercourse and the exploitation of boys (or children) in brothels as the immediate consequence of the Roman imperial conquests.[82] By contrast, marital chastity and abstention from sex with male children are characteristic of the Jews as a people.[83] But it is worth noting that this stigmatization of the Romans as prone to sex with boys appears in this Jewish text in the period when Romans express their own anxieties about sex with boys in the *Lex Scantinia*. The particular emphasis on brothels may reflect the recognition that Jewish children were at risk of becoming spoils of war. Again in the early second century CE, in the wake of the first Jewish War and perhaps also the revolts of 117–18, the *Fifth Sibylline Oracle* inveighs against sex with boys or children as particularly Roman (lines 166, 387) and complains that the Romans have made (female) prostitutes of those who were once pure.[84] Similarly, when *Testament of Levi* (17.11) castigates certain priests as child-corrupters, the accusation is preceded with the charges of being idolaters and adulterers.

A less polemical tone appears in the magisterial serenity of the *Sentences of Pseudo-Phocylides*. Apparently the work of an Alexandrian Jew of the late first century BCE or early first century CE, this didactic poem presents itself as the moral counsels of a sixth-century-BCE Greek poet.[85] Thus, like the Sybils, Phocylides was a figure of the Greek world; the Jewish authors who used their voices were deliberately invoking cultural norms of Greece.[86] The text also shows its concern with the imperial morality enshrined in Augustus's *Leges Iuliae*. The moralist insists that beautiful children are a trial to parents. They must take care not to let a boy child grow long hair, and to guard him against the many who "are mad for intercourse with a male." Similarly, a virgin must be locked up in the house to keep her safe.[87] Here the moral concerns of the Jewish author are represented as entirely harmonious with those of the Greek-speaking *paterfamilias* of the imperial period.

Philo, a philosophical interpreter of Judaism of the first half of the first century CE, was also a spokesman for the Jews of Alexandria to the emperors and their servants.[88] His interpretation of the Mosaic laws categorizes pederasty among sexual sins. He describes the stringency of the law in *Hypothetica*, the most explicitly apologetic of his works:

> if you engage in pederasty (*paiderastēis*), if you commit adultery, if you rape a child—do not mention a male child, but even a female—likewise if you prostitute yourself, if also you submit to (*pathēis*) something beyond the age—or think of it, or intend it— the penalty is death.[89]

Although Philo treats the severity of the law as extraordinary and unique to Judaism, he expects the Greek-speaking Roman reader to approve this severity, to see it as evidence of the moral superiority of Judaism. This of course assumes that the reader will also see the specific prescriptions against sexual transgressions as laudable; thus Philo almost certainly expects the reader to share his disapprobation of pederasty as well as adultery and rape. The actual sexual prohibitions of the Hebrew Bible are of adultery (Ex 20:14, Dt 5:18), lying with a male as with a woman (Lv 18:22, 20:13), and rape of a virgin (Dt 22:23–29, cf. Ex 22:16–17). Philo has rearticulated them in contemporary terms that make clear that Jews are forbidden by their ancestral piety those things that transgress the imperial laws and mores: pederasty, raping a boy, and "submitting to something beyond the age" as violating the provisions of the *Lex Scantinia*, and adultery and rape of a girl as violations of *Lex Iulia*.

In the less polemical context of *On the Decalogue*, Philo explains all the sexual sins as subsumed under the commandment against adultery in the "ten words," which he treats as summaries of the special laws. He seems to distinguish corrupters and pederasts, while treating them as parallel criminals; perhaps the first refers specifically to men who seduce or rape (commit *stuprum* with) young unmarried girls.[90]

Reflection on the damaging nature of the sexual exploitation of the young appears in Philo's *On the Contemplative Life*.[91] In describing the Essene banquets, Philo contrasts them with those of Xenophon and Plato, whose discourses were concerned with *eros*, not only with "the desires that tithe to nature, but also those of men for males differing from them only in age" (*On the Contemplative Life*, 59). Whereas Plato's Aristophanes classes the love of boys as more manly, Philo sees it as infecting young boys with the "feminizing disease" rather than instructing them in manliness, and damaging lover as well as beloved: "having wrought havoc with the years of boyhood and reduced the boy to the grade and condition of a girl besieged by a lover it inflicts damage on the lovers also in three most essential respects, their bodies, their souls and their property" (60–61).

The idea that the beloved boy becomes "a girl besieged by a lover"[92] evokes the advice Tibullus's Priapus gives to the pursuer of boys: that pursuit and coercion will turn the resistant beloved boy compliant, indeed ardent. When he claims that pederasty infects boys with the female disease, Philo probably envisions something like the process by which the coerced boy learns to like the "kisses."[93] But he spares little concern for the fear, pain, and confusion the pursuit brings. More serious, in his view, is the injury visited upon the public good when the elite do not reproduce (62). And his concern for the status of the boys reinforces the inferior and subordinate status of women and girls.

Despite the strongly apologetic tone of most of these references, the appearance of pederasty in Philo's interpretation of the decalogue suggests that these sexual sins are not entirely confined to Gentiles, and that Jews also must guard against such temptations. There in fact is evidence that the erotic attraction of boys was not so unheard of in Jewish contexts. The *War Scroll* from Qumran, probably from the end of the first century BCE or the beginning of the first century CE excludes women and boys from eschatological camps.[94] The context shows that the issue is one of the purity of the warriors. The implication is either a youth or a woman might inspire lust and therefore cause the fighters to have sex (or at least to ejaculate) and render themselves impure.[95] The castigation of the wayward priests as child-corrupters in *Testament of Levi* 17.11 likewise shows that Jews could be suspected of sex with children by other Jews (or perhaps Christians).[96] At a later date, a Mishnaic ruling prohibits unmarried men (and all women) from teaching children.[97]

The Jewish texts, then, do not so much introduce a new moral stricture against homosexuality as marshal the ambiguities of Greek pederastic tradition, Roman social practice and strictures, and philosophical reflection into a condemnation of Roman rule. They do so in order to claim the moral high ground for the law of Moses as offering a firmer basis for the good order of the patriarchal family and the society it grounds. It may be that the condemnation of corrupting children in Jewish texts acquires a special poignancy from Jewish vulnerability: because Jewish children had been enslaved and prostituted and continued to be at risk, Jews were more deeply conscious that the sexual use of boys destroyed their autonomy and that the sexual use of girls alienated their submission from its appropriate goal.

EARLY CHRISTIANS

As I mentioned above, the prohibition of "child-corrupting" appears in apologetic contexts in the very early years of Christianity, in part as a stigmatization of Roman imperial mores. In the two earliest texts it appears in the instruction of the "two ways," among commandments that delineate the choice Christians have made or should make. One version of the two ways opens the *Teaching (Didache) of the Twelve Apostles*, while another closes the *Letter of Barnabas*.[98] In describing the "way of life" *Didache* allots the prohibition to "the second commandment of the teaching," which begins with a summary of the laws that appear in and are derived from the second half of the decalogue.[99] The commandment "you shall not commit adultery" is extended with the commands "you shall not child-corrupt, you shall not fornicate."[100] While the *Didache* is unlikely to be directly dependent on Philo's interpretation, the text probably reflects the traditions of Jewish apologetic interpretation. References to corrupting children in 2.2 and to corrupters of God's formation in 5.2 are usually interpreted as referring to abortion.[101]

The letter to Barnabas also refers to "child-corrupting" in its version of the two ways: "you shall not fornicate, you shall not commit adultery, you shall not corrupt children" (19.4). The context does not suggest that these commandments are an interpretation of the decalogue. Earlier in the text, Barnabas interprets Moses's prohibitions of eating certain unclean animals as allegorical prohibitions of child-corruption, adultery, and fellatio. The prohibited animals include the hyena (not actually proscribed in the biblical codes) as well as the hare and weasel. Barnabas's zoological explanations are less than fully intelligible, as well as bizarre.[102]

The cryptic character of these references makes them difficult to interpret beyond pointing to the continuities with the Jewish texts discussed above.[103] It is certainly the case that they envisage a prohibition of pederasty—that is, of sexual use of citizen boys. It may be that the term *paidophthor-* combines for these early Christian authors what Philo distinguishes: "corruption" of young girls and pederasty—in Roman terms, *stuprum* with either a boy or a girl.

CLEMENT OF ALEXANDRIA

At the turn of the second to third century, the prohibition against child-corrupting surfaces in the sophisticated and ambitious work of Clement of Alexandria. Like the earlier apologists, he identifies the prohibition with the laws of Moses that distinguish Christians from pagans[104] and good Christians from bad (that is, antinomian heretics).[105]

More helpfully, Clement also integrates the prohibition into a developing Christian code in his *Paidagōgos*, a manual of Christian morals and manners written to mold an emerging Christian elite.[106] Its title, which has been translated as the *Instructor* or *Christ the Educator,* evokes the image of a household slave whose role it was to oversee the young child, supervising clothing, manners, and behavior, and guiding and protecting the child outside the house, for instance on the way to and from school.[107] The opening of the *Paidagōgos* presents Christ as trainer in morals to all Christians, who in relation to God and Christ are children—men and women, wise and simple.

Clement's premise that virtue is the same for women and for men might have offered the grounds to challenge the gendered arrangements of his world. Only in this world do men and women marry and only in this world is female distinguished from male (*Paidagōgos,* 1.4.10.3, citing Luke 20:34). Even in the present, Clement asserts, "all those who have put off fleshly desires are equal and spiritual (*pneu-matikoi*) before the Lord" (1.6.31.2), citing Galatians 3:28 as a testimony.[108] The names "human being" (*anthrōpos*) and child (*paidarion*) are common to both men and women (1.4.10.3, 11.1).

Despite this opening acknowledgement of equality, the *Paidagōgos* is a profoundly "this worldly" text, focused upon discipline of desire, and especially of sexuality, and covering everything from true belief through table manners and footwear. The arrangements of gender are central to the discussion throughout, so that while the addressee is conceived as male, women must be given specialized counsel about clothing, ornament, and so forth (see, for example, 2.10.111–12.129). Clement consistently attempts to harmonize Biblical directives and examples with citations of and references to the philosophical tradition and the poets, especially Homer and the tragedians. Plato in particular is invoked throughout, and presented as the philosopher who learned from Moses—but the *Symposium* plays no role in Clement's discussion of *eros* and sexual union.

Clement turns to the question of sexual union in book 2, chapter 10, described by Foucault as "the first great Christian text devoted to sexual practice in married life."[109] Clement begins from the restriction of sexual union to married partners, explaining, "[t]he goal and end (*telos*) of the married is childbearing and being well supplied with children" (83.1). Using an agricultural metaphor he derives in part from Plato, he warns against sowing on rocky soil.[110] He follows Barnabas in interpreting the Biblical proscriptions of eating hare or hyena (supposedly) as metaphoric proscriptions of pederasty and adultery respectively (83.4–5).[111] These animals are proscribed lest eating them contaminate the Christian with their sexual voraciousness.

The threefold sexual prohibition "you shall not fornicate, you shall not commit adultery, you shall not corrupt a child" (*Barnabas* 19.4) Clement attributes to Moses, speaking "no longer under a figure but with head unveiled" (89.1).[112] Presumably Clement understands the prohibition to be a completion of the explicit command against adultery in the decalogue rather than to be derived from the food laws. These prescriptions, he insists, must be kept. Violating them constitutes *hubris;* this is shown by Plato's image of the chariot, in which the lower part of the soul is represented by an unruly horse, which the philosopher names *Hubristes*.[113] The burning of Sodom is made a warning of the punishment of (generic) lust by fire (89.3). "It is necessary to consider children as sons and women (wives?) not one's own as daughters, and essential to conquer the pleasures of the belly and rule over those below the belly" (90.1). This sentence is particularly informative. The first clause suggests that, although he calls attention to the inclusive meaning of *pais/paidarion*, Clement thinks primarily in terms of boys. At the same time it illustrates the subordinate status of all women: whether they are unmarried young girls or wives of other men, they are to receive the protective regard that a virgin daughter would receive. Thus for Clement one paramount concern is protection of the status of the family, particularly the father and the husband. The second clause illustrates that his second concern is the self-control of the adult male Christian and head of household. The rest of the discussion in chapter ten weighs heavily on that concern. It is based on the conviction that although marriage is to be esteemed, sexual intercourse within marriage is justified only for the purpose of procreation (95.3, 98.2); mere pleasure sought even in marriage is both unjust and against reason (92.2).[114] Clement adopts the claim that "sexual intercourse benefits in no way, except that it harms the beloved" (98.2), but he does not elaborate on the harm done to the beloved, whose gender is ambiguous.[115] Far more attention is devoted to the claim that "everyone who sins acts unjustly, not so much against his neighbor, if he commits adultery, but against himself, because he has become an adulterer" (100.1).[116]

Clement's ability to rethink the moral life in baptismal terms is limited. In regard to sexual mores, obligations remain the same as they are for the imperial gentleman and the Stoic moralist: to preserve and foster familial good order, and to rule over himself. In stigmatizing the decadence of imperial society, Clement expresses pity for slave boys displayed by the traders as sexual wares (3.3.21.1) and horror that men who visit brothels may have sex with a son or daughter they exposed in the past (3.3.22.5). But concern for the autonomy and relationality of the slaves or sex workers plays no role in his arguments for limiting sex to procreation within marriage.

As Foucault noted, Clement stands at the beginning of a long history of Christian reflection and prescription on sexuality. But the premises from which that reflection began are already clear in the *Paidagōgos*. The mastery of the self against the weakening effect of pleasure, limitation of procreative sex as the standard of nature, and the protection of the patriarchal family are central issues. The social order and moral imperatives protect the autonomy of elite men and foster the autonomy of elite boys. Women, girls, and lesser men and boys are put in a double bind in that they are expected to maintain moral autonomy while the subordinate status required of them deprives them of the power to protect their physical integrity. This pattern provided few resources for change in the Christianization of the social order.

IN CONCLUSION

As this schematic overview has shown, while it is possible to keep the children of antiquity at the center of an investigation, it is not possible to put them at the center of the ancients texts. They are not there. The ancient texts, like most contemporary writing, centers on its source: the desires of powerful adults, in antiquity nearly all of them male. Is it still possible to offer "lessons from history" for moral approaches to the current crisis? Is it possible either to draw wisdom from antiquity or to use its deficits as correctives for the concerns of the present? Some aspects of this history are suggestive.

First, the very absence of the children is significant, pointing to a version of the sameness, the continuous and repetitive features of abuse that McKinnon underlined. Both the erotic literature of antiquity and the self-justifications of the abusive priests exhibit denial or elision of the pain, reluctance or confusion of the young boy or girl who is the object of *eros*, and attribute to the victim the role of tyrant or aggressor.[117] The complete silence of ancient victims and the long silences of more recent ones attests to the success of this technique.

At the same time, Foucault's recognition of the difference of ancient constructions of sexual experience deserves attention. This insight has helped to undermine the reification of the modern categories heterosexual and homosexual, alerting readers of ancient texts to the operation of power in the production of both homoeroticism and erotic relations with the opposite sex. It also offers an important alternative to explanations of the crisis that suggest that the crisis has been primarily caused by homosexual priests pursuing minors, and that compulsory celibacy has made the priesthood particularly attractive to homosexuals.[118] The reverse should also be considered: that the current structures of priesthood might not only attract those with homoerotic desires but also valorize boys as objects of desire and so produce homoerotic desire. The simplest and probably most important of these structures is access. The desire to control sexuality and promote chastity has fostered a policy of segregating children by sex, especially to segregate teenage boys from girls in schools and youth groups, and this policy has given priests limited access to teenage girls but virtually unlimited access to boys.

Access is complicated by the intersection of structures of power and gender. Priests function in a literally patriarchal structure continuous with the arrangements of antiquity to a degree that is encountered in few other settings: power is held by a limited number of privileged males (called, as in the Roman structure, fathers) over women, children, and other males. Especially in seminaries and schools, they associate largely with other priests and have been encouraged to see an ontological distance between themselves and other Christians, particularly women, whose exclusion from the priesthood has been increasingly treated as a theological and ontological necessity. In part in the interest of enforcing this exclusion, recent papal and Vatican theologizing has insisted on gender complementarity to a degree that approaches a doctrine of two distinct human natures and is based in the ancient construction of sexuality along an axis of "activity" and "passivity," disguised in recent years as "receptivity."[119] These factors taken together make boys of higher status in the ecclesiastical order than girls, and therefore perhaps also more desirable as sex objects. At the same time, it should be remembered that the difference in numbers is known only through reporting. The very same factors that elevate the status of boys in the system constantly remind girls and women of their lower value to the hierarchy, making them less willing to report.

Vatican pronouncements on sexuality and on women make clear the enduring character of the ancient paradigm. Here too sexual experience is constructed on an axis of activity to passivity. Activity is defined by penetration and identified with masculinity, and sex counts only when penetration takes place. The persistence of this construction is sometimes recognized in "Mediterranean," Latin, or African cultures, which can be defined as more primitive or less critical than "ours."[120] But I would argue that it is far more pervasive. The "ancient" and "modern" constructions exist side by side, interacting in ways that intensify the potential for violence and abuse. This potential emerges, for instance, in assaults in which the male aggressor uses rape to stigmatize the male victim as gay, while distancing himself from any lack of masculinity.[121] In less violent manifestations, it eroticizes imbalances of power. Thus those "inequities in social and economic status, age and maturity, professional identity, etc.," that "render sexual relations inappropriate and unethical" become central determinants of the erotic not only in ancient poetry but in contemporary liquor ads.[122] They further contribute to misogyny by its disparate valuing of male "activity" and female "passivity."

The collaboration of ancient and modern constructions of sexuality also emerges in the theologizing of gender that appears in the host of church documents and theological writings that reassert the identification of maleness with activity and initiative and femaleness with receptivity. Male and female "natures," defined by their relation to the act of penetration and ejaculation, are used to justify the rejection of women from ministerial priesthood, of "artificial" contraception, and of gay marriage. Homosexuality is "disordered" in light of these definitions. Thirty years ago, Farley described the ways that rigid concepts of activity and receptivity allied respectively with maleness and femaleness enable unjust and inequitable gender roles.[123]

This problematic anthropology is coupled with inadequacies of moral resources that have marked the Christian (and Western) tradition from its beginning. For too long, moral theology has focused on a chastity defined by sexual abstinence whose goal is to produce individual self-mastery and to protect the rights of the family and its head to the fertility of its female members. This focus has left a substantial majority in every generation in the bind of the vulnerable of antiquity: women, children, and subordinated men have been made morally responsible for their own physical integrity, while the power to protect it is withheld from them. It will not be enough simply to reiterate the demand for celibacy on the part of priests, whether straight or gay, and to focus on protecting children solely or primarily through restricting their activities and the knowledge about sexual matters.

What is required to reorder the moral power of the tradition is a form of distributive justice, an understanding of chastity as a right to physical integrity and autonomy owed by all to every human being, including children. Recentering moral thought in the church will require foregoing a wide variety of disorders that have marked the development of sexual mores in the West: promoting self-mastery as inherently good, denigrating desire and pleasure as inherently bad, defining gender in terms of activity and passivity, using "spousal imagery" to reinscribe the inequities of ancient forms of marriage, limiting chastity to abstinence, innocence to ignorance, and sexuality to reproduction. Rethinking and rearticulating anthropology and moral theology so as to promote the autonomy and relationality central to the being and well-being of every human person, adult or child, will not be easy for some sectors of the church. It demands much energy and honesty, and a willingness to listen before pronouncing. But the benefits of this level of reordering will be major. First and foremost, it will provide the moral impetus to fully endorse sex education for children, including education on protecting themselves from contact they do not desire and from infection through sexual contact.

Margaret Farley's work offers the deep grounding in tradition and reflection that can enable the reordering that is so badly needed.[124] In the context of the HIV/AIDS crisis, perhaps truly the greatest moral crisis that now faces the church and the world, she has articulated the norms of truly compassionate respect for persons, one that acknowledges the needs and potential of a humanity that need not be defined differently for men and women, straight and gay, child and adult. They can also speak to the real, though lesser crisis created by the hierarchy's years of tolerance of child abuse, serving as a description of what is needed now to address the realities of the victims of the past and the children of the present and future:

the maximization of autonomy insofar as possible, the protection of bodily integrity in some significant sense, the provision of knowledge and competent care, fidelity to commitments, honor to personal stories and deeply human hopes.[125]

NOTES

1. Margaret A. Farley "History, Spirituality, and Justice," *Theology Digest* 45, no. 4 (1998): 331.

2. Farley, "History, Spirituality and Justice," 334.

3. *A Report on the Crisis in the Catholic Church in the United States Prepared by the National Review Board for the Protection of Children and Young People* (Washington, DC: United States Conference of Catholic Bishops, 2004).

4. *The Nature and Scope of the Sexual Abuse of Minors by Catholic Priests and Deacons in the United States: A Research Study Conducted by John Jay College of Criminal Justice* (Washington DC: United States Conference of Catholic Bishops, 2004), 69.

5. *Report on the Crisis,* 8, 25.

6. See Michel Foucault, *History of Sexuality,* 3 vols., trans. Robert Hurley (New York: Random House, 1978), 2:215–20; John J. Winkler, *The Constraints of Desire: The Anthropology of Sex and Gender in Ancient Greece* (New York: Routledge, 1992), esp. 17–23; Eva Cantarella, *Bisexuality in the Ancient World,* trans. Cormac Ó Cuilleanáin (New Haven, CT: Yale University Press, 1992) viii; Marti Nissinen, *Homoeroticism in the Biblical World,* trans. Kirsi Stjerna (Minneapolis: Augsburg Fortress, 1998); Craig A. Williams, *Roman Homosexuality: Ideologies of Masculinity in Classical Antiquity* (New York: Oxford University Press, 1999); Mary Rose D'Angelo, "Perfect Fear Casteth Out Love: Reading, Citing and Rape," in *Sexual Diversity and Catholicism,* ed. Patricia Beattie Jung, 175–97 (Collegeville, MN: Liturgical Press, 2001).

7. On the problematic character of these concepts, see Williams *Roman Homosexuality,* esp. 4–8, who yet uses them, as does Cantarella; *Bisexuality,* throughout.

8. Margaret A. Farley, "Response to James Hannigan and Charles Curran," in *Sexual Orientation and Human Rights in American Religious Discourse,*

ed. Saul Olyan and Martha Nussbaum (New York: Oxford University Press, 1998), 102.

9. Two important articles that do directly engage the topic have appeared since this essay was substantially finished. They are Christian Laes, "Desperately Different: Delicia Children in the Roman Household," in *Early Christian Families in Context: An Interdisciplinary Dialogue*, ed. David L. Balch and Carolyn Osiek, 298–324 (Grand Rapids, MI: William B. Eerdmans, 2003); and John Pollini, "Slave-Boys for Sexual and Religious Service: Images of Pleasure and Devotion," in *Flavian Rome: Culture, Image, Text,* ed. A. J. Boyle and W. J. Dominik, 149–66 (Leiden: Brill, 2003).

10. Cantarella, *Bisexuality,* 40.

11. Margaret Farley, "A Feminist Version of Respect for Persons," *Journal of Feminist Studies in Religion* 9 (1993): 183–98; *Compassionate Respect: A Feminist Approach to Medical Ethics and Other Questions* (New York: Paulist Press, 2002), 32–39.

12. Margaret Farley, "An Ethic for Same-Sex Relations," in *A Challenge to Love: Gay and Lesbian Catholics in the Church,* ed. Robert Nugent (New York: Crossroad, 1983), 101.

13. Ibid., 102.

14. Farley, "History, Spirituality and Justice," 330–31.

15. Foucault, *History of Sexuality,* 1:81–102.

16. Catherine A. McKinnon, *A Feminist Theory of the State* (Cambridge, MA: Harvard University Press, 1988), 126–54.

17. Foucault, *History of Sexuality,* 2:22–23.

18. Frederick William Danker translates "to engage in same-sex activity with a young male, *commit sodomy*"; *A Greek-English Lexicon of the New Testament and Other Early Christian Literature,* 3rd ed. (Chicago: University of Chicago Press, 2000), 750. All translations are my own unless otherwise acknowledged. References to classical and early Christian works use the numbering systems from the standard editions.

19. So Kurt Niederwimmer, *The Didache: A Commentary,* trans. Linda M. Mahoney, ed. Harold W. Attridge, Hermeneia (Minneapolis: Fortress, 1998), 89n7.

20. See also *Clementine Homilies* (Edinburgh: T. & T. Clark, 1870), 4.16.

21. Foucault, *History of Sexuality,* 2:187–254.

22. See Foucault 's account of the conventions of pederastic love in *History of Sexuality,* 2:234–35; here he relies largely on Xenophon's *Symposium*. Cantarella offers a much wider treatment of texts, and addresses the scholarly debate about the status of pederasty and the question of whether it permitted consummation; see *Bisexuality,* 17–44.

23. Xenophon, *Symposium* 8.12–43, esp. 32.

24. See Foucault's treatment of Plato's *Symposium* in *History of Sexuality,* 2:232–46.

25. Plato, *Symposium* 211c, 210d–e.

26. Cantarella marshals a collection of citations that suggest psychic difficulty in this transition; *Bisexuality*, 36–39.

27. The work of Sappho (7th/6th c. BCE) has sometimes been read as deriving from such a context, but if this reading is accurate, it derives from a much earlier period.

28. See, e.g., Isomachus's description of his education of his not-yet-fifteen-year-old bride in Xenophon's *Oikonomikos*, 7.4–9.1.

29. See Henry George Liddell and Robert Scott, *A Greek-English Lexicon*, rev. Sir Henry Stuart Jones and Roderick McKenzie, 9th ed. (Oxford: Clarendon Press, 1996), s.v. *phtheirō*, 3b; see, for example, Philo, *Special Law*, 3.65–70, 4 Macc 18:8.

30. Plato, *Apology*, 24b. The accusations as reported by Xenophon and by Diogenes Laertius's citation of the *antomosia* are essentially the same; see John Burnet's note on 24b in *Plato's Euthyphro, Apology and Crito* (Oxford: Clarendon, 1924), 101–2.

31. See further on this, Mary Rose D'Angelo, "Early Christian Sexual Politics and Roman Imperial Family Values: Rereading Christ and Culture," in *Papers of the Henry Luce III Fellows in Theology*, vol. 6, ed. Christopher I. Wilkins, 23–48 (Pittsburgh: Association of Theological Schools, 2003).

32. Plutarch, *Amatorius, Moralia* 750–67e; Achilles Tatius, *Leucippe and Cleitophon* 2.35–38. Cantarella also looks at the debate in the *Greek Anthology* (*Bisexuality*, 73–74) and the later dialogue of Pseudo-Lucian called *Amores* (*Bisexuality*, 74–77).

33. Cantarella describes the debate, focusing heavily on the significantly later (third–fourth c.) *Dialogue on Love* attributed to Lucian; Foucault discusses the Plutarch text in detail; *History of Sexuality*, 3:189–97.

34. Foucault, *History of Sexuality*, 3:189–92.

35. ... [D]*a mihi floridam iuventam, / da mihi ut pueris et ut puellis / fascino placeam bonis procaci / lusibus frequentibus iocisque / dissipem curas animo nocentes / nec gravem timeam nimis senectam*; citation and translation from Williams, *Roman Homosexuality*, 22.

36. This material has been surveyed by Cantarella, *Bisexuality*, 120–41, and is cited throughout Williams, *Roman Homosexuality*.

37. Cantarella, *Bisexuality*, 145–54; Williams, *Roman Homosexuality*, 20–22, 198–99.

38. Trimalchio also recounts his early career as the beloved of his former master (Petronius, *Satyricon*, 75).

39. John R. Clarke, *Looking at Lovemaking: Constructions of Sexuality in Roman Art 100 B.C.–A.D. 250* (Berkeley: University of California Press, 1998), 188, 341n163, plates 1 and 2, and figures 7–8 and 25–27.

40. Williams (*Roman Homosexuality*, 188) points to Apuleius's identification of the *puellae* of the great lyricists with Roman matrons; *Apology* 10

identifies Catullus's Lesbia as Clodia, Propertius's Cynthia as Hostia, and Tibullus's Delia as Plania. But it should be remembered that the identification comes nearly two hundred years after the poems were written, and the possibility of excavating real women from the *scriptae puellae* is dubious. See Maria Wyke, *The Roman Mistress: Ancient and Modern Representations* (Oxford: Oxford University Press, 2002),18–45, on the difficulties of constructing a Cynthia from the work of Propertius.

41. The jurist Paulus makes "slave" the first meaning of *puer,* distinction of male from female the second, and the *aestas puerilis* only the third; *Digest* 50.16.204 (Paulus 2 *Epitomarum Alfeni*).

42. He suggests that the ceremonial *depositio barbi,* shaving and burning of the first beard, be seen as a sort of definitive close to this period; Williams, *Roman Homosexuality,* 19–28, 72–77.

43. Clarke, *Looking at Lovemaking,* plates 2 and 1, respectively.

44. See on this Cantarella, *Bisexuality,* 74–75.

45. Susan Treggiari, *Roman Marriage: Iusti Coniuges From the Time of Cicero to the Time of Ulpian* (Oxford: Clarendon, 1991), 39–43.

46. Legal sources speak of girls who are married when "not yet capable of a man" (*non* or *nondum viripotens*) designating them as betrothed (*sponsa*) rather than wife; Treggiari, *Roman Marriage,* 41.

47. Susan E. Wood, *Imperial Women: A Study in Public Images, 40 B.C.– A.D. 68* (Leiden: Brill, 1999), 30–31, 35.

48. Richard P. Saller, *Patriarchy, Property, and Death in the Roman Family,* Cambridge Studies in Population Economy and Society in Past Times 25 (Cambridge: Cambridge University Press, 1994), 25–41; Bruce W. Frier, "Roman Demography" in *Life, Death, and Entertainment in the Roman Empire,* ed. D. S. Potter and D.J. Mattingly, 85–109 (Ann Arbor: University of Michigan Press, 1999), 90–94.

49. Treggiari, *Roman Marriage,* 180.

50. Saller, *Patriarchy,* esp. 37–40. See also Aline Rouselle's description of these years in *Porneia: On Desire and the Body in Antiquity,* trans. Felicia Pheasant (Oxford: Basil Blackwell, 1988), 59–61.

51. On the husband as teacher, see Plutarch, *Conjugalia Praecepta* 48, *Moralia* 145C.

52. Seneca the Younger, *Letter* 122; trans. Williams, *Roman Homosexuality,* 238; I find "indignity" less forceful than the *contumeliae.* See also Williams, *Roman Homosexuality,* 83–86, on *exoleti.*

53. Williams, *Roman Homosexuality,* 18–47; Cantarella, *Bisexuality,* 101–6.

54. So also Williams, *Roman Homosexuality,* 97–101.

55. The Latin reads, *non facis mihi officium; multum ille huic in officiis versatur.* Seneca, *Controversies* 4, *Preface* 10.

56. Williams, *Roman Homosexuality*, 96.

57. Ibid., 97.

58. See the discussions in Cantarella, *Bisexuality*, 106–14, and Williams, *Roman Homosexuality*, 119–24.

59. "[I]f anyone shall be said to have removed the attendant of a *materfamilias*, a boy in the *toga praetextata*, or a girl in the *toga praetextata*, or to have accosted or followed him or her against good mores [he shall be liable to punishment]." The citation is from Williams, *Roman Homosexuality*, 121; I have retranslated to make the details slightly more explicit. See further discussions in Cantarella, *Bisexuality*, 115–19.

60. See on this Mary Rose D'Angelo, "*Eusebeia*: Roman Imperial Family Values and the Sexual Politics of 4 Maccabees and the Pastorals," *Biblical Interpretation* 11 (2003): 139–65.

61. Discussions in Cantarella, *Bisexuality*, 110–14; Williams, *Roman Homosexuality*, 119–24.

62. *Discourses* 7.151–52.

63. Catharine Edwards, *The Politics of Immorality in Ancient Rome* (Cambridge: Cambridge University Press, 1993), 63–97.

64. See also Williams's discussion of Seneca the Younger and Musonius Rufus, *Roman Homosexuality*, 234–42, and Foucault, *History of Sexuality*, 3:168–74.

65. Rousselle, *Porneia*, 11–20.

66. This does not mean that women or "inferior" males were never able to attain any measure of independence. Women who survived a first marriage and who owned property or had professional qualifications might well be able to act on their own behalf to either remain single or contract a second marriage, and even slaves could under some circumstance pursue freedom. See Tregiarri, *Roman Marriage*, 135 on the ability of women to initiate second marriages; on the potential and barriers to manumission see Keith R. Bradley, *Slaves and Masters in the Roman Empire: A Study in Social Control* (New York: Oxford University Press, 1987), 80–112.

67. See, e.g., Plato's claim that the desire of the boy is similar to that of the lover but weaker, and his description of the awakening of that desire in *Phaedrus* 255e–265c.

68. Ovid, *Art of Love* 2.683–84; Cantarella, *Bisexuality*, 138–39, connects the claim to Ovid's treatment of Tiresias (*Metamorphoses*, 3.316–38). Thomas Habinek has suggested that Ovid invented heterosexuality; see "The Invention of Sexuality in the World-City of Rome," in *The Roman Cultural Revolution*, ed. Thomas Habinek and Alessandro Schiesaro, 23–43 (Cambridge: Cambridge University Press, 1997).

69. For Ovid's expressions of preference for women, see Cantarella, *Bisexuality*, 138–41, and Williams, *Roman Homosexuality*, 8.

70. *Tunc tibi mitis erit, rapias tum cara licebit / oscula: Pugnabit, sed tibi rapta dabit / rapta dabit primo, post adferet ipse roganti / post etiam collo se implicuisse velit*; Tibullus, *Elegies*, 1.4.53–56.

71. Williams, *Roman Homosexuality*, 186.

72. On sexual use of slaves, see Bradley, *Slaves and Masters*, 116–21; Jennifer A. Glancy, *Slavery in Early Christianity* (New York: Oxford University Press, 2002), 21–24.

73. Plutarch, *Conjugalia Praecepta* or *Advice to Bride and Groom* 2; *Moralia* 138E. See also *Moralia* 48 where the picture of husband as teacher of the wife also responds to the age differential that is usual in elite Roman marriages.

74. See, e.g., Cantarella, *Bisexuality*, 147–49; Williams, *Roman Homosexuality*, 19–21.

75. *Percidere, puer, moneo, futuere puella / barbatum furem tertia poena manet, Carmina priapea* 13. The translation is from Williams, *Roman Homosexuality*, 21; see the passages cited there and on 87, and in Cantarella, *Bisexuality*, 145–46, and Williams's discussion of Roman celebration of the phallus, 86–95.

76. Martial, *Epigrams* 5.46, translation cited from Cantarella, *Bisexuality*, 149.

77. For descriptions of the reversal in elegy that contextualize it in regard to the genre and writing practices of elegy, see Wyke, *Roman Mistress*, 33–35, 166–91; Ellen Greene, *The Erotics of Domination: Male Desire and the Mistress in Latin Love Poetry* (Baltimore: Johns Hopkins University Press, 1998); Kathleen McCarthy, "*Servitium Amoris: Amor Servitii*," in *Women and Slaves in Greco-Roman Culture: Differential Equations*, ed. Sandra R. Joshel and Sheila Murnaghan, 172–92 (London: Routledge, 1998).

78. Patricia Clark, "Women, Slaves and the Hierarchies of Domestic Violence: The Family of St. Augustine," in Joshel and Murnaghan, *Women and Slaves*, 109–29, esp. 117–22.

79. Wilhelm Dittenberger, *Sylloge inscriptionum Graecorum*, vol. 3 (Hildesheim: Olms, 1960; orig. pub. 1898–1901), no. 885, lines 25–31 and 35–39, pages 117–18; trans. Frederick W. Grant, *Hellenistic Religions: The Age of Syncretism* (New York: Liberal Arts Press 1953), 29.

80. Cantarella concludes that the eventual proscription of homoerotic behavior in the late empire derives from the Hebrew Bible and is an enforcement of Christian mores (*Bisexuality*, 191–210).

81. John J. Collins, *Between Athens and Jerusalem: Jewish Identity in the Hellenistic Diaspora*, 2nd ed., Biblical Resource Series (Grand Rapids, MI: Eerdmans, 2000), takes particular note of Jewish condemnation of homosexuality, but points out that the Jewish texts can be seen as joining a Greek debate (esp. at 159).

82.   "But those men / will have a great fall when they launch on a course of unjust haughtiness / Immediately compulsion to impiety will come upon these men. / Male will have intercourse with male and they will set up boys (children) / in houses of ill-fame," lines 182–87, trans. John J. Collins, in *Old Testament Pseudapigrapha,* vol. 1, ed. James H. Charlesworth (Garden City, NY: Doubleday, 1983), 366.

83.   "Greatly, surpassing all men, / they are mindful of holy wedlock, / and they do not engage in impious intercourse with male children / as do Phoenicians, Egyptians, and Romans / spacious Greece and all Asia, transgressing / the holy law of immortal God which they transgressed"; lines 594–600, ibid., 375. Cf. lines 762–66.

84.   It should be noted, however that this oracle also accuses the Romans of matricide, various forms of incest, and bestiality.

85.   For the date, see Pieter Willem van der Horst, *The Sentences of Pseudo-Phocylides: With Introduction and Commentary* (Leiden: E.J. Brill, 1978), 81–83.

86.   On the pseudonym, see ibid., 58–63.

87.   Ibid., 213–17.

88.   See his description of his ambassadorial role in *Legation to Gaius,* and the interpretation of Maren Niehoff, who regards his politics as pro-Roman; *Philo on Jewish Identity and Culture.* Texte und Studien zum antiken Judentum 86 (Tübingen: Mohr Siebeck, 2001).

89.   The *Hypothetica* 7.1 is drawn from Eusebius's lengthy citations in his Preparation of the Gospel, 8.7.1.

90.   "The first summary of the other [pentad] is the one against adulterers, under which are subsumed a plethora of prescriptions: against corrupters (*phtoreis*), against pederasts, against those who live dissolutely and engage in lawless and unbridled practices and unions" (Philo, *On the Decalogue,* 168).

91.   Philo, *On the Contemplative Life,* trans. W. H. Colson, vol. 9, Loeb Classical Library (Cambridge, MA: Harvard University Press, 1941), 149.

92.   The Greek is *tēs erōmenēs.* Colson's translation, "a girl besieged by her lover," extrapolates slightly but does an excellent job of making Philo's emphases explicit.

93.   See Diana M. Swancutt, "'The Disease of Effemination': The Charge of Effeminacy and the Verdict of God (Romans 1:18–2:16)," in *New Testament Masculinites,* ed. Stephen Moore and Janice Capel Andersen, Semeia Studies, 193–234 (Atlanta: Society of Biblical Literature, 2003).

94.   For the date, see Philip Davies, "War of the Sons of Light against the Sons of Darkness," *Encyclopedia of the Dead Sea Scrolls,* ed. Lawrence Schiffman and James Vanderkam (Oxford: Oxford University Press, 2000), 2:965–68 (66–67).

95. *War Scroll*, 1Q33 (=4Q496), col. 7, 3–4.

96. Some portions of *Testament of the Twelve Patriarchs* appear to have undergone Christian redaction.

97. *Kiddushin* 4.13.

98. A Latin version appears to be either a translation of the two-ways portion of the *Didache* or of its source. See the stemma and comments in Niederwimmer, *Didache*, 40.

99. On the relation to the decalogue and the order of the commandments, see ibid., 88–91.

100. *You shall not kill* (Ex 20:14, Dt 5:18), *you shall not commit adultery* (Ex 20:13, Dt 5:17), you shall not corrupt a child (*paidophthoreseis*), you shall not fornicate, *you shall not steal* (Ex 20:15, Dt 5:19), you shall not practice magic, you shall not make potions, you shall not kill an offspring (*teknon*) by corruption (*phthora*, old Latin "by abortion"), nor slay what is begotten/born, *you shall not lust for your neighbor's belongings* (Ex 20:17, Dt 5:21), you shall not forswear, *you shall not bear false witness* (Ex 20:16, Dt 5:20). Similarly the commandment against adultery is expanded in Matthew by prohibitions of the lustful gaze and of divorce (Mt 5:27–32).

101. For 2.2, see Niederwimmer, *Didache*, note 81; in 5.2 "the way of death" enumerates vices and evil-doers, including, toward the end of the list, "killers of children, corrupters of God's formation (*plasmatos*)." *Plasma* might refer to the creation of the first (and every) human being (Gn 2:7) or of animals (Gn 2:19). Niederwimmer translates: "child murderers, who destroy what God has formed, who turn away from the needy person" (*Didache*, 115), and follows the old Latin in referring the phrase to abortion, pointing out that the phrase pairs abortion and infanticide as 2.2 seems to do; *Didache*, 117–18. But the word group to which "corrupt" and "corruption" belong has a wide range of meaning. "Corrupter of God's formation" is ambiguous: adultery, seduction, and castration are all possible referents for this phrase, and all, from the perspective of ancient Judaism and Christianity, pervert and destroy creation.

102. A very literal translation of *Barnabas* 10.6–8 reads:

> But also, "you shall not eat the hairy-foot" why? Do not be, he says, a child-corrupter, or be made like such as these. Because the hare each year multiplies the offcasting. As many years as it lives, so many holes it has. But "neither shall you eat the hyena." Do not be an adulterer or a child-corrupter, or be made like these. In what regard? Because that animal year-by-year changes its nature and is sometimes male and sometimes female. But he also rightly hated (shunned?) the weasel. Do not be such a one, of which we hear that they do wickedness with the mouth on account of uncleanness, nor

cleave to unclean women who do wickedness with the mouth. For this animal conceives through the mouth.

The problems arise with the hare. The word I translated off-casting can mean either privy or excrement, and the word I translated holes can mean burrow, anus, intestine (among other things).

103. The "two ways" is an important genre of biblical and ancient Jewish wisdom texts, and the two versions in the *Didache* and *Barnabas* may have had a Jewish origin. See Niederwimmer, *Didache,* 35–42.

104. Clement's *Protreptic to the Greeks* 10.108.1 reads, "If you enroll yourself, heaven will be your native country, God your lawgiver. What are the laws? 'You shall not kill, you shall not commit adultery, you shall not child-corrupt, you shall not steal, you shall not bear false witness, you shall love the Lord your God.'"

105. Clement's *Stromateis* 3.4.36.5 reads, "Besides, if your aim is to undo the lawgiver's commandments, why on earth do you aim to undo by your immorality 'you shall not commit adultery' and 'you shall not corrupt boys' and all that bears on self-control?"; trans. John Ferguson, *Clement of Alexandria Stromateis* 1–3, The Fathers of the Church 85 (Washington, DC: Catholic University of America Press, 1991), 277–78; 276n114 identifies the opponents with the Severians through Epiphanius, *Panarion* 45.2.

106. On Clement's audience, see Simon P. Wood, *Christ the Educator;* Fathers of the Church 23 (Washington, DC: Catholic University of America Press, 1954), ix.

107. The former by William Wilson in *The Writings of Clement of Alexandria,* vol. 1 of *The Ante-Nicene Fathers* (Edinburgh: T. & T. Clark, 1867), 111–346, the latter in Wood, *Christ the Educator.* For the meanings of *paidagōgos,* see Liddell and Scott, *Greek-English Lexicon,* 1236.

108. Clement is rejecting a distinction between the simple (*psychikoi*) and the enlightened (*gnōstikoi*) rather than between male and female in the context of making the claim that Christ is the teacher of all, and all children before him.

109. Foucault, *History of Sexuality,* 2:126.

110. See Plato, *Laws* (838e, 841).

111. His explanations actually seem more appropriate for the reverse (85–88).

112. The order of the discussion suggests that Clement depends on the *Letter of Barnabas* (his rather different explanation of the prohibition of eating hare probably attests to the use of other interpreters as well—or it may simply be his inventive dealing with the cryptic character of Barnabas's reading).

113. Clement, *Paidagōgos,* 89.2; cf. Plato, *Phaedrus* 238a, 254c–e.

114. Strong verbal correspondences suggest that Clement is directly dependent on Musonius's *Diatribe,* 12.64.3–4 in this passage.

115. "Beloved" here translates *agapēton,* a two-termination adjective that can be either masculine or feminine. The dictum is attributed to Epicurus. See Wood, Christ the Educator, 175n34.

116. This sentence appears to be a revision of Musonius Rufus's conclusion that one who has sex with a prostitute is culpable even though he does not commit adultery because although he does not injure a neighbor, he injures himself (*Diatribe,* 12.65.6–10).

117. The claim that the child is the seducer is a frequent theme in the priests' accounts of sexual abuse; see, e.g., Maurice Grammond's disclaimer of responsibility on the grounds that children would "throw themselves" at him, reported in "Oregon Archdiocese Files for Bankruptcy," *New York Times,* July 7, 2004, A12.

118. Donald Cozzens makes a sophisticated argument that the priesthood and seminaries are attracting a large percentage of gays; see his *Sacred Silence: Denial and the Crisis in the Church* (Collegeville, MN: Liturgical Press, 2004, 89–139.

119. See Susan Ross, "The Bridegroom and the Bride: The Theological Anthropology of John Paul II and Its Relation to the Bible and Homosexuality," in *Sexual Diversity and Catholicism: Toward the Development of Moral Theology,* ed. Patricia Beattie Jung with Joseph Andrew Coray, 39–59 (Collegeville, MN: Liturgical Press 2001).

120. Cantarella, *Bisexuality,* 117.

121. This was apparently the case in the murder of Matthew Shepard. For another account from a rape victim see John Andrew Murphy, "Hate and Homosexual Rape," *Common Sense* 13, no. 2 (1998): 1, 5; cited in D'Angelo, "Perfect Fear Casteth out Love," 175–76.

122. Farley, "An Ethic for Same-Sex Relations," 102.

123. Margaret Farley, "New Patterns of Relationship: Beginnings of a Moral Revolution," *Theological Studies* 36 (1975): 627–46, esp. 33–40; see also her "Sources of Sexual Inequality in the History of Christian Thought," *Journal of Religion* 56 (1976): 162–76.

124. Since this essay was completed, Farley's work in sexual ethics has been made more readily accessible in her *Just Love: A Framework for Christian Sexual Ethics* (New York: Continuum, 2006).

125. Farley, *Compassionate Respect,* 123.

Chapter Nine

The Sexual Abuse Scandal in the Catholic Church

Implications for Sexual Ethics

Brian F. Linnane, S.J.

THE DIMENSIONS OF THE SCANDAL

During the early years of the twenty-first century, the Roman Catholic Church in the United States has faced what is arguably the gravest crisis in its history. This crisis was sparked by the sexual abuse of children by members of the clergy, and specifically by the criminal trial in early 2002 of John Geoghan, a laicized priest of the Archdiocese of Boston. Attention to the misconduct of Roman Catholic priests by the criminal and civil courts—and so by the media—was by no means a novel event in 2002. There had been a series of well-publicized accounts of priest pedophilia and ephebophilia in Louisiana, Texas, and Massachusetts dating back to the mid-1980s. What was different about the Geoghan case was the unprecedented access to archdiocesan records that the courts allowed prosecutors. These records indicated that officials of the Archdiocese of Boston had repeatedly acted to protect abusive priests and to discount the harmful experiences of the survivors of this abuse. They did so by continuing to reassign priests credibly accused of the sexual abuse of minors to new parishes after minimal treatment and without adequate supervision.[1] The pattern that emerged from these documents was one of avoidance and cover-up aimed at preventing scandal and preserving the good name of the Catholic Church.

The public reaction to this flood of information on the archdiocese's response to allegations of the sexual abuse of minors by priests provoked the outrage and scandal that the cover-up was designed to avoid. Both attendance at Sunday Mass and contributions to the Catholic Church plummeted. As harmful as the actual crimes and cover-ups were, the response of the church authorities to the unfolding crisis was equally troubling for many persons. In Boston, where many were hoping for some acknowledgement of wrongdoing and compassion for survivors, the archdiocesan officials tended to respond in hostile or defensive fashion that appeared to be influenced more by liability concerns than pastoral considerations. That the spiritual leaders of the Catholic Church in Boston could seem to be relatively indifferent to and defensive about the crimes committed by some priests against vulnerable young persons while expressing compassion and concern for those who committed these crimes deepened the scandal affecting the church.[2]

ISSUES FOR CATHOLIC SEXUAL ETHICS

To refer to the crisis in the Catholic Church that is the result of sexual abuse of minors by some members of the clergy as a scandal is, of course, to invoke a particular, technical understanding of what has transpired in the early years of the twenty-first century. To call this crisis a scandal does not refer to negative or embarrassing publicity or only to the many shocking and disgraceful elements that have been revealed as the story of this abuse crisis has unfolded. Scandal used in this context refers to "an attitude or behavior which leads another to do evil";[3] it has, as Margaret Farley has suggested, a morally negative sense, "in that it 'offends' in a way that raises an obstacle to faith or that leads someone else to sin."[4] While Farley's own work on the Catholic Church as a source of scandal to the faithful does not directly address the sexual abuse crisis, it does demonstrate the ways in which the public pronouncements of those in positions of authority within the Church can undermine its prophetic witness in the public arena and so be an obstacle to maintaining and sustaining Christian identity. This is particularly significant for understanding the scandalous effects of the present crisis because the cover-up of the abuse by diocesan authorities and the official response to the unfolding crisis had a far greater negative impact on believers than the actual abuse itself. The sexual abuse crisis can be understood as a scandal insofar as it has undermined the faith and trust of many Catholics in the Church and in its leaders as sources of moral and spiritual insight. With regard to questions and concerns about sexual morality, this paper will argue that the moral vacuum created by the crisis is acute. The issue is not that Catholics and others will necessarily become more sinful (although this cannot be discounted), but rather that because of this scandal they may lack the effective moral guidance necessary to avoid harmful or destructive choices in the area of sexuality. There is a need, then, for a renewed and morally compelling Catholic sexual ethic. Such a renewed ethic will be effective insofar as it draws on both the rich traditions of Catholic morality and the lived experience of contemporary persons. This essay will suggest that some essential elements for this ethic can be found in the work of Margaret Farley.

That there were a relatively small number of priests who exploited their positions of trust to sexually violate the vulnerable and the young was bad enough, but it was, in some sense, comprehensible. Every dimension of western society has been affected by such violations: the family, the classroom, youth organizations, and the like. Thus while these violations are in themselves intolerable, it is not unduly surprising that a small number of religious professionals would be guilty of such abuse.[5] For many persons, the real source of scandal was the evidence that suggested that bishops and their associates systematically failed to protect the vulnerable, protected the abusers, and resisted attempts to begin a dialogue on issues of reform in the life of the Catholic Church. Similarly, a tendency to shift blame for the crisis to dissenting theologians, deficient moral theology, homosexual priests, or the decadence of contemporary society while resisting analyses of the roles of the clerical culture, hierarchical authority, and a patriarchal sexual ethic tended to reinforce views that perceived the response of Church leaders to the scandal as disingenuous or, worse, mean-spirited. Andrew Sullivan speaks for many when he writes, "How can it [the institutional Church] have ever been so blithe about the sexual abuse of children and minors? How could it have covered it up? How could it have compounded the hurt by scapegoating good gay priests for the crimes of others?"[6]

It is well known that the laity's acceptance of and adherence to official Catholic teaching on sexual ethics has declined dramatically in the decades following the close of the Second Vatican Council (1962–1965). Many commentators have linked this decline in the authority of Catholic sexual teaching to the widespread theological dissent and general nonreception of the affirmation of the traditional ban on artificial birth control in the encyclical *Humanae Vitae* (1968). Those who teach Catholic morality to undergraduates are aware of their frequent assertion that the Church's teaching on sexual morality is seriously "out of date," (even while they fail to establish why prevailing sexual norms in western society would be an improvement). The present scandal—rooted as it is in sexual misconduct and the perceived indifference to it on the part of Church authorities—has surely served to increase the gap between official teaching and its reception by the faithful. To quote Andrew Sullivan once more, "it's fair to say that very few people in my generation of 40-year-olds and younger can take the church's sexual teaching seriously again. When so many church leaders cannot treat even the raping of children as a serious offense, how can we trust them to tell us what to believe about the more esoteric questions of contraception, homosexuality, or divorce."[7] The issue that Sullivan and others point to is the diminished credibility of an abstinence-based sexual ethic.

To refer to Catholic sexual ethics as abstinence-based is to point to a long-standing suspicion about human sexuality in the Christian tradition and the ancient preference for celibacy that many argue continues to inform contemporary Catholic ethics. While this suspicion about human sexuality reflects legitimate concern for the genuine harm that disordered sexual passion can inflict on persons and communities, it also can be understood as interpreting sexuality negatively, as problematic and shameful in itself. Mark Jordan's analysis of Christian texts from the patristic, medieval, and Reformation periods and their implications for contemporary Christian ethical discourse on human sexuality leads him to claim that while there is a place for sexual activity in Christian marriage, "it is both small and temporary. Wife and Husband are meant to become Mother and Father, and perhaps Sister and Brother."[8] In other words, sexual desire finds legitimate expression in a procreative marital union in which sexual partners quickly become parents with the hope of eventually transcending the need for sexual intimacy.

In light of this, many would argue that the deepest impulses in the Christian tradition with regard to human sexuality are to limit, channel, and contain it. Whatever appeal such an ethic and its rationale may have had for contemporary persons has been further undermined by the sexual abuse crisis. If we accept that Catholic sexual morality is abstinence-based, it would seem that the celibate clergy would be the "gold standard" of this ethic. The sexual abuse scandal, then, brought unprecedented attention to the sexual behavior of Catholic priests. Most persons were, of course, shocked by the gross sexual misconduct of religious persons publicly committed to celibacy and by the tolerant and forgiving attitudes of bishops when they became aware of these behaviors. This in turn raised questions about the role of the discipline of clerical celibacy in generating the crisis and about the numbers of priests sexually active with adults.[9] That so many Catholic priests, who are believed to be called and sustained in a divinely ordained vocation, are unsuccessful in achieving sexual continence suggests that an ethic that places such a strong emphasis on sexual continence may no longer be fully adequate to contemporary understandings of the human sexuality and personhood. That so much of the official response to the sexual abuse crisis argues for greater fidelity to traditional articulations of Catholic sexual morality and indeed blames the crisis on a general failure to adhere to Catholic moral teaching in its fullness suggests a profound impasse between many members of the faithful and the Church's leadership.[10] As the experience of many committed Catholics leads them to question the viability of an abstinence-based sexual ethic, Church leaders are working to reinforce its authority. The unwillingness of Church authorities to engage in dialogue on matters of sexual morality or other areas perceived to be in need of reform, and the tendency of those authorities to discipline or marginalize those persons or groups calling for such dialogue, has become for many a source of scandal.

ABSTINENCE IN CATHOLIC SEXUAL ETHICS

To refer to Roman Catholic sexual ethics as abstinence-based is not entirely accurate or fair to the tradition's self-description. This moral tradition does not present itself as negative toward sexuality and the body. It has always viewed human sexuality as a gift from God ordered toward the human good. While it is the case that the tradition has understood human sexuality to be affected by the disorder of original sin, it is also the case that the tradition sees that every dimension of the human condition has been so affected. Thus sexual expression is not proscribed in itself; rather it is limited to contexts understood as particularly appropriate. In this sense, it can be described as a chastity-based ethic. Yet there is reason to wonder if regulation and abstinence is not at the heart of the rhetoric of chastity as Mark Jordan has suggested. In the Roman Catholic perspective, the concept of chastity means "the successful integration of sexuality within the person"[11] and suggests that persons must seek to develop their affectivity and sexuality in a manner appropriate to their particular vocations or states of life. It is, in this sense, a virtue that promotes human growth and freedom in personal relationships, or what James Keenan has referred to as a "functionary virtue."[12] In addition to the integrative function of chastity, Keenan also argues that this virtue, as it is employed in Catholic moral teaching, also serves a more regulatory function in its promotion of abstinence. Insofar as this regulatory function dominates pastoral teaching and popular perception, the Catholic ethic of sexuality can be construed as abstinence-based.

This regulatory function operates, Keenan suggests, in both a narrow and broad way; narrowly in that it proscribes any marital sexual relations that are not open to procreation, and broadly by forbidding any intimate sexual expressions outside of heterosexual marriage. While Keenan emphasizes the great value of Christian chastity in that it "promotes a considerable Christian realism about the challenges of sexuality in the modern world,"[13] his essay also reflects a particular tension between the implications of Christian chastity for homosexual persons and current theological and ethical reflection on same-sex attraction. This tension has important implications for the argument we have been making about the declining effectiveness of Catholic sexual teaching in the wake of the clerical sex abuse crisis.

Keenan notes that while there are "theologians and pastors who contend that homosexual tendencies must have some *in se* moral legitimacy," chastity in the Catholic context counsels homosexual persons to avoid union with another person; they should instead unite themselves "to the cross wherein they will hopefully find inner freedom."[14] After the sexual abuse crisis, however, new questions about the efficacy of union with the cross for achieving a healthy, affectively integrated sexual continence in homosexual persons—or any unmarried persons—who do not experience a divine call to a chaste life are raised in the minds of many when there is significant evidence of sexual dysfunction among Catholic priests (called and sustained, presumably, by the person of Christ).[15] In the context of his powerful affirmation of the need of contemporary Christians for a renewed sense of the virtue of chastity in order to ensure a proper appreciation and appropriation of the gift of human sexuality, Keenan acknowledges that the failure to consider the experience of mature adults on matters of sexual orientation limits the effectiveness of appeals to this virtue.[16] The problem is that insofar as chastity is interpreted and enforced as abstinence-based and negative toward sexuality, the richness of the Catholic perspective on the virtue of chastity as a source of human integration is undermined and, perhaps, even lost. The evidence suggests that it is not simply the appeal to abstinence—narrowly or broadly construed—that is undermined by the current situation in the Catholic Church, but that the tradition's ability to provide constructive moral guidance on the significance of commitment, fidelity, and love in sexual relations is also undermined.[17] The danger is that

Catholics, particularly younger Catholics, are deprived of an effective moral teaching on the meaning of human sexuality and so are subject to cultural trends that result in the commodification and commercialization of intimate personal relations. This trend was well advanced by the start of the current century, but the clerical abuse scandal and its aftermath have surely exacerbated it. This suggests that one of the important challenges before the Catholic Church is to find an effective means to reestablish its legitimacy as a teacher in the realm of human sexuality and so communicate a just and humane ethic of sexuality. In the next section of this paper, we will consider the ways in which Christian feminist thought, particularly the contributions of Margaret Farley, might help to renew Catholic moral reflection on human sexuality. The central methodological dimensions of this feminist approach, as we will see, include a commitment to attention to the richness of human experience and to the central role of justice in human relationships.

RENEWING CATHOLIC SEXUAL ETHICS

The response to the sexual abuse crisis by many of those in authority in the Catholic Church has tended to resist any suggestion of a need to examine and reevaluate the Church's teaching or authority structure. The problem that the sexual abuse crisis exposes, on this view, is not internal to the Church but rather is the moral effect of a corrupt culture on weak individuals.[18] Indeed, those in authority tend to argue that the solution to the issues raised by the scandal is not be found in dialogue about morality or authority but rather by a renewed commitment to traditional Catholic sexual ethics. We can find evidence of this strategy in the seminary visitation program, with its special attention to the teaching of orthodox moral theology, currently underway in the United States and in the recent Vatican instruction prohibiting homosexual seminarians.[19] Many bishops in the United States believe that *The Charter for the Protection of Children and Young People* with its provision of "zero tolerance" for those priests who abuse minors is the only institutional reform necessary. Thus with the abusers removed from ministry and protective procedures in place in each diocese, the scandal "is history" in the words of Bishop Wilton Gregory, former president of the U.S. Conference of Catholic Bishops.[20] This approach to the crisis and its aftermath does not, however, take adequate account of the disillusionment and loss of trust experienced by many of the faithful. Nor does it take account of those theological and scientific analyses that suggest that the scandal is, in fact, symptomatic of deeper problems in the life of the Church.

In an essay on the evaluation and treatment of abusive priests, Leslie Lothstein, a psychologist with extensive clinical experience in this area, argues that the crisis in the Catholic Church is ultimately a theological one. He writes,

> It is my opinion that if real change is to take place, it must be systemic. Catholic moral theologians need to develop a developmentally and scientifically appropriate narrative of human sexuality for parishioners and clergy. Until a healthy sexual narrative is established, we will continue to see faith communities become devastated by a combination of a clergy's sexual mayhem (the enactment of a perverse scenario) and the cover-up by the church hierarchy.[21]

What is interesting to notice is that at the conclusion of a paper devoted to psychological explanations of clerical sexual abuse, Lothstein proposes a theological solution. Further, he does not suggest that the discipline of clerical celibacy is itself particularly problematic psychologically. Rather, Lothstein's experience as a clinician treating sexually abusing priests is that this abuse is symptomatic of certain dimensions of a sexual ethic that fails to adequately promote human integration and flourishing. This call for "a healthy sexual narrative" raises important questions about what such a renewed Catholic ethic of sexuality will look like and what resources are available for its formation.

The Role of Experience

Feminist ethicists, for example, have long been acutely aware that prospects for a renewed and compelling Catholic sexual ethic would require careful attention to which voices are heard in the process of its formulation. For as Susan Secker has pointed out, those "whose voice has access and influence in the formulation of moral teaching has decisive impact on the content of those teachings."[22] This insight suggests that the traditional Catholic sexual ethic may be deficient insofar as it has been formulated largely by celibate, male religious professionals, and that a successful reformulation would have to attend and respond to the experience of the diverse populations it will address. If it is the case that the traditional sexual ethic suffers from a loss of credibility, a loss worsened by the current abuse crisis, any attempt at its reformulation will be authoritative insofar as it "makes sense" or is consistent with the experience of the persons and communities it addresses. Margaret Farley notes in this regard that "the moral authority of any source is contingent upon our recognition of the 'truth' it offers and the 'justice' of its aims."[23] Feminist theories are particularly attentive to the role of experience in the formation of ethical norms because of the awareness that such norms have usually been formulated without the input of women and without adequate attention paid to their lived experience. In other words, feminist analysis would hold that all moral norms, even those presented as abstract, universal, and principle-based, are experience-laden. The question is, whose experience counts? Insofar as questions of inclusion and exclusion are questions of power and ultimately of justice, feminists generally acknowledge a particular commitment to the experience of all marginalized persons and victims of injustice as a starting point for ethical reflection.[24] A renewed, Catholic ethic of sexuality would have to take the experience of survivors (minors, women, vulnerable men) of sexual abuse by clergy seriously. This would necessarily involve a frank assessment of power relationships within the Catholic Church and their connection to patterns of abuse.[25]

While the role of experience in ethical analysis does involve careful attention to particular histories of real persons and groups of persons, it includes other important dimensions as well. These dimensions include attention to the cultural conditions shaping moral choice, the insights of scientific research, and shared moral insight into the human condition.

A consideration of the social and cultural contexts that shape the possibility of moral discernment and choice is a significant element of experience. Margaret Farley's work on the AIDS epidemic in Africa highlights this dimension of experience when she points to the unspoken cultural and religious assumptions about sexuality and gender that serve to undermine an effective and humane response to this growing crisis.[26] Farley shows that while religious organizations are very vocal about the relationship between poverty and the spread of AIDS, they are largely unwilling to even talk about those religious teachings, practices, and assumptions that actually serve to further the spread of this disease. Thus their often stern affirmations of traditional sexual morality ring hollow in this context insofar as they imply an experience of autonomy in sexual decision making that simply may not be available to women and vulnerable persons.

Scientific Insight to Human Experience

The insights of the natural and social sciences are similarly an important source of ethically relevant human experience. As Secker has shown, these disciplines serve to provide the factual basis necessary for sound ethical discernment.[27] The findings of disciplines such as biology, psychology, and anthropology during the past century, for example, have served to shape both contemporary understandings of human sexuality and sexual morality.[28] Insofar as these disciplines attempt to examine various aspects of the human experience of sexuality with some degree of objectivity, they provide a type of "reality check" for beliefs and assumptions about this experience and its moral meaning. Farley notes that sociological surveys of sexual behavior "reveal massive discrepancies between accepted sexual norms and actual behavior," which in turn can have the effect of undermining some of the arguments supporting the particular norms. Thus statistical data showing that the vast majority of men engage in autoerotic behavior at some point in their lives challenges the claim that masturbation causes mental illness. In addition, she points to the significant ethical implications of the American Psychiatric Association's decision to remove homosexuality from the list of diseases in its diagnostic manual.[29]

Farley's own analysis of moral issues surrounding same-sex relations provides a helpful example of the ways in which ethical analysis is enhanced by the access to human experience provided by scientific inquiry. While acknowledging that much of insight gained into the nature of homosexuality is not definitive, she argues that enough has been learned from biological, social scientific, and psychoanalytical studies to challenge many of the assumptions that informed traditional proscriptions of same-sex relations. In Farley's view, the empirical sciences do not show the homosexual orientation to be harmful in itself (although they do not demonstrate it to be benign, either); that it can be construed as "natural" insofar as it is usually a given rather than chosen orientation, which cannot be reversed by treatment or therapy; and, that this sexual orientation need not constitute a denial of one's gender or embodiment.[30] In light of these findings and the challenges they pose for traditional moral evaluations of homosexuality and homosexual behavior, Farley argues that an absolute prohibition of same-sex relations is difficult to sustain.[31] Her concern, then, is to evaluate the conditions or standards under which same-sex relations are morally permissible and it is here that she argues for a sexual ethic that applies consistently to both heterosexuals and homosexuals.[32]

Although Farley's conclusions about the morality of same-sex relations differ significantly from official Catholic Church teaching on this matter, there are important similarities between her dependence on the insights of the contemporary sciences and the natural law methodologies that have been so influential in the formulation of official teaching on matters of sexuality. Insofar as natural law is a type of moral realism, it is dependent upon collective experience and shared knowledge about the behaviors and circumstances that lead to human flourishing or destruction. Its very credibility hinges, to a large degree, on its ability to appropriate new insights into the human reality (the difficulties of identifying and knowing "reality" notwithstanding). For many contemporary persons in the West, the methodologies of modern scientific research provide the best window on reality and so must be taken into account in the formulation of ethical norms. This is not to suggest that a natural law approach to sexual ethics simply translates the insights of science into norms, but rather that a natural law that ignores the findings of science does so at its peril.

A tension between scientific evidence and the articulation of traditional sexual norms is sometimes seen in official Catholic teaching. The Congregation for the Doctrine of the Faith's "Declaration on Certain Questions Concerning Sexual Ethics," for example, begins by situating its discussion in the context of scientifically based accounts of human sexuality.[33] The document's treatment of the moral issues surrounding homosexual relations and masturbation does acknowledge scientific research that seems to challenge traditional Catholic evaluations of this behavior, but any possibility of revision is immediately rejected. It is the case that the declaration's understanding of homosexuality, drawn from modern sexology, is a change from earlier Catholic interpretations, which did not recognize a homosexual orientation but rather linked same-sex behavior to self-indulgent licentiousness or corrupt moral formation. While this insight fails to provoke a reevaluation of the morality of sexual relations between persons of the same gender, it does affect the evaluation of the moral status of homosexual persons in that the declaration is clear that the orientation itself is morally blameless.[34] The document's discussion of masturbation acknowledges that modern psychology views it as part of normal sexual development and that sociological study finds widespread evidence of the practice and that it does not inflict personal or social harm. Nonetheless, the authors write, "[w]hatever force there may be in certain biological or philosophical arguments put forward from time to time by theologians, the fact remains that both the magisterium of the Church, in the course of a constant tradition, and the moral sense of the faithful have been in no doubt and have firmly maintained that masturbation is an intrinsically and gravely disordered action."[35] The disordered nature of the action is, like same-sex relations, established by its failure to respect the marital meaning of human sexuality because it contradicts "the finality of the sexual faculty," according to this account.[36]

In this respect the declaration surely does reflect the consistent prohibition of these behaviors, but the question remains as to how persuasive the appeal to "finality" is for contemporary Catholics given the perspectives offered by scientific research. The pride of place given to finality, or the procreative potential of human sexuality, may not conform to experience of many thoughtful Catholics who, while acknowledging this procreative potential, would understand the primary meaning of sex to be an expression of love and personal intimacy. Indeed, this problem of persuasiveness is likely to have become even more acute as a result of the sexual abuse crisis and its aftermath. One can helpfully contrast Andrew Sullivan's previously cited harsh rejection of the teaching authority of the bishops as a result of their handling of the sexual abuse and his more docile attempt to appropriate Catholic teaching on same-sex relations to his own life as it is reflected in his 1994 essay, "Virtually Normal."[37] Whatever else can be said about Sullivan's personal reflection on recent church teaching about this matter, it is not closed to being instructed by the church and he does not simply reject church teaching in a rash and thoughtless manner. He approaches the 1975 declaration and "The Pastoral Care of Homosexual Persons" (1986) respectfully, willing to be taught by his church and acknowledging what he finds to be the strengths of the teaching.[38] That Sullivan is ultimately unable to appropriate this teaching in his own life does result in a rejection of the legitimacy of the church's teaching authority. The tone in his 2002 essay, "Is the Church Dying?"[39] could not be more different. It is angry and despairing in the face of the bishops' response to the scandalous abuse crisis. Sullivan's willingness to engage the magisterium's teaching on human sexuality has evaporated. It may be the case that many other Catholics have become less willing to attend to a sexual ethic already somewhat remote from their experience as a result of the institutional church's handling of this crisis.

Experience as Shared Insight into the Human Condition

Farley has identified what might be referred to as "shared moral wisdom," which constitutes a third dimension of human experience that is significant for ethical reflection. This experientially derived shared wisdom serves to generate an inclusive account of the person and of its obligating features. As such it provides a basic normative foundation for moral decision making. Farley is well aware that many feminists, influenced by postmodern thought, are critical of attempts to develop foundational accounts of the human person. Critiques of this sort raise questions about the very possibility of an objective and universal description of the person, especially in light of an awareness that such descriptions are often "constructed" by particular cultures in ways that reflect and maintain prevailing power relationships.[40] Insofar as these accounts of the person are based on the generalized experience and interests of the powerful, they are harmful to and oppressive of the weaker and more vulnerable, and so critics argue that they must be rejected. Further, such normative descriptions of the person are, in this view, inevitably products of particular cultures and historical periods and so can only speak cross-culturally with limited success, if at all.[41]

As compelling as these critiques are at unmasking the power relations implicit in the Kantian autonomous subject, for example, the difficulty is that they do so at the expense of a commitment to what Farley has referred to as "the obligating features of persons."[42] These obligating features refer to the understanding that there are some features of persons that engender a requirement of respect and that these obligating dimensions of personhood, while conditioned by the exigencies of particular cultures, are ultimately experienced across cultures. To reject a commitment to the idea that there is something intrinsically valuable and morally compelling about persons in themselves that in turn engenders certain common obligations to persons can suggest that norms regarding the treatment of persons are culturally and historically relative. This relativism is particularly dangerous for vulnerable persons and others whose lives are marked by experiences of injustice, in Farley's view, insofar as it serves to "abandon the field to the powerful" and "limits or eliminates the possibility of a common cry for justice."[43] In other words, Farley understands that to concede that human experience does not generate a common appreciation of the need to respect persons is also to concede that there are no objective standards by which to criticize or protest social or cultural arrangements perceived to be destructive of persons. Thus Farley believes that it is important for feminists to search for reasons to protect the inviolability of persons, and she argues that evidence from experience will support such an ethical commitment.

Instead of finding diversity to be an obstacle to a person-centered common morality based on experience, Farley argues that "[a]ttention to diversity disallows false universalization from limited experience, but it allows new ways to common moral insight."[44] Because her feminist methodology takes the experience of women and other oppressed persons seriously, the insight and wisdom it yields about the human condition will not be skewed to unduly reflect the interests of the powerful. In light of this it is possible to identify common dimensions of human experience and derive ethical norms from them. In this regard Farley writes,

> Whatever differences in human lives, however minimal the actuality of world community, however unique the social arrangements of diverse peoples, it is nonetheless possible for human persons to weep over commonly felt tragedies, laugh over commonly perceived incongruities, yearn for common hopes. And across time and place, it is possible to condemn commonly recognized injustices and act for commonly desired goals. The range of universal moral norms may be narrower than traditional ethical theories supposed, but it does exist.[45]

The shared capacities of persons for self-determination and for relationship are, in Farley's view, chief among the human attributes that serve to generate moral claims. The human ability to enter into and sustain relationships is, in this account, as significant as the capacity for autonomy.[46] In asserting the real capacity for and moral significance of self-determination, Farley is not simply reiterating traditional, abstract, and individualistic notions of personal autonomy. Rather, autonomy exists and finds it meaning in the context of human relationality. This capacity for relationship, then, both enables meaningful freedom and is a source of the particularity that limits and conditions it. In light of this, it is possible to argue that while the histories of real persons can and often do give witness to harsh limitations on personal self-governance, the possibility of relationship with other persons and affective commitment persist as a significant realm of self-determination. Autonomy in this sense is not the freedom to become or do whatever one might want, but rather it is the ability to commit oneself to human flourishing, both one's own and that of others.[47]

With regard to sexual ethics, Farley shows that respect for self-determination and relationality are essential to what she has referred to as a "just love." Human relations are characterized by justice insofar as they affirm persons "according to their concrete reality, actual and potential."[48] This understanding of justice as it relates to sexual morality confirms human experience of sexuality and sexual desire as bearing the potential to affirm or harm persons in profound ways. In Farley's account, a just love that involves sexual intimacy will be informed by a series of norms understood to be generated by the human capacities for autonomy and relationality. These norms include consent, mutuality, commitment, equality, fruitfulness, and the like.[49] The final section of this paper will examine these norms as a source for evaluating the moral appropriateness of particular sexual relationships and as dimensions of character conducive of a renewed understanding of the virtue of chastity. What is important to emphasize at this point is that Farley's understanding of that common moral wisdom about the obligating features of persons suggests that there are some experience-derived norms that serve to order and integrate sexual experience in a manner that protects individuals, relationships, and communities. Before turning to the final section it will be important to consider the relationship of experience as a source for ethical reflection to other sources of moral wisdom.

An appeal to experience as a central resource for ethical analysis is not to claim that experience is, or can be, the exclusive source. For Christians, the insights derived from scripture and from the theological tradition play a vital role in moral discernment. Ultimately, scripture and the theological tradition are, of course, themselves based on human experience insofar as the scriptures reflect the encounter of individuals and communities with God's revelation, while the theological tradition reflects Christian communities' attempts to interpret scripture in light of new conditions or concerns. In the ideal, the evidence drawn from experience—both personal experience in its diversity as well as the insights of scientific research—and the wisdom drawn from scripture and tradition should be sources for a cohesive and compelling Christian ethic. It is, however, the case that the interpretations of the Christian sources and of human experience used in the pursuit of moral insight can conflict, and this raises the question of how to adjudicate among these conflicting insights.

In regard to this question, Farley has addressed the critique that suggests that feminist appeals to experience can undermine the authority of the scriptural and theological tradition because they project "selfish human desires" onto traditional formulations.[50] She argues that those who claim a primary authority for the moral tradition as derived from scripture and doctrine cannot reject experience simply because it fails to conform to those sources. A religious tradition that is unwilling or unable to speak to and help interpret human experience is in danger of becoming irrelevant. Moral teaching that "contradicts the fundamental convictions that make sense in and to human experience" is unlikely to be effective.[51] This gap between religious authority and appeals to human experience is often, as we have seen, particularly wide in the area of sexual ethics. Farley points to Catholic teaching in support of the prohibition against artificial birth control, which suggests that the love of couples who use these methods to avoid pregnancy is intrinsically selfish and exploitative. This argument is flawed, she argues, insofar as it contradicts the experience of many married couples "whose whole lives bear witness to their unselfishness."[52] The argument and the norm it supports, do not "make sense" in light of the experience of these couples, and so it can be perceived by them as morally unintelligible and demanding blind obedience. Such a situation is very problematic from the perspective of Catholic ethics, Farley argues, precisely because the Catholic moral tradition is committed to the basic intelligibility of its norms.[53] This tradition, then, does not have the intellectual or pastoral "luxury" of ignoring or discounting the authentic experience of the persons it addresses. Its norms must reflect the wisdom of revelation and the theological tradition interpreted in light of lived experience. The current crisis in the Catholic Church, with its particular implications for the credibility of church teaching on matters of human sexuality, makes it all the more imperative that the church teach in such a way that the faithful recognize the truth of it as generating a moral claim on them. An authentic moral claim, even one that is very challenging, does not "coerce the human person but obligates her; in this process, it also frees her to do what is most true to herself."[54] In an attempt to generate a sexual ethic that is true both to the insights of the Christian tradition and to contemporary experience, the final section of this essay will consider the norms proposed by Margaret Farley, informed as they are by commitments to relationality, self-determination, and justice.

JUST LOVE: RENEWING THE VIRTUE OF CHASTITY

The experience of sexuality is an essential dimension of the human condition, in which persons experience their deepest longings for interpersonal intimacy and union. Contemporary Christians reject any suggestion that human sexuality is sinful or shameful in itself. Rather, they understand sexuality to be part of God's design, capable of sustaining multiple human goods, including committed love, embodied pleasure, and the potential for new life. Yet it is also the case that this realm of human experience is also susceptible to genuine harm by means of manipulation, betrayal, and violence. So then, while a sexually intimate relationship can be the most affirming and profound of life's experiences, it is also the case that such relationships can be destructive of persons when they fail to respect the fundamental dignity or value of persons and the relational meaning of human sexuality. Further, human history demonstrates that given the multiple meanings inherent in the experience of sexuality persons can "miss the mark" insofar as they can easily fail to attain the humanizing goods possible in a sexual relationship or easily inflict harm on themselves or others by means of their sexual choices. This history of experience necessarily raises the question of the conditions and circumstances that can be understood to safeguard persons in sexual relationships and so promote human flourishing. One obvious and popular answer to this concern is that interpersonal love provides the moral justification for sexual intimacy. But, as Farley has noted, this appeal to love may beg the question or even be part of the problem. This is the case because love itself still requires greater specification in order to determine the nature of a good love and, ultimately, to what Farley refers to as a just love.[55] The norms or values that she proposes for a sexual relationship characterized by justice are derived from the fundamental human capacities for self-determination and relationality. These values include: free consent, commitment, mutuality, equality, fruitfulness, and justice.[56] If a sexual relationship is to be the sort of relationship that truly respects the dignity and vulnerability of both partners while demonstrating a concern for the common good, none of these basic values can be dispensed with or ignored.

An awareness of the human capacity for self-determination generates a minimal requirement that all sexual relations reflect the free and effective consent of both partners. This requirement rules out manipulation, coercion, and violence in sexual relationships as well as inequities of power in the relationship. Inequitable power relationships always undermine the possibility of free and effective consent. A failure to respect the importance of free consent is, of course, at the heart of all relationships characterized by abuse. With regard to the current crisis in the Catholic Church, it is important to emphasize that the power inequities inherent in a relationship between an adult and a minor always undermine the prospects for effective consent. The same thing is true with regard to relationships between a member of the clergy and a parishioner or client. If consent is to be meaningful it also implies the need for a basic honesty between persons who are in an intimate relationship.

The human capacity for relationality serves to generate a norm of commitment in sexual relationships. Farley argues that sexuality and sexual desire are of such central importance in human life that they need to be "nurtured, sustained, as well as disciplined, channeled and controlled."[57] This need is not likely to be realized in brief or multiple sexual relationships. She is well aware of the problems with traditional understandings of committed intimate relationships—particularly for feminists—and she is unwilling to claim that uncommitted sexual encounters are necessarily without value. Nonetheless, human experience in all of its diversity does give evidence to support the view that the full potential of human relationality with its promise "of knowing and being known, of loving and being loved" is best achieved in a covenantal relationship between two persons.[58] Furthermore, insofar as sexual relations can involve interpersonal sharing at the deepest level of human vulnerability, a norm of faithful commitment will serve both to help protect these vulnerabilities and promote a spirit of trust between the partners.

The nature of a commitment consistent with an ethical sexual relationship must be further specified by attention to the values of mutuality and equality. Concern for mutuality in personal commitments follows from the ethical requirements of autonomy and relationality because it serves to safeguard the dignity of persons *within* their sexual relationships. Consent to a sexually intimate relationship never permits sexual activity that one partner finds demeaning or that satisfies one partner alone. It must entail, in Farley's view, "activity and receptivity on the part of both persons—mutuality of desire, of action, and of response."[59] Mutuality, then, must reflect a basic equality between the partners within the sexual relationship. A requirement of equality suggests that neither partner is dominant in the relationship, that neither partner must necessarily subordinate his or her needs and aspirations to those of the other. A sexual relationship requires an equality of power. Inequities of power that result from disparities of age, social standing, or professional status within a sexual relationship undermine the prospects for authentically free consent and so are a clear indication of an ethically inappropriate relationship. As was evident in the discussion of the general implications of autonomy for sexually intimate relationships, the exploitation of power differences is always at the heart of an abusive relationship.

As relational beings, the ethical significance of human choice and action is understood to have social and communal implications. In this light, even the most intimate activities are not simply private. All authentically human sexual relationships should move the partners to become more loving in all of their relationships. This concern for the social and communal dimensions of sexual relationships has traditionally expressed itself within Christianity as a fundamental commitment to a procreative norm. The procreative power of these relationships generates a requirement of responsibility in sexual decision making, not only between partners but also for the reproductive implications of sexual activity. But social responsibility is not limited to questions of human reproduction and the education of offspring alone. Committed and loving relationships that are not in themselves open to biological reproduction nevertheless share the ethical requirement of fruitfulness and social responsibility. Authentic interpersonal love should never be selfishly turned in on itself, but also must serve the family, the local community, and human society generally.

Concerns about the larger social dimensions of relationality necessarily raise questions about justice. Farley notes that the classical interpretation of justice as rendering each person his or her due might be understood helpfully in the context of contemporary intimate personal relations as generating a basic requirement for sexual partners to respect and promote the dignity and integrity of each other.[60] A concern for justice also raises questions about the ways in which personal choices help to shape communities and particular moral climates. A community whose members legitimate random, uncommitted sexual relations marked by minimal consent or tolerate the eroticization of dominant power relations may generate a community atmosphere harmful to its more vulnerable members.[61] From a Catholic perspective any account of a just ordering of relationships would have to be particularly attentive to its affects on weaker persons.

Farley's norms for sexual relationships, generated from her appreciation of the central human capacities for self-determination and relationality shared by all persons, make an important contribution to the ethical discernment of contemporary persons. These norms provide ethical criteria for evaluating choice and action in particular relations so as to safeguard the dignity of all persons and promote the full human potential of sexual relationships. Free consent, commitment, mutuality, and the like can help persons discern the objective moral quality of particular types of sexual relations and serve as a guide for those discerning the level of intimacy appropriate for their personal relationships. From the perspective of the current sexual abuse crisis affecting the Catholic Church, they help persons to see that the profound harm done to victims of abuse is ultimately an attack on these capacities that experience suggests are vital to prospects for human flourishing. This is evident in the testimony of so many persons abused by members of the clergy (and others) as minors. The depression, addiction (chemical and sexual), and a lack of a sense of self-worth experienced by so many survivors inhibited any capacity for meaningful self-direction, while an inability to trust and an inner drive to become dominant in sexual relations in response to the experience of abuse undermined the possibility for a fulfilling personal relationship for many.

In addition to understanding the norms for sexual ethics proposed by Farley as providing criteria for evaluating and discerning the appropriate contexts for ethical sexual relations, one might also view them as particular states of character necessary for entering into and sustaining an integrated and humane sexual relationship with another person.[62] Reflection on the human experience of relationality suggests that most persons view a lifelong intimate relationship as central to their aspirations for a successful and fulfilling life. Further reflection indicates that such relationships are entered into and happily sustained for both partners insofar as they themselves are persons capable of committed fidelity, equality, mutuality, fruitfulness, and justice. These qualities of character must be ingrained in persons long before such relationships are entered into. If Farley is correct when she argues that sexual desire must be nurtured *and* disciplined, sustained *and* controlled if it is to be a source of human self-realization, it should not be surprising that social patterns and personal histories that trivialize, instrumentalize, and commodify the sexual dimension of personhood make the appropriation of those virtues necessary for a committed and satisfying intimate personal relationship difficult in the extreme. The norms of Farley's sexual ethic can, then, be understood as a rearticulation of the virtue of chastity in that they "promote the successful integration of sexuality within the person and thus [the] inner unity of . . . bodily and spiritual being."[63] This integration is possible because Farley's norms challenge persons to discipline and order the gift of human sexuality in accord with the demands of relational justice in the service of personal and communal flourishing.

While there are considerable similarities between Farley's norms of sexual justice and Catholic understandings of the virtue of chastity, some critics would certainly cite what they perceive to be significant departures from this tradition. There is no question that these norms require careful attention to values central to Catholic understandings of sexual morality. As in Keenan's account of the Christian virtue of chastity, Farley's norms suggest that "sexual desires need to be checked by a realistic appraisal of one's own maturity and the willingness to commit to another."[64] Farley's willingness, however, to reinterpret the procreative norm found in official Church teaching on sexual ethics in order to articulate a sexual ethic that is "consistent,"[65] that is appropriate for heterosexual and homosexual persons alike, can be viewed as a major shift away from traditional teaching and the ethic of sexual abstinence it supports. Ultimately, it may be more helpful—especially in light of the crisis of credibility facing official Catholic sexual ethics— to view this reinterpretation as an affirmation of basic principles. Farley herself notes that there has been considerable development of the meaning of the procreative norm in the Catholic tradition. She writes, "[t]raditional arguments that if there is sex, it must be procreative have changed to arguments that if sex is procreative it must be within a context that assures responsible care of offspring."[66] To this one can also add the relatively recent requirement that procreative sexual activity must always be an expression of marital love. This supports a view that the norm itself is not closed to further development. Farley supports this norm insofar as she recognizes both a need for the responsible reproduction of the human species *and* for fruitfulness on the part of those committed couples—heterosexual and homosexual alike—whose relationships do not ultimately produce offspring.

A further consideration in this regard is the distinction between principles and the practical judgments involved in applying them. Charles Curran has noted, for example, that recent Catholic ethical teaching on matters of social and political morality presupposes agreement among Catholics on fundamental principles while acknowledging the likelihood of difference in the implementation of these principles.[67] Indeed it is understood that the application of these principles must be different given the diverse social contexts to which they are applied. While this distinction between absolute principle and diversity of implementation has not applied to official Church teaching on sexual morality, the present crisis may present an occasion to reflect on its potential usefulness in this area. Farley's approach, then, affirms the principle of relational fruitfulness while understanding that persons of good faith will respond to this human good in light of their particular context.

It is certainly the case that the credibility and persuasiveness of the official teaching of the Catholic Church on matters of sexual ethics have declined dramatically in recent decades. Further, this decline has been exacerbated in the United States in the aftermath of the clerical sexual abuse crisis and its perceived cover-up. The result is not that many Catholics adopt other reasoned moral positions on sexual morality—although some persons do—but rather that many Catholics are simply "adrift" with regard to sexual morality.[68] Margaret Farley's insightful and respectful Christian interpretation of the norms surrounding the experience of human sexuality can be understood to be a vitally important resource as the Catholic community attempts to move forward from this time of crisis and disarray. The norms she identifies, based on human experience in light of the Christian theological tradition, are themselves experienced not as abstract commands but as truths about the human condition and its deepest relational aspirations. As such they are capable of generating mature moral discernment around issues of human sexuality and so serve to promote authentic human liberation and self-realization.

NOTES

1. For a full account of the events in the Archdiocese of Boston, see *Betrayal: The Crisis in the Catholic Church*, the Investigative Staff of the *The Boston Globe* (Boston: Little, Brown and Co., 2002).

2. See the letters from Cardinal Bernard Law to John Geogan and Paul Shanley, two of the most serious offenders, *Betrayal*, 226 and 246.

3. *Catechism of the Catholic Church*, 2284.

4. Margaret A. Farley, "The Church in the Public Forum: Scandal or Prophetic Witness," *Proceedings of the Catholic Theological Society of America*, 55 (2000): 87–101, at 88.

5. An independent study commissioned by the U.S. Catholic Conference estimates that 4 percent of the 109,694 Roman Catholic priests active

in the ministry between 1950 and 2002 have had allegations of abuse leveled against them. See *The Nature and Scope of the Problem of Sexual Abuse of Minors by Catholic Priests and Deacons in the United States: A Research Study Conducted by the John Jay College of Criminal Justice* (Washington, DC: United States Conference of Catholic Bishops, 2004), 2. www.usccb.org/nrb/johnjaystudy.

6. Andrew Sullivan, "Is the Church Dying? Sex Abuse is Just the Symptom," *Time Magazine*, June 10, 2002 (available at http://www.andrewsullivan.com/faith.php?artnum=20020610, last accessed April 2007).

7. Ibid.

8. Mark D. Jordan, *The Ethics of Sex* (Oxford: Blackwell Publishing, 2002), 130. Also see Michael J. Hartwig, *The Poetics of Intimacy and the Problem of Sexual Abstinence* (New York: Peter Lang, 2000).

9. The research of A. W. Richard Sipe suggests that about fifty percent of the Catholic priests in the United States are practicing celibacy in an integrated manner at any given time. He claims that six percent are sexually involved with minors; see his *Sex, Priests, and Power: Anatomy of a Crisis* (London: Cassell, 1995), 69. To refer to instances of the sexual misbehavior of priests with adults is not to suggest that those behaviors need not be abusive. Violations of the discipline of celibacy with parishioners or clients are abusive due to the power inequities necessarily involved.

10. See, for example, Pope John Paul II's address to the U.S. cardinals and bishops at the extraordinary meeting called to address the abuse crisis, in which he refers to scandal as "a grave symptom of a crisis affecting not only the Church but society as a whole. It is a deep-seated crisis of sexual morality. . . ," April 22, 2002 (text available at www.zenit.org/english/visualizza.phtml?sid=19598; last accessed Jan. 2007). On their part, the cardinals and bishops, in their final statement at this meeting, recommitted themselves to "promote the correct moral teaching of the Church and publicly reprimand individuals who spread dissent," and called for an apostolic visitation of seminaries "with a particular emphasis on the need for fidelity to the Church's teaching, especially in the area of morality," April 25, 2002 (text available at www.zenit.org/english/visualizza.phtml?sid=19702, last accessed Jan. 2007).

11. *Catechism of the Catholic Church*, 2337.

12. James Keenan, S.J., "Virtues, Chastity and Sexual Ethics," Catholic Common Ground Initiative Lecture Papers (text available at www.nplc.org/commonground/papers/keenanpaper.htm, last accessed Jan. 2007).

13. Ibid.

14. Ibid. With regard to the extensive discussion about the moral legitimacy of homosexual tendencies and genital expression of same-sex attraction, see James Keenan, S.J., "The Open Debate: Moral Theology and

the Lives of Gay and Lesbian Persons, *Theological Studies* 64, no. 1 (2003): 127–50.

15. I am not suggesting that pedophilia, clinically understood as acting on a persistent and powerful attraction to prepubescent minors, is primarily a failure of celibacy (the chaste state of priests). Classic pedophiles make up a very small percentage of the priests accused of abusing minors. Nor am I suggesting that the discipline of celibacy caused the sexual abuse of minors. My argument is that the abuse crisis further undermined the credibility of Catholic sexual ethics by exposing substantial dysfunction with the "gold standard" of this ethic and the relative indifference of the Bishops to it.

16. Keenan, "Virtues, Chastity and Sexual Ethics," op cit.

17. A 1999 special report on U.S. Catholic attitudes, beliefs, and behavior in the *National Catholic Reporter* found that only 20 percent of Catholics in the United States believed that the church leaders should have the final say on the morality of same-sex relations, while 23 percent believed that these leaders should have a determinative voice on the morality of extra-marital relations; Dean R. Hoge, "What is Most Central to Being a Catholic?" *National Catholic Reporter*, October 29, 1999 (available at http://natcath .org/NCR_Online/archives2/1999d/102999/102999j.htm, last accessed April 2007). A more recent survey (2002) of Roman Catholic students at the College of the Holy Cross, found that while there was a high level of agreement with Catholic doctrine and practice generally, only 16 percent of those surveyed found "the teaching authority claimed by the Vatican" to be "very important." This percentage was significantly lower than the Catholics surveyed in the 1999 NCR survey (www.holycross.edu/departments/ socant/rsinglet/sp02majf.htm, last accessed April 2007). Further, Peter Steinfels cites Andrew Greeley's assertion of "the catastrophic collapse of the old Catholic ethic" and his example that Catholics in the United States are far more likely than Protestants to agree that premarital sex is "not wrong at all"; Peter Steinfels, *A People Adrift: The Crisis of the Roman Catholic Church in America* (New York: Simon and Schuster, 2003), 259.

18. See Mary Gail Frawley-O'Dea, "Psychosocial Anatomy of the Church Sexual Abuse Scandal," *Studies in Gender and Sexuality*, 5, no. 2 (2004): 121–37, at 125.

19. See "Concerning the Criteria for the Discernment of Vocations with regard to Persons with Homosexual Tendencies in View of their Admission to the Seminary and to Holy Orders," Congregation for Catholic Education, 2005 (text available at http://www.zenit.org/english/visualizza .phtml?sid=80825, last accessed Jan. 2007).

20. At a press conference on February 27, 2004, accepting the reports of the National Review Board and the John Jay study, Bishop Gregory said, "The terrible history recorded here is history."

21. Leslie M. Lothstein, "The Evaluation and Treatment of Sexually Abusing Priests," *Studies in Sexuality and Gender* 5, no. 2 (2004): 167–95, at 191–92.

22. Susan L. Secker, "Human Experience and Women's Experience: Resources for Catholic Ethics," in *Dialogue about Catholic Sexual Teaching,* Readings in Moral Theology 8, ed. C. Curran and R. McCormick, 577–99 (New York: Paulist Press, 1993), 591.

23. Margaret A. Farley, "The Role of Experience in Moral Discernment," in *Christian Ethics: Problems and Prospects,* ed. L. S. Cahill and J. Childress, 134–51 (Cleveland: The Pilgrim Press, 1996), 147.

24. Ibid., 141.

25. See Brian F. Linnane, "Celibacy and Sexual Malpractice: Dimensions of Power and Powerlessness in Patriarchal Society," in *Theology and the New Histories,* ed. G. Macy, 227–44 (Maryknoll, NY: Orbis Books, 1999).

26. Margaret A. Farley, *Compassionate Respect: A Feminist Approach to Medical Ethics and Other Questions* (New York: Paulist Press, 2002), 9–17. Susan Secker makes a similar observation with regard to Farley's writings on the question of abortion, "Human Experience," 583–84.

27. Secker, "Human Experience," 579.

28. See Margaret A. Farley, "Sexual Ethics," in *Encyclopedia of Bioethics,* revised edition, ed. W. Reich, 2363–75 (New York: Simon and Schuster, 1995), 2370–71.

29. Ibid., 2371.

30. Margaret A. Farley, "An Ethic for Same-Sex Relations," in *A Challenge to Love,* ed. R. Nugent, 93–106 (New York: Crossroad, 1983), 98–99.

31. Farley's willingness to find moral justification for same-sex relations is also informed by what she takes to be an inconclusive moral evaluation of same-sex desire in the scriptures and in the theological tradition; see ibid., 94–97.

32. Ibid., 105.

33. Congregation for the Doctrine of the Faith, "Declaration on Certain Questions Concerning Sexual Ethics," 1975 (text available at http//www.vatican.va/roman_curia/congregations/cfaith/documents/rc_con_cfaith_doc_19751229_persona-humana_en.html, last accessed Jan. 2007), I.

34. Ibid.

35. Ibid., IX.

36. Ibid.

37. Andrew Sullivan, "Virtually Normal," *The South Atlantic Quarterly* 93, no. 3 (1994): 659–74. This essay was later incorporated into a book with the same title (New York: Alfred A. Knopf, 1995).

38. Sullivan cites the acceptance of the evidence of psychology and sociology that supports the understanding of homosexuality as a given and

unchangeable orientation in the Declaration ("Virtually Normal," 664–65) and Cardinal Ratzinger's affirmation of the dignity of homosexual persons insofar as he invokes the morally significant language of personhood in his 1986 letter ("Virtually Normal," 666–67).

39. Sullivan, "Is the Church Dying?"

40. On this point, see Seyla Benhabib, "The Generalized Other and the Concrete Other," in *Ethics: A Feminist Reader*, ed. E. Frazer, J. Hornsby, and S. Lovibond (Oxford: Blackwell, 1992), especially 280–86.

41. A full treatment of this issue is beyond the scope of this essay. See Brian F. Linnane, "The Dignity of Persons and the Catholic Intellectual Vision," in *As Leaven in the World*, ed. T. Landy, 191–212 (Franklin, WI: Sheed and Ward, 2001).

42. Margaret A, Farley, "A Feminist Version of Respect for Persons," *Journal of Feminist Studies in Religion* 9 (Spring/Fall 1993): 183–98, at 183.

43. Margaret A. Farley, "Feminism and Universal Morality," in *Prospects for a Common Morality*, ed. G. Outka and J. Reeder, Jr., 170–90 (Princeton, NJ: Princeton University Press, 1993), 178.

44. Farley, "Role of Experience," 146.

45. Farley, "Feminism and Universal Morality," 178.

46. Ibid., 182.

47. Also see Linnane, "Dignity of Persons," 205–7.

48. Farley, "An Ethic of Same-Sex Relations," 100–101.

49. Ibid., 100–105.

50. Farley, "Role of Experience," 142–43.

51. Ibid., 142.

52. Ibid., 150n39.

53. Margaret A. Farley, "Ethics, Ecclesiology, and the Grace of Self-Doubt," in *A Call to Fidelity*, ed. J. O'Connell, J. Walter, and T. Shannon, 55–75 (Washington, DC: Georgetown University Press, 2002), 66–67.

54. Ibid., 67–68.

55. Farley, "An Ethic for Same-Sex Relations," 100.

56. The discussion of these values follows Farley's treatment of them in "An Ethic for Same-Sex Relations," 100–106, and is also influenced by her Mooney lecture, "Current Issues in Sexual Ethics," unpublished paper, Fairfield University, March 23, 1995. Some of this material was first presented in my essay, "Sexual Decision-Making and Human Values: A Call to Discernment and Dialogue," written for the Division of Student Affairs, College of the Holy Cross.

57. Farley, "An Ethic for Same-Sex Relations," 103.

58. Ibid., 104.

59. Ibid., 102.

60. Ibid., 100–101.

61. See Karen Lebacqz, "Love Your Enemy: Sex, Power, and Christian Ethics," *The Annual of the Society of Christian Ethics* 10 (1990): 3–23, esp. 3–9.

62. I am grateful to David O'Brien for this insight.

63. *Catechism of the Catholic Church*, 2337.

64. Keenan, "Virtues, Chastity, and Sexual Ethics."

65. See Rich Barlow, "Arguing for a Consistent Sexual Ethic," an interview with Margaret Farley, *The Boston Globe*, November 23, 2002, B2.

66. Farley, "An Ethic for Same-Sex Relations," 104.

67. Charles E. Curran, "Official Catholic Social and Sexual Teaching: A Methodological Comparison," in Curran and McCormick, *Dialogue,* 536–58, esp. 555.

68. Steinfels, *A People Adrift*, 253–306.

Chapter Ten

"Framework for Love"

Toward a Renewed Understanding of Christian Vocation

Anne E. Patrick, S.N.J.M.

> The word of the Lord came to me thus: "Before I formed
> you in the womb I knew you, before you were born I
> dedicated you, a prophet to the nations I appointed you."
>
> (Jeremiah 1:4–5, *New American Bible*)

In an age when people expect to have at least two or three
careers, and when they regularly witness changing commitments of
persons who married or made religious vows, what value remains
with the notion of "vocation"? Is the concept hopelessly destabilized
by the fluctuations of our fast-paced social context, our postmodern
culture that prizes spontaneity and independence? Or is the notion a
potential resource for living a centered and productive life in an increasingly unstable world?

John W. Gardner, who founded the citizens' movement Common Cause, observed four decades ago that in a world of constant
change, "[t]he only stability possible is stability in motion."[1] Could
the theological idea of vocation help us to achieve such equilibrium,

such empowering stability in the course of a lifetime "in motion"? I suggest that an affirmative answer is possible if we are willing to confront the myth and mystery of vocation with discerning minds and generous hearts. My inquiry takes its inspiration from several works by Christian ethicist Margaret Farley, especially her ground-breaking study from 1986, *Personal Commitments.*[2] Although Farley has not focused directly on the idea of vocation, her reflections on commitment and related issues offer help for thinking in new ways about this concept, which retains great potential as a resource for the Christian life. Her metaphor of "framework for love," I maintain, is an especially valuable contribution to a renewed understanding of Christian vocation.

Before discussing Farley's insights, however, it is appropriate first to enlarge on the phrase used above, the "myth and mystery of voca-tion." By vocation I refer not only to the special states of life such as marriage, the priesthood, or membership in a vowed religious com-munity, but also to such secular callings as that of artist, teacher, doc-tor, or politician. I refer as well to the fundamental call to respond to the good news of salvation by living a holy life, which the Sec-ond Vatican Council emphasized in the *Dogmatic Constitution on the Church*: "Thus it is evident to everyone that all the faithful of Christ of whatever rank or status are called to the fullness of the Christian life and to the perfection of charity" (*Lumen Gentium,* 40). The opera-tive assumption here is that "vocation" involves both a story-saturated symbol of tremendous power *and* a mystery that eludes any attempts at full certainty about what one should be doing with one's life. Fur-thermore, both the symbol and the mystery are religious in the gen-eral sense of being associated with the human experiences of ultimacy and transcendence, whether or not specific language about the sacred is employed.

THE MYTH OF VOCATION

In his volume *Stories of God* theologian John Shea describes religious myth as a story that shapes consciousness, encourages attitudes, and suggests behaviors. "Myth," he observes, "is that story or formulation which establishes the world within which we live and out of which we act."[3] It is in this rich sense that one can speak of the myth of vocation. As Andrew Greeley stresses in *The Jesus Myth*, "There is nothing more real than [human] symbols and myths," understanding the latter in the sense of narratives that convey the fullest possible truth about the meaning of human existence.[4] For persons influenced by the Christian tradition, the idea of particular callings in life is grounded in many biblical accounts of God or Jesus summoning people to tasks and indeed to life-projects. The early chapters of Genesis establish a pattern whereby God speaks with human beings, and this metaphor of conversation between Creator and creature often extends to stories of a special divine summons. The story of the covenant with Israel is a prime example, as is the episode where Jeremiah is called to be a prophet. Likewise the gospels portray Jesus calling fishermen to abandon their nets and become "fishers of men," offering discipleship to a rich young man who is unable to leave his possessions, summoning a tax-collector to abandon that work and become an apostle, and sending Mary Magdalene to tell the disciples the news of his resurrection.

From such narratives has arisen the notion of vocation, the idea that individuals have a life task they are destined to figure out and fulfill. The concept is deeply etched into western consciousness, affecting believers and nonbelievers alike, although in different ways. Fundamentalists tend to speak confidently of being or expecting to be called by God as if it were an actual summons, as if there were a "thing" called vocation out there somewhere to be experienced and known. Less literal Christians may not expect such clarity or certainty, but often they operate under the assumption that there is a calling specifically designed for them. Even when people no longer interpret biblical narratives as literal accounts of events but rather understand these stories as post facto theological interpretations of the significance of something that happened in the past, their imaginations have been profoundly affected by stories of God's summoning individuals for particular tasks in life. Moreover, religious and secular persons alike still speak of being called by the community or by the times or by one's deepest self to undertake this or that life-project. And once language of vocation is adopted, ethical judgments soon follow, particularly judgments about fidelity and infidelity. The good person is faithful to the demands of her calling, the good parent puts the welfare of the child above his own, the good artist is true to her vision.

THE MYSTERY OF VOCATION

The powerful myth that there is such a thing as a life-calling should be balanced by a counterweight, namely the recognition that the meaning and purpose of any life is ultimately a religious mystery, to be discerned gradually over the course of one's earthly existence. The biblical stories of callings and the subsequent literature of vocation are misleading if they are not interpreted in the full context of the Mystery that created us and sustains us in being. Since God transcends our knowledge, and since the meaning and purpose of our lives is finally bound up in our relationship with God, there can be no complete resolution of the question of our particular life-calling within the finite frame of our existence. What this means is not that the idea of vocation is worthless but simply that our process of discernment must proceed with an appropriate degree of humility. The question of "vocation" amounts to a collection of repeated articulations of what James M. Gustafson has identified as the basic question of Christian ethics: "What is God enabling and requiring me to be and to do?"[5] not just in this or that particular moment of my life but for a significant portion of my life, and maybe even the "rest of my life."

Furthermore, although everyone's vocation is ultimately a religious mystery, there remains value in doing the hard work of conceptual and ethical analysis about the matter. As Farley has indicated, "It is possible . . . to enter more deeply into the questions—to take a lantern, as it were, and walk into what may ultimately be a mystery to us, but which we do not deserve to call a mystery until we have entered it as far as we can go."[6] An individual's vocation can be analyzed as a composite that involves three sorts of callings. For everyone there is the basic summons to holiness, which is a succinct way of stating the biblical command to love God with our whole heart and soul and strength and our neighbor as ourselves (Mt 22:37–39). Beyond that is the sense of being invited to focus love and creativity (and sexual energy) in a particular life-context. This is the meaning that *vocation* has had for most Catholics. They are accustomed to link the idea with the sacraments of matrimony and holy orders, or with a call to practice celibacy in community or individual life, speaking of these various "states of life" as things that God invites one to enter. Finally there is the matter of the many possible occupations that become vocations to the extent that they are seen as more than mere jobs. This third sort of calling, to productive secular activity, was emphasized especially by the reformers Luther and Calvin, who felt that the Roman Catholic stress on the clerical and vowed religious states had tended to obscure the baptismal vocation to holiness that belonged to all believers.

The distinction between a vocation in this occupational sense and a mere job depends on factors that are elusive but nonetheless real. A given occupation fits somewhere on a continuum that is defined at one extreme in terms of economic utility ("what I do to earn a living") and at the other in terms of meaning and fit with one's unique capacities and inclinations ("the work I was born to accomplish"). Frederick Buechner's oft-cited characterization of vocation as "the place where your deep gladness meets the world's deep need" describes the latter very well.[7] This occupational sort of vocation goes beyond what we think of as a job or career to include our sense of being called to devote time and energy to various persons, projects, and causes. Whether through a career or through an avocation in this latter sense, one's experience of meaning and fit (with one's particular gifts and talents) in the way one spends one's hours contributes significantly to overall meaning and satisfaction in life.

The three sorts of vocations outlined above—the fundamental call to holiness, the call to a state of life such as marriage or the religious sisterhood, and the call to particular occupations, activities, or causes—are intimately connected with each other. Each concerns the love of God and neighbor, which is the fundamental obligation of every human being. The call to holiness is another way of stating this universal commandment to love God with one's whole heart, mind, soul, and strength, and one's neighbor as oneself. A vocation to a "state of life" such as marriage or celibacy establishes a focus and context for interpersonal love and sexual expression or abstinence. And a vocation to an occupation, cause, or enterprise establishes the setting for labor suffused with love. The responses to these multiple callings can be separated out for purposes of analysis, and there are often conflicts over which demand takes precedence on a given day, but ultimately they are united in the will to love.

Having established the three basic types of callings and their common relationship to love, we still face many questions about this matter of vocation. What is it that lends such solidity to the amorphous idea of vocation? What gives it power and substance, the ability to demand countless small deeds of fidelity over years and even decades of a lifetime? What is it that dissolves that substance and frees one from a formerly felt sense of obligation, or perhaps instead realigns that sense of obligation? I believe that the power attaching to the concept of vocation depends on a quality of relationship developed by a process that combines the passive experiences of attraction and insight and the active response of commitment. The former involves the reception of a gift, known theologically as a "grace," and the latter a series of decisions in response to this gift, including the choices to attend to what is attractive, to affirm the love that is evoked, and to promise future deeds of love. The power builds from the interaction of the passive and active aspects of the experience, sustained by a religious conviction that the ultimate source of the inclination is God, the creator of one's very life. In embracing the vocation one feels that this will be the appropriate context in which the faithful practice of neighbor love can be substantively linked with a loving response to the gifts of God. Furthermore, in the Christian religious context the notion of vocation operates by analogy, that is, by a thought process that recognizes both similarities and differences between what the contemporary believer experiences and what certain biblical personages experienced. What is happening to me in this attraction, this sense that here indeed is the situation where my own "deep gladness meets the world's great need," is like what those first disciples of Jesus experienced when they heard him say, "Come, follow me." And at the same time it is an altogether different experience, unique to my circumstances today.

FARLEY'S "ETHICS OF COMMITMENT" AND
THE RECONSIDERATION OF VOCATION

Although Farley's writings do not deal explicitly at length with the concept of vocation, her insights constitute a rich resource for ethical reflection on this topic. Most obviously relevant here is her important study from 1986, *Personal Commitments*, which can be read as a highly successful reinterpretation of the ethical significance of vocation that derives its power in part from an avoidance of this theologically freighted term. Nowhere does Farley directly reject the rhetoric of vocation, and there are occasional references to "calling" and "vocation" in this book as well as in her other writings, but these are rather rare for an author so centrally preoccupied with commitment.

One may speculate that several factors contribute to Farley's tendency to give the rhetoric of vocation a rest. In the first place, Roman Catholic understandings of vocation as a state of life have been linked with a problematic tendency to moral absolutism, especially where sacramental marriage is concerned. The longstanding tendency to absolutize the "marital bond" even in abusive situations has caused suffering and scandal for many Catholics, which the post–Vatican II liberalization of the annulment process has not fully remedied. It is precisely this situation of a tradition imposing impossible demands on individuals that *Personal Commitments* is designed to counter.[8] In an article on sexual ethics published in 1983 Farley had made brief reference to "weariness with the high rhetoric that has traditionally surrounded human covenants," seeking to replace it with a more "limited" rhetoric that recognizes that "commitment is itself only a means, not an end."[9] Moreover, Roman Catholic teaching has historically relegated marriage to a lesser status than that of virginity chosen "for the sake of the Kingdom." An effort was made by the Second Vatican Council to offset this elitism by stating in the *Dogmatic Constitution on the Church* that all members of the People of God share "a common dignity" and "the same vocation to perfection."[10] Nearly two decades after the council, however, Farley lamented the fact that the church's recent emphasis on the universal call to holiness had not altered an entrenched elitism. "Twentieth century efforts in the Roman Catholic tradition to move beyond a ranking of higher and lower ways of Christian living," she observed in 1983, "are countered still by largely unanalyzed beliefs which hold the family to an inferior place."[11] Instead of making an explicit argument against vocational elitism in *Personal Commitments*, Farley takes what marriage and religious or priestly vows have in common, namely, the formal promise of binding oneself to future deeds of love within a particular "framework," and she analyzes these commitments on an equal basis. Her choice to treat examples from various walks of life on the same plane is a subtle but effective way of countering the elitism to which she objects. Furthermore, Protestant understandings of vocation have been associated with debates about matters such as the extent to which biblical meanings have been misapplied to worldly concerns and Christian moral energies have been co-opted by secular powers.[12] Important as they may be, these debates are not central to Farley's purpose, and it makes sense to avoid engaging them by employing new language.

Finally and most importantly, both Roman Catholic and Protestant understandings of vocation have been implicated in the sort of gender injustice that Farley's feminist ethic so strongly opposes. For all of church history Christian women have suffered under male definitions of their vocational possibilities and duties. These range from literal applications of the Pauline exhortation, "Wives should be submissive to their husbands as if to the Lord," (Eph 5:22), to claims that only men are called to the priesthood. In her 1983 essay on "The Church and the Family: An Ethical Task," Farley observed:

> Women, unlike men, have received a double message about vocation to marriage and family life. On the one hand, the call to transcend it has been given to them . . . [and] on the other hand, they have been taught that they have a special call to the family. The family is a refuge for men, and hence the object of *eros*, a selfish love. But it is the responsibility of women, and hence the place of self-sacrificial love, of unlimited Christian *agape*.[13]

Several years earlier Farley had called for a revolution in patterns of relationship between women and men. Writing in *Theological Studies* during 1975, which the United Nations had designated International

Women's Year, Farley declared that patriarchal family and church structures are "inadequate, based on inaccurate understandings of human persons, preventive of individual growth, inhibitive of the common good, conducive to social injustices, and in the Christian community not sufficiently informed by or faithful to the teachings of Christ." Then, in a carefully reasoned discussion of what authentic love and justice require, she went on to conclude that both family and church are "better served by a model of leadership which includes collaboration [of men and women] between equals."[14] These ideals of mutuality and collaboration, however, were far from realized in 1986, when Farley published *Personal Commitments,* and the situation is not much better today.

In light of all this, there is considerable wisdom in Farley's move to consider the issue of vocational obligations in fresh language. In *Personal Commitments* the term she employs instead of "vocation" is "framework for love." This phrase respects two realities that an uncritical application of the concept of vocation otherwise obscures: the role that our own freedom plays in contributing to the sense of bundled obligations that a particular "calling" entails, and the ultimate mystery of the divine-human relationship that grounds all our proximate responsibilities. A framework is useful but provisional, and so are the settings in which human beings are meant to respond to God's love for us. The frameworks have moral weight, but they are not ultimately binding in themselves because God alone is the proper object of an absolute love (Farley, *Personal Commitments*, 120; subsequent parenthetical references cite page numbers from this book).

Farley's book on commitment is an excellent example of the process that Paul Ricoeur's hermeneutical theory of "second naïveté" enjoins on our age, namely the task of rethinking the classical religious symbols and stories that provide meaning for our lives in the light of new, "critical" knowledge. In articulating this theory at the close of *The Symbolism of Evil*, his cross-cultural investigation of ancient stories about such figures as Adam and Eve, Pandora, and Oedipus, Ricoeur distinguishes three possible ways of relating to traditional myths. There is in the first place an unquestioning acceptance of the story as literally true, which he characterizes as "primitive naïveté."

Typical for children, fundamentalists, and many premodern thinkers, this approach to myth assumes that the things narrated in biblical accounts happened just as they are told, whatever degree of fiction may be involved in myths from pagan sources. The reward for this stance is a high level of meaning, although the sort of simplicity entailed here cannot stand up to the new gains of knowledge brought about by modern history, science, and philosophy.

Thus there often emerges a second attitude to myth, which Ricoeur calls "criticism." Here the story is again understood literally, but this time it is judged as false. The character Sportin' Life from Gershwin's *Porgy and Bess* captures this attitude well in his song about biblical stories, "It Ain't Necessarily So." In naming this attitude, Ricoeur had in mind such great critics of religion as Nietzsche and Freud, thinkers who made significant gains of truth at the expense of meaning. Finally, Ricoeur proposes a way to get beyond the "meaning versus truth" impasse that modernity had reached with respect to biblical narratives. He does this by describing the possibility of a third stance toward myth, which combines aspects of the first two stances, "primitive naïveté" and "criticism." This third stance he calls "second naïveté." His use of the word "naïveté" here is paradoxical, for this stance involves a sophisticated ability to interpret the story symbolically rather than literally, and thus the adjective "second" is crucial to the concept. Ricoeur's reason for retaining the term "naïveté" in this secondary sense is to convey that some of the immediacy and power felt by those who relate uncritically to myth can be regained if educated persons will undertake a dialectical process. The first step in this process toward second naïveté is to make a sort of Pascalian wager that the narrative offers significant truth about human existence. Following this act of trust, one seeks to embrace all that criticism can supply by way of scientific or factual knowledge relevant to this myth. Ricoeur envisions a continuing dialectic in which the powers of imagination are unleashed by the wager of trust and then informed by the knowledge gained through critical thought and research so that *both* meaning *and* truth are realized. He offers the image of a "hermeneutical circle" to describe the ongoing dialectical process by means of which the truth available in the myth is discovered "in and through criticism."[15] Farley's endorsement of the possibility and desirability of reaching "second naïveté" understandings of key theological ideas is clear from what she says at the outset of *Personal Commitments*:

> [J]ust as special revelations (whether through sacred scriptures or through the voice of the community or through whatever sources) may illuminate all of our commitments and enable us to covenant forever, so our philosophical reflection on our experience of commitment can, as Paul Ricoeur testifies, "set off the horizon of significance where [God's word] may be heard."[16]

And her skill in navigating the hermeneutical circle is evident in the book's final chapter, which takes the biblical myth of God's covenant with Israel in precisely this fashion.

Farley's preceding chapters have involved the descriptive and normative analysis of the human experience of commitment, and she waits until the book's conclusion to unpack its religious presuppositions in a chapter entitled, "Commitment, Covenant, and Faith." Her espousal of a second naïveté approach to the biblical myth of God's covenant with Israel is apparent when she acknowledges the critical insight that the covenant tradition is ambiguous and problematic. To begin with, there are conflicting interpretations, and the tradition of these interpretations and the theologies shaped by them has displayed "an alarming potential for the oppression of groups and individuals—in spite of its remarkable possibilities for liberation and for life." She cites the scandals of religious chauvinism and anti-Semitism, as well as the tradition's acceptance of atrocious violence and its "massive dependence" on imagery of domination, as in "lord-servant and husband-wife relationships." Nevertheless she proceeds to make her Pascalian wager on the fundamental truth of the symbol: "Despite all of these difficulties, however, the Covenant tradition can, I believe, illuminate important aspects of commitment. If it is interpreted with sufficient caution, it retains a power to express the convictions of a fundamentally strengthening and freeing faith" (112). She recognizes the narrative basis of faith claims concerning God's love and fidelity to human beings. She prefers the terms "story" or "narrative" to "myth," but there is no doubt that Farley is well acquainted with the critical literature of biblical studies regarding Covenant stories, citing as she does figures from Gerhard von Rad through Katherine Doob Sakenfeld. She speaks of a "narrative kernel" (114) that continues through biblical accounts of creation and the covenants with Noah, Abraham, and Moses. What the people receive in various instances, she observes, is God's "promise of a relationship, a promise of unconditional love and ongoing presence: 'I will be your God. You shall be my people'" (116). In Ricoeur's terms, it is this symbol of God's covenant of unconditional love and care for humanity that has "given rise" to Farley's own thought on analogous human commitments in the book's earlier chapters. She ends the work by affirming that the "Covenant *story* provides a context and a ground for all our commitments to love" (134; emphasis added).

Embedded but not developed in this chapter is the language of call, which Farley links directly with God's promise: "God's promise is addressed to human persons in a way that takes account of their reality as persons and that thereby calls for and makes possible a responding personal and communal commitment" (117). Indeed, the fact that the chapter subsequently speaks of calls to love and action (122) and to responsibility (133) suggests that a theology of vocation is present here at a deep level:

> Out of the relationship that is the substance of the Covenant, then, emerges the call and the responsibility to oppose the forces of evil in the world, to nurture the sources of human well-being, to form structures that respect human dignity. Whatever can serve this labor falls within the scope of the Covenant. Always any given labor may end in exile, or in destruction of the land, or in death. Yet the word remains; the relationship holds; hope and responsibility can continue. (133)

MERCY VOCATIONS AND FARLEY'S THEOLOGICAL ETHICS

If Farley had reason for keeping explicit references to vocation to a minimum when she published *Personal Commitments* in 1986, the situation today is different. In recent years there has been a resurgence of this rhetoric in U.S. Christian circles, in part because of the generous funding the Lilly Endowment has provided for religious scholars and college educators and students to probe this theme. There is now a vigorous discussion of vocation among Catholic and Protestant scholars, and although Farley herself has not been involved in this discussion, the ethical insights she has developed over the years can contribute much to it.[17]

Farley's ideas on commitment and related topics are particularly useful for the contemporary reassessment of Christian vocation because she understands both Catholic and Protestant experiences so well and because she has integrated feminist insights so thoroughly into her work. A Catholic Sister of Mercy who taught for more than three decades in a historically Protestant seminary at a secularized university (Yale Divinity School), Farley was trained in philosophy before undertaking studies of Christian ethics under James Gustafson at Yale. Gustafson, a pathbreaking Protestant scholar who later taught at the University of Chicago and Emory University, brought an ecumenical spirit and an openness to diverse disciplines and methods to his theological and ethical work, and encouraged his students to pursue projects related to their backgrounds and interests. Farley began teaching full-time in New Haven in 1971, shortly before Gustafson moved to Chicago, and during her tenure at Yale Divinity School she was an active participant in important vocational struggles involving herself and other Sisters of Mercy. Experiences during the period just prior to the publication of *Personal Commitments* in 1986 included tensions with the Vatican over demands that the sisters (elected leaders and many members) found inimical to their sense of what God was calling them to be and do. Three cases were profoundly significant for these women religious: a 1982 Vatican directive to the Mercy General Administrative Team halting consideration of whether their hospitals should provide tubal ligations; a 1983 ultimatum that Sister Agnes Mary Mansour should resign as Director of the Michigan Department of Social Services; and various pressures brought on Farley herself during 1984–1985 to disavow a judgment concerning diversity among Catholics on the abortion issue. This last instance had involved a 1983 survey published as an advertisement in the *New York Times* just prior to the 1984 U.S. presidential election. By late 1984 Farley and 23 other Catholic sisters faced the possibility of being dismissed from their communities if they did not publicly disassociate themselves from the advertisement.

Each of these cases involved complex issues and a "trial by fire" of the vocations of the sisters affected. Their ideals, intelligence, faith, and staying power were tested by pressures from within and without. Farley offered an analysis of the tubal ligation crisis to colleagues at the June 1982 convention of the Catholic Theological Society of America (CTSA) under the title, "Power and Powerlessness: A Case in Point." She explained that concern for the well-being of patients in hospitals operated by the Religious Sisters of Mercy of the Union had led the elected leaders of the community to sponsor a theological and ethical study of the policy banning tubal ligations in Catholic hospitals. These officers were persuaded by the study to recommend that tubal ligations should be made available in Mercy hospitals, which then comprised the largest network of private nonprofit hospitals in the country. This put them in a position of dissent from the hierarchical authorities, since the policy had been established by the National Conference of Catholic Bishops. Although the Mercy General Administrative Team did not order a change in hospital policy, they informed hospital administrators of their belief that tubal ligations should be available "when failure to provide [them] would cause unjust injury to persons," and they expressed their "desire to draw concerned persons into dialogue on the issue." After some discussion between Sisters of Mercy and U.S. bishops on the matter, a directive of Pope John Paul II ended the dialogue with an ultimatum that the Mercy officers should withdraw their letter to the hospitals and accept magisterial teaching on tubal ligation. This Vatican directive posed a crisis of conscience for the Mercy leadership team, which they resolved in favor of submitting to Church authorities. Their submission entailed informing the Vatican officials on May 11, 1982, that although "they had personal disagreements" with official teaching on tubal ligations, "they would not in the light of present circumstances take a public position in opposition to it" and "they would withdraw their letter to the Community's hospitals."[18]

Farley's analysis of the reasons for this submission is instructive for a theology of vocation. She points out that three values were at stake—ministry, truth, and community—and all three had to be respected in the decision. Recognizing that public standoffs between the Vatican and women's religious congregations had led to the dissolution of American communities of sisters in the recent past, and knowing that not all Sisters of Mercy shared their own vision, the officers judged it prudent not to "take this Community 'to a wall' on this particular issue forced to a time-line by external authorities."[19] Their concern for community survival was not about preserving community for its own sake but about preserving the conditions for the possibility of continuing a healing ministry in their hospitals and maintaining a corporate voice capable of raising the question of truth again in a more favorable time. To employ the metaphor from *Personal Commitments,* they were willing to compromise their vision of truth and justice in order to preserve the "framework for love" that had served ministry so well in the past and still had such promise for the future.[20] Their capitulation was justified by Farley in terms of a traditional moral principle that allows for material cooperation in evil for the sake of a "proportionate good," with a proviso that the decision needs ongoing assessment from within and beyond the Mercy community. "[T]his story is unfinished," she concludes. "The wisdom of the decision of the Sisters of Mercy may become manifest only when their voice is once again heard."[21]

Shortly after the tubal ligation case had been temporarily resolved, Mercy leaders were again confronted with Vatican pressures overriding their authority, this time with regard to appointing sisters to ministerial positions. The case of Sister Agnes Mary Mansour, a member of Farley's own Detroit Province of the Religious Sisters of Mercy, involved complex issues of political ministry, government service, and abortion. In 1982 Mansour had been President of Mercy College of Detroit for eleven years, and with the support of provincial leaders she decided to implement Mercy chapter statements about justice and systemic change by accepting a political appointment by the governor-elect of Michigan, James Blanchard. Sister Helen Marie Burns, Provincial Administrator, writes that she "telephoned Archbishop [Edmund]

Szoka who expressed his approval for the appointment and reflected his concern—should it be the Department of Social Services—for a clear stand relative to the abortion issue."[22] Mansour spoke with Szoka on December 29, the day the governor-elect announced her appointment, and felt uncertain of the archbishop's support. It was clear, however, that he wanted her to state her opposition to abortion and to Medicaid payments for abortions, although her post would require her to uphold the law that mandated them. Burns quoted a December 31, 1982, *Detroit Free Press* article that indicated to her the archbishop's support for Mansour was "clear and firm":

> "A lot is being made about the fact that the [Department of Social Services] (uses Medicaid funds) to pay for abortions," [Szoka] said. "It's creating a problem where there is none. . . . As a sister, Sister Mansour must be in accord with the church. But in her job she has to follow the laws of the state, even if she doesn't agree with them. . . . The fact that her appointment encompasses so many of the areas women religious have traditionally worked in—poor, foster children, welfare—could give a powerful witness to the Christian dimension of the D.S.S."[23]

Between the Governor-elect's announcement and the March 8 confirmation hearing, however, pressure from right-to-life groups led Archbishop Szoka to ask Mansour to relinquish the appointment unless she made a clear statement against Medicaid funding for abortions. Mansour was decidedly against abortion, but she had reached a more nuanced view of the Medicaid situation than would allow her to comply with Szoka's wishes, which she subsequently described thus:

> I'm opposed to abortion and consider it a violent solution to a human problem. I don't consider myself pro-choice; I am pro-life. I also recognize that those who are pro-life need to be more convincing in changing attitudes than in controlling what is done in a pluralistic society. Living in a morally pluralistic society, one must respect the fact that other people may conscientiously come to other decisions regarding abortion. We should not attempt to control their

decisions through public policy when no consensus exists. Neither do I feel it would be appropriate to withdraw resources for the poor as long as abortion is legal in our society. It would be illegal to withdraw [M]edicaid funds for abortion.[24]

On February 23 Szoka called for Mansour to resign the position, and Mercy leaders then sought in various ways to gain time to consider the issues. Burns and her administrative team named these issues in a March 5 press release: "a) the religious community's traditional involvement in social services; b) their support for Sister Agnes Mary Mansour in accepting the appointment as Director of Social Services; and c) their respect for the Archbishop's authority."[25] Church authorities, however, took swift action to address what they regarded as a simple matter of obedience and insisted that Mercy leaders confront Mansour with a stark choice. On March 23 the apostolic delegate, Archbishop Pio Laghi, gave Mercy general administrators Sister M. Theresa Kane and Sister Emily George a letter indicating that the Vatican Congregation for Religious and Secular Institutes (CRIS) required Kane to order Mansour to resign or else face dismissal from the congregation. After extensive consultation the Mercy leaders (provincial and general) sought an alternative solution to the dilemma. On April 11 Kane requested formal reconsideration of Rome's decision, with a provision that Mansour would be granted a leave of absence from the Sisters of Mercy during her term of political office, effective April 20, 1983. The leadership team expected there would be time for discussion of this alternative with the Holy See, but instead their authority was bypassed by Roman officials, who sought a direct confrontation with Mansour. CRIS had delegated Bishop Anthony Bevilacqua of Brooklyn, New York, to "approach Sister Agnes Mary directly and to require, in the name of the Holy See and by virtue of her vow of obedience, that she immediately resign as Director of the Department of Social Services," and he did this during a momentous meeting on May 9, 1983.[26] The Mercy sisters in attendance—Agnes Mary Mansour, Helen Marie Burns (the Detroit provincial leader), and Emily George (a Detroit Province member then serving on the general administrative team)—were surprised by the nature of this meeting, having expected an opportunity to discuss the issues with church authorities. Mansour knew that Bevilacqua had been delegated by Pope John Paul II to convey the Holy See's decision concerning her government appointment, but neither she nor the Mercy leaders realized she would be expected to come to an immediate decision about her future as a woman religious.

On May 9 at the Mercy provincial house in Detroit, Bevilacqua presented a long document from the Holy See to Mansour. This "formal precept" summarized the Vatican interpretation of events since December and the official policy on leaves of absence, and concluded with the following points:

> 3. In virtue of this mandate and as *ad hoc* delegate of the Holy See, I hereby require, in the name of the Holy See and by virtue of your vow of obedience to the Holy Father, that you immediately resign your position as Director of the Department of Social Services in the State of Michigan.
> 4. Should you refuse to obey this precept to resign immediately . . . I shall be compelled to initiate immediately the canonical process that subjects you to the penalty of imposed secularization entailing dismissal from the religious Congregation of the Sisters of Mercy and the loss of your canonical status as a Religious Sister.[27]

Mansour later observed that the meeting offered "no due process" and "there wasn't even a full understanding of my rights." She feared dismissal from her community and scandal. Burns's account of the meeting's outcome accords with that of Mansour:

> After discussion, argumentation, reflection, and prayer, Sister Agnes Mary regretfully requested dispensation from her vows. She had asked what alternatives were open to her and was offered none. She had stated that she did not wish to be in defiance of the Holy Father and did not wish to be dismissed. She asked for dispensation, then, as the only means possible to avoid resigning from a position she felt was in accord with the mission of the Sisters of Mercy and to avoid defiance of the Holy Father by forcing the Holy See to dismiss her from the Sisters of Mercy.[28]

Bevilacqua had brought to the meeting an official document of dispensation from vows, which Mansour and he signed, along with Mercy leaders Burns and George.[29] Mansour left the meeting officially separated from the religious community to which she had belonged for thirty years.

Later efforts by Mercy leaders to have the case reconsidered because the process had impinged on Mansour's freedom without benefit of canonical legal advice proved unsuccessful. In the fall of 1983 the Eleventh General Chapter of the Sisters of Mercy of the Union voiced deep concern over the matter, objecting to the lack of mutuality and due process in the Vatican's handling of Mansour's case.[30] Mercy general administrators soon faced further difficulties concerning political ministry, this time involving two sisters from Rhode Island, Arlene Violet (who was running for state Attorney General) and Elizabeth Morancy (who sought a fourth term in the state legislature). Although Bishop Louis Gelineau of Providence had given Morancy a diocesan award in 1981 for her "work with the handicapped," including "her successful sponsorship of two bills providing subsidy programs for parents of handicapped children," by 1983 he opposed the political ministries of both Morancy and Violet.[31] Each sister sought ways of continuing political work without leaving the congregation, and the Twelfth General Chapter sent a formal petition to the Holy See for an indult that would allow Morancy to remain a legislator, which Rome denied.[32] By the time Theresa Kane completed her term as General Administrator of the congregation in July 1984, both Violet and Morancy accepted dispensations from their vows in order to continue political ministries originally undertaken in response to Mercy chapter decrees.

These developments had meanwhile alerted other women religious to issues of Vatican power and due process of canon law, and the Mercy cases were kept in mind during a third critical confrontation between Rome and U.S. sisters, which took place during 1984–1986. The immediate cause of the confrontation was a display advertisement published October 7, 1984, in the *New York Times* by a lay organization called Catholics for a Free Choice (CFFC) during the presidential race between Republican Ronald Reagan and Democrat Walter

Mondale. Geraldine Ferraro, a Catholic congresswoman from New Jersey, was Mondale's running-mate, and the first female candidate to be nominated for vice-president in U.S. history. Many Catholics were dismayed by the way some prominent members of the hierarchy had attacked Ferraro during the campaign because, although expressing a personal stance against abortion, she assumed a political stance of tolerance in view of its legality. They noted that Catholic male politicians, such as Mario Cuomo and Edward Kennedy, did not receive the sort of treatment that Ferraro did. Thus as the election neared, CFFC sought to inform voters that Catholic thinking on abortion and related public policy was not limited to the positions of Cardinals Bernard Law or John O'Connor. In 1983 the pro-choice group had surveyed a number of Catholic thinkers and obtained their endorsement of a statement that included these claims:

> a diversity of opinion regarding abortion exists among committed Catholics: a large number of Catholic theologians hold that even direct abortion, though tragic, can sometimes be a moral choice; [and], according to data compiled by the National Opinion Research Center, only 11% of Catholics surveyed disapprove of abortion in all circumstances. . . . Finally, while recognizing and supporting the legitimate role of the hierarchy in providing Catholics with moral guidance on political and social issues and in seeking legislative remedies to social injustices, we believe that Catholics should not seek the kind of legislation that curtails the legitimate exercise of the freedom of religion and conscience or discriminates against poor women.[33]

Among the ninety-six names published as endorsing this statement were those of twenty-four women religious, including Farley, who like many other signers had responded to a 1983 CFFC survey without knowing that the document would eventually be published as an advertisement. Although the statement was the work of lay theologians and CFFC, it was the clergy and members of religious communities among the signers who felt the direct force of Vatican objections to the advertisement. Of these, three men promptly withdrew their endorsement in December 1984 and a fourth had settled by May 1985, but twenty-two sisters held out for nearly two years until they were able to "clarify" their positions in a way that both their consciences and Rome could accept.[34] They had managed, during an arduous process that taxed the energies of signers and community officers alike, to retain community membership without backing down from their claim that signing the statement had been appropriate in view of the situation in the United States at the time.

The *New York Times* case affected a number of religious congregations and put pressure as well on the officers and staff of the Leadership Conference of Women Religious (LCWR), the national organization of elected leaders of women's communities. LCWR called for a day of prayer and fasting in March 1985 on behalf of "a just and peaceful resolution to the situation," and supported the officers by trying to communicate with the Vatican behind the scenes. The organization also sought to educate its members by focusing the program of its September 1985 convention in New Orleans on ethical decision making, inviting Margaret Farley as a plenary speaker. Despite the fact that two prominent members of the hierarchy cancelled their plans to attend and celebrate the liturgy because Farley was speaking, LCWR went ahead with their program.[35] Farley's presentation, "From Moral Insight to Moral Choice: Decision-Making in the Christian Community," was a general one that did not mention her own situation as a signer, although in discussing natural law she declared that "'authority' to teach is the power to evoke consent, the power to enable to see. Truth . . . does not come in the form of extrinsic imposition, in the form of juridical power."[36] Neither the Mansour case nor that of the Vatican 24 has been the subject of an ethical essay by Farley comparable to her treatment of the tubal ligation case in 1982. These three cases, however, were unfolding during the years she prepared *Personal Commitments* for publication in 1986. They have informed her subsequent work as well, including an essay occasioned by the Vatican's removal of moral theologian Charles Curran from his tenured position at the Catholic University of America in 1986. In her 1987 essay, "Moral Discourse in the Public Arena," Farley observed that "[w]e have had long centuries in which to learn the counterproductiveness of coercive measures when the issue becomes not truth but power."[37]

Farley waited until the occasion of her presidential address to the Catholic Theological Society of America in 2000 to make a full statement of her reasons against the hierarchy's "overwhelming preoccupation" with abortion policies and its effort to control internal debate on moral questions. Arguing that these approaches are counterproductive and scandalous, she recommended that opposition to abortion "should be removed from the center of the [church's political] agenda until the credibility gap regarding women and the church is addressed."[38] Although abortion policy should remain part of the agenda, Farley invited speculation on gains to be made if racism or welfare rights were to become the central focus instead.[39] She also argued that efforts by the hierarchy to curtail debate among theologians are unhelpful. Not only do they diminish the "effectiveness of the Church's voice in the public political arena," but they also cause confusion among the faithful and discourage the "best and the brightest" from pursuing a "vocation in theology."[40] The aim of this critique is to restore the possibility that the church can bring a prophetic witness to the public arena. In her estimation, a reconfigured agenda and a reasonable degree of tolerance for theological diversity will allow the church to regain credibility in the wider society. This will permit its voice to summon everyone "to the imperatives of justice and the respect and care of those among us who are wounded or ignored." The tradition itself, in its enduring respect for reason and human freedom and its ideal of love for one another, has the resources needed to restore trust between those "whose vocation is theology and those whose vocation is church leadership."[41] The willingness of Pope John Paul II to pray for forgiveness at the Western Wall in Jerusalem during Lent of the Jubilee Year 2000 exemplifies the sort of "humility, respect, and deepest compassion" required for the church in the United States to influence the wider society for the good.[42]

As one looks back over the tensions between the Sisters of Mercy and the hierarchy that affected Farley so profoundly during the 1980s and then observes the appreciative way she invokes the image of papal leadership while seeking to deflect the U.S. bishops from a counterproductive public strategy, there are several things to note. The first is the way Farley's theological work is so thoroughly Catholic, shaped by the characteristic conviction that tensions between faith and reason, authority and freedom, individual conscience and the common good, are creative and enduring ones. The vocations of theologians and church leaders are different, and each role affords a different vision of what circumstances require. Although church officials should have the last word, this word will be the wiser if leaders listen well to the wide range of church members' experiences before teaching on controversial issues. Also noteworthy is the irony that the Vatican made such strong efforts in the early 1980s to control the behavior of women religious—whose political actions and statements issued from concern for the poor and marginalized, and, whatever one thinks of their wisdom, were legal and well meant—during the very years when the hierarchy missed its opportunity to stem the sexual abuse crisis by taking strong action against the criminal behavior of priests. If only the wrath of Rome had fallen on abusive priests with half the force expended on Agnes Mary Mansour or Elizabeth Morancy! And finally, it is intriguing to note that although Farley regularly stresses that women's experience is a crucial resource for feminist ethics, she has rarely written about the experiences of herself and other Sisters of Mercy. The brief treatment of the tubal ligation case she presented to colleagues of the CTSA in 1982 was exceptional in this regard. Nevertheless these experiences inform her choice of topics and the ethical insights she reaches, and they undoubtedly contribute as well to the theology of vocation that grounds her work. Although she does not often employ the rhetoric of vocation or call, the occasional instances are telling, perhaps none more so than the following passage from her 1985 address to LCWR, offered in a discussion of conflicts of value:

> When it comes to making radical choices—choices that involve explicit decisions about what we will love absolutely and how we will integrate all of our other loves and all of our actions in relation to our absolute love—we need a method of discernment that goes beyond rational assessment of situations and consideration of

principles. We need a method that enables us to discern the call of God—a call not always able to be understood only as a call to "right" rather than "wrong," or even "good" rather than "evil," but a call to the way along which we are to go if we are to be faithful to what we love above all else.[43]

This ideal of fidelity to the divine call, we may infer, is what enabled the various Sisters of Mercy to sacrifice different finite goods and loves, even their treasured identity as members of this religious congregation, when confronted with an ultimatum that would take them off the path their consciences had discerned as the way of fidelity to God, who called them to care especially for the poor and marginalized. Farley said as much at the December 21, 2004, funeral of Agnes Mary Mansour:

> It was a painful truth that she had to leave [the Sisters of Mercy], that the church declared her officially not a member. There was suffering in the community, and also for her. When she left she was quoted as saying that she would always be a Sister of Mercy in her heart. And that has absolutely been the case. She continued in works of mercy all her life.[44]

Farley's vocational metaphor from 1985 of the "way along which we are to go" seems to anticipate the metaphor of "framework for love" associated with her largely implicit theology of vocation in *Personal Commitments*. Both metaphors suggest the idea of a context for living as a Christian, one capable of allowing the agent to relate finite loves appropriately to their divine Source.

INSIGHTS CONTRIBUTING TO A THEOLOGY OF VOCATION

With these experiences and writings of Farley in mind, we are now in a position to draw out some implications of her ethics for today's discussion of vocation. As was mentioned earlier, in recent years there has been a resurgence of interest in the topic of vocation in the United States, thanks in part to funding from the Lilly Endowment. Two works of note that Lilly has supported are Sandra M. Schneiders's trilogy-in-progress, *Religious Life in the New Millennium*, of which the first two volumes (*Finding the Treasure* and *Selling All*) were published in 2000 and 2001, and Douglas J. Schuurman's 2004 study, *Vocation: Discerning Our Callings in Life*.[45] The former is a masterful treatment of the Catholic vowed religious life, with particular attention to the situation of contemporary women who have chosen this "organic life-form," to use Schneiders's language. The latter is a more general exploration of the topic of vocation from a Protestant perspective. Each makes a distinctive contribution to contemporary understanding of the religious reality of vocation, and both can be effectively complemented by some ethical insights Farley has developed over the years. Here are some of the ideas from Farley's ethics that are particularly useful for the contemporary discussion of vocation.

Active Receptivity and Framework for Love

The metaphor of framework, derived from the human activity of building, takes away the "mystique" of vocation and assigns human responsibility properly. Frameworks have been humanly built. This metaphor counters the passivity of precritical understandings of vocation and highlights the active dimension of the experience, which is recognized by Schneiders, Schuurman, and others. Farley has also written on the notion of "active receptivity," an idea that offers philosophical and theological grounds for recognizing our role as cocreators of our own vocations and complements the efforts of contemporary analysts of vocation to demystify the experience. Schuurman, for example, stresses that it is a "misconception" to think of vocation as providing a "blueprint" for life or an "unmistakable, miraculous call." Rather the "call" is mediated in "numerous and quiet ways," and is essentially a matter of employing "one's God-given gifts to be of use to the broader community."[46] Schneiders is similarly concerned to minimize miraculous interpretations of the imagery of the call to a religious vocation. Faith in God's presence and guidance does not require that this call must occur outside normal processes of attraction and influence. Far from being a thunderclap from the sky, the experience of vocation involves a

> convergence of interior factors such as attraction, talent, interest, experience, desires, ideals, and even realistic fears and awareness of personal limitations, with exterior factors such as people I admire, work that interests me, opportunity presenting itself, needs that move me, structures that facilitate exploration, invitation from another. This convergence is usually a rich mixture that is both confusing and exciting and leads a person to begin to explore what this might mean.[47]

What Farley has observed concerning the "active receptivity" involved in the love of God and neighbor is indeed congruent with what these contemporaries are noting about the experience of Christian vocation: "[A]ll this receptivity at the heart of Christian existence is not in any way only passivity. . . . The receiving which is each human person's from God, and from one another within a life shared in God, is an active participation in the active receptivity of Christ, awakening, growing, reaching to the coincidence of peak receptivity with peak activity."[48]

Value of Institutions

As structures, frameworks are valuable and necessary; they are not mere scaffolding. Keeping them serviceable is a worthy task, and whenever possible the frameworks for love should be preserved and strengthened. The Mercy leaders who decided in 1982 to submit to a Vatican directive they judged to be wrong did so with the awareness that this "material cooperation with evil" seemed necessary to prevent greater harm, namely the loss of the institutions that expressed the Mercy ministry. Schneiders prefers an organic metaphor for the institution of vowed religious life, treating it as a "lifeform" at some risk in a postmodern era, one whose evolution (or possible extinction) is in large measure in the hands of religious themselves. Farley's structural metaphor complements this organic one nicely, inviting awareness of the ways that institutions are needed to support life, just as skeletal structures are needed for complex organisms.

Egalitarianism and a New Natural Law Sexual Ethic

Although official Catholic teaching no longer promotes an elitist view of celibacy as superior to marriage, the magisterial positions on sexual ethics have not kept pace with these developments in ecclesiology. The classic Christian ethic has tended to view celibacy and marriage as islands of grace in a sea of sexual sin. Farley is a leader in developing a more adequate sexual ethic, one that respects the complexity of sexual sin and grace and the diversity of human beings. Proposing that justice is a better norm for sex than either the traditional "taboo morality" or the vague subjectivism of "love," she argues that sexual relations, to be just, must respect the "concrete reality" of the partners, which she analyzes in terms of their autonomy and relationality. This leads her to develop several criteria for judging the appropriateness of sexual relations: avoidance of unjust harm, free consent, mutuality, equality of power, commitment, fruitfulness, and social justice. The list comprises a stringent set of norms that apply equally to heterosexual and homosexual couples.[49] The pioneering work Farley has done in the area of same-sex relationships is also a resource for vocational exploration by homosexual and other differently gendered persons, including the increasingly wide consideration of gay marriage.

Analysis of the Relation Between Justice and Love

Farley has devoted much attention to this topic. Her 1975 essay, "New Patterns of Relationship," examined the historical reasons for bringing a new feminist approach to the question and argued persuasively for understanding justice and love to be dialectically related, for "justice itself is the norm of love," while love (mutuality, communion) is the goal of justice:

> What is required of Christians is a just love, a love which does indeed correspond to the reality of those loved. . . . Minimal justice,

then, may have equality as its norm and full mutuality as its goal. Justice will be maximal as it approaches the ultimate goal of communion of each person with all persons and with God.[50]

Farley's detailed analysis of justice as a norm for love would be especially helpful as a complement to Schuurman's discussion, which emphasizes love as "vocation's guiding moral norm" and shalom as "its orienting ideal." Schuurman recognizes that a proper understanding of vocation ought to "criticize hierarchies—whether based on gender, race, or class" and "transform asymmetric relations." A fuller treatment of what constitutes a love that is *just* would enhance this discussion considerably.[51] Farley's 1975 analysis of *agape*, equal regard, self-sacrifice, and mutuality in light of the recognition of women's full human dignity offers ways of advancing the revolutionary changes required in intimate and public relationships if the aims Schuurman expresses are to be achieved.[52]

Attention to the Problems of Postmodernity for Love and Commitments

Farley returned to the analysis of love and justice with new force and insight in her 2002 Madeleva Lecture, *Compassionate Respect: A Feminist Approach to Medical Ethics and Other Questions*. This time the analysis is conducted mainly in conversation with philosophical ethics and theories of postmodernity rather than Christian texts, with particular attention to the current debate between schools of ethics emphasizing care and those stressing autonomy, respect, and justice. She argues that the debate is misconceived, and maintains that when care is thought of in terms of compassion it becomes evident that "only if they [compassion and respect] are integrated, each requiring the other, will their full meaning be conceptually clear and practically useful in moral discernment."[53] She describes compassion as "a way of 'seeing' that evokes a moral response," and maintains that this way of seeing brings a "stronger affect" to the notion of care because it attends to the concrete reality of suffering human beings.

Attention to the concrete reality of suffering human beings is a theme threaded through Farley's writings of the last decade. Postmodernity, she is quite aware, has challenged traditional understandings of the unified "self" and posed philosophical problems for claims about "reality," and the possibility of commitment and love. And yet, she maintains, the seemingly decentered postmodern self ("no longer preoccupied with self-certainty in settled truth") is paradoxically "freed for relationship," particularly when it is willing to respect the destabilizing experiences of beauty and the pain of others, and to respond with reverence and compassion.[54] However attenuated our freedom may be, it remains the case that human beings have some ability to focus our attention and bind ourselves to future deeds of love. Indeed, as she argued in *Personal Commitments*, it is precisely the instability of our experiences of desire that leads us to bind up our futures by making commitments, for commitment is "love's way of being whole when it is not yet whole, love's way of offering its incapacities as well as its power."[55] Schneiders's treatment of the need for "perpetual commitment" to Jesus Christ in religious life is explicitly dependent on this work of Farley, although she does not probe the factors that can sometimes justify seeking a dispensation from religious vows once the commitment has been publicly expressed. Further conversation with Farley on this matter seems warranted, as well as on whether or not there is a theological difference between Farley's claim that only God is to be loved absolutely and Schneiders's assertion that "[t]he commitment that constitutes Religious Life is absolute, total, and unconditional, whereas the implicated commitment to the congregation is relative, partial, and conditional" because the essence of religious life involves "the commitment to love Jesus Christ totally, absolutely, and forever and to express and embody that love . . . in the complete and exclusive self-gift of consecrated celibacy."[56]

Schuurman's discussion of vocation would likewise benefit from more explicit attention to the demands and limits of commitment, for it presently is more concerned with arguing the value and possibility of vocation than with pondering what constitutes fidelity to vocation once it is embraced. He shares the basic position of Farley and Schneiders that one's ultimate relationship is with God, and this leads him to recommend always being "open to the possibility that God will call us to other forms of paid work, to new social relations, to a different marital status, to different roles in our churches and communities."[57] One senses that he would welcome the sort of clear criteria Farley provides for changing "frameworks for love" as a way to balance the openness to change that his theological position commends.

Schuurman and Schneiders both share with Farley the recognition that the Christian's vocation is linked with concern for the needs and sufferings of others, and their discussions will be enriched by Farley's increasingly explicit emphasis on the call to "drink the cup" of suffering, and to combat vigorously the "unnecessary" suffering that is caused by injustice, including injustice for which the Christian tradition bears some responsibility.[58] In her recent work Farley has elaborated this concern in terms of the need to see how religions, particularly fundamentalist versions, are putting the health of persons, especially women, at great risk. The inability of most Catholic bishops to tolerate the use of condoms as part of a comprehensive program to prevent spread of the AIDS virus is surely a factor in Farley's articulating this concern about fundamentalist religion. Undoubtedly her earlier experience of tensions over health care issues between the Vatican and the Sisters of Mercy contributes to her insistence that the suffering we see in the global HIV/AIDS pandemic should inspire Christians to examine their own attitudes and actions in light of the gospel mandate to imitate God's mercy:

> Like God's mercy, genuine human mercy is formed by respect for what God has made—for human freedom, relationality, embodiment, historical and cultural formation, uniqueness, and the potentiality of fullness of life in an unlimited future. Like God's mercy, genuine human mercy is made true by its justice.[59]

Mercy, we do well to note, is the distinctive charism of her religious congregation, and there is no doubt that her years of contemplating this particular gift have contributed to Farley's insights on what works of mercy and justice are demanded in our time. We should hardly be surprised that her writings argue so strongly that attention to the sufferings of others is essential to love, in a postmodern or any other world, or that poised as she is between the world of the Religious Sisters of Mercy and that of the secular academy, she probes, again and again, the connection between compassion/care and rationality. She has further enriched the contemporary discussion of vocation by her occasional remarks on the Christian vocation to prophecy, something Schneiders claims is central to the "organic lifeform" of religious life, and by her own willingness "to speak the truth in love" to a wide audience of secular and religious readers, including church authorities who might encounter her works.[60]

The stakes for rethinking the meaning of vocation in a world of systemic violence and injustice are as high today as ever. Farley's ideas on "frameworks for love," on the relation between justice and compassion, on how to love justly in a postmodern world, and on the process and obligations of personal commitments constitute an invaluable resource for this task.

NOTES

1. John Gardner, *Self-Renewal: The Individual and the Innovative Society* (New York: Harper and Row, 1963), 7. Gardner credits Peter Drucker's *Landmarks of Tomorrow* (New York: Harper and Brothers, 1959), chapters 1 and 2, as the source of this insight.

2. Margaret A. Farley, *Personal Commitments: Beginning, Keeping, Changing* (San Francisco: Harper and Row, 1986).

3. John Shea, *Stories of God: An Unauthorized Biography* (Chicago: Thomas More Press, 1978), 52.

4. Andrew M. Greeley, *The Jesus Myth* (Garden City, NY: Doubleday and Company, 1971), 13. Greeley's prefatory Note begins with a defense of his title: "The word 'myth' is used in the title of this volume in a specific and definite sense. A myth is a symbolic story which demonstrates, in Alan Watts' words, 'the inner meaning of the universe and of human life.' To say that Jesus is a myth is not to say that he is a legend but that his life and message are an attempt to demonstrate 'the inner meaning of the universe and of human life.'" I concur with Greeley's judgment that there is great value in employing this term that is so "common among historians of religion, literary critics, and social scientists" and that Christians should overcome their fear of the word "myth" and appropriate it as a valuable tool for understanding their faith (12).

5. James M. Gustafson, *Can Ethics Be Christian?* (Chicago: University of Chicago Press, 1975), 179.

6. Farley, *Personal Commitments*, 11.

7. Frederick Buechner, *Wishful Thinking* (San Francisco: HarperSanFrancisco, 1993), 119. Cited here from Parker J. Palmer, *Let Your Life Speak: Listening for the Voice of Vocation* (San Francisco: Jossey-Bass Publishers, 2000), 16.

8. Farley, *Personal Commitments*, 22, 84, 92, 99, and elsewhere.

9. Margaret Farley, "An Ethic for Same-Sex Relations," in *A Challenge to Love*, ed. Robert Nugent (New York: Crossroad, 1983), 103–4.

10. Vatican II, Dogmatic Constitution on the Church (*Lumen Gentium*), 32. All citations from the Second Vatican Council are from Walter M. Abbott, ed., *The Documents of Vatican II* (New York: America Press, 1966).

11. Margaret Farley, "The Church and the Family: An Ethical Task," *Horizons* 10 (1983): 56.

12. For a full treatment of Protestant discussions, see Douglas J. Schuurman, *Vocation: Discerning Our Callings in Life* (Grand Rapids, MI: Eerdmans, 2004).

13. Farley, "The Church and the Family," 63.

14. Margaret Farley, "New Patterns of Relationship: Beginnings of a Moral Revolution, *Theological Studies* 36 (1975): 628 and 645.

15. Paul Ricoeur, *The Symbolism of Evil*, trans. Emerson Buchanan (Boston: Beacon Press, 1967), 351.

16. Farley, *Personal Commitments*, 10. Farley is quoting here from Ricoeur's *Essays on Biblical Interpretation*, ed. Lewis S. Mudge (Philadelphia: Fortress, 1980), 97.

17. In addition to other vocation-related grants to scholars and to seminaries and divinity schools, the Lilly Endowment awarded $176.2 million to 88 church-related colleges and universities during 2000–2002 through its Programs for the Theological Exploration of Vocation (PTEV) initiative. According to the PTEV website, the purpose of these grants is to help the schools "establish or strengthen programs that 1) assist students in examining the relationship between faith and vocational choices, 2) provide opportunities for gifted young people to explore Christian ministry, and 3) enhance the capacity of a school's faculty and staff to teach and mentor students effectively in this area" (http://www.ptev.org/history.aspx, last accessed January 2007). The "History" section on this site provides details about the grants made in 2000 and 2001, and the recipients are listed under "Participating Schools." Information on the 2002 awards ($79.2 million) was supplied by PETV Program Coordinator Kim Maphis Early in an e-mail message sent to me April 29, 2004.

18. Margaret Farley, "Power and Powerlessness: A Case in Point," *Proceedings of the Catholic Theological Society of America* 37 (1982): 116–17. I have discussed these issues more fully in Anne E. Patrick, *Liberating Conscience* (New York: Continuum, 1996), 41–48.

19. Farley, "Power and Powerlessness," 118.

20. In making this decision Mercy leaders were vividly aware of two cases from the late 1960s in which women's religious communities had been drastically reorganized after hierarchical interventions short-circuited internal debates on post–Vatican II renewal. In both cases (Glenmary Sisters and Sisters of the Immaculate Heart of Mary of Los Angeles) the majority of sisters had responded to Vatican interventions by reluctantly requesting dispensations from their vows and forming noncanonical religious organizations. For recent accounts of these events, see Helen M. Lewis and Monica Appleby, *Mountain Sisters: From Convent to Community* (Lexington: The University Press of Kentucky, 2003), and Anita M. Caspary, *Witness to Integrity: The Crisis of the Immaculate Heart Community of California* (Collegeville, MN: Liturgical Press, 2003).

21. Farley, "Power and Powerlessness," 119. The eminent moral theologian, Richard A. McCormick, S.J., had been involved in the study originally commissioned by the Mercy leaders, and with bioethicist Corrine Bayley, C.S.J., had published some findings in "Sterilization: The Dilemma of Catholic Hospitals," *America* 143 (1980): 222–25. He later commented in *Health and Medicine in the Catholic Tradition* (New York: Crossroad, 1984), 103–4, that "In 1980, I coauthored . . . an article in *America* arguing that some sterilizations were morally defensible. A bishop friend of mine remarked to me, 'I can name you at least one hundred bishops who agree with you—but none who will say so publicly.' That is, of course, profoundly saddening for anyone who treasures the free flow of information in the Church."

22. Helen Marie Burns, R.S.M., "Case Study: The Experience of Sisters of Mercy of the Union in Public Office," in *Authority, Community, and Conflict*, ed. Madonna Kolbenschlag (Kansas City, MO: Sheed and Ward, 1986), 5.

23. Quoted in ibid., 6. Archbishop Szoka's account of events in December differs from that of Burns, according to his letter of February 23, 1983, which is reproduced as an appendix to Kolbenschlag, *Authority*, 155–57.

24. Agnes Mary Mansour, interviewed by Annie Lally Milhaven, ed., *The Inside Stories: 13 Valiant Women Challenging the Church* (Mystic, CT: Twenty-Third Publications, 1987), 66.

25. Burns, "Case Study," 8.

26. Ibid., 12.

27. Kolbenschlag, *Authority*, 173. The full text of the formal precept is found on 168–73.

28. Burns, "Case Study," 12.

29. The Indult of Secularization is reprinted in Kolbenschlag, *Authority*, 174.

30. Burns, "Case Study," 15.

31. The diocesan award is mentioned in a lengthy Petition from the Twelfth General Chapter of the Sisters of Mercy to CRIS, included as "Document 29" in Kolbenschlag, *Authority*, 201.

32. See "Document 29" (196–205) and "Document 30" (205–6) in ibid.

33. The full text is reprinted in *Origins* 14 (December 6, 1984), immediately following a November 15, 1984, statement of Archbishop John R. Quinn, then chair of the U.S. Bishops' Committee on Doctrine, "Abortion: A Clear and Constant Teaching," which criticizes the CFFC statement (413–14). I have discussed this episode of the "Vatican 24" more fully in *Liberating Conscience*, 118–28 and 134–43.

34. Two of the original twenty-four, however, came to advocate a "pro-choice" position, eventually deciding to leave their congregation. See Barbara Ferraro and Patricia Hussey with Jane O'Reilly, *No Turning Back: Two Nuns Battle with the Vatican over Women's Right to Choose* (New York: Poseidon Press, 1990).

35. Archbishop Pio Laghi, Papal Pro-nuncio to the United States, and Archbishop John R. Quinn of San Francisco cancelled plans to attend the LCWR convention, but Archbishop Philip Hannan of New Orleans did celebrate the liturgy there. See Florence Herman and Jerry Filteau's story in the Washington, DC, *Catholic Standard* for September 12, 1985, "Archbishops Boycott Meeting Because of Abortion Ad Signer." Former executive directors of LCWR, Lora Ann Quiñonez and Mary Daniel Turner, describe the careful thought involved in LCWR's convention decisions in their *The Transformation of American Catholic Sisters* (Philadelphia: Temple University Press, 1992), 133–40.

36. Margaret A. Farley, "From Moral Insight to Moral Choice: Discernment and Decision-Making in the Christian Community," (unpublished typescript, 1985), 11.

37. Margaret A. Farley, "Moral Discourse in the Public Arena," in *Vatican Authority and American Catholic Dissent: The Curran Case and Its Consequences,* ed. William W. May (New York: Crossroad, 1987), 184. For a related recent article, see Margaret Farley, "Ethics, Ecclesiology, and the Grace of Self-Doubt," in *A Call to Fidelity: On the Moral Theology of Charles E. Curran,* ed. James J. Walter and Thomas A. Shannon, 55–75 (Washington, DC: Georgetown University Press, 2002).

38. Margaret A. Farley, "The Church in the Public Forum: Scandal or Prophetic Witness?" *Proceedings of the Catholic Theological Society of America* 55 (2000): 89–92.

39. Ibid., 95.

40. Ibid., 96–97.

41. Ibid., 98–99.

42. Ibid., 101.

43. Farley, "From Moral Insight to Moral Choice," 9.

44. Margaret A. Farley, quoted in Arthur Jones, "She Answered to Her Conscience: Agnes Mary Mansour, Who Left Mercys at Vatican Ultimatum, Dies at 73," *National Catholic Reporter* (January 7, 2005), 7.

45. Sandra Schneiders, I.H.M., *Finding the Treasure: Locating Catholic Religious Life in a New Ecclesial and Cultural Context*, vol. 1 of *Religious Life in a New Millennium* (New York: Paulist Press, 2000), and *Selling All: Commitment, Consecrated Celibacy, and Community in Catholic Religious Life*, vol. 2 of *Religious Life in a New Millennium* (New York: Paulist Press, 2001); Douglas Schuurman, *Vocation: Discerning Our Callings in Life* (Grand Rapids, MI: Eerdmans, 2004).

46. Schuurman, *Vocation*, 127 and 164.

47. Schneiders, *Selling All*, 12–13.

48. Farley, "New Patterns of Relationship," 639.

49. Margaret A. Farley, *Just Love: A Framework for Christian Sexual Ethics* (New York: Continuum, 2006), 215–31.

50. Farley, "New Patterns of Relationship," 643 and 646.

51. Schuurman, *Vocation*, 79 and 114.

52. Farley, "New Patterns of Relationship," 632–46. See also Farley, *Just Love*, 196–206.

53. Margaret A. Farley, *Compassionate Respect: A Feminist Approach to Medical Ethics and Other Questions* (New York: Paulist Press, 2002), 4. Farley had made a similar point in her February 24, 1997, Henri de Lubac Lecture at St. Louis University, when she voiced a question that informs her work: "How shall compassion and justice 'kiss,' as the psalmist says, so that justice keeps compassion straight and true, and compassion tests and tests again the truth in every theory of justice?" See her "History, Spirituality, and Justice," *Theology Digest* 45 (Winter 1998): 335.

54. Margaret A. Farley, "How Shall We Love in a Postmodern World," *The Annual of the Society of Christian Ethics* (1994): 17–18.

55. Farley, *Personal Commitments*, 134.

56. Schneiders, *Selling All*, 80.

57. Schuurman, *Vocation*, 162.

58. Margaret A. Farley, "History, Spirituality, and Justice," 335; and, *Compassionate Respect*, 69–79. In the latter work Farley draws attention particularly to the unjust suffering associated with the worldwide HIV/AIDS pandemic and maintains that patriarchal religions must be challenged about their role "in making women invisible" if there is to be a "compassionate response to the crisis of AIDS" (17).

59. Farley, *Compassionate Respect*, 79.

60. See, for example, Farley, "The Church in the Public Forum," 98–99. Schneiders maintains that "as an essentially prophetic vocation and state of life in the Church, Religious Life should constitute a continual call from within the Church to ongoing reform and increasing fidelity to the Gospel"; see her *Finding the Treasure*, 252–53.

Chapter Eleven

Virtuous Decision Makers and Incompetent Patients

The Case of the Conjoined Twins

M. Cathleen Kaveny

In August 2000, a set of Maltese conjoined twins, known to the public by the pseudonyms "Jodie" and "Mary," were born in a Manchester, England, hospital. They were ischiopagus tetrapus conjoined twins, which means that they were joined in the pelvic region and had four lower limbs between them. Viewed externally, the twins shared a single torso, with one baby's head attached on either end. Their legs extended at right angles from the middle of the torso, and their external genitalia appeared on the side of the body. According to medical testimony, with the exception of a large, shared bladder, each twin possessed her own set of internal organs.[1] Nonetheless, Mary's lungs and heart were severely abnormal; she would not have survived long after her birth had it not been for the fact that her circulatory system was able to draw upon Jodie's for a continuing supply of oxygenated blood.[2]

Soon after their birth, the twins became the center of an international controversy regarding whether they should be surgically separated. Without the operation, the twins were predicted to die, probably before their first birthday, because Jodie's heart would not be able to sustain the burden of supporting both herself and her twin. With the operation, Jodie was predicted to live a long and virtually normal life, although she might need several reconstructive operations to repair her urogenital tract. The parents, who were devout Roman Catholics, objected to the operation on a number of grounds, including their belief that the operation would constitute the unjustified killing of Mary. They were supported in their opposition to the procedure by Cormac Murphy-O'Connor, the Cardinal Archbishop of Westminster, who submitted a statement to the Court of Appeal raising a number of objections both to the procedure in itself and to any order to proceed with it over the strong objections of the babies' parents.[3] Nonetheless, the three judges of that Court unanimously decided to authorize the operation,[4] which was performed on November 6, 2000.[5] As expected, Mary died in the twenty-hour operation. As hoped, Jodie returned home to Malta with her parents less than eight months later.

About seven months after the operation, the twins' parents reflected upon their experience in an interview with an English newspaper. The following is an excerpt from a news story about that interview:

> Mr. Attard [the twins' father] said: "Of course we are glad to have Gracie [Jodie's real name] alive but it is still not nice to say we are happy, because Rosie [Mary's real name] died.
>
> "We only have one baby daughter instead of two and as much as we love Gracie we miss Rosie. Maybe Gracie is more special to us because she was saved." Mr. Attard, a builder, and his 35-year-old wife had fought a legal battle to prevent the separation.
>
> Mrs. Attard [the twins' mother] said: "We were upset that we lost the cases because we always thought we should have the right to say what was best for our children and that the taking of life was wrong.
>
> "The decision was taken out of our hands in the end, but we are happy that the decision to separate was taken by the judges. It meant we didn't say, 'Yes, kill Rosie to save Gracie.'
>
> "There would be great guilt if we had.
>
> "I do not know how any parent could decide to end the life of one of their babies."[6]

These reflections on the part of the babies' parents are marked by a very understandable ambivalence about the events that took place in the previous year. On the surface, they may even appear to be internally inconsistent. I think, however, it would be a mistake to dismiss their reflection too quickly on those grounds. In my view, Mr. and Mrs. Attard can be coherently understood as suggesting that the particular demands of their parental roles place certain limits upon the decisions they can make with respect to their twin daughters, which extend beyond the limits of general justice and fairness binding upon everyone.

In my view, the nature of role-related obligations deserves more attention from those reflecting on medical-moral decision making, particularly with respect to the situation of surrogate decision makers acting on behalf of incompetent patients. I believe that this perception is not only consistent with Margaret Farley's work in medical ethics, but in no small measure inspired by it.[7] She has integrated the humane wisdom of the Catholic casuistical tradition on end-of-life decision making with the feminist insight that the demands of justice cannot remain at an abstract level, but must take into account the needs of particular persons—especially the needs of the most marginalized members of society, who are very often women. Calling for "compassionate respect," she invites her readers and students to transcend the apparent dichotomy between honoring the autonomy of others and caring for them in their weakness—to transcend, in other words, the apparent dichotomy between justice and mercy.

Compassionate respect for other human beings begins with the capacity to see them in all their particularity: their strengths, their weaknesses, their hopes, their fears, their medical options, their social and familial contexts. It requires the willingness to engage the situation sympathetically, from their point of view, although it does not demand that their point of view be accepted without comment or challenge. It is my hope that this essay exemplifies, at least imperfectly, the virtue of compassionate respect toward Mr. and Mrs. Attard. As we grapple with the legal and moral issues their case raises, Margaret Farley would caution us not to forget the human dimensions of the situation. The Attards were far from home, without the status conferred by wealth, power, or an elite education, and confronting the full force of the English medical and legal systems. Most importantly, however, they were new parents faced with an almost unimaginable trial of love, justice, and loyalty with respect to their newborn baby daughters.

THE PARENTS' MORAL CLAIMS

There are at least four ways of interpreting the parents' claims to the English newspaper, three of which are not ultimately morally tenable, and one of which I believe turns out to be so. The first two options focus on the moral acceptability of the procedure itself. We could interpret the parents as saying that the operation is morally impermissible, either because it involves the intentional killing of Mary, or because it is unfair knowingly to cause her death under these circumstances. Although these arguments have been persuasive to many persons of good will and intelligence, they are not in my view correct. As I have argued elsewhere, the operation is not in itself morally impermissible.[8]

The third and fourth options focus not on the acceptability of the procedure itself, but rather on the parents' reluctance to be directly involved in authorizing it. The third option interprets the parents' motivations in an uncharitable way, charging them with simple moral hypocrisy on the grounds that they refused to consent to a procedure from which they were so clearly reaping the benefit of having at least one living daughter. That interpretation, however, may very well be incorrect. There is a fourth way of interpreting the parents' concerns that is far more sympathetic to their moral integrity. More specifically, one could understand them as saying that "it is wrong for *us*, as Mary's mother and father, to give our consent—our approval—to a medical procedure that will bring our daughter no benefit, but only harm." On such an understanding, the parents would be making a claim about what actions are permitted and prohibited to *them*, as determined by the requirements of their roles as *parents*.

Obviously, this claim is subject to immediate challenge on the factual grounds that the operation is not harmful to Mary, given the only alternative available to her. If she died during surgery, her death would be quick and painless; if the surgery were not performed, she would die slowly of cardiovascualar failure, all while being jostled and dragged about by her more active older sister. The degree to which she would suffer pain under these circumstances was not clear.[9] Nonetheless, it is at least arguable that the operation was *not* in Mary's best interests, because it significantly cut short the only life she had.[10] Moreover, even if one is not convinced by this argument, it is possible to preserve the theoretical point explored below by hypothetically altering the facts to make the harm to Mary far more clear-cut; suppose, for example, the operation would deprive her of one or two years of a relatively happy and peaceful childhood before the one functioning heart gave out.

Under these circumstances, then, can the parents coherently claim that it is inconsistent with their roles as mother and father to Mary for them to consent to an action that will bring no benefit, but only harm, to her? Moreover, how can their claim be accommodated within the traditional Catholic (and broadly Christian) framework for making medical-moral decisions, which asks decision makers to consider whether a proposed treatment is an "ordinary" or an "extraordinary" means of medical treatment? Note that accommodating such a claim within the framework of ordinary/extraordinary means analysis would require a broadening, if not a shift, in attention. More specifically, the analytical focus would need to expand from the proposed treatment considered in the abstract or even in terms of its effect on the patient to the particular surrogate decision maker's choice to authorize it. The parents' argument would not be that the *treatment* is extraordinary per se or in this case, but rather that the *decision* to authorize it is extraordinary for them to take as surrogate decision makers, given their particular relationship to the two little girls affected by it.

ORDINARY MEANS, EXTRAORDINARY MEANS, AND VIRTUE

In order to discern how to accommodate our formulation of the parents' moral claim within the traditional categories, it first is necessary to step back for a minute and look more closely at the rationale for the distinction between ordinary and extraordinary means of medical treatment. When medical ethicists, both Catholic and Protestant, re- trieved the distinction as a powerful way of dealing with the incentives for overtreatment dominating the American health care finance and delivery system from the time of the 1960s through the mid-1980s, they had two major objectives.[11] First, they emphasized that the focus of the distinction is not the treatment considered in isolation, but rather a particular patient's understanding and experience of the treatment. There are no lists of "mandatory" and "optional" treatments that guide the treatment of all patients, no matter what their circumstances. Sec- ond, and relatedly, they recognized that the patient-centered focus of the decision to accept or refuse treatment made the most appropriate decision maker the conscious and competent patient herself rather than the patient's family members, the patient's physician, or the majority vote of a hospital ethics committee.[12]

If no treatment can be said to be either ordinary or extraordinary in itself, and the determination about which category applies must be made by the patient herself with respect to a particular option, is not the distinction rather devoid of content? Yes, if one believes the dis- tinction ought to provide clear-cut rules that exhaustively determine each person's obligations in a way that can be evaluated conclusively by an external observer. No, if one sees it as providing the patient with some practical wisdom regarding living well at the end of life, as signposts in the *ars moriendi*. In my view, the latter interpretation of the distinction is the correct one.

The process by which a competent patient determines which means are ordinary and which are extraordinary in her particular case is one of discernment, not deduction. It calls upon the patient to assess honestly the range of available treatment options and make a decision about what to do in light of the potential benefits and burdens upon herself, family, and the broader community associated with each op- tion. Such a patient, therefore, is called to exercise *phronesis*: to make a determination in a particular case that takes into account a range of factors including far more than her medical prognoses with and without treatment. These factors encompass the burdens and benefits directly associated with the treatment as well as its indirect and more remote consequences. In contemplating aggressive treatment for cancer, for example, a patient might consider how much pain she can bear, whether she is emotionally strong enough to tolerate life in a severely compromised state (for example, with one or more amputated limbs), and whether she feels called to seek treatment in order to complete some necessary task or to be present for her family members a little while longer. In addition, a patient is invited to consider what would be appropriate, given her particular vocation in life. For example, a member of a religious community dedicated to the corporal works of mercy on behalf of the most marginalized members of developing countries might very well decide to decline expensive life-saving treatment, even if her wealthy family offered to pay for it. She might discern, for example, that preventing her own death in such a manner would be inconsistent with the values by which she lived her life, which had long been focused on radical solidarity with the poor.[13]

The development of the distinction between ordinary and extraordinary means by Christian moralists, and its application by Christian patients attempting to die well, is fully intelligible only within a particular account of human flourishing, and of the actions, habits, and dispositions that allow persons fully to partake of such flourishing. That account understands human persons as embodied, essentially social, and created for eternal fellowship with God and with one another. It assumes that mortal life is a good, but not an absolute good; it understands the pain, suffering, and isolation associated with death as evils that have been defeated by Christ, but not fully overcome until the full realization of the kingdom of God on earth. Finally, it presupposes that God has called each person by name to a unique vocation, and that God will not abandon her as she prayerfully discerns its nature and scope.

In this context, one might say that the distinction between ordinary and extraordinary means can be understood as a helpful way of framing the concerns that a virtuous person facing death must ponder. Formally, we are all called to fortitude rather than cowardice or rashness, to charity rather than selfishness, and to faith and hope rather than despairing unbelief. What responding to that call will require of each of us materially will differ from person to person. The distinction, therefore, does not give particular answers; it guides competent patients in considering the appropriate questions.

In the case of competent patients, therefore, the contemporary formulation of the distinction between ordinary and extraordinary means can straightforwardly be incorporated into a virtue-oriented perspective on the moral life; the relevant moral agent and the patient are the same person. Obviously, the same unity of agent and patient is not possible in the case of incompetent patients; such a patient is by definition incapable of making a decision on her own behalf. The decision regarding her medical treatment must be made by a surrogate decision maker—usually a relative, a court, or a court-appointed guardian.

The decisions made by surrogate decision makers to accept or refuse life-saving treatment for incompetent patients have been the subject of heated debate within bioethics for nearly thirty years. That debate, however, has been cast in a particular way, which presupposes a particular account of what should count as relevant in evaluating decisions made with respect to incompetent patients. Since it is impossible in their case to maintain the unity between an agent-centered and a patient-centered focus in analyzing such decisions, most bioethicists have virtually abandoned the former in order to focus on the latter. In fact, for the past thirty years the fundamental issue of morality and public policy with respect to incompetent patients has been the formulation of a legal standard that will appropriately guide treatment decisions—which will, in other words, produce the appropriate result.[14] In the American context, the "substituted judgment" standard has generally been held to be applicable; it directs surrogate decision makers to make treatment decisions according to what they believe the patient herself would have chosen, were she competent to make the choice. In the case of patients with respect to whom it is impossible to apply this standard, the "best interests of the patient" standard is frequently applied instead. Although the merits of both standards have been hotly debated, virtually no one has called into question the fundamental premise that the focus of moral analysis should be the development of an action guide that reliably selects the appropriate treatment in light of its effect upon the incompetent patient.[15]

In the bulk of these discussions, the specific identity of the surrogate decision maker, and the relationship of the act of deciding to her character, has been virtually invisible in the discussion. She is simply treated as the agent who is legally authorized to apply the appropriate standard and cause the appropriate result to come to pass. From this perspective, all surrogate decision makers would ideally be fungible; substituting one for another would not change the result. To the extent that the particular identity and role of the surrogate decision maker receives consideration, it is generally limited to minimizing potential bias and abuse in the application of the standard in question.[16] If, for example, the decision maker is a court, will it have the knowledge base from which to consider the benefits and burdens of treatment from the point of view of the patient? If the decision maker is a relative, will she inappropriately privilege her own interests in the outcome? If the decision maker is not handicapped in any way, will she inappropriately impose her own sense of the difficulties of living with a disability upon the patient? Of course, all of these questions are extremely important. Nonetheless, they do not actually expand the real focus of moral analysis beyond the effect of the treatment decision on the patient.

In my view, the failure of the dominant approaches to take seriously the moral agency of the surrogate is extremely problematic. First, it seems to me to occlude an important aspect of the moral reality of the situation. As I argued above, when a competent patient has the opportunity to accept or refuse life-saving treatment for herself, she is making a decision that both reflects and constitutes her unique identity, that shapes her particular character in relationship to herself, other persons, and God. Cannot the same be said of a surrogate decision maker deciding upon a treatment option for an incompetent person within her charge?

Second and more generally, the exclusive focus on the recipient of the action, to the exclusion of the agent, is inconsistent with some of the best insights of contemporary moral theory, both religious and secular. More specifically, in recent years, much Catholic moral theory has reaffirmed and renewed its Thomistic (and Aristotelian) heritage; it has recognized both the strength and the flexibility of its intention-based, virtue-oriented action theory that locates its primary moral description of human action in the perspective of the acting agent. The insights from both feminist theory and virtue theory have converged to teach us that acting agents are not fungible abstractions. They are particular human beings, with particular strengths and weaknesses, called to be faithful to particular relationships and particular vocations.[17] Their moral obligations are in part determined by the particular roles they inhabit. Not only the actions but also the habits, thoughts, and feelings required of them are to some degree determined by the exigencies of those roles.

How, then, would we go about developing a way of incorporating virtue theory into the evaluation of the decisions made by surrogates with respect to incompetent patients? How can we argue, not that a particular *treatment* is extraordinary per se, but rather that a decision to authorize that treatment is extraordinary when made by a particular decision maker? As I indicate in more detail below, the way forward requires us to consider more carefully the moral requirements and limitations incumbent upon persons who inhabit certain roles and who may be called upon to function as surrogate decision makers.

VIRTUES, ROLES, AND PRACTICES

A virtue-oriented approach to the moral life places at the center of the discussion the intimate relationship between the acts an agent performs, the habits (both virtues and vices) she develops through them, and the person she becomes—and the character that she develops—in the course of her life as an acting agent. The character that she develops is not entirely of her own choice, of her own making: it is thoroughgoingly social. She relates to other persons in part through the particular role(s) that she inhabits. But what, precisely, is a "role"?[18] It is a socially defined way for a person to participate in one or more socially constituted practices, to relate those practices to one another fruitfully over time, and to promote those practices by fostering the goods internal to them. This includes both building up the institutions that will allow such practices to extend through time and protecting them from the distortions to which being embedded in institutional life subjects them. Not insignificantly, as feminist ethicists have forcefully reminded us, it also includes reforming and reshaping the requirements of the role to meet new demands and to respond to changing circumstances.

The roles we inhabit shape our understanding of ourselves and our expectations of one another. In part, they are constitutive of our identity. Inhabiting a role faithfully requires a person to develop her abilities and personality in certain ways. Ideally, her character—the stable pattern of intellectual, moral, and emotional traits that shape her identity—should equip her to appreciate the goods internal to the practices constitutive of her role, not simply to seek the external goods that the role may be instrumental in acquiring. Her character should also enable her to relate to other persons through the practices constitutive of the role with reliability and integrity.

Roles and practices, then, are intrinsically related. But what is a practice? Alasdair MacIntyre defines it as:

> any coherent and complex form of socially established cooperative human activity through which goods internal to that form of activity are realised in the course of trying to achieve those standards of excellence which are appropriate to, and partially definitive of, that form of activity, with the result that human powers to achieve excellence, and human conceptions of the ends and goods involved, are systematically extended.[19]

According to MacIntyre, an activity must involve a certain form of complexity to qualify as a practice; he notes that tic-tac-toe and bricklaying do not qualify, but that chess, architecture, and farming do.[20] Correspondingly, in my view, an occupation must entail a certain level of complexity to qualify as a role within the context of a practice. Many jobs do not meet the criteria, while many states of life for which one receives no compensation do. Being a checkout clerk at a supermarket is not a role, but being a parent is.

Our assessment of the particular actions performed by particular agents, then, must take into account a number of criteria that are sensitive to the particular role such an agent occupies and the exigencies of the practices constitutive of that role. Of course, occupying a particular role does not give a particular agent license to perform actions that are prohibited to everyone; Aquinas, for example, makes it clear that no one, no matter how politically powerful, is justified in intentionally killing the innocent.[21] Moreover, it is equally clear that occupying a particular role legitimates and even requires actions that are prohibited to others who do not occupy such a role. The question remains, however, whether occupying a certain role also rules out certain actions that are permitted to other persons.

It seems to me that the response to this question must be "yes." There are certain actions that must not be performed by persons occupying particular roles, despite the fact that the same actions are permitted to others occupying other roles. Moreover, the rationale for this restriction must be grounded in holistic reflection on the relationship between an agent's act, her character (including feelings as well as habits of mind), her role, the practices in which she is characteristically engaged, and the relationships to other persons mediated by those relationships.[22]

Two examples used by Thomas Aquinas will furnish us with the material to begin addressing these issues more concretely. First, consider Thomas's response to the question whether it is licit for clerics to kill malefactors. Although he believes that it is just—indeed morally obligatory—for the state to execute certain criminals, he maintains that it is morally impermissible for clerics to carry out the sentence. More specifically, Aquinas contends that it is not "becoming" or "fitting" for clerics to kill malefactors.[23] Second, in another passage, he suggests that a woman who possesses a good will may legitimately wish that a sentence of execution directed against her husband, a thief, not be carried out, despite the fact that the sentence is just and imposed for the benefit of the common good.[24]

While Thomas is dealing with the same general issue in both responses, the questions he considers differ slightly from one to the other. The question about the cleric focuses on external acts suitable for a priest, while the question about the wife pertains primarily to inner acts: dispositions, feelings, and attitudes appropriate to her role

and relationship with her husband and family. Between them, therefore, the two questions cover the full scope of issues and concerns
about character and role-related obligations. Taken together, the remarks that Aquinas makes about each case are extremely illuminating
regarding what is at stake in both.

Thomas does not object to a cleric carrying out an execution because he believes capital punishment is immoral per se; he takes it
for granted that the practice accords with justice and therefore fur-
thers the common good.[25] It is rather that the cleric, because of his
role, is not called to further justice in this particular manner. More
specifically, Aquinas says that it is not "fitting" for him to do so, for
two interrelated reasons. First, it is unfitting because every cleric
has been chosen for the ministry of the altar; he therefore represents
the passion of Christ, who "when He was struck did not strike." Second, it is unfitting because clerics are "entrusted with the ministry
of the New Law, wherein no punishment of death or bodily maiming
is appointed."

The concept of moral "fittingness" has an aesthetic component that
is best elucidated by elaborating upon the relationship between the
cleric's actions, his character, the practices in which he is engaged,
and the way in which his participation in those practices enhances the
ability of other participants to appreciate the goods internal to them.
A nuanced description and particular assessment of all these factors is
required; generalizations will not suffice. For example, while Aquinas
recognizes that while we are called upon to imitate God and the saints,
he also states that we are not all called to do so in the same way.[26] The
Priests and the Levirites of the Old Testament were appointed ministers of the Old Law, so it was appropriate for them to kill malefactors.
But their role is not the same as that of a Christian cleric, whose central responsibility in the life and practice of the Christian community
is to represent Christ, the nonresisting sacrifice, as well as Christ the
giver of the New Law.

The potential dissonance between engaging in a particular action
and the requirements of a role can have moral implications for both the
inhabitants of that role themselves and the other persons who relate to
them through it. If a cleric engages in an action that is utterly alien to

the heavenly kingdom, how will he shape his character, emotions, and responses according to its ways? If he does not shape his character accordingly, how will he be able to interact with persons in the particular Christlike manner that he, by virtue of role, is assigned to imitate? How will others be able to view him as making present to them a particular aspect of God's identity, namely, the loving and merciful savior, if he engages in an action so inconsistent with Christ's pattern of relating to sinners? If they cannot reasonably view the cleric as representing Christ's forgiveness, how will they participate wholeheartedly in the sacramental life with him?

What about the situation of the thief's wife? Aquinas notes that she "has to consider the private good of the family, and from this point of view she wishes her husband, the thief, not to be put to death."[27] Doubtless, part of what Aquinas had in mind regarding the wife's wish that her husband not be executed has to do with the material harm to the family's social status and well-being that will result from it. Surely, however, her concern extends to other matters as well. Aquinas believes that the bond of *fides* that unites a husband and a wife connects them in a powerful and unique way, ideally uniting them in the greatest friendship as they share bodily union and the intimacies of household life.[28] In most cases, the community of husband and wife has expanded to include the children it has produced; consequently, their relationship both affects and is affected by the relationship they each have with their children. All of these relationships will be irremediably altered by the execution of the husband, and the familial practices mediating and mediated by those relationships will be permanently destroyed. Consequently, as she considers the good of her family, the wife is being entirely morally reasonable in wishing that her husband not be put to death.

But why is the thief's wife allowed to consider only the good of her family? Why should she not be expected to look at the broader good of the political community, which Aquinas would have no doubt believed to be served by her husband's execution? Clearly, however, she is not expected to take the so-called "broader view" in evaluating the prospect of his death. Otherwise Aquinas would not have condoned her wish that he be saved, although he might have excused it, perhaps by arguing that her stressful situation mitigated her moral culpability. Instead, he justifies the wife's wish, and in so doing obviously refuses to dismiss her attitudes and feelings as a rankly sentimental, although understandable, refusal to consider the "big picture" and the needs of the broader community.[29] We can glean some insights about why this is the case by considering more carefully the conditions of good family relationships and Aquinas's conception of the proper relationship between families and the state.

Aquinas's discussion of the thief's wife occurs in the context of a question considering whether the human will must conform to the divine will in order to be good. His response to that question makes it clear that he recognizes that various spheres of relationships can in some sense be ranked from less to more inclusive in terms of the universality of the good that they encompass. For example, he notes that the thief's wife has concern for the private good of her family, the judge has concern for the common good (of earthly life), and God has concern for the good of the whole universe.[30] Nonetheless, Aquinas appears to make a sharp division between the common good of the family and the political community, on one hand, and the divine and universal common good, on the other. The first two are *both* limited and finite in scope; in fact, one might say that only the divine and universal common good can truly be called the "common good" *simpliciter.*

Moreover, he clearly does not believe that these various spheres of good can be neatly nested inside one another like Russian dolls, so that the good of the family is entirely subsumed in the political common good, which in turn is subsumed under the most inclusive common good, that is, God's "own goodness, which is the good of the whole universe." In fact, if the various spheres of flourishing could be neatly nested in such a manner, the wife would be obliged to will that her husband would be executed in order to serve the political common good, assuming such an execution was just.

Aquinas's primary justification for his position is epistemological: materially, the object of our will is determined by the particular, finite good apprehended by our intellect; the good that we intellectually apprehend is determined by the sort of beings we are, which in turn is determined by God. It is not our province, because it is beyond our power, to situate intellectually the particular finite goods that are materially the object of our will within the one truly comprehensive and infinite good, which is the divine and universal good.[31] Consequently, there is and should be some pluralism regarding the matter perceived and promoted by persons with good wills in the fabric of human society, because no human being, by nature possessed only of a finite intellect, is capable of locating the good that she seeks, under the precise aspect that she perceives it as a good, in its proper place within the context of the divine plan.

Consequently, Aquinas's theory has significant room to accommodate legitimate tension between and among good people regarding the goods that they perceive, and therefore the goods that they will. In his perspective the competing good wills of the judge and the wife is not an anomaly, it is a divinely ordained aspect of human society. He writes:

> Now a thing may happen to be good under a particular aspect, and yet not good under a universal aspect, or vice versa, as stated above. And therefore it comes to pass that a certain will is good from willing something considered under a particular aspect, which thing God wills not, under a universal aspect, and vice versa. And hence too it is, that various wills of various men can be good in respect of opposite things, for as much as, under various aspects, they wish a particular thing to be or not to be.[32]

How, then, are the "competing" good wills reconciled? In Aquinas's view, it must be remembered that this sort of tension is not truly opposition. This statement holds not only with regard to the competing wills of two human beings, but even with respect to the competing wills of human beings and God. In affirming that a son is not required to will the death of his father just because God wills it, he writes that "there is no opposition of wills when several people desire different things, but not under the same aspect: but there is opposition of wills, when under one and the same aspect one man wills a thing which another wills not."[33]

Aquinas proposes a three-pronged strategy to ensure that tension born of human finitude does not degenerate into opposition. First, he insists that "in order that a man will some particular good with a right will, he must will that particular good materially, and the divine and universal good, formally." All human persons must refer the immediate objects of their willing to the one all-encompassing end, although they cannot describe that end with any degree of particularity. Second, he reminds us that God has designed the universe so that persons intellectually apprehend particular finite goods, and will them precisely as such. It is God's job, not the job of human beings, to order the finite goods (for example, both the good of the family and the good of the *polis*) in service of the divine and universal good. Third and finally, to the extent that human beings will something from charity, as God wills it, our will formally conforms to the divine will, because the last end is the proper object of charity.

A vision of human familial and political life animated by the thought of St. Thomas, then, must be prepared to accept a great deal of tension; it must allow (in fact, it must encourage) persons to pursue the well-being of the practices and the communities to which their vocations and roles call them, while at the same time placing limits on the degrees to which persons operating in one sphere can obstruct the projects of those operating in another. Those limits, too, are generated by the epistemological humility of Thomas's approach. All parties involved need to recognize and honor both the requirements and the limits of role-related obligations, both their own and those of other persons.

For example, while recognizing that the wife may mourn the execution of her husband, Aquinas does not suggest she may interfere with it. Similarly, while Thomas states that the cleric may not kill, he does not imply that they may prevent a lawful execution.[34] Restrictions in the opposite direction are also immediate corollaries of his argument. If it is impermissible for clerics to kill, it is impermissible for a Christian state to employ them as executioners in order to shore up the theological legitimacy of governmental policies. If a woman may legitimately will that her husband is not executed, it is impermissible for a government to enlist her as a cog in the machinery that leads to his death.

THE PARENTAL ROLE AND SURROGATE DECISION MAKING

How does the foregoing analysis illuminate the case of surrogate decision makers making choices about medical treatment for incompetent patients? First, it is important to recognize that being a surrogate decision maker is not inhabiting a role; rather, it is performing a function. It is not a complex way of ordering one's participation in one or more practices and appreciating the goods internal to them. Second, it is a function that may be required of persons who inhabit any one of a number of roles, including that of court, parent, and child. In the case of the conjoined twins, of course, the salient role is the parental role. The question we must ask is whether Mary and Jodie's parents may have been justified in thinking that their role-related obligations placed certain restrictions on the choices that they could make when asked to make medical decisions on behalf of their twins. In my view, the best way to begin answering it is by thinking about the crucial requirements of the parental role, with a central focus on the practices and relationships entailed by it.

The most basic obligations of parents are to protect and care for each of their children while they are unable to protect themselves, and to educate them, not only so that they will be materially self-sufficient, but also so that they are able to appreciate the goods internal to a number of worthwhile practices. The primary good internal to the practice of parenthood is love: unselfish love given to the child, in the hopes of nurturing a person who is able to love unselfishly in return. It seems to me that the particular role-related obligations of parents, along with the primary good internal to the practice of parenthood, can generate the following claim: it is "unfitting" for parents to authorize or cooperate with the physical or psychological treatment of a child in a way that will bring that child no benefit, but only harm. The reasons supporting the claim are analogous to those we teased out with respect to Aquinas's treatment of the two cases discussed above.

More specifically, the dual obligations of parents to care for and to educate their children mean that there will be a number times that a parent will need to perform (or authorize a third party to perform) an action that the child herself considers distasteful, threatening, or even positively harmful. In the case of education, children frequently find the lessons assigned to them tedious and unhelpful; they would much rather be doing something else. In the case of medical care, the problem can be far more dramatic: parents may find themselves needing to authorize physicians to perform painful procedures on their terrified children. In all such cases, the child may not herself grasp the fact that what is being done is ultimately for her own benefit; against her own best perceptions of the situation, she is asked to trust her parents, to believe their assurances that this is so. The basis of such trust must be the child's justified belief that "my parents would never knowingly do (or knowingly authorize another person to do) anything that seriously harms me without any corresponding benefit." By articulating and supporting a role-related claim that it is "unfitting" for parents to engage in behavior of that type, we create a context that makes sense of a child's choice to trust her parents in ways necessary to ensure her own well-being.

There seems to me also to be a second reason supporting such a judgment of "unfittingness," which relates to the goods internal to parenthood and the countervailing temptation for some parents to use their relationship with their children to obtain external goods instead. Internal to parenthood is the good of self-gift: the opportunity to realize the possibility of choosing to place the well-being of another before one's own immediate desires and goals, and in the process to discover that one's conception of one's own flourishing has in fact expanded to encompass that of the other, to whom one is united in the bond of love. But instead of seeking this good internal to the practice of parenthood, it can at times be tempting instead to use one's children to obtain an external good, such as social approval, ego gratification, or the chance to recapture opportunities lost in one's own youth. Some cases are common and may only be mildly problematic; for example, many parents express the desire that their children excel at the same sports that they themselves played in high school. Others can be devastating, when parents engage in physical, emotional, or sexual abuse in order to force their children to serve their own desires and purposes.

Instrumentalization of children is one of the most dangerous temptations to wrongdoing endemic in the practice of parenthood. Moreover, precisely because they are immature and lack good judgment, children cannot always differentiate between cases where parents or other authority figures are acting appropriately for the good of the child (for example, authorizing unpleasant medical care or providing appropriate education or discipline) and when they are merely using them for their own ends. Because we cannot expect children to protect themselves, the common judgment that it is "unfitting" for parents to act in a way that harms their child helps protect them, by protecting the goods internal to the practice of parenthood, by ruling out particularly destructive ways in which parents might sacrifice the well-being of their children to pursue goods external to that practice.[35]

Against this background conception of the practice of parenthood and the goods internal to that practice, the refusal of the parents of the Maltese twins to consent to the surgery that they knew would kill Mary is entirely intelligible. They can plausibly argue that it is "unfitting" for them as Mary's parents to cooperate in any way with the infliction of physical harm on her in a way that is not in some sense for her ultimate benefit.[36] They might also reasonably believe that they are called to love both of their children equally, and in particular to refuse to make any comparisons of their relative merits for purposes of determining favorable treatment, even in ways that are appropriate for third parties to do in a society committed to the equal dignity of all persons.[37] So doing, they might believe, is required of them to promote the "common good" of their family life.

On such a basis, the parents could legitimately claim that it would be an extraordinary means for them to consent to the surgical separation because it would be morally unfitting for them to do so given the demands of their role. Such a claim would not logically differ from that which could be made by Mother Theresa: that it would be an extraordinary means for her to consent to life-saving treatment because it would be morally unfitting for her to do so given the demands of her role. The latter deals with the role-related obligations of competent patients, while the former deals with the role-related obligations of surrogate decision makers.

The parents' claim that it would be wrong for them to authorize the operation is tied to the particular requirements of their role. It does not entail the judgment that it is wrong for another agent, namely, the court, to give permission to the physicians to proceed with the operation. As the example from Aquinas about the condemned family man suggests, the role-related obligations of judges are quite different from those of parents. Nor does that claim entail the judgment that the parents are entitled actively to interfere with the court's decision in this matter, such as by attempting to remove the babies from the jurisdiction.[38]

Rather, it suggests that courts and parents should not be treated as fungible decision makers each charged with protecting the "best interests" of the children in an undifferentiated way, so that the court is charged with stepping in only when the parents make a clear "mistake," or (what may be worse) that the parents are viewed as having an authority somehow derivative from the court's *parens patriae* power to protect the well-being of the citizenry, particularly children.[39] Instead, parents and courts should be seen as occupying two distinct roles, both of which generate distinct role-related obligations, which at times are in tension, and both of which are important to protecting children, families, and the common good, despite this tension.

Needless to say, it is beyond the scope of this essay to outline exhaustively the role-related obligations of parents and courts with respect to medical decision making in the case of minor children. The salient questions are both numerous and complex. Still, I think one or two points can be made. I have already said a few words about the role-related obligations of parents. What about the courts? Their primary role is to further what Aquinas calls the virtue of "general justice" or "legal justice," which is concerned with the common good.[40] The object of justice is *jus*, the right, which is best understood not in contemporary terms as a single individual's moral property, but as a *situation* of right relations described from an external point of view.[41] Unlike the virtues of fortitude and temperance, which focus their efforts internally, on regulating the passions of the acting agent, the virtue of general justice as such focuses primarily on the *external* and other-directed aspects of human actions, particularly how they affect the just claims of other people.[42] Consequently, the court's basic role-related obligation is to promote the virtue of legal justice as citizens of the community, which in the case of children focuses on insuring that they receive just and fair treatment, particularly with respect to the material aspects of their lives on this earth.

In the case of Jodie and Mary, then, I think it is possible to argue that both the parents and the courts fulfilled their role-related obligations with integrity. As parents, Mr. and Mrs. Attard legitimately concluded that they were morally unable to authorize the operation because they reasonably and in good faith believed that it would bring no benefit, but only harm, to one of their twin daughters. As members of the judiciary, the judges who heard the case concluded that they were morally required to authorize the operation. In fact, one could plausibly maintain that it was the only fair course of action because it was the only way to free Jodie from her bodily link to her sister, which was extinguishing Jodie's own life while not preserving Mary's for more than a very short time.[43] Viewed externally, from the perspective of legal justice, no child can rightly be expected to provide bodily life support to her sibling, especially at the cost of her own life.

IDENTITY AND AGENCY

The case of Mary and Jodie is a liminal case, which presses our normal categories of moral analysis to their limits and, in so doing, forces us to reexamine their adequacy. As Margaret Farley has taught all of us over the years, that reexamination must take into account not only factors such as theoretical rigor and consistency, but also considerations such as adequacy to the lived experience of those affected by the situation, especially of those whose experience has previously been ignored or discounted.[44] The tension between theory and practice, between vision and lived experience, is not destructive but constructive, as it presses us to be ever truer to the basic insight that moral claims must "make sense" in a life-giving way. As both her students and her readers well know, Professor Farley has always insisted that this insight is consistent with the best in both natural law and feminist approaches to moral discernment.

If my analysis in this paper is correct, the lived experience of the babies' mother and father reveals an inescapable divergence, at least in this exceptional case, between the particular, role-related obligations of parents not to authorize acts harmful to one of their children and the general obligations of the courts to bring about a situation of just relations between Jodie and Mary. Accounting for that divergence, and accommodating the integrity of the parents' experience, may require us to reconsider the adequacy of how we have formulated the task of surrogate decision makers charged with authorizing or declining life-saving treatment on behalf of incompetent patients. More specifically, it may require us to take seriously the identity of surrogate decision makers as particular moral agents, who are situated within particular roles, practices, and institutions, and who are accountable to other people on that basis.

On a broader level, the divergence between the role-related obligations of the parents and the courts in this case presses us to attend, in perhaps a slightly different way, to the tension between particularity and universality, which has been of central concern to Catholic feminist ethicists.[45] On the one hand, many feminist theorists have insisted that human beings are not abstract choosers; we live our lives in and through a complicated set of relationships that are structured by roles, institutions, and the patterns of interaction and expectation embedded within them. Taking seriously the experience of women requires taking seriously the particularities of their lives, which includes their responsibilities and their aspirations within these concrete contexts. Embodied, social, and historical beings, human persons will never escape the need for such contexts. On the other hand, it is impossible to deny that for many persons, particularly women, the opportunity both to flourish themselves and to contribute to the flourishing of the community has been dramatically constricted by roles, practices, and institutions that have been understood too narrowly, that have been constructed and maintained without imagination or hope.

At some times, we are morally required to criticize and reform the roles, practices, and institutions that shape our lives. The role of "parent" for example, should never have been understood as encompassing the power of a Roman *paterfamilias* over the lives of his children. At other times, we are called to acknowledge our finitude, to admit the partiality of our own perspective as acting agents, and to recognize that we function within roles that are good and valuable, but not comprehensive in their apprehension of the good. Loving parents need not take on the perspective of courts in every respect, any more than just judges need to take on the perspective of parents. Discerning which course of action is called for in a particular situation is not easy. It calls not only for technical knowledge and proficiency in ethical theory but also for moral wisdom. To those of us blessed by the opportunity to study with her, Margaret Farley has not only exemplified that quality in her own life, she has also encouraged her students to pursue it with faith, hope, and love as we go about our own vocations as teachers and scholars.

NOTES

1. *Re A (children) (conjoined twins: surgical separation)*, 4 All ER 961, 972 (Ward LJ 2000).
2. Ibid., 975.
3. Cormac Murphy-O'Connor, "The Conjoined Twins Mary and Jodie: Ethical Analysis of their Case," *Origins* 30 (5 October 2000): 269–72.
4. *Re A (children) (conjoined twins)*, 961.
5. Clare Dyer, "Conjoined Twins Separated After Long Legal Battle," *British Medical Journal* 321 (11 November 2000): 1175.
6. Peter Allen, "Home at Last, Our Gorgeous Gracie," *Daily Mail,* June 18, 2001, 8–9.
7. See, e.g., Margaret Farley, *Compassionate Respect: A Feminist Approach to Medical Ethics and Other Questions* (New York: Paulist Press, 2002).
8. M. Cathleen Kaveny, "The Case of Conjoined Twins: Embodiment, Individuality, and Dependence," *Theological Studies* 62 (2001): 752–86. See also M. Cathleen Kaveny, "Conjoined Twins and Catholic Moral Analysis: Extraordinary Means and Casuistical Consistency," *Kennedy Institute of Ethics Journal* 2 (2002): 115–40.
9. These facts so impressed the lower court judge who heard the case that he held that the operation was in the best interests of both babies. *Central Manchester Healthcare Trust and Mr. and Mrs. A and Re A Child,* High Court Justice-Family Division, Case No. FD0P10893 (2000).

10. The three appellate judges who heard the case held accordingly, see *Re A (children) (conjoined twins)*, 961.

11. See, e.g., Paul Ramsey, *The Patient as Person* (New Haven, CT: Yale University Press, 1970), chap. 3.

12. See, e.g., National Conference of Catholic Bishops, *Ethical and Religious Directives for Catholic Health Care Services,* 4th ed. (Washington, DC: United States Catholic Conference), directives 56 and 57.

13. For a helpful discussion of the historical development of the distinction, see Kevin Wildes, S.J., "Ordinary and Extraordinary Means and the Quality of Life," *Theological Studies* 57 (1996): 500–512.

14. See, e.g., *In Re Quinlan,* 70 N.J. 10 (1976); *Superintendent of Belchertown State School & Another v. Joseph Saikewicz*, 373 Mass. 728 (1977).

15. See, e.g., Richard A. McCormick's summary and evaluation of the state of the debate in 1981, in "The Preservation of Life," in *Notes on Moral Theology 1981 through 1984* (University Press of America, 1984) 27–37. See also Paul Ramsey, *Ethics at the Edges of Life* (New Haven: Yale University Press, 1978, chaps. 5, 7, and 8, and Germain Grisez's discussion in *The Way of the Lord Jesus* (vol. 2): *Living a Christian Life* (Quincy, IL: Franciscan Press, 1993), 524–32. Grisez does take into account the particular role of the agent more specifically in *The Way of the Lord Jesus* (vol. 3): *Difficult Moral Questions* (Quincy, IL: Franciscan Press, 1997), 209–25.

16. These worries are apparent in Gilbert Meilaender's response to Kevin Wildes's article, "Ordinary and Extraordinary Means and the Quality of Life." See Gilbert Meilaender, "Ordinary and Extraordinary Treatments: When Does Quality of Life Count," *Theological Studies* 58 (1997): 527–31, and Kevin W. Wildes, S.J., "When Does Quality of Life Count? A Response," *Theological Studies* 59 (1998): 505–8.

17. See Nancy Sherman, *The Fabric of Character* (Oxford: Clarendon Press, 1989), chap. 2, for an account of the importance of particularity in a virtue-oriented theory of moral decision making.

18. My account here is obviously deeply indebted to Alasdair MacIntyre's work in *After Virtue,* 2nd ed. (Notre Dame, IN: University of Notre Dame Press, 1984) and *Whose Justice? Which Rationality?* (Notre Dame, IN: University of Notre Dame Press, 1988).

19. MacIntyre, *After Virtue*, 187.

20. Ibid.

21. Thomas Aquinas, *Summa Theologica*, trans. Fathers of the English Dominican Province (Westminster, MD: Christian Classics, 1981), II-II, q. 64, art. 6.

22. For a helpful account of the relationship of the emotions to the virtues, see Nancy Sherman, *Making a Necessity of Virtue* (Cambridge: Cambridge University Press, 1997).

23. Aquinas, *Summa Theologica*, II-II, q. 64, art. 4. The Latin words are "competit" and "congruit."

24. Ibid., I-II, q. 19, art. 10.

25. Obviously, the idea that the role of the state legitimately includes the infliction of capital punishment is one that many today would call into question.

26. "Wherefore everyone should imitate God in that which is specially becoming to him"; Aquinas, *Summa Theologica*, II-II, q. 64, art. 4, rep. ob. 1.

27. Ibid., I-II, q. 19, art. 10.

28. Thomas Aquinas, *Summa Contra Gentiles*, trans. Vernon J. Bourke (Notre Dame, IN: University of Notre Dame Press, 1975), bk. 3, pt. II, chap. 123. See John Finnis, *Aquinas: Moral, Political, and Legal Theory* (Oxford: Oxford University Press, 1998), 143–53, and Lisa Sowle Cahill, *Between the Sexes* (Philadelphia: Fortress Press and New York: Paulist Press, 1985), chap. 6. Both of these treatments highlight Aquinas's insistence on the intensity of the friendship between husband and wife.

29. Aquinas, *Summa Theologica*, I-II, q. 19, art. 10.

30. Ibid.

31. But Aquinas maintains that "in the state of glory, every one will see in each thing that he wills, the relation of that thing to what God wills in that particular matter. Consequently he will conform his will to God in all things not only formally, but also materially"; ibid., I-II, q. 19, art. 10, rep. ob. 1.

32. Ibid., I-II, q. 19, art. 10.

33. Ibid., I-II, q. 19, art. 10, rep. ob. 2.

34. On the general topic of interfering by force with lawful sentences of death, see ibid., II-II, q. 69, art. 4; II-II, q. 10, art. 12, rep. ob. 2.

35. Leon Kass has made such an argument with respect to the practice of medicine, arguing that three negative absolute prohibitions are necessary to enable both physicians and patients to realize the goods internal to that practice. More specifically, he argues that the prohibitions against doctors disclosing patient confidences, engaging in sexual relations with their patients, and giving them deadly drugs are essential to the undistorted practice of medicine. See his "Neither for Love nor Money: Why Doctors Must Not Kill," *The Public Interest* 94 (Winter 1989): 25–46.

36. One might object that there must be an exception in cases involving the defense of others; a parent, for example, certainly may defend one child against the vicious bullying of another, even though she knows that her actions will inflict physical harm on the bully. That objection, of course, raises a valid point—but one that is only relevant in the case of the Maltese conjoined twins if the relationship between the twins is understood as Mary "harming" Jodie by overloading her cardiovascular system. I have

argued elsewhere that understanding the relationship between the twins in this way is defensible, but not inevitable. See Kaveny, "Case of Conjoined Twins."

37. For example, Lord Justice Ward's opinion in the Court of Appeal includes physician testimony describing Jodie as "very sparkling really, wriggling, very alert, sucking on a dummy and using her upper limbs in an appropriate manner, very much a with it sort of baby"; *Re A (children) (conjoined twins)*, 973. Another physician gave testimony about Mary: "What we see at present is a child whose responses are extremely primitive. They are more like mass movements to a stimulus, be it what is regarded as a pleasurable stimulus or a painful stimulus. They are withdrawal type and grimacing and such like"; ibid., 983. In an interview taken nearly a year after the birth, the parents distanced themselves from this sort of objective assessment of their daughters. Her father said: "I know it was very easy for people who didn't know Rosie [Mary's real name] to say 'Sacrifice her.' They didn't know Rosie, but we loved her. Yes, she was poorly and she couldn't shout because her lungs were so underdeveloped—but you could tell if she was crying or if she was happy"; Carole Aye Maung and Amanda Stocks, "When I First Saw Our Babies I Recoiled," *The News of the World*, June 17, 2001, 2.

38. The parents indicated in an interview that they had considered this option. Maung and Stocks, "When I First Saw Our Babies I Recoiled."

39. Unlike the American courts, the English courts do not currently understand themselves as possessing the broad power of *parens patriae*, that is, the power to usurp the rights of the natural parent.

40. Aquinas also recognizes the existence of particular justice, which guides individuals with respect to actions affecting themselves, or other particular persons; Aquinas, *Summa Theologica*, II-II, q. 58, art. 7.

41. Ibid., II-II, qq. 57–58.

42. Ibid., II-II, q. 58, art. 9, rep. ob. 2. I have argued elsewhere, however, that the legal system cannot ignore the substantial and complicated relationship between legal justice and the other virtues. See, e.g., M. Cathleen Kaveny, "Ethics/Civil Law and the New Millennium," in *Ethical Dilemmas in the New Millennium,* vol. 1, ed. Francis A. Eigo, O.S.A., 161–88 (Villanova University Press, 2000).

43. Unfortunately, the Court of Appeal that considered the case made the judgment that under English law (which equates the effects of an action that the agent foresees as virtually certain with intended effects), the operation constituted the intentional killing of Mary. In my view, that judgment is not correct; Mary's death was the foreseen and unintended effect of the operation.

44. Margaret A. Farley, "The Role of Experience in Moral Discernment," in *Christian Ethics: Problems and Prospects*, ed. Lisa Sowle Cahill and

James F. Childress, 134–51 (Cleveland: The Pilgrim Press, 1996). See also her "Feminist Theology and Bioethics," in *Women's Consciousness, Women's Conscience*, ed. Barbara Hilkert Andolsen, Christine E. Gudorf, and Mary D. Pellauer (San Francisco: Harper & Row, 1985).

45. See, e.g., Cristina L. H. Traina, *Feminist Ethics and Natural Law: The End of the Anathemas* (Washington, DC: Georgetown University Press, 1999).

Part 4

Truth and Love in
Ecclesial Community

INTRODUCTION

The essays in this final section explore issues connected with morality, authority, and the sources for Christian ethics. Jean Porter's analysis of the long-standing Catholic ban on the use of contraceptives explores the possibilities for doctrinal development, particularly in light of a growing perception of the importance of gender equality in interpretations of moral norms for sexuality and marriage. Porter draws from scholastic conceptions of natural law to suggest a richer way of understanding the process of ecclesial discernment than is often defended, taking fuller account both of historical developments and of the participation of the community. Leslie Griffin shows how the Catholic Church's failure to develop a full theology of freedom, to germinate the seeds sown by Vatican II, ultimately compromises its public credibility. For Griffin, unwillingness to fully promote freedom of discourse within the ecclesial community, often in matters pertaining in particular to women's lives, undermines the Church's own affirmation of the nature of freedom in its defense of religious liberty, that is, that freedom pertains to the dignity of each individual and is "indivisible," it cannot be denied within its walls and defended beyond. Charles Curran's essay, "John Paul II's Understanding of the Church as Teacher of Truth about Humankind" traces the influence of the late pope on the development of contemporary moral theology. Echoing Farley's observation that ecclesial leadership demands "the grace of self-doubt," Curran argues for a view of doctrinal development that rests on the dual role of the church as teacher and learner. Focusing on debates over women's ordination, William O'Neill underscores the questions of credibility and the church's public witness raised by Griffin and earlier by Brian Linnane. Feminist commitments to the human rights of all individuals, on the one hand, and, on the other, to the importance of a particular set of institutional and social conditions in the achievement of human dignity, help resolve internal contradictions within Catholic social teaching and enrich its public voice. At the same time, he shows that they raise important and inescapable questions of ecclesial polity, of the Church's own ability to organize for human dignity.

Chapter Twelve

Contraceptive Use and the Authority of the Church

A Case Study on Natural Law and Moral Discernment

Jean Porter

The moral teachings of the Catholic Church are sometimes regarded as a set of clearly formulated precepts, backed by the authority of the magisterium and irreversibly in place. And there is perhaps some truth in this picture, depending (in part) on the way in which we understand the magisterium, and the extent to which we expect moral norms to be clear and fixed. Nonetheless, as soon as we try to apply this picture to actual moral debates, it becomes apparent that matters are more complex than it suggests. Margaret Farley, in her ground-breaking work on feminism, sexual ethics, divorce and re-marriage, and related topics, has done as much as any Catholic theologian in the past quarter-century to show that our moral beliefs and practices are embedded in historical processes and cannot be understood, much less evaluated, without some sense of those processes. Correlatively, any adequate account of the teaching authority of the Catholic Church must take account of the historical character of our collective moral discernment.

In this paper, I shall explore these issues by focusing on one much-discussed moral question, namely, the licitness of the use of artificial contraceptives. In an article published in *Theological Studies* in 1978, Germain Grisez and John Ford argued that the ban on the use of contraceptives is an infallible teaching of the ordinary magisterium, although not formally defined as such.[1] This claim was challenged by Francis Sullivan in his 1983 book on the magisterium and defended in a subsequent article by Grisez, thus initiating a debate that continued for several years.[2]

It may seem that there is nothing more that can usefully be said on the topic of contraceptive use. Yet as the Grisez/Sullivan exchange indicates, this issue continues to be debated, and there are good reasons why this should be the case. Precisely because the official ban on contraceptive use is so controversial, it raises important questions about the nature and scope of the church's teaching authority in moral matters. At the same time, because the history of this ban has been so thoroughly documented, in John Noonan's classic study and elsewhere, it provides a useful focus for framing these issues in terms of the historical development of moral doctrine.[3] In addition, the issue of contraceptive use raises issues of sexual ethics and social justice that are central to Farley's own work, but to the best of my knowledge she has not devoted extensive attention to this particular topic. We will therefore have an opportunity to consider how her perspectives on sexual ethics might be developed to help us to address a question that she herself does not consider in detail.

Finally, the issue of contraceptive use provides a valuable focus for reflecting on the church's teaching authority because it raises very fundamental questions about the sources for Christian ethics, and the scope and limits of authoritative judgments based on those sources.[4] In particular, reflection on this topic draws us immediately into a consideration of the natural law and its relation to scriptural and theological considerations, and this topic is of course a long-standing locus of debate for Christian ethics. A natural law ethics is often regarded as the antithesis of an approach grounded in history, but, as I will attempt to show, this assumption rests on one contestable construal of what the natural law is. When we examine the medieval construal of the natural law, we find an approach that is more open to historical development, and by the same token more theological in its orientation, than the purely philosophical approach to which we are now accustomed. This reorientation of our thinking on the natural law, in turn, suggests ways of reframing the issue of moral authority, both with respect to the teaching on contraceptive use and more generally—or so I will try to show.

THE THEOLOGICAL CHARACTER
OF THE NATURAL LAW

Since the early modern period, the natural law has generally been understood, by both defenders and critics of the idea, as more or less equivalent to moral reasoning, operating without any necessary reliance on revelation, or on distinctively Christian doctrinal or moral commitments. So understood, the idea of natural law has played an ambiguous role in Catholic moral theology. On the one hand, those who accept this idea of natural law regard it as providing a firm foundation for Catholic moral teachings, and as such, this idea has probably contributed as much as any other factor to the assumption that these teachings are timeless and fixed. On the other hand, the purely philosophical character of the natural law stands in a paradoxical relation, to say nothing more, to a distinctively Christian ethic—a point that has frequently been made by Protestant critics of the idea. This ambiguity is neatly illustrated in the debate over the authority of magisterial teachings on contraceptive use.

In a 1993 article on the secondary object of infallibility, Sullivan observes that "whatever principles or specific norms of the natural law are also contained in the deposit of revelation belong, by that fact, to the primary object of infallibility. What we are concerned with here are those questions of moral law to which the answers are not found in the revealed word of God. . . . The question we are asking is whether such moral issues belong to the secondary object of infallible teaching by the Church."[5] The question, in other words, is whether specific moral norms, other than those contained in, or (perhaps) directly implied by revelation, can be so closely connected to the core truths of revelation that they can be appropriate objects of an infallible definition, calling for an assent of faith.

In Sullivan's view, such norms cannot be appropriate objects of an infallible definition because they are grounded in human reason applying the fundamental principles of morality to particular situations. Hence, they cannot be considered to be necessary conditions of nor implications of the central truths of revelation, such that it cannot be faithfully transmitted unless they are affirmed. As he adds, probably a majority of Catholic moral theologians would share this view. Indeed, there are some who go further. For example, the Australian theologian Frank Mobbs has recently argued that the magisterium has no authority at all to teach on nonrevealed matters of the natural law since its authority is limited to expounding what has been revealed.[6]

In contrast, Grisez and Ford hold that the magisterium can infallibly teach some specific norms connected to the natural law, even though they cannot be said to be revealed in any obvious sense. Their argument is straightforward: the ban on the use of contraceptives meets the generally accepted criteria for an infallible teaching of the ordinary magisterium; but this is not a revealed moral norm; therefore, since actuality is the best possible proof of possibility, it must be possible for a nonrevealed, specific moral norm to be the object of an infallible teaching. Correlatively, we know that the precept forbidding the use of contraceptives is necessarily connected to revelation because it has been infallibly taught—even though we may not know *how* it is connected. At the risk of oversimplifying, Grisez and Ford appeal to a procedural criterion for determining whether a given teaching is infallible, whereas Sullivan believes that we need substantive as well as procedural criteria for making such a determination.

As I will argue below, Sullivan's substantive approach is more satisfactory than Grisez's procedural approach, and for this reason, among others, I find Sullivan's arguments about the status of the teaching on contraceptives to be generally persuasive. However, considered as two ways of interpreting the theological significance of moral norms, neither of these approaches appears to me to be fully satisfactory because they seem to presuppose an overly simplified account of the natural law and its relation to revelation. On this account, natural and revealed morality comprise two distinct bodies of moral norms, which partially overlap. On Sullivan's view, we can make some independent judgments about which norms fall into which set, whereas on Grisez's view, we can only know this (sometimes, anyway) as a result of magisterial teaching. Both presuppose, however, that natural and revealed morality stand over against each other as two independent yet intersecting sources for moral judgment.

But as Norbert Rigali has pointed out in a different context, any such sharp separation of natural and Christian morality overlooks the fact that human morality, as such, never exists in a pure state; what we find instead are the historically and socially conditioned moralities of particular communities.[7] It need not follow that these particular moralities have nothing in common, or that they cannot be interpreted as expressions of more fundamental natural or rational exigencies. Although I cannot argue the point here, I think it is in fact the case that all moral systems are grounded in fundamental prerational tendencies and patterns of interaction that we share with the other primates.[8] However, if Rigali is right, as I believe him to be, we cannot derive a full-fledged morality from these exigencies, which would somehow be prior to and more basic than the specific moralities of particular communities. The natural givens of human social existence shape our moral beliefs and practices, but at the same time, on almost any plausible construal of the relation between nature and morality, the former underdetermines the latter.[9]

This claim might seem to be inconsistent with a classical Catholic natural law approach to morality, and indeed it would be inconsistent with most interpretations of the natural law developed from the early modern period onward. However, it would not be inconsistent with an earlier medieval concept of the natural law, and by the same token that concept offers us a new perspective—new, that is, to us—on the issues before us.

The concept of the natural law that I have in mind is the one that developed among canonists and theologians in the first flush of scholasticism, between the mid-twelfth and the end of the thirteenth centuries.[10] As is well known, this was a period of consolidation, following on the institutional and intellectual reforms of the eleventh and early twelfth centuries.[11] As one part of their attempt to systematize Christian practice and doctrine, the scholastics in this period developed a coherent concept of the natural law, which in turn provided a frame-work for thinking about a number of theological, exegetical, and prac-tical questions.

When we turn to an examination of these authors, we are likely to be struck by the extent to which they emphasize the theological char-acter of the natural law. At the beginning of his synthetic compilation of the canons of the church commonly known as the *Decretum*, writ-ten in about 1140, Gratian writes,

> The human race is ruled by a twofold rule, namely, natural law and custom. The natural law is that which is contained in the law and the Gospel, by which each person is commanded to do to others what he would wish to be done to himself, and forbidden to render to others that which he would not have done to himself. Hence, Christ [says] in the Gospel, "All things whatever that you would wish other people to do to you, do the same also to them. For this is the law and the prophets."[12]

Many commentators have dismissed these comments as a confused commingling of two distinct sources for moral reflection.[13] But this judgment itself reflects one particular contestable and (as I believe) unjustified perspective on the natural law. Gratian's remarks reflect a distinctive way of construing the natural law, which dominated scholastic thought, at least among canon lawyers and theologians, in the twelfth and thirteenth centuries. On this view, the natural law is warranted by scripture and correlatively, it is to be understood and interpreted in theological terms. In particular, the specific normative implications of the natural law were interpreted in accordance with scriptural norms—particularly the Golden Rule and the precepts of the Decalogue—which were regarded as especially perspicuous sum-maries of the immediate implications of natural law principles. While the scholastics in this period do recognize a distinction between natu-ral and divine, or scriptural, law, they do not consider the latter to be a form of positive law; rather, they insist that natural and divine law are two complementary and mutually interpreting expressions of God's providential wisdom and governing will.

In a recent survey and assessment of current natural law perspectives on homosexuality, Stephen Pope identifies one such current paradigm as "revealed natural law," according to which "human beings, given the great limits of finitude and the corruption of sin, must rely on revelation if we are to attain reliable and clear knowledge of the human good."[14] On this view, we are thus dependent on divine revelation for any kind of moral knowledge that we may possess. This view, it should be noted, is not Pope's own. While he acknowledges the importance of emphasizing the role of scripture in theological ethics, he argues that this approach gives too little weight to reason and experience, even seen from a traditional Catholic perspective, and that it promotes a one-dimensional perspective on human nature. These criticisms seem to me to be on target.

Yet it might appear that I am attributing a similar perspective on the natural law to the scholastics. Admittedly, their views do resemble the "revealed natural law" approach in one respect, namely, the centrality of scripture for their interpretation of the natural law. Yet it would be just as misleading to regard the natural law as the scholastics understood it as purely "revealed" in Pope's sense, as to regard it as an early stage on the way to the development of purely rationalistic theories. Rather, the scholastic approach to the natural law combined elements of what we now regard as two disparate approaches to moral discernment—namely, rational reflection and reliance on revelation—and they did so in a characteristic way.

More specifically, the scholastic concept of the natural law emerged out of a scripturally informed and selective appropriation of earlier Christian, Jewish, and classical thinking on the natural law.[15] The resulting account of the natural law was in turn applied to specific scriptural texts as a basis for interpretation. On this basis, they distinguished between those scriptural norms that are genuinely moral norms and those that are not, and in addition they interpreted and extended the meaning of those norms, such as the precepts of the Decalogue, which they took to be incontrovertibly moral norms. In a way, the scholastics' procedure was circular, but not, I believe, in a vicious sense. They began with assumptions about nature and the moral order informed by many sources, including Christian and Jewish authorities as well as a wide range of philosophical sources. As they developed these assumptions, they uncovered inconsistencies or difficulties, which they sometimes corrected through analysis and argument, and sometimes by revising their interpretations of their sources. Always, they aimed to preserve the overall harmony of these sources and to safeguard the inerrancy of scripture.

There is a further reason why we cannot conclude that, just because the natural law as the early scholastics understood it is not comprised of a set of purely rational precepts, therefore it must consist of a set of revealed precepts. That is, the scholastics were hesitant to identify the natural law with precepts, that is to say, specific moral rules, except in a derivative or secondary sense.[16] This does not at all mean that they regarded the natural law as a purely formal or abstract entity that has no direct substantive implications. After all, they considered the precepts of the Decalogue to be expressions of the natural law, and it is hard to imagine a more important set of substantive norms than these. Nonetheless, with very few exceptions they identified the natural law in its primary sense with our basic capacities for moral judgment, or with the basic principles through which that judgment operates.

This, it should be noted, is itself a scriptural approach to the natural law, at least as the scholastics, following a long tradition of patristic interpretation, understood scripture. We find this view summarized in a much-quoted passage from the Ordinary Gloss, the standard compilation of patristic commentaries on scripture, commenting on Romans 2:14:

> Paul said above that the Gentiles are damned if they act badly and saved if they act well. But since they do not have a law, as it were being ignorant of what is good or evil, it would seem that neither should be imputed to them. Contrary to this, the Apostle says: Even if one does not have the written law, one nonetheless has the natural law, by which one understands and is inwardly conscious of what is good and what is evil, what is vice insofar as it is contrary to nature, which in any case grace heals. For the Image cannot be so far extirpated from the human soul by the stain of earthly desires, that none of its lineaments should remain in it. For that is not

altogether removed which was impressed there through the Image of God when the human person was created. Accordingly, when vice has been healed through grace, they naturally do those things which pertain to the law. Grace is not denied on account of nature, but rather nature is healed through grace; which being restored in the inner individual, the law of justice, which fault deleted, is re-inscribed through grace.[17]

Given this approach, we can more readily see why the scholastics did not perceive any incongruity between asserting the primordial character and universality of the natural law (as they did), and interpreting it in light of a theologically informed construal of human nature. If the natural law is fundamentally identified with a capacity for moral discernment, which is itself privileged on theological grounds as the distinctive mark of humanity, then it is easier to see how a ubiquitous natural law might at the same time be expressed through precepts that are more or less specific to a particular set of circumstances and convictions.

This brings us to a further point. The scholastics' identification of the natural law in its primary sense with fundamental capacities or principles of discernment, as opposed to specific precepts, undermines the distinction between rational and revealed morality from another direction. If the natural law is primarily either a power of discernment or a set of abstract first principles, then just how do we arrive at specific precepts of the natural law? Generally speaking, specific precepts of the natural law are discerned through rational reflection on the needs and inclinations of human life.[18] However, the scholastics do not understand this rational reflection in terms of deduction from fixed principles, nor do they identify it with any one procedure or formula. Rather, on their view we move from first principles to specific norms through complex processes of discernment and practical determination. Through these processes, we arrive at concrete norms that are grounded in the natural law in its primary sense and can be justified in terms of it, but that cannot be said to be contained in that natural law prior to human deliberation.

If this is so, then it is misleading to speak of precepts of the natural law that we discover in contrast to precepts that are revealed to us. We cannot quite say that the precepts of the natural law are *either* discovered, in the sense that scientific laws are discovered, *or* revealed, as the dogmas of faith are revealed. To a considerable degree, at least, they are constructed, as laws in the ordinary legal sense are constructed.[19] This process of construction operates within constraints, both practical and theological in nature, and for that reason the analogy with positive law should not be pressed too far. Nonetheless, there is a real sense in which the natural law, understood as a body of precepts, is also a law in the sense of being the product of deliberative prudence.[20]

Of course the scholastics believe that there are some specific precepts of the natural law that God has revealed to us, including the precepts of the Decalogue and certain of Jesus's moral injunctions. However, even those precepts of the natural law that are revealed by God cannot be translated directly into social practices without a considerable degree of interpretation. In this sense, there is some room for human construction even with respect to the fundamental moral precepts that stem from the natural law. To quote Aquinas,

> these precepts of the Decalogue, with respect to the rational character of justice which they contain, are unchangeable. But with respect to some determination through application to individual acts, whether for example this or that is murder, theft or adultery, or not, this indeed is changeable; sometimes only by the divine authority, namely in those things which are instituted by God alone, as for example marriage and other things of this sort; and sometimes by human authority, with respect to those things which are committed to human jurisdiction. For with respect to those things, human persons act as the vicar of God, not however with respect to all things.[21]

Aquinas does not say that human authority in the interpretation and application of the precepts of the natural law is unlimited, but he does consider it to be very extensive. (And as the history of ecclesial marriage law indicates, there was practically a great deal of room for interpretation even with respect to those practices "instituted by God alone.") In this respect, his view is typical of the scholastics in the period we are considering.

THE NATURAL LAW AND THE TEACHING AUTHORITY OF THE CHURCH

What does this way of understanding the natural law imply about the church's teaching authority with respect to moral questions? At the very least, it calls into question Mobbs's view, according to which the magisterium cannot teach on matters of the natural law at all. If the natural law is foundationally theological, then it would seem that the whole of it is, in principle, a fit object for the church's teaching authority. Indeed, on this view the substantive precepts of the natural law, at least as these are articulated within the church itself, are necessarily the result of the church's discerning and selective moral reflection—*if* by the church we understand the whole of the Christian community, and if we assume that much of this activity will be expressed through prereflective practice rather than through theological argument or official pronouncement.

This brings us to a crucial point, because of course we must draw a distinction between the authoritative moral discernment of the church, that is to say, the believing community taken as a whole, and the activity of the magisterium, whether ordinary or extraordinary, in articulating that discernment. Even though we cannot draw the simple line that Mobbs suggests, this does not mean that we can simply assume that the magisterium has unlimited and unconditional authority to teach on moral matters. At the very least we must ask whether the theological judgments pertaining to moral matters are analogous to the discernment that is called for in matters of doctrine. And if not, what relevance does this fact have for our understanding of magisterial authority?

We sometimes refer to four sources for Christian moral reflection, namely, scripture, tradition, reason, and experience. The scholastic concept of the natural law suggests a different, and I believe a more satisfactory way of construing these four "sources"—not as four distinct sources that we consult in the formation of moral norms, but rather as four components of a communal process of ecclesial moral discernment, which can be separated at the level of analysis but which are always interconnected in practice. Our reception of scripture as a moral document, that is to say, as a text that provides us with norms for action, cannot be understood as if it were equivalent to the discovery or contemplation of independent truths contained in the text. From its first moment, this reception proceeds by way of a reasoned construal of the scriptural texts, guided (as we hope and trust) by the Spirit of Christ and understanding reason broadly to include the prerational exigencies of human nature. By the same token, there is no point at which rational moral discernment within the church can be said to operate in a "purely human" way, if that implies a way of operating that is wholly independent of its ecclesial context. Moral reasoning within the church community is always shaped by theological and ultimately scriptural starting points, saliencies, and concerns. Similarly, this process of moral discernment is always situated within a history and a context of current practices and concerns, which give it a definite shape, and which it in turn directs—so that, if we mean by "tradition and experience," something like, "history and reflection on current practice," then moral discernment within the church is always shaped by tradition and experience. Indeed, the ongoing processes of practice, reflection, and the correction of practice that comprise tradition and experience are nothing other than an extended process of rational discernment, which is also always a process of reflection on the practical meaning of scripture in the sense just indicated.

If this approach is accepted, then we will need to rethink what it might mean to say that moral truths are revealed in scripture, and correlatively which specific precepts we consider to be revealed moral truths. In my view, we cannot speak in terms of moral truths revealed in scripture, if by that we mean something like, "Moral norms that are given in scripture, antecedently to the reflective discernment of the Christian community." We *can* speak in such terms, if by that we mean something like, "Moral norms which the Christian community has drawn from scripture by incorporating them into its practices and articulating them through reflection on those practices." Hence, there is a sense in which some norms of the natural law may be said to be revealed. Yet the process of revelation, so to speak, is not prior to the appropriation and application of scriptural norms, but *is* that process. And correlatively, the norms that are revealed in this way cannot be separated from the practices that give them meaning. That is, there can be no fundamental distinction between the norm and its application, such that one is revealed and the other is not.

What does this line of analysis imply for the question of the church's authority in matters of the natural law? In the first place, it is difficult to see how, on this view, *any* moral precept, including those traditionally said to be revealed, can be said to be a proper object of infallible teaching. That is, even such norms, considered as moral norms and not as bare scriptural texts, are themselves constructs of the Christian community, and it seems odd to say that such constructs can be objects of supernatural faith. (I am focusing here on the reception of scripture as a more or less formed text, but of course scripture is itself in some sense a communal construct—in just what sense, we can, mercifully, pass over for now.)

Yet secondly, it does not follow that the Christian community cannot teach authoritatively or even definitively on moral matters. On the contrary, I would argue, there is a sense in which the church does teach definitively on moral matters, through a process of discerning that a given norm is so integrally connected to the Christian faith that it will always necessarily be incorporated into any authentic Christian community. Such teaching will take the form of practical efforts to incorporate the norm in question and to draw out its specific consequences in a variety of circumstances, as well as more self-reflective attempts to articulate the norm and to comment on its significance. In this sense, the church can arrive at moral teachings that are definitive and irreversible, both because such teachings are centrally connected to revelation, and because they are built into the practices of the church at so many points as to shape all further reflection, and to be practically inextricable from its communal life. I say the church advisedly, because it appears to me that any authentic magisterial teaching on moral matters will necessarily stem from and depend on the practices of the community as a whole.[22] However, I can see no reason to deny that the magisterium can reflectively express the results of communal moral discernment in such a way as to articulate definitive, irreversible moral teachings.

Are there examples of moral teachings that are irreversible in this sense? It would take us well beyond the scope of this paper to explore this question adequately, but let me at least suggest two candidates for such teachings. First, I would argue that Gratian is right to identify the natural law with the Golden Rule as articulated in scripture—right, that is, to identify this as a foundational principle of Christian moral reasoning and to identify it as the central core of the moral witness of scripture.

It should be noted that this claim is not original to Gratian, and indeed it would weaken my case if it were.[23] He reflects a long-standing view, which we find articulated throughout the patristic and early medieval traditions, and which continues to be articulated after the medieval period, that the natural law is encapsulated in the Golden Rule. The Golden Rule is in turn spelled out in terms of a commitment to non-maleficence grounded in an intelligent appreciation of another's point of view: by emphasizing the importance of the claims of others, and especially by building on empathy for another as the basis for social morality, this approach gives relatively greater weight to our commonalities, while it de-emphasizes the moral importance of our differences. In this way, the scholastic appeal to the Golden Rule as the epitome of the natural law both expresses and reinforces a more fundamental Christian moral commitment to normative equality.[24]

The rapid social changes of the past century have given a new saliency to equality as a moral norm, and have occasioned a rich literature on the meaning and justification for this norm. A commitment to equality is sometimes seen as one expression of a distinctively secular liberal worldview, which as such is fundamentally alien to the church—for better or for worse.[25] Margaret Farley, in contrast, has been at the forefront of those Christian scholars who have defended a commitment to some form of normative equality on theological grounds. As she has argued, a norm of equal regard is not only implied by a right understanding of Christian love, it is also a necessary presupposition for the intimacy that we expect in marriage and other interpersonal relationships, and a precondition for the good order of the Christian community itself.[26] On this view, a commitment to normative equality is central to the Christian moral tradition because it stems from fundamental theological commitments and is enmeshed in the life and practice of the church in rich and complex ways. It will be apparent that I follow Farley in her assessments of the validity and centrality of normative equality as a standard for Christian ethics. I would only add that this commitment has historically been central, even though ambiguously affirmed, and that it qualifies as an irreversible moral teaching if anything does.

I can envision at least two challenges to this claim. The first would simply observe that there is nothing distinctively Christian about a commitment to normative equality; in some form or other, this norm is central to moral and judicial institutions throughout much of the world. The second is at least implicit in Farley's own writings, because even as she has defended the theological exigency of a commitment to equality, she has also been deeply critical of the historical failures of Christianity to defend this commitment. In particular, as she forcefully argues, the embrace of a genuine norm of equality in gender and family relations would be a new departure for Christian ethics, in fact "a revolution," since until very recently Christian sexual ethics and sacramental practice have been deeply shaped by assumptions about and even explicit defenses of the deep inequality of the sexes.[27] This at least implies that a Christian commitment to normative equality has been more verbal than real, although so far as I recall she never frames her conclusions in quite this way.

In response to the first point, it is certainly true that a commitment to normative equality is not unique to Christianity, although neither is it universally held.[28] However, it is appropriated within the Christian community on specifically theological grounds and developed accordingly. Again, it would take a much longer discussion adequately to defend this claim, but let me at least illustrate what I mean by focusing on one strand of scholastic thinking on this issue.

We have already noted that for the scholastics the natural law in its primary sense is usually identified either with reason itself or with the first general principles through which reason operates. As we

have seen, this does not necessarily imply that the natural law understood in a secondary sense as a body of concrete precepts is universally accessible to all. Nonetheless, on their view the natural law in
its primary sense is intimately bound up with capacities for reason,
judgment, or free action, which all persons share.[29] Understood in
this way, the natural law is one fundamental expression of the equality of moral capacity that the scholastics believe to be shared by all
normal adults. Hence, just as every mentally normal adult, man or
woman, good or bad, naturally possesses some capacities for moral
discernment and action, so every human being necessarily possesses
some knowledge of the natural law, or alternatively some inclination towards moral goodness, which is tantamount to the natural
law. While this knowledge (or inclination) has been dimmed and
distorted by sin, it cannot be extinguished, as we are frequently reminded, not even in Cain himself—just as the patristic tradition mediated through the Gloss held.

So far, the theological interpretation of this appeal to shared humanity would seem to be focused on negative claims, forestalling false
interpretations. However, this appeal lends itself to a more positive
theological expression because, still guided by scripture as mediated
through the Gloss (among other sources), the scholastics also tended
to identify the biblical Image of God with the human capacity for rational self-direction.[30] And since this capacity is integrally connected
to the natural law, it follows that the natural law is also an expression of the divine image in which we are created. This line of interpretation, in turn, helps to indicate how a commitment to natural
equality, interpreted by reference to the image of God motif, is tied
to doctrinal commitments, and why it is so central to the moral life of
the Christian community. That is, on this view, by respecting the capacity for self-direction that is present, actually or potentially, in each
human being, we are paying reverence, as best we can, to God as we
apprehend God through the neighbor.

What are the implications of this interpretation of the *imago Dei*
motif? Most importantly, an appeal to the doctrine that we are created in the image of God serves to qualify and develop the general idea
that we are equal in virtue of a shared humanity.[31] Given a different

set of values, it might be said that a capacity for depth of feeling, or courageous and spirited self-assertion, is central to moral agency and forms the basis for the respect that we owe to others.[32] The moral vision that gives central place to reason and free judgment does not originate with Christianity, but in the period we are considering, it is reinforced and given theological depth through its association with the *imago Dei* motif. Secondly, and correlatively, this interpretation leads the scholastics to a commitment to respect for the free self-direction of the other. Seen from our standpoint, this commitment is regrettably limited, yet it does have genuine practical effects, for example, the protection of the freedom to marry (more on this below); the development of limits on obligations of obedience; and among some scholastics in this period, although not all, the beginnings of a development of a doctrine of subjective rights.[33]

This brings me to the second objection noted above. I suspect that the differences between Farley's interpretation of earlier Christian moral teachings and the one just sketched is to some degree a matter of emphasis. If there were no basis at all for a commitment to equality within the Christian moral tradition, then a present-day affirmation of that norm would call for more than a new departure within the Christian tradition: it would amount to adopting an altogether new moral approach. This is clearly not what Farley advocates.[34] It is also certainly true that the Christian commitment to equality has developed within a context of deep and pervasive inequalities, which to some degree at least have themselves been defended on theological grounds.[35] Nonetheless, I would still argue that when we study the history of Christian moral and political thought, we do find a progressive elaboration of the meaning of this commitment, both theoretical and practical in nature. These elaborations, in turn, or some of them at any rate, become part of the meaning of normative equality itself, at least as understood and practiced within the Christian community, and in this way they become irreversibly part of Christian moral belief and practice, just as is the commitment to normative equality itself. Other specifications are not so centrally important, of course; sometimes only discernment and time will enable us to distinguish central from nonessential qualifications of a basic commitment.

I would suggest a second candidate for an irreversible moral teaching which is perhaps more directly relevant to the topic with which we
began. That is, it seems to me that the goodness of marriage and procreation has also been irreversibly determined over the course of Christian
moral reflection. This is again an example of a moral commitment that
is, of course, not uniquely Christian, but at the same time it is a still
clearer example of a commitment that is affirmed within the Christian
community on specifically theological grounds. As Farley observes, the
history of Christian attitudes has included pervasive elements "of deep
ambivalence, sometimes open hostility, towards marriage and family
life," periodically leading to dualist denials that marriage is an acceptable way of life for the Christian, or that procreation is in any way
good.[36] This history of ambivalence towards, and outright denials of,
the goodness of marriage and procreation has led in turn to repeated
affirmations of the goodness of these fundamental human experiences.
It is important to realize that fundamental theological issues were at
stake in these conflicts. The dualist position on sexuality has generally
been grounded in a more fundamental rejection of the goodness of the
material world and ultimately its status as God's creation; by the same
token, the church's affirmation of the goodness of marriage is centrally
connected to its affirmation of the doctrine of creation, and serves to
draw out the immediate practical implications of that affirmation.

The doctrinal significance of marriage within the Christian tradition has, in turn, shaped the way in which Christian marriage has been
understood and practiced. Most importantly, it has led to a normative connection in Christian teaching and practice between marriage
and procreation; that is, it has led to the view that marriage is ideally
or normatively oriented towards procreation, and serves in turn to
provide the appropriate social context for procreation. This linkage
is so deeply imbedded in our thinking and practice that it is likely to
seem obvious. Yet as Noonan points out, it would have been possible
to develop the scriptural starting points in another way, perhaps by
building on the Pauline view that in this time between the times,
marriage serves essentially as a way of managing our sexual needs.[37]
Similarly, in contemporary society we see another model of marriage
as a compact for companionship and mutual support, including but

not limited to sexual expression. Such a model is attractive and admirable, but as Lisa Cahill suggests, it is not finally consonant with a Christian vision of marriage, precisely because it recognizes no normative link at all between marriage and children.[38]

At the same time, the Christian understanding of marriage also incorporates other ideals and commitments, including some that are arguably even more fundamental than the value of procreation. In particular, Christian reflection on marriage has provided one critical context for reflecting on, and thereby constructing, the practical meaning of the commitment to equality. This may seem surprising, given the long history of a Christian defense of gender inequality. But this view has from the beginning been qualified and (as I believe) progressively undermined by concrete affirmations of equality. As Jo Ann MacNamara has argued, the early Christian insistence on safeguarding the freedom to marry or not to marry had the perhaps unintended effect of breaking down patriarchal family structures, which in turn offered women in particular opportunities for freedom outside marriage, and parity within marriage, that they had not previously enjoyed.[39] A number of scholars, including Farley herself, have pointed out that the Christian prohibition against divorce tended likewise to safeguard women's interests in the context of late antiquity and the medieval period.[40] Moreover, the insistence that men and women should abide by the same sexual norms, and should enjoy the same sexual freedoms within marriage, worked to undermine the idea of a dual morality at the very point at which it was most powerful.

Finally, the patristic and medieval defense of an almost unlimited freedom to marry, which was expressed in a variety of ways in this period, reflected and extended the commitments to normative equality and freedom discussed above.[41] The widely held doctrine that the mutual consent of a couple is sufficient to establish a valid marriage functioned as a powerful safeguard for the right to marry; as such, it opened up a space in which people could act freely in a matter of fundamental importance, whatever their place in a social hierarchy. This implied ideal of natural equality was also defended in other ways, for example, by explicit assertions of the rights of those in a state of servitude to marry, as we find in Gratian's *Decretum* (C.29, q.2). Although this view was contested, it was subsequently incorporated into church law in 1155 by a decree of Hadrian IV, *Dignum est*, which unequivocally affirms the right of unfree persons to marry without the approval of their masters.[42] These reforms give substance to Aquinas's claim that "in things which pertain to the nature of the body, one person is not held to obey another, but only God, since all persons are equal in nature" (*Summa theologiae* II-II 104.5).

When we speak of a natural law account of marriage within the Christian context, we must take note of those aspects of human nature that this account privileges, while at the same time attending to the theological commitments underlying it. In particular, this account does imply a particular understanding of sexuality according to which there is a normative link between sexuality and procreation, but it also embodies other ideals and commitments, not necessarily related to sexuality per se, which must also be taken into consideration. These commitments, in turn, provide the context within which to assess Christian teachings and practices on contraception.

I think it is fair to say that the Christian understanding of marriage and procreation implies that there is something problematic about the use of contraceptives. If procreation is a human good, and if we have serious doctrinal reasons for insisting on this teaching and incorporating it into our common life, then it does seem to follow that there is something incongruous from the Christian standpoint in the use of contraceptives. This incongruity helps to account for what might otherwise be hard to understand, namely, why it is that we within the Christian community identify the use of contraceptives as a moral issue at all. Furthermore, it helps to explain why we find a consistent condemnation of the use of contraceptives throughout the history of Christian reflections on sexuality.

Yet none of this necessarily implies that this condemnation need be strictly binding on us today. Indeed, it is by no means obvious that a strict prohibition on the use of contraceptives is necessary to preserve the fundamental Christian affirmation of the goodness of marriage and procreation. On the contrary, as any number of theologians both within and outside the Catholic context have argued, there is a good case to be made that it is not.[43]

This brings us back to the questions with which this essay began. What is the status of the magisterium's teaching on the use of contraceptives? In the next section, I will take up this issue.

THE MORAL MAGISTERIUM AND
THE BAN ON CONTRACEPTIVE USE

According to Grisez and Ford, the received Catholic teaching on contraceptives meets the criteria set forth by Vatican II for an infallible teaching of the ordinary magisterium; that is to say, throughout history it has been taught by all the Catholic bishops as something to be held definitively by all the faithful. As they admit, this is to some extent an argument from silence. They consider it to be powerful nonetheless, since no one has yet offered a clear counterexample, in spite of the extensive study that this subject has received.[44]

In response, Sullivan asks what I think is the critical question: "[H]ow do they understand what it means to teach something as to be held definitively?"[45] As he goes on to observe, for them "definitive" seems to be equivalent to "binding in conscience," or sometimes, "scripturally based." The practical consequence of this view would be that every moral teaching of the ordinary magisterium is infallible; that is to say, the distinction between authoritative and infallible teachings would be rendered meaningless. This, in turn, would imply that the teachings of the magisterium can never develop in substantive ways, since once the magisterium has infallibly defined something, of course it cannot reverse itself later on.[46] In Sullivan's view, such an interpretation is not consistent with the understanding of infallibility set forth in both Vatican councils:

> Against such a view I would argue that if it were true, there would be no point at all in the insistence of Vatican I and Vatican II that the magisterium can speak infallibly only on matters of faith and morals. It would have been necessary to say only this: whenever the magisterium speaks in a definitive way it must be speaking infallibly, because the very fact that it speaks in a definitive way would

guarantee that what it speaks about would be a proper matter for infallible teaching. What then would have been the point of mentioning the limits of the matter about which the Church can teach infallibly? It seems to me that the supposition underlying the argument of Ford and Grisez would open the door to absolutism in the exercise of magisterium.[47]

Let me add one further point. It is perhaps obvious, but worth noting nonetheless, that any attempt to apply Vatican II criteria for infallible teaching to earlier periods cannot be understood as a simple appeal to an objective matter of fact having to do with what "the church has taught." In the process of applying these criteria, we are making an interpretative theological judgment about the significance of consensus (in the case at hand)—to say nothing of the further judgments that must be made in determining what counts as a consensus, who counts as the church, and the like.

This is particularly germane to any assessment of church teaching in the premodern period. In today's Catholic church, any magisterial teaching presupposes an extensive and well-organized institutional and legal structure, in which the weight of specific teachings can be minutely analyzed and closely debated. But no such structure was in place in the patristic or medieval church.[48] The episcopal structure of the church was loose and its theological significance was disputed. There was no systematic compilation of canon law in the Western church until the publication of Gratian's *Decretum* in 1140, and officially sanctioned collections of canons did not begin to be published until the next century.[49] Until about the twelfth century, there was not even a practical, consistently reliable way of determining what bishops, councils, and popes had taught or were teaching, because there was no practical way of systematically accessing the records of the past or effectively communicating across any distances in the present. In addition, throughout much of this period the relation between Eastern and Western churches was an open question in the minds of many on both sides of that tragic division. Given all this, it is not at all clear how a consensus of church leaders and theologians could have been established in this period, nor can we say with confidence just what individuals would have understood practically by teaching in accordance with such a consensus.

Of course none of this prevents us from interpreting their teachings as authoritative for the church as a whole. However, my point is that in that case what we are doing is precisely interpreting the historical record on the basis of a particular set of theological judgments about the structure of the church and the normal exercise of its teaching office. We cannot assume that in such a case we are simply verifying that an objective criterion for authoritative teaching has been met.

This is particularly relevant to the question that Sullivan presses: What exactly would it have meant for bishops and others to propose a teaching as definitive in the context of the early or high middle ages, before the structures of the modern Western church were in place? Certainly, when a bishop in, say, the ninth century pronounced a particular kind of act to be sinful, we can assume that he believed that he had Christian tradition behind him, and presumably he would have expected his brother bishops to agree with him. But can we say anything more than that? In particular, can we assume that he would have thought of himself as articulating a particular teaching in concert with all his brother bishops, and as thereby sharing in the expression of a definitive teaching? It seems to me unlikely that he would, particularly since his chances of ever knowing what his brother bishops were teaching was so small. One does not readily think in terms of a worldwide church (at least, not as a social and institutional reality) when one's world is effectively limited to the carrying power of one's horse. Again, my point is not that the consensus of bishops in the ninth century should have no weight for us today. Nonetheless, we cannot just assume that the fact of consensus then, if it could be ascertained, would have had the same meaning for them as episcopal consensus would have for us today.

So far, this line of argument would apply to the assessment of any church teaching. Further issues arise when we turn to the assessment of moral teachings in particular. In the last section, I argued that moral discernment should not be equated with the contemplation of speculative truths. Given the constructive element in moral discernment, it is more like devising laws than discovering truths. Of course, this comparison would need to be carefully qualified; my point is that the evaluation of the history of moral thought needs to be approached with questions similar to those that lawyers bring to the interpretation of laws. When considering a particular moral norm, we need to ask not only what is being said, but in what context and to what purpose this norm has been articulated.

The development of the ban on contraceptive use offers a good illustration of this point. Certainly, so far as we know, this ban has been universally affirmed. But what was the significance of this ban? Has it always been seen as a central expression of the church's moral commitments?

As Noonan shows, there have been periods in the church's history when the answer to the latter question would almost certainly have been positive. Yet it is not so clear that this would always have been the case. James Brundage offers the startling suggestion that Gratian himself considered the use of contraceptives to be only venially sinful, on the basis of two passages from the *Decretum*.[50] In my view, this is overreading the texts, because in neither place does Gratian say that the use of contraceptives is venially sinful; what he says (quoting Augustine, in the earlier passage) is that it is venially sinful to engage in sexual intercourse within marriage simply in order to satisfy sexual desire. At the same time, in both passages Gratian's condemnation of the use of contraceptives envisions a context in which the partners have entered into a relationship solely for the purpose of mutually satisfying their sexual desire, and the question he is considering is whether such a relationship should count as a marriage or not. In other words, Gratian is not interested in the sinfulness of contraceptives per se, although he clearly presupposes it, but in working out the proper definition of marriage. Of course this does not mean that he would have approved of the use of contraceptives within a full-fledged marriage, but it does suggest that for him the use of contraceptives is not a focus for concern.

Even more tellingly, the use of contraceptives does not appear to receive much explicit attention in this period. A number of scholastic theologians either do not mention the use of contraceptives at all, or they discuss them in their earlier works only to drop the subject later on.[51] This does not mean that they did not consider the use of contraceptives to be sinful—without doubt, they did—but it does suggest that for most of them, this particular sin was not significant enough to merit explicit mention, much less extensive discussion. It might be said that references to unnatural sexual acts, to spilling seed outside the intention of procreation and the like, would be understood to include the practice of contraception. That is probably true, at least in many cases, but the same could be said of masturbation or homosexual acts, both of which are regularly singled out for explicit mention in catalogues of sexual sins. Nor can this be explained by the relative absence of contraceptive practices in medieval practice. On the contrary, knowledge of contraceptive practices was widely available. The medical historian Roy Porter mentions one medieval treatise, *The Treasury of the Poor*, attributed to Peter of Spain, later Pope John XXI, which offered more than one hundred prescriptions for fertility, aphrodisiacs, and contraceptives.[52] It is difficult indeed to believe that this information would be circulated if nobody was interested in using it.

This is another argument from silence, and I would not place too much weight on it. Nonetheless, it does at least suggest that references to the received teaching on contraceptives stand in need of careful qualification. Even though the use of contraceptives does seem to have been universally condemned up until modern times, it is not at all clear that this condemnation has always been understood as something central to the integrity of Christian faith and moral practice.

It has often been argued, both within and outside the Catholic community, that a commitment to the goodness of procreation and its integral place within marriage does not necessarily rule out the use of contraceptives. The evidence from the scholastic period, limited though it is, seems to support this conclusion. What this evidence suggests is that in one period, at least, the sinfulness of contraception was viewed as an implication, and not a centrally important implication, of certain views of sexuality and marriage. Given later reassessments of the sinful or problematic character of sexual desire—a process that itself began in this period—we can understand how the Christian community could qualify its views on the sinfulness of contraceptive use without thereby reversing its fundamental commitments to the goodness of marriage and procreation.[53]

Moreover, there is a case to be made that some acceptance of contraceptive use, within the context of an institutional commitment to both marriage and procreation, is actually necessary to safeguard other natural law commitments, which are arguably even more central to Christian moral practices, and which have also progressively transformed our understanding of marriage. In *Sex, Gender and Christian Ethics*, Cahill points out that given the conditions of modern industrialized society, the full equality of women both within marriage and within society as a whole requires some regulation of births, which can only practically be implemented through judicious use of contraceptives.[54] It would be easy to dismiss this as an attempt to challenge church teachings by the standards of contemporary liberal values, but on the contrary the ideal of equality is itself a natural law ideal, and one that is central to Christian belief and practice. Moreover, as Farley has powerfully argued, a commitment to equality is central to a fully adequate Christian understanding of marriage.[55] Given this, a judicious use of contraceptives, which respects the overall openness of the marital relation to children, can actually be a way of safeguarding and expressing natural law principles in a contemporary context.

If this conclusion were to be adopted by the magisterium, would this amount to a reversal of a previously held moral teaching, and if so, what would be the implications of that fact? These questions raise further issues that cannot be explored here in any detail, but I would like to touch on them briefly by way of conclusion.

First of all, the distinction between a reformulation or qualification of a previously held teaching, and its flat reversal, is not always clear. Much depends on just what one identifies as the teaching in question. If we consider the teaching in question to be the goodness of procreation and its centrality in Christian marriage, then it makes sense to say that by allowing for the licitness of contraceptive use, we would be qualifying and extending a fundamental moral commitment in light of current circumstances, but not repudiating anything centrally important to a Christian understanding of marriage. Nonetheless, it is difficult to deny that such a move would involve a reversal of teaching at some level. Once we said that the use of contraceptives is always sinful; now we say that it is not. If this does not count as a reversal, what does?

Many theologians and church leaders have resisted this conclusion, because it seems to have untenable consequences. In *Magisterium*, Sullivan quotes the minority report of the Preparatory Theological Commission set up to study the question of contraceptive use as follows:

> [T]here is no possibility that the teaching itself is other than substantially true. It is true because the Catholic church, instituted by Christ to show men the sure road to eternal life, could not err so atrociously through all the centuries of its history. The Church cannot substantially err in teaching a very serious doctrine of faith or morals through all the centuries—even through one century— a doctrine constantly and insistently proposed as one necessarily to be followed in order to attain eternal salvation.[56]

And why not? Because, the minority report continues a little further on, "The Catholic Church could not in the name of Jesus Christ offer to the vast multitude of the faithful, everywhere in the world, for so many centuries an occasion of formal sin and spiritual ruin on account of a false doctrine promulgated in the name of Jesus Christ."[57]

To this argument, Sullivan replies, "One problem with this argument is that if it were valid, and its conclusion were true, it would also have to be true that the Church has never erred when it has taught something to be gravely sinful. The argument would have to be able to stand up to the test of history."[58] Sullivan himself leaves it as an open question whether there are examples of erroneous teachings of this kind.

In fact, it seems fairly clear that there are some such. This needs to be qualified, because again much depends on how one identifies the teaching in question. For example, it is often said that the magisterium reversed itself on the question of usury, but this claim depends on a particular view of what counts as usury, namely, charging any interest at all (which is no longer condemned) or charging excessive interest (which is still condemned).

We might perhaps point to a better example that is also more directly relevant to the question of contraceptive use. I am referring to the teaching on the marriage debt, that is to say, the obligation on the part of either partner to offer sex to the other on request.[59] This, it was said, is a grave obligation that can only be refused on penalty of serious sin. Not only was this a consistent and very nearly universally held theological teaching, but the obligation to pay the marriage debt was embedded in canon law from (at least) the early twelfth century, and the corresponding right was enforced in church courts throughout the medieval period. Yet we no longer speak of the marriage debt in these terms, or indeed in any terms, as far as I can determine. It is difficult to imagine any priest or counselor in a Catholic context telling someone that he or she has a serious obligation to offer sexual gratification to the spouse on demand; nor would this be likely to occur to most Catholic couples. We seem to have simply dropped the idea.

It might be said in reply that this is not an example of a magisterial reversal; the magisterium never declared that the received teaching regarding the marital debt has now been canceled, it simply stopped mentioning it. To the best of my knowledge that is true, but then it is easy to imagine something similar happening in the case of the current teaching on contraceptive use. It is difficult to imagine that any future pope or council of bishops would explicitly repudiate this teaching, but it is easy to imagine, in fact it seems probable, that at some point in the near future the magisterium will just stop talking about it.

This possibility does raise real theological problems, as the minority report suggests. But as Sullivan goes on to observe, these problems do not arise solely in the context of moral teaching:

> [T]his argument [i.e., the Minority Report argument] seems to suppose that we know how much spiritual harm God is prepared to allow the leaders of the Church to be the occasion of. How can it be shown that erroneous moral teaching would cause more spiritual harm than has been caused by the scandalous conduct of which Church leaders have certainly been guilty? If God has permitted the latter, why could He not permit the former as well?[60]

Probably most Catholic theologians would agree that the church, and by extension the magisterium, safeguards revelation and represents God's will in a definitive or a paradigmatic or an indispensable way. None of this implies, however, that it does so in a transparent way, free from all the limitations of its humanness. In order fully to address these problems, it would be necessary to sort out the different ways in which these limitations affect the processes of ecclesial discernment and magisterial formulation. That, happily, is a task for another day.[61]

NOTES

1. Germain Grisez and John Ford, "Contraception and the Infallibility of the Ordinary Magisterium," *Theological Studies* 39 (1978): 258–312.

2. Francis A. Sullivan, S.J., *Magisterium: Teaching Authority in the Catholic Church* (Mahwah, NJ: Paulist Press, 1983); Germain Grisez, "Infallibility and Specific Moral Norms: A Review Discussion," originally published in *The Thomist*, reprinted in *Dissent in the Church*, Readings in Moral Theology 6, ed. Charles Curran and Richard McCormick, 58–96 (Mahwah, NJ: Paulist Press, 1988); Francis A. Sullivan, "The 'Secondary Object' of Infallibility," *Theological Studies* 54 (1993): 536–50; Germain Grisez and Francis Sullivan, "The Ordinary Magisterium's Infallibility," *Theological Studies* 55 (1994): 720–38.

3. John Noonan, *Contraception: A History of Its Treatment by the Catholic Theologians and Canonists* (Cambridge, MA: Harvard University Press, 1965; reprinted by New York: Mentor/Omega Books, 1967). All references in this paper are taken from the 1967 edition.

4. Throughout this paper, I focus on a distinctively Catholic set of questions having to do with the scope and limits of the authority of the magisterium. However, the account of natural law and moral discernment to be developed below would apply generally to any Christian community. By the same token, a full account of moral discernment within the Catholic Church would need to take account of the ways in which this process is shaped by conversations with other churches, and indeed with other religious and secular communities as well.

5. Sullivan, "The 'Secondary Object' of Infallibility," 543.

6. Frank Mobbs, *Beyond Its Authority? The Magisterium and Matters of the Natural Law* (Alexandria, Australia: Dwyer, 1997).

7. Rigali has often made this point; see in particular Norbert Rigali, "Christ and Morality," originally published in 1978, reprinted in *The Distinctiveness of Christian Ethics*, Readings in Moral Theology 2, ed. Charles E. Curran and Richard A. McCormick, S.J., 111–20 (New York: Paulist Press,

1980); "Moral Pluralism and Christian Ethics," *Louvain Studies* 13 (1988): 305–21; "The Uniqueness and Distinctiveness of Christian Morality and Ethics," in *Moral Theology: Challenges for the Future*, ed. Charles E. Curran, 74–93 (New York: Paulist Press, 1990); and "Christian Morality and Universal Morality: The One and the Many," *Louvain Studies* 19 (1994): 18–33.

8. Although this view was widely rejected by Catholic moral theologians (and others) during the last century, it has once again begun to receive sympathetic consideration; see for example Stephen Pope, *The Evolution of Altruism and the Ordering of Love* (Washington, DC: Georgetown University Press, 1994).

9. For a defense of this point, developed in the context of a very helpful analysis of the issues at stake, see John Kekes, "Human Nature and Moral Theories," *Inquiry* 28 (1985): 231–45.

10. In this paper, I draw extensively on an earlier study in which I attempted to reconstruct the scholastics' conception of the natural law, and to suggest what some of its contemporary implications might be; see Jean Porter, *Natural and Divine Law: Reclaiming the Tradition For Christian Ethics* (Grand Rapids, MI: Eerdmans, 1999). I should add that while I sometimes refer to "the scholastics" for convenience's sake, this is strictly speaking inaccurate; the secular jurists in this period, sometimes known as the civilians, would have had a somewhat different understanding of the natural law from that of the canon lawyers and theologians on whom I focus.

11. There is a very extensive literature on this period. In my own work, I have been especially influenced by R.W. Southern's *Scholastic Humanism and the Unification of Europe* (Oxford: Blackwell, 1995).

12. Gratian, *Decretum* D.1, introduction. This and all subsequent translations from Latin texts are my own. Augustine Thompson has published a fine English translation, with extensive notes, of the first 20 distinctions of the *Decretum*, and I checked my translation of Gratian against his. See *Gratian: The Treatise on Laws (Decretum DD. 1–20), with the Ordinary Gloss*, Augustine Thompson, translator of Gratian, and James Gordley, translator of the Gloss, with an introduction by Katherine Christensen (Washington, DC: Catholic University of America Press, 1993).

13. Yves Congar, however, offers a more sympathetic and accurate appraisal of Gratian in his "Jus divinum," in *Eglise et Papaute: Regards historiques*, 65–80 (Paris: Cerf, 1994), at 66–67.

14. Stephen J. Pope, "Scientific and Natural Law Analyses of Homosexuality: A Methodological Study," *Journal of Religious Ethics* 25, no. 1 (1997): 89–126, at 104.

15. I argue for this in more detail in Porter, *Natural and Divine Law*, 121–86.

16. See Porter, *Natural and Divine Law*, 88–91 for further details.

17. I take this from Minge's *Patrologiae Cursus Completus* (Paris, 1852), 114:475–76; I also checked the facsimile text published as the *Biblia Latina cum Glossa Ordinaria*, vol. 4 (Brepols: Turnhout, 1992). The Ordinary Gloss was an early twelfth-century collation of patristic comments on scripture, arranged in the form of a running commentary on the texts, referred to as "Ordinary" because it came to be the standard scriptural gloss for the scholastics, and as such served as a basic research tool (not unlike a standard commentary would do today). It later came to be attributed, wrongly, to Walafrid Strabo (d. 849), and is published under his name in Minge. For a comprehensive account of the formation of the Gloss and its later significance, see Beryl Smalley, *The Study of the Bible in the Middle Ages* (Notre Dame, IN: University of Notre Dame Press, 1964, a reprint of the 1952 Blackwell edition), 46–65.

18. Again, the details may be found in Porter, *Natural and Divine Law*, 85–98.

19. There is a case to be made that dogmas of faith are also constructed, in the sense that they are articulated through a process of communal discernment on the meaning of scripture as it unfolds through the experiences of the faithful community. To the extent that this point of similarity is emphasized, it might be argued that dogmas are closer to moral teachings than I assume, but in such a way as to assimilate dogma to moral precept, rather than the reverse. I certainly would agree that the expressions of dogmatic truths are historically conditioned, and to that extent contingent. That being said, however, I do think that dogmatic formulae express truths that exist independently of the practices of the community, in a way that moral precepts, properly understood, do not. To put the matter in old-fashioned terms, I believe that there is a relevant difference between speculative and moral reasoning. However, I am unsure how far to push this difference in this context, and am happy to leave dogma to the systematic theologians.

20. For a similar interpretation, limited in this case to Aquinas, see Pamela Hall, *Narrative and the Natural Law: An Interpretation of Thomistic Ethics* (Notre Dame, IN: University of Notre Dame Press, 1994). In contrast, Ford and Grisez remark at one point that "the teaching of moral truths" is a "quite different function" from making church law; see their "Contraception and the Infallibility of the Ordinary Magisterium," 276. To be sure, there is a distinction to be drawn between moral discernment and the creation of canon law, but it does not appear to me that this distinction is so sharp as they presuppose.

21. Thomas Aquinas, *Summa Theologiae* I-II 100.8 *ad* 3. It is interesting to compare Aquinas and Albert with the decretalist Raymond of Penyafort, who states that the precepts of the natural law can be interpreted by the

Pope—a restriction which neither Albert nor Aquinas mentions. See his *Summa Juris* I.10.

22. Of course, this raises further questions, which I do not have the fortitude to tackle at this point. I do not want to say that the magisterium is so dependent on the practices of the church community that it could never challenge or correct sinful practices, or exercise a prophetic function within the community. Yet it seems inconceivable to me, on both philosophical and theological grounds, that the magisterium could formulate a moral norm that had no grounding whatever in the practices of the church. A full discussion of these issues would also have to take account of the divergence of practices among different communions. Finally, I do mean "authentic" rather than "authoritative" here; cf. Sullivan, *Magisterium,* 26–28.

23. Gratian's immediate source for his definition of the natural law is probably Hugh of St. Victor, who offers a very similar definition at *De sacramentis* I 11.7. More remotely, the identification of the natural law with the Golden Rule appears to have been a patristic commonplace, and it certainly becomes a commonplace in subsequent scholastic discussions of the natural law.

24. The centrality of an ideal of equality to Christian moral and political thought is argued at length in R. W. Carlyle and A. J. Carlyle, *A History of Medieval Political Theory in the West,* 6 vols. (Edinburgh: W. Blackwood and Sons, 1903–36, last reprinted in 1970). The views of the Carlyles have since been challenged. Nonetheless, without wanting to commit myself to every detail of their analysis, and recognizing that they overstate their claims, I am still convinced that they are fundamentally right. For a helpful assessment of this book and its critics, see J. H. Burns, "Introduction," in *The Cambridge History of Medieval Political Thought: c. 350–c. 1450,* ed. J. H. Burns, 1–10 (Cambridge: Cambridge University Press, 1988). In Orlando Patterson, *Freedom,* vol. 1 of *Freedom in the Making of Western Culture* (New York: Basic Books, 1991), 347–401, Patterson argues that freedom is the central moral and social ideal in the Middle Ages. However, since the ideas of equality and freedom are closely linked for the scholastics, this interpretation is not inconsistent with the view being offered here. Finally, I have argued in more detail for the centrality and the distinctively theological character of the natural law ideal of equality in scholastic thought in Jean Porter, "A Tradition of Civility: The Natural Law as a Tradition of Moral Inquiry," *The Scottish Journal of Theology* 56, no. 1 (2003): 27–48.

25. For a good illustration of this line of argument, decidedly unfriendly to contemporary liberalism, see Stanley Hauerwas, *A Community of Character: Towards a Constructive Christian Social Ethic* (Notre Dame, IN: The University of Notre Dame Press, 1981), 72–86.

26. These claims run throughout Farley's work. In developing this summary, I rely particularly on the following: "Sources of Sexual Inequality in

the History of Christian Thought," *Journal of Religion* 56, no. 2 (1976): 162–76; "Moral Imperatives for the Ordination of Women," in *Women and Catholic Priesthood: An Expanded Vision,* ed. Anne Marie Gardiner, 35–51 (New York: Paulist, 1976), together with "The Dialogue Continues" (response to George Tavard), ibid. 58–61; "New Patterns of Relationship: Beginnings of a Moral Revolution," in *Women: New Dimensions,* ed. Walter Burkhardt, 51–70 (New York: Paulist Press, 1977); "An Ethic for Same-Sex Relations," in *Dialogue about Catholic Sexual Teaching,* Readings in Moral Theology 8, ed. Richard McCormick and Charles Curran, 330–46 (New York: Paulist Press, 1993; essay originally published in 1983); "The Church and the Family: An Ethical Task," *Horizons* 10, no. 1 (1983): 50–71; "Feminism and Universal Morality," in *Prospects for a Common Morality,* ed. Gene Outka and John Reeder, 170–90 (Princeton, NJ: Princeton University Press, 1993); and "A Feminist Version of Respect for Persons," *Journal of Feminist Studies in Religion* 9 (Spring/Fall 1993): 182–98.

27. This point is made in most of the essays just mentioned, but it is argued most forcefully in the earliest essays, particularly "Sources of Sexual Inequality," "Moral Imperatives for the Ordination of Women," and "New Patterns of Relationship: Beginnings of a Moral Revolution."

28. For example, many forms of classical Hinduism appear not to have incorporated such a norm, but this is of course contested; for a good overview of the issues, see Lina Fruzzetti, Àkos Östör, and Steve Barnett, "The Cultural Construction of the Person in Bengal and Tamilnadu," in *Concepts of Person: Kinship, Caste, and Marriage in India,* ed. Lina Fruzzetti, Àkos Östör, and Steve Barnett, 8–30 (Cambridge, MA: Harvard University Press, 1982).

29. This point is particularly stressed by Brian Tierney, who sees this as a central presupposition for the emergence of a doctrine of natural rights; see his *The Idea of Natural Rights: Studies on Natural Rights, Natural Law and Church Law, 1150–1625* (Atlanta: Scholars Press, 1997), 43–77. Aquinas expresses a general consensus when he says that knowledge of the natural law cannot be altogether extirpated from the human soul, although it can be distorted or obscured; see the *Summa Theologiae* I-II 94.6.

30. There are many, many instances of this connection in scholastic thought; see, for example, William of Auxerre, *Summa Aurea* III 18.4, Bonaventure, *De Per. Evan.* IV 1 *ad* 4, and Aquinas, *Summa theologiae* II-II 66.1.

31. This brings me to a point at which I would disagree with Farley's interpretation of the Christian tradition. Farley claims that in patristic and medieval theology, women were not seen to participate in the Image of God, except in a secondary sense: "Christian theology for centuries refused to attribute the fullness of the *imago dei* to women. All persons are created in the image and likeness of God, but men were thought to participate in

the *imago dei* primarily and fully, while women participated in it secondarily and partially"; Farley, "Moral Imperatives," 40.

In my view, this is not accurate, at least with respect to that slice of the tradition that I know best, early medieval scholasticism. So far as I have been able to determine, the scholastics held that both men and women participate fully in the Image of God understood in the primary sense, that is to say, in rationality and the capacity for self-direction. It is true that women do not participate in the Image in a secondary sense, insofar as they do not represent rule and authority (as men do). But I would suggest that there is nonetheless a significant difference between claiming that women participate in the Image in a secondary and partial way only, and claiming that they participate in the Image in its primary sense, but not in a secondary sense. The former would indeed undermine claims for equality grounded in human nature, but it is not apparent to me that the latter claim necessarily does. Certainly, the scholastics' attitudes towards women left a great deal to be desired, but my point is simply that they were committed, in principle, to the fundamental natural equality of women. This indeed caused them some embarrassment. Gratian remarks at one point that the exclusion of women from the office of judge is based on custom rather than nature, and more specifically, it does not presuppose that women lack the power of judgment; *Decretum* C.3.7.1.1.

In particular, the scholastics were aware that the church practice of denying ordination to women gives at least the appearance of injustice, and they attempt to justify this practice through an analysis of the different symbolic or social roles played by the two sexes. Aquinas asserts that women and men are equal with respect to the possession of the image of God, understood in its primary sense as the capacity for reasoned self-governance: "Scripture, after saying, 'To the image of God he created him,' adds, 'Male and female he created them,' not inasmuch as the image of God is considered to follow the distinction of the sexes, but because the image of God is common to both sexes, since it is in accordance with the mind, in which there is no distinction of sexes"; Aquinas, *Summa theologiae* I 93.6 *ad* 2; cf. I 93.4 *ad* 1. On this basis, he defends the propriety of women exercising the charism of prophecy or acting as teachers and counselors in a private capacity; *Summa theologiae* II-II 177.2. Nonetheless, because women are subordinate to their husbands in marriage, he argues, the social status of women carries with it an implication of subordination, and this is why a woman cannot represent Christ, who holds authority within the church; ibid., and also see *Summa Theologiae* II-II 183.1 and Bonaventure, *Commentary on the Sentences* IV.25.2.1a). Bonaventure, for his part, argues that a woman cannot be ordained because she cannot be a natural sign of Christ, but he considers the opposite opinion to be credible; *Commentary* IV.25.2.2. Like Aquinas, he insists that women and men are equally created in the image of God, but the image, he adds, pertains to the rational nature of the human person, whereas ordination concerns the bodily existence of the person as well; ibid. IV.25.2.2 *ad* 3. At the same time, both Aquinas and Bonaventure note that the exercise of secular political authority by women is entirely legitimate, ibid., IV.25.2.1a and IV.25.2.2 *ad* 1, respectively.

32. John Casey makes this point in some detail in his *Pagan Virtue: An Essay in Ethics* (Oxford: Oxford University Press, 1990); see in particular 51–103.

33. Both Bonaventure and Aquinas discuss the limits of the obligation of obedience; see, respectively, *De perfectione evangelica* 4.1 and the *Summa theologiae* II-II 104.5. With respect to the development of a doctrine of individual rights, see Tierney, *Idea of Natural Rights*, 69–76; note especially that this was not just a theoretical doctrine, but was given juridical effect, as Tierney points out at 74.

34. Again, all the articles mentioned above are to some degree works of retrieval, as well as critique; see in particular her "New Patterns of Relationship" and "Church and the Family."

35. It is important to resist the temptation to identify those aspects of the Christian tradition that we like with foundational Christian or theological commitments, while relegating those aspects we don't like to cultural accretions. Christianity and culture cannot be so neatly divided from one another. As Farley notes, "Theology . . . is quite capable of incorporating sociologically based ideas into itself; and in this instance [that is, the status of women] it incorporated societal definitions and norms in a way that reinforced what it might otherwise have served to correct"; "The Dialogue Continues," 60. At the same time, I think it is legitimate to argue that some moral norms are more closely tied to central theological commitments than others, and in that sense have a better claim to be regarded as centrally or essentially Christian. But this line of argument presupposes that we have first identified central doctrinal commitments on theological grounds.

36. Farley, "Church and the Family," 53. She does not refer specifically to dualist movements at this point, although she briefly discusses their impact; see 60–61. Noonan offers an especially helpful account of the influence of Catharism and similar movements on the sexual ethics of the twelfth and thirteenth centuries in his *Contraception*, 211–44; also see James Brundage, *Law, Sex, and Christian Society in Medieval Europe* (Chicago: University of Chicago Press, 1987), 429–31.

37. Noonan, *Contraception*, 332–62.

38. Cahill has often made this point; see in particular, Lisa Cahill, "Current Teaching on Sexual Ethics," in McCormick and Curran, *Dialogue about Catholic Sexual Teaching*, 525–35 at 533–34; and *Sex, Gender, and Christian Ethics* (Cambridge: Cambridge University Press, 1996), 108–20.

39. Jo Ann MacNamara, "Wives and Widows in Early Christian Thought," *International Journal of Women's Studies* 2 (1979): 575–92; for a similar view, see Cahill, *Sex, Gender, and Christian Ethics,* 166–216.

40. Cahill summarizes these arguments in her *Sex, Gender, and Christian Ethics,* 183–99.

41. More specifically, this freedom was defended through a series of reforms initiated by the reform movement of the latter eleventh century; on these reforms and their consequences, see Brundage, *Law, Sex, and Christian Society,* 176–228.

42. On this and subsequent church legislation on the marriage of unfree persons, see Antonia Bocarius Sahaydachcy, "The Marriage of Unfree Persons: Twelfth-Century Decretals and Letters," 483–506 in *De Iure Canonico Medii Aevi: Festschrift für Rudolf Weigand,* Studia Gratiana 27, ed. Peter Landau, 483–506 (Rome: LAS, 1996). As Sahaydachcy goes on to show, *Dignum est* was subsequently challenged, but the popes consistently upheld the validity of the marriages of unfree persons. In addition, Michael Sheehan suggests that the then-majority scholastic view that consent alone is sufficient to establish a marriage was adopted as a safeguard for the right of unfree persons to marry; see Michael M. Sheehan, C.S.B., "Theory and Practice: Marriage of the Unfree and the Poor in Medieval Society," *Mediaeval Studies* 50 (1988): 457–87.

43. Including Noonan himself; see his *Contraception,* 565–631.

44. Grisez and Ford, "Contraception and the Infallibility of the Ordinary Magisterium," passim.

45. Sullivan, *Magisterium,* 145; the subsequent argument is summarized from 145–48.

46. Ford and Grisez insist on this point; see their "Contraception and the Infallibility of the Ordinary Magisterium," 259. Sullivan, for his part, clearly wants to hold open the possibility of substantive development of moral teachings; see his *Magisterium,* 146–47.

47. Sullivan, *Magisterium,* 144–45.

48. Southern is particularly illuminating on this point; see his *Scholastic Humanism,* 235–63.

49. This is not to say that there were no compilations of church canons before Gratian, but his seems to have been the first to arrange them in accordance with an analytic account of church law. See James Brundage, *Medieval Canon Law* (Essex: Longman, 1995), 44–70, for further details.

50. Brundage, *Law, Sex, and Christian Society,* 241; he cites Gratian, *Decretum* D.25.3.7 and C.32.3.5.

51. According to Noonan, theologians and pastors were reluctant to discuss contraceptive use explicitly, focusing instead on "the sin against nature" or "sodomy" in a marital context; see his *Contraception,* 270–77.

Both Albert and Aquinas discuss the contraception in their commentaries on Lombard's *Sentences,* as Noonan points out (ibid., 284–85), but so far as I can tell neither returns to the topic in later works.

52. Roy Porter, *The Greatest Benefit to Mankind: A Medical History of Humanity from Antiquity to the Present* (San Francisco: Harper Collins, 1997), 129. More generally, see Noonan, *Contraception,* 245–80.

53. To my knowledge, the first theologian to question the sinfulness of sexual desire is William of Auxerre, who claims that sexual delight would have existed in Paradise and should therefore be distinguished from sinful lust; see his *Summa aurea* 17.1.1.

54. Cahill, *Sex, Gender, and Christian Ethics,* 201.

55. See in particular Farley "Church and the Family," but again, this is a theme running through almost all the essays cited in note 26 above. If we expand the statement of this theme to include the necessity for equal regard in intimate relationships more generally, it may fairly be said to run through all of them.

56. Sullivan, *Magisterium,* 141–42.

57. Ibid., 142.

58. Ibid., 142.

59. On the doctrine of the marriage debt and its place in canon law, see Noonan, *Contraception,* 343–45, and Cahill, *Law, Sex, and Christian Society,* 282–84, 358–60, 505–7.

60. Sullivan, *Magisterium,* 142.

61. An earlier draft of this paper was read at the annual meeting of the Catholic Theological Society of America, June 1999, and I am grateful to those present for many helpful suggestions and comments.

Chapter Thirteen

The Second Great Argument about Freedom

Leslie Griffin

The Second Vatican Council promulgated the landmark *Dignitatis Humanae* (hereafter, DH), the Declaration on Religious Freedom, in December 1965.[1] DH identified religious freedom as a right of the human person that must be protected by civil law and identified the dignity of the human person as the basis for that right. The text of DH, however, did not address the question of religious freedom within the church and did not include a "theology of freedom" for Catholics.[2] In 1965 as in 2007, "[t]he issue of freedom within the Church [was] neuralgic."[3] Nonetheless, in one introduction to DH, John Courtney Murray, the American Jesuit who developed the argument and led the drafting of the Declaration, predicted that "[i]nevitably, a second great argument will be set afoot now—on the theological meaning of Christian freedom."[4]

THE THEOLOGICAL MEANING OF CHRISTIAN FREEDOM

Pietro Pavan, Murray's coauthor of DH, endorsed this perspective in a 1977 lecture that rejected the argument that the Declaration had no implications for the internal life of the church. If the human person has a right to religious freedom, he insisted, "obviously, the right holds for Catholics as such, as members of the Church."[5] Pavan thought that the repercussions of DH were already evident within the church in "a process of readjustment . . . not yet in sight of its end." That process included "a re-ordering of the relations between laity and hierarchy and between the various grades of the hierarchy itself, aimed at giving a *more ample air of liberty*—understood and lived as an exercise of responsibility—*to all members of the Church*, making them share more consciously and actively in its life."[6] Both Murray and Pavan recognized the interconnection of the two freedoms, civil and ecclesial, and anticipated that it would be problematic for the church to advocate the former but not the latter. Having led the church to support a civil right to religious liberty in the first great argument about freedom, the two priests set the stage for a second great argument focused on freedom within the internal life of the church.

The originality of Murray's Declaration was his decision to ground the civil right to religious freedom on the dignity of the human person instead of on the rights of conscience or the truth of any religion. In turn, Margaret Farley understood that the dignity of the unique human person is also the starting point for any theology of freedom. At the time of the council, Farley was already an assistant professor at Mercy College in Detroit; by then, Jesuit philosopher Jules Toner had sparked her interest in freedom. After the council, Farley met the challenge of Murray and Pavan by developing a theology of human freedom that begins with individual dignity. Her writings (on freedom, commitment, sexuality, and feminism) have displayed a steady commitment to recognizing the freedom of the human person and promoting that freedom within the church.

Consistent with the call of Murray and Pavan for the development of a theology of freedom, Farley crafted a description of the moral agent with freedom at her core. As she explains, "freedom is in the first instance the action of individuals upon their desires and loves," not compliance with the laws of the state or the teachings of the church.[7] Her work confirms the insight that freedom is whole, so that ecclesial freedom cannot be divorced from civil freedom. Her phenomenology of human freedom teaches that personal freedom cannot be imposed by states *or* churches but must be "lived out by [individuals] deciding for it at each creative juncture."[8]

Careful thinkers that they were and are, Murray, Pavan, and Farley anticipated the implications of the council's argument about the dignity of the human person. If the right to religious freedom is grounded in the nature of the human person, then it must be both ecclesial and civil. It must belong preeminently to individual believers, not to institutional churches, and individuals' freedom must be protected—even over the objections of religious institutions—in civil law.

Farley also added an additional element that the fathers neglected: she extended the full principle of freedom to the lives of women. If freedom is the right of the human person, then it belongs to women as well as men. Indeed, Farley recognized that Christian women must make a special effort to claim their freedom "by exercising both self-legislation and self-determination. Women need to take hold of their own lives, to refuse the subordinate position that rendered them passive in relation to an active male, to trust their own insights and articulate their own self-understanding."[9] To Murray and Pavan's recognition that freedom should be part of the internal life of the church, Farley added the insight that women must enjoy equal freedom within the church and in civil society.

According to Farley, such new freedom for women leads to "new patterns" of life and relationships, including sexual relationships. For example, "new emphases on the element of freedom in the complex structure of the person give rise to norms for sexual behavior that place greater emphasis on the need for the free consent of both sexual partners."[10] Once freedom was experienced and lived by men and women in their personal and sexual lives, both traditional cultural norms and church teachings were confronted by demands for change. "Women's growing awareness of the dissonance between past teachings regarding their nature and role on the one hand and their own experience of themselves and their possibilities on the other has become a key source of insight for challenging laws and structures, attitudes, and patterns of behavior."[11] These structures include the structures of the church, where women have particular reasons to emphasize a new theology of freedom.

If the ecclesial and civil aspects of DH, as well as women's claim for freedom, had been emphasized in the postconciliar era, that second great argument about Christian freedom within the church might have occurred. Instead, under the leadership of Pope John Paul II, the church defended a different interpretation of freedom. On that account, the right to religious freedom belongs primarily to the institutional church instead of to the individual. Hence, over the years since DH emerged from the last session of the council, the church has often sought to protect religious freedom by defending its right to participate in the public arena and by supporting civil laws that protect the freedom of the institutional church. This decision to protect the institution over individuals is evident in the American church, where the hierarchy, following John Paul's direction, regularly attempts to promulgate the church's moral teachings into civil law. Moreover, while it sought to protect its institutional freedom in civil society, John Paul's church did not permit the internal dialogue about freedom to occur within the church. Instead, the church ordered individual Catholics to obey its moral teachings unquestioningly and silenced theologians who called traditional teachings into question.

It is noteworthy that the church has sought to establish its moral teachings into law and damped the internal church debate precisely in those areas that most affect the lives of women, including sexuality, where Farley has explained that freedom is essential. Because the church seeks to influence civil law, the freedom of both Catholics and non-Catholics is at stake. In opposing individual freedom, the church thus ignores the lesson of theologians like Murray, Pavan, and Farley, that the foundation of human freedom is the dignity of every human person, not the moral or theological teaching of the Roman Catholic Church, or any other church. It also neglects the point that freedom is indivisible, and that the church loses credibility when it defends freedom outside but not inside its doors. In her presidential address to the Catholic Theological Society of America, Farley explained how the lack of freedom within the church has undermined the church's promotion of freedom in civil society:

[C]urrent efforts within the church to repress internal discourse (and therefore, also, thought) have an effect on the church's participation in the secular political arena. The public perception of the Roman Catholic Church as prohibiting a free and responsible exchange of ideas within its own boundaries weakens the effective-ness of the church's voice in the public political arena. . . .

Any policy of repression of discourse within the church has con-sequences both for the church itself and for the church's relation-ship with other churches, organizations, and the wider society.[12]

Freedom is not divided; for that reason, Pavan and Murray supported a second great argument about freedom, in which Farley has partici-pated throughout her career.

In the following pages, I explain how the church has ignored DH's lessons by promoting its institutional interests over personal freedom, especially on subjects that affect the lives of women. The conclusion is that Murray's, Pavan's, and Farley's hopes for a theology of free-dom were never realized because the church sought to limit freedoms in the civil sphere instead of welcoming the second great argument about freedom within its own ranks.

THE DECLARATION ON RELIGIOUS FREEDOM

The absence of a full theology of Catholic freedom from DH was in-tentional, a product of the intense disputes among the council fathers over the meaning of religious freedom and the content of the Vatican Declaration. The initial, preconciliar drafts were theological in focus and emphasis. The draft of the Theological Commission (the lead-ing preparatory commission for the council) endorsed the theological argument that the right of religious freedom was for the one, true, Catholic religion only because "error has no rights."[13] The Secretariat for Christian Unity, which was formed by Pope John XXIII to pro-mote ecumenism at the council, focused on the moral, theological, and ecumenical question of how Catholics relate to people who do not share their faith.[14] Moreover, the first two schemata presented at the council identified freedom of conscience (not the dignity of the human person) as the basis of religious freedom.[15]

Murray and Pavan redirected the argument from the moral and theological to the legal and political. The basis for the right to religious freedom became the objective dignity of each human person, not the subjective freedom of conscience. The legal focus is evident in the following text from DH, which summarizes the document's central argument that religious freedom requires immunity from coercion and restraint.

> This freedom means that all men are to be immune from coercion on the part of individuals or of social groups and of any human power, in such wise that in matters religious no one is to be forced to act in a manner contrary to his beliefs. Nor is anyone to be restrained from acting in accordance with his beliefs, whether privately or publicly, whether alone or in association with others, within due limits.[16]

With its legal focus, the document ignored contentious issues about the internal freedom of the church and the subjective rights of conscience while insisting that religious freedom "demands recognition and sanction in the constitutional law whereby society is governed."[17]

Murray identified the second immunity from restraint as "the new thing" at the council.[18] The first immunity, from coercion, was old and accepted. The preconciliar church did not hold that the state could *coerce* the individual to believe. It had already accepted the first immunity from coercion "even during the post-Reformation era of confessional absolutism. . . . The principle was gradually established that even the absolutist prince may not compel a man to act against his conscience or punish him for reasons of conscience."[19] For the preconciliar church, however, it *was* appropriate for the government to *restrain* the practice of erroneous religion. Only the true religion had the right to public worship; erroneous religions could be prohibited from it. "Error had no rights" until DH recognized the individual's immunity from restraint as well as coercion.[20]

The influence of the First Amendment to the United States Constitution on Murray's thought was evident in DH's legal and political argument.[21] The "juridical guarantee" of religious freedom was defined as a negative immunity, not a positive entitlement. In other words, religious freedom was a "freedom from."[22]

The argument that the right of religious freedom was rooted in the dignity of the human person, rather than in the truth of the Catholic faith or the individual's conscience, allowed the church to accept both that the Catholic Church was the one true religion and that everyone (Catholic and non) is entitled to religious liberty. That line of reasoning, however, established "contradictory characteristics" within the document. As a perceptive American commentator observed in 1966, in contrast to the First Amendment, DH's "primary commitment . . . is to religion, not to freedom."[23] The paradox is that religious freedom was "endorsed as a human right, but tied to the conviction that its proper use will lead to a predetermined religious truth."[24] That tension increased in the church's life since 1978 as John Paul's church repeatedly advocated religious truth over democratic freedom.

Despite the legal emphasis of the argument about religious freedom in the first part, the second half of the Declaration retained a theological argument about freedom, emphasizing the roots of religious freedom in revelation. The theological section also proclaimed the "necessary freedom of the act of Christian faith"[25] and the importance of the church's institutional freedom. On the freedom of human faith, article ten affirms quite simply: "man's response to God in faith must be free."[26] Farley later deepened our understanding of the meaning of the individual's free response to God:

> Mutuality between God and human persons depends on the *free response of human persons*. Just as it is always possible for any one person to choose (unilaterally and unconditionally) to *love* another, but not possible for that person unilaterally to choose friendship with the other (since friendship requires a responding mutual love); so it is possible for God to commit God's own love unconditionally, but not to effect friendship (mutuality) with human persons without their response. [27]

This "free response of human persons," in other words, the freedom to relate to God, is the heart of religious freedom, the fundamental immunity that neither church nor state may coerce.

The theological section of the Declaration also included the church's assertion of its own institutional freedom of religion. On that subject, as Murray noted, "The freedom of the Church is the fundamental principle in what concerns the relations between the Church and governments and the whole civil order."[28] Again, however, the paradox emerges. The *legal* claim of the document was the recognition of every *individual's* freedom from coercion and restraint. Nonetheless, much of DH's theological language prefers the *institutional* to the individual right. "DH is unusually loquacious" about the freedom of the *church*, as Russell Hittinger noted.[29]

A return to the First Amendment clarifies this institutional focus and suggests an incomplete aspect of DH's legal argument. Murray's immunities parallel the free exercise clause of the First Amendment, which protects the individual's beliefs from government coercion and restraint.[30] But the American First Amendment also contains an establishment clause that is lacking in DH.

In contrast to the First Amendment, DH avoided the question of establishment. It did so in order to protect the freedom of the institutional church. The text of article three stated that "[g]overnment, therefore, ought indeed to take account of the religious life of the people and *show it favor*, since the function of government is to make provision for the common welfare. However, it would clearly transgress the limits set to its power were it to presume to direct or inhibit acts that are religious." Murray later noted that this "general and somewhat enigmatic phrase" appears to recognize a positive role for government in promoting religion (not merely a negative role of avoiding constraint and restraint).[31] Murray explained that the council fathers did not want to support a completely secular or laicist account of the state and so included the enigmatic passage. "[O]ne of the difficulties with the whole Declaration is that it did not want to get into the broader problem of Church and state; it simply wanted to prevent such a Declaration from appearing to favor an older laicist or secularist conception of the problem of Church and state."[32] The ambiguity was not lost on American commentators, however, who could interpret the text to support government aid to religion, a violation of the establishment clause.[33]

Murray and the council fathers had good theological and practical reasons to avoid the DH equivalent of the establishment clause. They had no commitment to disestablish the church from Catholic nations. European Catholics were content to keep establishment whenever it had worked for the church and would accept it willingly wherever governments chose it. Moreover, Murray himself criticized the U.S. Supreme Court whenever it denied aid to Catholic institutions.[34] From the church's perspective, resolving the free exercise question was necessary but addressing establishment was not.

Nonetheless, there are good reasons to include an establishment principle in a declaration about religious liberty. The establishment clause protects individuals by setting limits on both state *and church*. The government may not establish a religion, even if a majority of citizens so desires. Furthermore, no matter how strong or accurate its claims to religious truth, no church may claim a right to establishment by the government. In a constitutional democracy, the roles of both church and state are limited for the protection of individual citizens. By emphasizing the freedom of the institutional church and ignoring the establishment principle, DH underprotected the religious freedom of individuals.

Murray acknowledged when the council was over that "the church [was] late" with its acceptance of legal protection for religious freedom; "religious freedom had long been recognized in constitutional law, to the point where even Marxist-Leninist political ideology [was] obliged to pay lip-service to it."[35] Within the Catholic world, however, DH made great strides in recognizing the right of all persons to public exercise of their religion. Given the opposition to religious freedom in the Curia, and the church's longstanding rejection of free exercise for non-Catholics, the acceptance of the Murray/Pavan argument was a major accomplishment.

Without an establishment principle, however, DH's legal argument remained incomplete. On the subject of its own freedom, the church preferred the theological demand for government favor to the legal argument of limitations on state support of religion. This combination—a weak establishment argument and a strong theological claim for the freedom of the institutional church—opened the possibility that, post-DH, the church would be oversolicitous of the institutional church and underprotective of individual rights. As Philip Denenfeld recognized, its "primary commitment . . . [was] to religion [i.e., to the church], not to freedom."[36]

POSTCONCILIAR RELIGIOUS FREEDOM

Although Murray lived less than two years after DH's passage, his writings indicate that he understood that DH's principle of religious freedom implied some limitations on the church's interventions on the content of civil law. Before Murray's death in August 1967, a majority of Pope Paul VI's Birth Control Commission recommended that the church's prohibition of contraception be lifted, while a minority argued that a change in the contraception teaching would undermine the church's authority. On the ecclesial side, Murray sided with the majority for change. About the church's opposition to contraception, he said: "The church reached for too much certainty too soon, it went too far. Certainty was reached in the absence of any adequate understanding of marriage."[37] In other words, the church emphasized certainty and truth instead of human experience and individual freedom. As Farley explains, too much certainty about the moral life is inconsistent with freedom: "It is simply not possible for us to settle our whole selves so that the task of freedom is once and for all completed."[38]

While the church was debating the morality of contraception during those last years of Murray's life, the law of contraception and reproductive technology was changing in the United States as the Supreme Court recognized a constitutional right to privacy. On the legal front, Murray argued that the church should not oppose the decriminalization of contraception in the law of Massachusetts. First he wrote that contraception is an issue of private, not public morality. In his words, "It is difficult to see how the state can forbid, as contrary to public morality, a practice that *numerous religious leaders approve as morally right*."[39] Then he referred to DH as an additional reason to decriminalize contraception. Because the government may not restrain its citizens from acting according to conscience on this private matter, he concluded, "laws in restraint of the practice [of contraception] are in restraint of religious freedom."[40] Murray understood that religious freedom does not permit the establishment of private morality into civil law.

In 1967, Murray recognized that the church was mistaken to reach for theological certainty on a difficult moral question, and then to impose that certainty through force of law. If the government may not restrict religious freedom, then the church should not encourage it to do so. Murray's successors have forgotten these fundamental lessons about freedom: that it must be protected in both the ecclesial and civil realms.

After the council, the church could have developed a stronger legal argument about freedom and a full theology of freedom within the church. Instead, it chose the opposite path of opposing both public and ecclesial freedom, especially on questions of sexuality. Within both the papacy and the American Catholic Church, the church's commitment to the freedom of the church took increasing priority over an individual right to religious freedom. In other words, the church went in reverse from Murray, Pavan, and Farley's suggestions. The theologians thought the church's support of freedom in the public sphere would increase freedom within the church. Instead the church opposed freedom within the church and, over time, became more willing to oppose the same freedoms in the public square, for Catholics as well as non-Catholics.

THE PAPACY

Within the papacy, Pope John Paul II repeatedly emphasized the priority of the church's truth over democratic freedoms. According to his most important encyclical on social justice, for example, "freedom attains its full development only by accepting the truth."[41] The pope persistently argued that the church's true moral teaching (on abortion, contraception, homosexuality, reproductive technology, euthanasia, and other topics) must become the universal law of every state.[42] This stance ignores Murray's core argument that the church's morality is not the same as public morality: "It is difficult to see how the state can forbid, as contrary to public morality, a practice that *numerous religious leaders approve as morally right*."[43] Although numerous religious leaders disagree with the pope's perception of moral truth, he repeatedly asked the state to enforce it as law.

In the United States, in many cases the legislation desired by the pope would infringe upon the constitutionally protected civil liberties

of non-Catholics. On John Paul's account of the truth, however, democratic institutions should follow the teaching of the church instead of
the incorrect will of the majority. In a commentary on Catholic participation in political life, for example, the Congregation for the Doctrine
of the Faith vigorously rejected the notion that "moral relativism" and
"ethical pluralism" are the "very condition for democracy."[44] Instead,
the document asserts that the church's truth must be the basis of political activity, and that Catholics must put truth into action. The "Church
teaches that authentic freedom does not exist without the truth. 'Truth
and freedom either go together hand in hand or together they perish
in misery.'"[45]

"The Participation of Catholics in Political Life" nods toward DH
by affirming "the rightful autonomy of the political or civil sphere
from that of religion and the Church."[46] It undermines this assertion,
however, by adding that "rightful autonomy" does not include the
state's autonomy "*from that of morality.*"[47] The state must be guided by
the church's moral teaching. This demand enlarges the spare, "general
and somewhat enigmatic phrase" of DH's article three that the government should show favor to religion. If Catholics obeyed this papal
teaching, they would vote to impose the church's moral teaching on
all citizens, Catholic and non-Catholic. The result, as Murray understood, would be "laws . . . in restraint of religious freedom."[48]

Current papal arguments about law and morality possess a troubling resonance to the pre-DH church of the 1940s and 1950s. In the
preconciliar era the church opposed the "rightful autonomy of the political or civil sphere from that of religion and the Church" and insisted
that non-Catholics should have no legal rights to public worship. In
1949, for example, French theologian Jacques Maritain warned that,
in the United States, "[m]any non-Catholics are afraid that . . . we are
invoking freedom for ourselves only in order to deprive them of it on
the day when we gain political power." The solution to this problem,
Maritain recommended, was "to make clear that for the Catholics of
contemporary democratic nations, . . . the recognition of equal rights
and liberties for all citizens is conceived of not as a matter of expedi-
ency, but of moral obligation."[49] Maritain's position was eventually
vindicated at the council.

Despite this legacy, today the church opposes the "rightful autonomy of the political or civil sphere from that of [morals] and the Church" and, through its efforts to change the laws of democracies, insists that non-Catholics should lose whatever civil rights (to, for example, privacy or liberty) conflict with Catholic teaching. Farley was accurate to complain to members of the Catholic Theological Society of America (CTSA) that the church's restriction on freedom within the church "awakens old fears (whether fairly or not) of nondemocratic organizations overly influencing a democratic society. It raises suspicions (whether legitimately or not) of hidden agendas, manipulation by external powers, and loyalties not appropriate for participation in a democratic process. Once again, the credibility of the church's political agenda, and its calls for justice, are compromised."[50]

Herminio Rico provides a different perspective on the legacy of John Paul II in implementing DH.[51] Rico argues that DH had a "second moment" when Catholics relied upon it to claim their freedom against Communist governments. "[W]hat this second moment did was to reorganize the balance of the reception of the document, putting more emphasis on what it demanded from governments than on what it committed the church to pursue and promote by example."[52] Although Rico praises this second moment, the church's focus on reforming the state instead of the church confirms the absence of both a theology of freedom and an establishment principle in the post-DH church. Whether in the Communist or democratic setting, the church fights for the institutional church's rights. In John Paul's church, DH has been interpreted to set limits on the state, not the institutional church.

THE AMERICAN CATHOLIC CHURCH

In a second postconciliar development, many members of the American Catholic community, bishops as well as theologians, conservatives and liberals, interpreted the council and DH to authorize a more active role for the church in the public arena.[53] David Hollenbach observes that "the Council has led to a growing awareness that the right to religious freedom empowers Christians to exercise positive and active responsibility for the shape of the wider societies in which they live."[54] The American bishops' pastoral letters on the economy and war were a specific instance of such participation, as was the development of "public theology" in the academic setting.[55] The public theologians were initially critical of Murray's philosophical style of analysis, arguing that it ignored important biblical and theological concerns. Over time they apprehended the increasingly secular and sterile quality of American public life, fearing that religion had grown more privatized. Hence they developed more explicitly religious, theological, and biblical arguments to guide public policy.[56]

The bishops' pastoral letters and the theologians' public theology shared a common goal: to persuade the American public of the wisdom of Catholic teaching. Although the bishops and theologians borrowed the secular language of economists, politicians, and philosophers, the impetus of their public interventions was theological rather than legal. A legal argument begins with analysis of the law, with legal principle and precedent, and legal rights instead of Catholic principles that impact political and legal questions. Pietro Pavan's argument proceeded in an opposite direction from the contemporary church. If the human person has a right to religious freedom, he stated, "obviously, the right holds for Catholics as such, as members of the Church."[57] Begin with the dignity of the human person and many freedoms follow. Instead, the church now begins with its teaching and asks for the law to follow. Most troubling, as Farley recognized, is that the church has been most vigorous in seeking to enforce its teaching on subjects that concern women, where the church has a "lack of credibility" because of its "less than happy record" on women's rights. That record has worsened in recent years as the church has campaigned across the United States against state laws promoting women's health.

THE LAW OF CONTRACEPTION

The church lost its battle to criminalize contraception when the United States Supreme Court recognized an individual right to privacy protected by the Bill of Rights.[58] The church has not accepted this result. In 1999, after six years of debate, the California legislature enacted the Women's Contraception Equity Act.[59] That act, like the laws of twenty-four other states[60] and the federal government, requires "certain health and disability insurance plans that cover prescription drugs [to] cover prescription contraceptives."[61] The legislation was meant to eliminate the discrimination against women that occurs because women pay 68 percent higher out-of-pocket healthcare costs than men due to the costs of contraception.[62] In addition to "health and safety concerns," the bill's authors "sought to promote and protect fundamental personal rights of individual employees to *privacy* and free *expression*, to *free exercise* of their respective religious and moral beliefs, and to *equal protection* in their access to prescription medications,"[63] in other words, the freedoms protected by the Bill of Rights.

In California, the Catholic Church was the only religious group to lobby against this bill.[64] Without its intervention, the legislation might not have included any exemption. In response to the church's concerns, however, the act contained an exemption for religious employers, but an exemption much narrower than the church desired. The church wanted all Catholic employers—churches, hospitals, schools, universities, and social service agencies—to be exempt from the insurance requirement. The legislature limited the exemption to religious employers "whose primary purpose is religious worship, religious teaching and religious service,"[65] in other words, primarily churches, synagogues, and mosques but not employers who offer secular services. The legislature crafted a narrow instead of a broad exemption because "permitting secular institutions . . . and the growing number of large hospitals and universities loosely affiliated with the Catholic Church to be exempt from the Act would deprive literally thousands of employees in th[e] state of access to nondiscriminatory health and disability insurance coverage.[66] Catholic hospitals alone employ over 52,000 people in the state of California.[67]

Catholic Charities of Sacramento is a non-profit organization that provides social services to the poor without regard to their religious background.[68] As it does in so many states, Catholic Charities provides valuable services and support to the poorest and neediest members of our society. In California, Catholic Charities "spends about $80 million a year on social services. About 60 percent of that money comes from taxpayers,"[69] and 74 percent of its employees are not Catholic.[70]

Catholic Charities filed suit to enjoin the application of the Women's Contraception Equity Act to its health insurance plan, arguing that the "case arises as a result of an *unprecedented assault* upon the religious freedom rights of the Catholic Church in California."[71] Charities' *legal* argument was that the First Amendment and California Constitution protect Charities and other Catholic institutions from such assault by granting them a complete exemption from this law. The *moral* argument at the heart of the case was that contraception is morally wrong for all men and women, Catholic and non-Catholic, married and nonmarried, without regard to "whether they choose to believe or accept" the teachings of the Catholic Church.[72] As Charities stated in one of its briefs: "Neither individual choice nor the personal religious convictions of the person seeking to engage in sinful or immoral conduct are *relevant*."[73] Contraception is always wrong.

So much for the freedom of the individual human person, Catholic or not. Charities wanted to receive government funding while blocking its employees from the benefits of civil law. The Catholic Church has fought this battle against contraception across the United States. In New York, for example, Cardinal Egan and the Catholic Conference lobbied against contraceptive coverage for women and threatened their own lawsuit against the state, which they filed after the state legislature finally passed a women's health bill.[74] To date, Catholic Charities has lost all its legal challenges to the women's contraceptive acts, including the case in California, as the courts have held that Charities must be held to the same law that governs all employers.[75] The courts have enforced the standard that the church is not above the civil law against church arguments that it is not subject to civil law and that its employees do not enjoy the law's benefits.

Murray understood by 1966 that sincere religious people disagree about the morality of contraception. Furthermore, since 1968 the church's teaching has been contested and defied internally, within the Catholic Church. Finally, in the United States the use of contraceptives enjoys legal protection as part of the constitutional right of privacy.[76] Faced with such moral pluralism, internal dissent, and a constitutional right, the church nonetheless uses the First Amendment and the courts to make it more difficult for individuals within its sphere of influence—employees of its institutions—to access that right.

This battle over contraceptive law reinforces the argument that religious freedom requires an establishment as well as a free exercise principle. The church believes that the free exercise clause of the First Amendment creates a special zone in which church organizations may follow their own law without regard to civil law. Moreover, their free exercise zone includes a demand to receive taxpayers' money and to employ non-Catholics who lose the protections of civil law.[77] Government funds, however, should never be used to establish a church teaching that violates constitutional rights. Religious freedom requires an establishment principle to protect individuals.

Establishing the church's teaching as civil law also limits freedom within the church. In addition to the ills of government funding and the imposition of the church's teaching on non-Catholics, exemptions like those the church demands in California place lay Catholics, especially women, at risk. As in all organizations, the lived reality of Catholic institutions is not exactly the same as what appears in official church documents or legal pleadings. By definition, most Catholic institutions are not sectarian but very worldly. They seek accreditation, high rankings, and funding from all sources, just like their secular peers. For this reason, Catholic *employees* may assume that their institutions do and should comply with the law, including the law of employment benefits. Meanwhile, few Catholic *employers* offer an explicit warning that their workplace is a zone in which the civil law does not apply.[78] What a surprise for Catholic and non-Catholic employees to discover that, whenever an employment dispute arises, or health benefits are withheld, their employer may invoke the First Amendment by asserting that its employment practices are exempt from civil law and resolvable only by church doctrine.

Catholic Charities argues that religious exemptions are necessary to protect religious freedom. The reality is that religious exemptions will protect some Catholics (those who run the institutions) at the expense of other Catholics (the people who work for them) as well as the majority of employees, the non-Catholics. There is a difference between institutional and individual freedom, and since DH the institutional church has fought more for the former than the latter.

The contraception laws indicate that the weak legal argument and the strong theological claims employed by the church post-DH are significant. A legal right should protect individuals rather than institutions. An establishment principle sets limits on the church. Both give priority to freedom over truth. Their decline explains why a theology of freedom never developed within the church. The church closed the avenues of individual freedom in order to protect the institution's truth, and the "second great argument . . . on the theological meaning of Christian freedom"[79] was muted.

Farley's writings remind us poignantly of the changes that the second great argument might have wrought after the council. During her CTSA address, she invoked John Courtney Murray to remind the audience that "Vatican II brought a turning point in the life of the church and in its participation in the world."[80] Quoting Murray, she described the turning point inspired by the Council: "It affirmed, in act even more than in word, the positive value of freedom within the People of God. [This] is the principle of doctrinal progress, of the growth of the church toward more perfect inner unity, and of the widening and strengthening of relations between the church and the world, both religious and secular."[81] That conciliar growth in the church, Farley observes, was met with "a new trust and confidence" by the rest of the world. Alas, the church has now lost that trust and confidence by its restrictions on freedom within the church and its unrelenting advocacy of restrictions on women's rights, including the rights to abortion and contraception.

Farley calls for freeing the voice of the institutional church so that it may accomplish its work of justice. The church's institutions should heed her call. Catholic Charities, for example, would have more time and resources to meet its mission of service to the poor if it were not actively lobbying and litigating against contraception.[82] If, however, the structure of the free response to God is as Farley describes, namely, rooted in our unique and personal desires and loves, then individuals need not wait for the institutional church. Instead free people who enjoy the blessings of civil freedom may "sketch a design and select the clay, the model, the tools" of their lives and decide for freedom "at every creative juncture,"[83] even in the absence of ecclesial freedom.

NOTES

1. Vatican Council II, *Dignitatis Humanae* (Declaration on Religious Freedom), in *The Documents of Vatican II,* ed. Walter M. Abbott (New York: Guild Press, 1966), 674.

2. John Courtney Murray, "The Declaration on Religious Freedom," in *War, Poverty, Freedom: The Christian Response*, Concilium 15 (New York: Paulist Press, 1966), 4.

3. Ibid., 5.

4. John Courtney Murray, "Meaning of the Document," in *Declaration on Religious Liberty and Declaration on the Relationship of the Church to Non-Christian Religions*, ed. John Courtney Murray and Robert A. Graham (New York: America Press, 1966), 5.

5. Pietro Pavan, "Repercussions of the Declaration 'Dignitatis Humanae' in the Life of the Church," *First World Congress on Religious Freedom* (March 21–23, 1977), 53.

6. Ibid.

7. Margaret A. Farley, "Fragments for an Ethic of Commitment in Thomas Aquinas," in *Celebrating the Medieval Heritage*, ed. David Tracy, *The Journal of Religion* 58 (Supplement, 1978): S152–53.

8. Margaret A. Farley, *Personal Commitments: Beginning, Keeping, Changing* (New York: Harper & Row, 1986), 45.

9. Margaret A. Farley, "Feminism and Universal Morality," in *Prospects for a Common Morality*, ed. Gene Outka and John P. Reeder, Jr. (Princeton, NJ: Princeton University Press, 1993), 181.

10. Margaret A. Farley, "Sexual Ethics," in *Encyclopedia of Bioethics*, ed. Warren T. Reich (New York: Free Press, 1978), 3:1586.

11. Ibid., 3:1584.

12. Margaret A. Farley, "The Church in the Public Forum: Scandal or Prophetic Witness?" in *The Catholic Church, Morality, and Politics,* Readings in Moral Theology 12, ed. Charles E. Curran and Leslie Griffin (Mahwah, NJ: Paulist Press, 2001), 215.

13. "Error has no rights," in *The HarperCollins Encyclopedia of Catholicism,* ed. Richard P. McBrien (San Francisco: HarperCollins, 1995), 476.

14. John Courtney Murray, "The Declaration on Religious Freedom: A Moment in Its Legislative History," in *Religious Liberty: An End and a Beginning,* ed. John Courtney Murray (New York: Macmillan, 1966), 16.

15. Ibid.

16. *Dignitatis Humanae*, no. 2.

17. Pietro Pavan, "The Right to Religious Freedom in the Conciliar Declaration" in *Religious Freedom,* ed. Neophytos Edelby and Teodoro Jimenez-Urresti (New York: Paulist Press, 1966), 39.

18. John Courtney Murray and Robert A. Graham, eds., *Declaration on Religious Liberty and Declaration on the Relationship of the Church to Non-Christian Religions* (New York: America Press, 1966), 10n5.

19. John Courtney Murray, "This Matter of Religious Freedom," *America* 112 (January 9, 1965): 40.

20. Ibid.

21. The First Amendment states that "Congress shall make no law respecting an establishment of religion, or prohibiting the free exercise thereof"; U.S. CONST. amend. I, § 1.

22. Murray, "This Matter," 40.

23. Philip S. Denenfeld, "The Conciliar Declaration and the American Declaration," in Murray, *Religious Liberty*, 120.

24. Ibid.

25. Murray, "This Matter," 41.

26. *Dignitatis Humanae*, no. 10.

27. Farley, *Personal Commitments*, 119 (emphasis added).

28. John Courtney Murray, "Annotations to Declaration on Religious Freedom," in Abbott, *Documents of Vatican II*, 693, no. 13, n. 53.

29. Russell Hittinger, "How to Read Dignitatis Humanae on Establishment of Religion" (available at http://www.catholic.net/rcc/Periodicals/Dossier/00MarApr/Article.html, last accessed January 2007).

30. *United States v. Ballard*, 322 U.S. 78 (1944).

31. John Courtney Murray, "The Declaration on Religious Freedom," in *Vatican II: An Interfaith Appraisal*, ed. John H. Miller (Notre Dame, IN: University of Notre Dame Press, 1966), 579.

32. Ibid., 580.

33. Victor G. Rosenblum, "The Conciliar Document: A Politico-Legal Excursus," in Murray, *Religious Liberty*, 112.

34. Some of Murray's arguments about aid to religious schools are included in John Courtney Murray, "Federal Aid to Church-Related Schools," in *Bridging the Sacred and the Secular*, ed. J. Leon Hooper (Washington: Georgetown University Press, 1994), 45–51, and "Law or Prepossessions?" *Law and Contemporary Problems* 14 (1949): 23.

35. John Courtney Murray, "Religious Freedom," in Abbott, *Documents of Vatican II*, 673.

36. Denenfeld, "Conciliar Declaration," 120.

37. John Courtney Murray, "Appendix: Toledo Talk," in Hooper, *Bridging the Sacred and the Secular*, 336.

38. Margaret A. Farley, "Freedom and Desire," in *The Papers of the Henry Luce III Fellows in Theology*, vol. 3, ed. Matthew Zyniewicz (Atlanta: Scholars Press, 1998), 67.

39. John Courtney Murray, "Memo to Cardinal Cushing on Contraception Legislation," in Hooper, *Bridging the Sacred and the Secular*, 83 (emphasis added).

40. Ibid., 84.

41. John Paul II, *Encyclical Letter* "Centesimus Annus" (Boston: St. Paul Books & Media, 1991), no. 66.

42. John Paul II, "Evangelium Vitae," *Origins* 24 (April 6, 1995): 689–727.

43. John Courtney Murray, "Memo to Cardinal Cushing," 83 (emphasis added).

44. Congregation for the Doctrine of the Faith, "Doctrinal Note on Some Questions Regarding the Participation of Catholics in Political Life," November 24, 2002, no. 2 (available at http://www.usccb.org/dpp/congregation.htm, last accessed January 2007).

45. Ibid., no. 7.

46. Ibid., no. 6.

47. Ibid.

48. Murray, "Memo to Cardinal Cushing," 84.

49. Jacques Maritain, "Supplementary Statement of Jacques Maritain Prepared for the Princeton Area Group Meeting on Church and State," January 16, 1949 (presented by Patrick J. Hayes, "Maritain and the 'Princeton Statement' on Church-State Relations: Reflections on a Little Known Text," Annual Meeting of the American Maritain Association, Princeton, NJ, October 17–20, 2002).

50. Farley, "Church in the Public Forum," 215.

51. Herminio Rico, *John Paul II and the Legacy of* "Dignitatis Humanae" (Washington, DC: Georgetown University Press, 2002).

52. Ibid., 10.

53. For analysis of the church's public role, see David J. O'Brien, *Public Catholicism* (Maryknoll, NY: Orbis Books, 1996).

54. David Hollenbach, "Freedom and Truth: Religious Liberty as Immunity and Empowerment," in *John Courtney Murray and the Growth of Tradition,* ed. J. Leon Hooper and Todd David Whitmore (Kansas City: Sheed & Ward, 1996), 129.

55. David Hollenbach, "Theology and Philosophy in Public: A Symposium on John Courtney Murray's Unfinished Agenda," *Theological Studies* 40 (1979): 700, and "Public Theology in America: Some Questions for

Catholicism After John Courtney Murray," *Theological Studies* 37 (1976): 290. See also Robert W. McElroy, *The Search for an American Public Theology: The Contribution of John Courtney Murray* (New York: Paulist Press, 1989). For a non-Catholic account of public theology, see Ronald F. Thiemann, *Constructing a Public Theology* (Philadelphia: Westminster, 1991).

56. John A. Coleman, "A Possible Role for Biblical Religion in Public Life," *Theological Studies* 40 (1979): 705.

57. Pavan, "Repercussions," 53.

58. *Griswold v. Connecticut,* 381 U.S. 479 (1965).

59. CAL. HEALTH & SAFETY CODE § 1367.25; CAL. INS. CODE § 10123.196.

60. Coalition of Labor Union Women, "State Contraceptive Equity Laws" (available at http://www.cluw.org/contraceptive-laws.html, last accessed June 2007).

61. *Catholic Charities v. Superior Court,* 85 P.3d 67, 74 (Cal. 2004).

62. Ibid.

63. Brief of Amici Curiae Jackie Speier & Robert Hertzberg at 6, *Catholic Charities of Sacramento v. Superior Court* (No. SO99822) (emphasis added).

64. *Catholic Charities v. Superior Court,* 109 Cal. Rptr. 2d 176, 191 (Cal. App. 3 Dist. 2001).

65. Brief of Amici Curiae Jackie Speier & Robert Hertzberg at 1, *Charities* (No. SO99822); see CAL. INS. CODE § 10123.196(d)(1): "(1) For purposes of this section, a "religious employer" is an entity for which each of the following is true: (A) The inculcation of religious values is the purpose of the entity. (B) The entity primarily employs persons who share the religious tenets of the entity. (C) The entity serves primarily persons who share the religious tenets of the entity. (D) The entity is a nonprofit organization pursuant to Section 6033(a)(2)(A)(i) or (iii) of the Internal Revenue Code of 1986, as amended."

66. Real Parties in Interest's Answer Brief on the Merits at 4–5, *Charities* (No. SO99822).

67. Real Parties in Interest's Answer Brief on the Merits at 5, n. 15, *Charities* (No. SO99822).

68. *Catholic Charities,* 85 P.3d at 75.

69. Don Lattin, "Catholicism and the Pill: Vatican Pushes Birth Control Edict Despite Court Ruling," *The San Francisco Chronicle,* July 8, 2001, A4.

70. *Catholic Charities,* 109 Cal. Rptr. 2d at 184.

71. Petitioner's Brief on the Merits at 1, *Charities* (No. SO99822) (emphasis added).

72. Petitioner's Brief on the Merits at 4, *Charities* (No. SO99822).

73. Petitioner's Brief on the Merits at 4, *Charities* (No. SO99822) (emphasis added).

74. Tom Precious, "Bishops Irate at GOP Shift on Covering Birth Control," *Buffalo News*, February 5, 2002, A6.

75. *Catholic Charities*, 85 P.3d 67 (Cal. 2004).

76. *Eisenstadt v. Baird*, 405 U.S. 438 (1972); *Griswold v. Connecticut*, 381 U.S. 479 (1965).

77. Seventy-four percent of Catholic Charities' employees in California are non-Catholic. *Catholic Charities*, 109 Cal. Rptr. 2d at 184.

78. Some states that recognize an exemption for religious employers have required the employer to notify the employee of this provision in their employment contracts; see the web page of the Coalition of Labor Union Women, www.cluw.org.

79. Murray, "Meaning of the Document," 5.

80. Farley, "Church in the Public Forum," 217.

81. Ibid. Farley, "Church in the Public Forum," 217, quoting John Courtney Murray, "Freedom in the Age of Renewal," in Hooper, *Bridging the Sacred and the Secular*, 185.

82. Farley, "Church in the Public Forum," 219.

83. Farley, *Personal Commitments*, 45.

John Paul II's Understanding of the Church as Teacher of the Truth about Humankind

Charles E. Curran

John Paul II, as Bishop of Rome for a quarter of a century, had a great impact on the life of the Catholic Church. That impact has been very prominent in the area of moral theology. John Paul II is the only pope in history to have written an entire encyclical dealing with moral theory and norms (*Veritatis splendor*) and has often written on moral matters. Three of his encyclicals deal with the social mission of the church and social justice, while *Evangelium vitae* discusses at length the approach to life issues, especially abortion and euthanasia. John Paul II's interest in moral teaching and moral theology is not surprising. He studied and taught philosophical ethics, but his philosophy was always intimately connected with his theology.[1]

As one would expect, John Paul II's moral teaching has been widely discussed and analyzed within the Catholic Church and even outside the church. In the area of social justice in the United States, not all agree in their interpretation of John Paul II's teaching. The United States bishops in their pastoral letters on peace and the economy together with many other theologians interpret the pope's position to call for some significant changes in the capitalist system to make it more just, but he is not opposed to capitalism as such. A group of

Catholic thinkers describing themselves as neoconservatives (Richard John Neuhaus, Michael Novak, and George Weigel) interpret the pope as being more supportive and less critical of capitalism especially as it is found on the United States scene. Discussions about papal social teaching primarily involve the language of interpretation. The commentators seldom express disagreement or dissent about such teaching. Papal social teaching tends to be rather general and thus allows for different interpretations. John Paul II pointed out that he is not proposing a specific model to be followed but only the principles that should be fleshed out in the economic and political orders.[2]

On issues of sexuality and life, the papal teachings are more specific and concrete, often spelled out in terms of absolute and universal norms that are always and everywhere obliging—for example, condemnation of contraception, direct sterilization, homosexual genital relationships, divorce and remarriage, direct abortion, euthanasia. Here, there is not much room for different interpretations. One either agrees with these positions or not. Significant numbers of Catholic moral theologians disagree with some of these specific teachings. Much discussion has taken place in the Catholic Church about such dissent. Generally speaking, more liberal Catholic theologians have disagreed with papal teaching in the area of sexual and life issues.[3] Margaret Farley, as a groundbreaking Catholic feminist ethicist, illustrates such an approach, but she is far from the only theologian expressing such disagreements. She has disagreed with papal teachings on contraception, sterilization, divorce, homosexuality, and direct abortion.[4] On the issue of capital punishment, which the *Catechism of the Catholic Church* condemned for all practical purposes, more conservative Catholics have disagreed.[5] This essay will not discuss specific moral issues but rather will focus on the basic presupposition of John Paul II that the church teaches the truth about humankind.

Any attempt to discuss the teachings of John Paul II runs into a very difficult problem. As pope, he wrote and spoke very often. In his almost 100 trips to foreign countries, he often spoke more than five times a day. Obviously, the pope has speechwriters and does not prepare most of these addresses himself. In addition, a scholar could never consult all these different sources. The only acceptable scholarly approach, especially in keeping with Catholic ecclesiology, concentrates on the more authoritative writings and teachings. Encyclical letters, while they do not include *ex cathedra* teachings, constitute the most authoritative form of papal documents. One can logically conclude that the pope spends more time and effort on these documents than on any others.

John Paul II wrote fourteen encyclicals in the course of his service as Bishop of Rome.[6] Three of his early encyclicals form a Trinitarian cycle—*Redemptor hominis* (1979), *Dives in misericordia* (1980), and *Dominum et vivificantem* (1986). *Redemptoris mater* (1987) deals with Mary, while *Redemptoris missio* (1990) discusses evangelization and missionary work. The three social encyclicals are: *Laborem exercens* (1981), *Sollicitudo rei socialis* (1987), and *Centesimus annus* (1991). *Veritatis splendor* (1993) discusses moral theology and some moral theological issues and norms in some depth, while *Evangelium vitae* (1995) concentrates on issues of life and death. *Ut unum sint* (1995) focuses on church and ecumenical issues, whereas *Fides et ratio* (1998) develops the perennial theme of faith and reason. *Ecclesia de eucharista* (2003) considers the role of the eucharist in the church. *Slavorum Apostoli* (1985) commemorates the evangelizing role of Saints Cyril and Methodius and has been characterized as an exhortatory encyclical and thus is not that significant for our purposes.[7]

THE THESIS: HUMANKIND AS THE WAY
FOR THE CHURCH

These various encyclicals do not develop in a systematic way the teaching role of the church, but they often refer to this function. In these documents, John Paul II clearly and often insists that the church teaches the truth about humankind.

Redemptor hominis, the first encyclical of John Paul II, sets the tone for much of his pontificate. In *Dives in misericordia* (1.2) he describes his first encyclical, *Redemptor hominis*, as devoted "to the truth about humankind—a truth that is revealed to us in its fullness and depth in Christ." According to the first encyclical, the church continues, in time and space, the mission of Jesus, the Redeemer, by fully revealing the meaning of the human and teaching the truth about humankind. "By Christ's institution the Church is its [truth's] guardian and teacher, having been endowed with the unique assistance of the Holy Spirit in order to guard and teach it [truth] in its most exact integrity" (12.2).

The 1986 encyclical, *Dominum et vivificantem*, spells out in greater detail the role of the Holy Spirit whereby the church continues the mission of Jesus. "The supreme and complete self-revelation of God, accomplished in Christ and witnessed to by the preaching of the Apostles, continues to be manifested in the church through the mission of the invisible Counselor, the Spirit of truth" (7.1). The first long chapter of this encyclical bears the title "The Spirit of the Father and of the Son Given to the Church." "The Holy Spirit, then, will insure that in the Church there will always continue *the same truth* which the apostles heard from their Master" (4). We see here the Trinitarian dimension of the church, which through the assistance of the Holy Spirit carries on the work of Jesus of teaching God's truth about the human person.

Three times paragraph 14 of *Redemptor hominis* refers to humankind "as the way for the Church." The insistence of *Redemptor hominis* that humankind is "the primary and fundamental way for the Church" (14.1) becomes a central point, if not the central point, in the encyclicals of John Paul II despite their dealing with a variety of subjects. The beginning of *Dives in misericordia* insists "that every individual human being is, as I said in my encyclical *Redemptor hominis,* the way for the Church. . . . In Jesus Christ, every path to humankind . . . has been assigned once and for all to the Church" (1.3). *Dominum et vivificantem*, the third of the Trinitarian encyclicals, also cites *Redemptor hominis* that humankind is the way for the church (58.2, 59.3).

In this context, it is no surprise that the three social encyclicals and the two encyclicals on moral teaching stress and develop the fundamental theme of *Redemptor hominis* that "humankind is the way for the Church." In the very opening paragraph of *Laborem exercens,* John Paul II justifies his devoting this document to human work and to humankind in the vast context of the reality of work by citing his insistence in *Redemptor hominis* that "humankind 'is the primary and fundamental way for the Church'" (1.1). Consequently, "it is necessary to return constantly to this way and to follow it ever anew in the various aspects in which it shows us all the wealth and at the same time all the toil of human existence on earth" (1.1).

The sixth chapter of *Centesimus annus*, the document written on the hundredth anniversary of *Rerum novarum* (1891), bears the title, "Humankind is the Way of the Church" (53). Why has the church developed its Catholic social teaching in the 100 years since Pope Leo XIII's encyclical *Rerum novarum*? "Her sole purpose has been care and responsibility for humankind, which has been entrusted to her by Christ himself" (53.1). "This, and this alone, is the principle which inspires the Church's social doctrine" (53).

Veritatis splendor (1993), according to the pope's own recognition, is the first papal encyclical to deal in depth with moral theology (115.1). Here, as is his want, John Paul II often cites Vatican II to make his point: "[T]he task of authentically interpreting the word of God, whether in its written form or in that of Tradition, has been entrusted only to those charged with the Church's living Magisterium, whose authority is exercised in the name of Jesus Christ" (27.3).[8] But notice that this citation does not deal specifically with moral issues, so the pope goes on to support this with a citation from canon law (canon 747.2) to make the point. "The Church, in her life and teaching, is thus revealed as 'the pillar and bulwark of truth' (1 Tim 3:15) including the truth regarding moral action. Indeed, 'the Church has the right always and everywhere to proclaim moral principles, even in respect to the social order, and to make judgments about any human matter insofar as this is required by fundamental human rights or the salvation of souls'" (27.3).

As he often does, John Paul II begins this encyclical by reflecting on a biblical passage—in this case the story of the rich young man who came to Jesus with the question: "Teacher, what good must I do to have eternal life?" (Mt 19:16). Papal commentary on this passage of scripture serves as the introduction and the justification of the whole body of the encyclical, which defends the church's moral teachings especially with regard to personal and immutable moral commandments. "This 'answer' to the question about morality has been entrusted by Jesus

Christ in a particular way to us, the Pastors of the Church; we have been called to make it the object of our preaching, in the fulfillment of our *munus propheticum*" (114.3). The whole structure of this encyclical, with its insistence on "the reaffirmation of the universality and immutability of the moral commandments, particularly those which prohibit always and without exception intrinsically evil acts" (115.3), builds on the understanding that Jesus, who answered the question of the rich young man about what is good, has now given that power and authority to the church to continue down through the centuries the function of teaching the moral commandments.

Evangelium vitae emphasizes the gospel of life which insists on "the greatness and inestimable value of human life even in its temporal phase" (21). But this gospel of life has a "profound and pervasive echo in the heart of every person—believer and unbeliever alike—. . . based on the natural law written in the heart" (cf. Rom 2:14–15) (2.2). Again, the encyclical appeals to *Redemptor hominis* to justify the church's need to teach the truth on the Gospel of life: "humankind—living humankind—represents the primary and fundamental way for the Church" (2.5). *Evangelium vitae* then develops the church's teaching on the dignity and value of human life and the evils of direct abortion and euthanasia.

The papal insistence on the fact that the church teaches the truth about humankind raises the two obvious questions about the understanding of truth and the understanding of the church as found in these encyclicals. The encyclicals by their very nature do not aim at providing an in-depth understanding of either truth or the church, but some things are said about each of these two important subject matters.

TRUTH

The papal encyclicals often speak about truth in a somewhat generic sense as in the often used phrase, "the truth about humankind." Also, the encyclicals have a somewhat general concept of the truth that is taught by the church. The beginning of *Veritatis splendor* illustrates such an approach. In the depths of our heart, we are all "yearning for absolute truth" (1.3). "No one can escape from the fundamental question: *'What must I do? How do I distinguish good from evil?'* Jesus is 'full of grace and truth (Jn. 1:14)' . . . the way and the truth and the life (Jn. 14:6). Consequently the decisive answer to everyone of humankind's questions, religious and moral questions in particular, is given by Jesus Christ, or rather is Jesus Christ himself, as the Second Vatican Council recalls: 'In fact, it is only in the mystery of the Word Incarnate that light is shed on the mystery of humankind'" (2.2). Jesus Christ sends the church "forth to the whole world to proclaim the Gospel to every creature (cf. Mk 16:15). Hence the Church . . . offers to everyone the answer which comes from the truth about Jesus Christ and his Gospel" (2.3). In this light at all times but particularly in the last two centuries the popes "have developed and proposed a moral teaching regarding the many different spheres of human life . . . with the guarantee of assistance from the Spirit of truth" (4.1). Hence there is a tendency to conflate and even equate the ultimate truth about human existence, the truth of the Gospel, and the moral truths taught by the church.

Different Types of Truth and Some Limitations

In fairness to the encyclicals, however, they also recognize different types of truth. *Fides et ratio* recognizes "the different faces of human truth" and "the different modes of truth." There is a mode of truth proper to everyday life and to scientific research. At another level, there exists philosophical truth attained by means of the speculative powers of the human intellect. Finally, there are religious truths, which are to some degree grounded in philosophy and which we find in the answers that the different religious traditions offer to the ultimate questions. In addition, there is the truth revealed in Jesus Christ (28–30.1).

With regard to the truths taught by the church the encyclicals also recognize different types of truths. Often these encyclicals refer to the truths of revelation and the truths of faith. Even with regard to the general category of revealed truth, or truths of faith, the encyclicals recognize some limitations. The most frequent limitation is the distinction between truth and its expression that is often supported by a reference to *Gaudium et spes* (n. 62). Thus, for example, *Veritatis splendor* notes "there is a difference between the deposit or the truths of faith and the manner in which they are expressed, keeping the same meaning and the same judgment" (29.2). *Ut unum sint* cites the 1973 declaration *Mysterium ecclesiae*: "Even though the truths which the Church intends to teach through her dogmatic formulas are distinct from the changeable conceptions of a given epic and can be expressed without them, nevertheless it can sometimes happen that these truths may be enunciated by the sacred Magisterium in terms that bear traces of such conceptions" (38.2). In this context, John Paul II points out: "One of the advantages of ecumenism is that it helps Christian Communities to discover the unfathomable riches of the truth" (38.3). *Ut unum sint* also refers in the same context to the famous opening address of John XXIII at Vatican II in recalling "the distinction between the deposit of faith and the formulation in which it is expressed" (81.3).

The basis for John Paul II's often recalled distinction between the truths of faith and their expression comes from the fact that "[r]evealed truth, to be sure, surpasses our telling. All our concepts fall short of its ultimately unfathomable grandeur (cf. Eph 3:19)" (*Veritatis splendor* 109.2). This distinction between the truths of faith and their expression also stands behind the recognition of the development of dogma with regard to the truths of faith (*Veritatis splendor* 28.2 and 53.3).

In addition to the truths of faith, John Paul II, especially in his encyclicals on moral matters, recognizes the truths of the moral life and especially truths of moral norms based on natural law, which are universal and unchanging. Such truths by their very nature differ somewhat from the truths of faith. In this context, *Veritatis splendor* fears that many contemporary thinkers so stress historicity and cultural diversity that they call into question the universality of the natural law. But human nature transcends all cultures. "[T]his nature is itself the measure of culture and the condition ensuring that the human being does not become the prisoner of any of his cultures, but asserts his personal dignity by living in accordance with the profound truth of his being" (53.2). There is a need "to seek out and discover the most adequate formulation for universal and permanent moral norms in the light of different cultural contexts. . . . This truth of the moral law . . . must be specified and determined . . . in the light of historical circumstances by the Church's Magisterium, whose decision is preceded and accompanied by the work of interpretation and formulation characteristic of the reason of individual believers and of theological reflection" (53.3). Thus, the formulation of universal and unchanging moral norms depends on natural law and a reasonable power of interpretation and formulation.

John Paul II, in these encyclicals, admits another type of Catholic truth—the truth involved in the social teaching of the church. According to *Centesimus annus,* the church's social teaching focuses on the human person involved in a complex web of relationships and societies. "The human sciences and philosophy are helpful for interpreting *the human being's central place within society* and for enabling him to understand himself better as a 'social being.' However, an individual's true identity is only fully revealed to him through faith, and it is precisely from faith that the Church's social teaching begins . . . while drawing upon all the contributions made by the sciences and philosophy" (54.1). *Centesimus annus* thus explicitly recognizes that the church's social teaching "has an important interdisciplinary dimension. In order to better incarnate the one truth about humankind in different and constantly changing social, economic, and political contexts, this teaching enters into dialogue with various disciplines concerned with humankind. It assimilates what these discipline have to contribute" (59.3).

The encyclicals of John Paul II thus expressly recognize that they are dealing with different types of truth—truths of faith, truths of moral norms, and truths of social teaching—and point out some limitations on all truths. But a study of these three different types of truth in church teaching shows more limitations and less certitude than John Paul II acknowledged in these encyclicals.

Greater Limitations and Less Certitude

Even on the level of truths of faith, John Paul II recognized the need for doctrinal development and even reformulation of truth. But the historical reality of such developments that have occurred in the truths of Catholic faith includes more discontinuity than John Paul II was willing to admit. The Christological and Trinitarian dogmas of the fourth and fifth centuries are definitely in continuity with the biblical teaching, but these also show quite a bit of discontinuity. The Greek terms of person and nature to understand the Trinity (three persons in one God) and Jesus Christ (two natures in one person) add considerably to the biblical understanding of God and Jesus. The development that has occurred in church teaching with regard to the sacraments is even more startling. For the greater part of its existence the Roman Catholic Church did not recognize the existence of seven sacraments. The church acknowledged marriage as a sacrament only in the twelfth century.[9] Of course, one must emphasize again that these encyclicals do not intend to give an in-depth discussion of the development of doctrine. But the development of dogma in the Catholic tradition thus exhibits greater discontinuity than recognized in the occasional formulations used by John Paul II in his encyclicals.

With regard to the truths of absolute moral norms, John Paul II recognized that these truths rest on natural law and the interpretation of reason. However, the effect of these factors on moral truths and the claims to certitude are more significant than the pope explicitly recognized. Take, for example, the universal and unchangeable moral norm on abortion found in *Evangelium vitae*. John Paul II, in a very solemn way, reasserts the teaching of the church condemning direct abortion (62.3). Notice that the condemnation does not include all abortion but only direct abortion. The pope thus invokes the philosophical distinction between direct and indirect to distinguish right from wrong with regard to abortion. This distinction is obviously based on a particular philosophical view and is far removed both from the core of faith and from more general ethical norms such as the respect due to all life, including nascent life. The magisterium arrived at the present understanding of direct and indirect abortion only in the twentieth century.[10] One cannot claim the same certitude on this level as one can regarding the more general ethical principles of respecting life or producing good. The more specific and concrete the universal moral norm becomes, the more circumstances and conditions are brought in, and one cannot claim a certitude that excludes the possibility of error. Long ago Thomas Aquinas recognized that the secondary principles of the natural law oblige as generally occurs but not always, precisely because of the more circumstantial elements that can enter in to change the case. He illustrates the point with the moral norm that deposits or goods being held for another should be returned. However, this is not true when the other has left a sword with you and now comes back and wants the sword returned, but is raving drunk and threatening to kill people.[11] Thus, the truth claims about direct and indirect abortion are limited by the very nature of the complex philosophical theory involved in such a distinction.

One should also note in the matter of abortion that the Catholic position and the teaching of the hierarchical magisterium have admitted theoretical doubt about the beginning of personal human life. We cannot have absolute certitude about when personal human life begins. However, in practice, one has to give the benefit of the doubt to the existence of a human person from the moment of conception.[12] Thus, the Catholic Church recognizes less certitude about the beginning of human life than John Paul II proposes in his obviously very short and limited discussion of abortion. On the matter of universal moral norms, including the condemnation of direct abortion, John Paul II explicitly denies any place for dissent from this teaching (*Veritatis splendor* 4.2–3, 26.2, 113). However, he proposes a quite limited understanding of "dissent in the form of carefully articulated protests and polemics carried on in the media" (113.2). One could conclude then that there might be room for some type of disagreement from the truths of absolute moral norms proposed by the church.[13]

With regard to the truths of the social teaching, John Paul II correctly recognizes the interdisciplinary nature of that teaching and its dependence on sources other than faith. Here too, as in the area of the truth of universal and unchangeable moral norms, one can only claim a limited certitude with regard to the teaching proposed. In the social area the church has undergone significant changes in its teaching as well, illustrated in its acceptance only in 1965 of religious freedom after a long denial of such freedom.[14] The church has also changed its social teaching on human rights, and on the best form of government with significant support for democracy only beginning in the middle of the twentieth century.[15] In *Veritatis splendor*, John Paul II points out some "principles which are primarily rooted in, and in fact derive their singular urgency from, the transcendent value of the person and the objective moral demands of the functioning of States" (101.1). Among these principles are, for example, "respect for the rights of political adversaries, [and] safeguarding the rights of the accused against summary trials and convictions" (101.1). Here again there has been significant change in church teaching and practice. For many centuries we did not respect the rights of political adversaries. In addition, the Catholic Church has changed its own teaching with regard to the rights of the accused to keep silent and not reveal their crimes.[16]

Three Difficulties

Three difficulties arise from the understanding of the truth about humankind found in the encyclicals of John Paul II. First, the generic use of truth insinuates that truth is a univocal term, but such is not the case. The beginning of *Veritatis splendor* well illustrates the problem. The introduction to the encyclical refers to the fundamental questions about human existence. Here Jesus Christ, who is the way, the truth, and the life, gives "the decisive answer to every one of humankind's questions, his religious and moral questions in particular" (85). But there exists a significant difference between the truths of faith regarding the ultimate questions of human existence and decisive answers to every one of humankind's questions, especially religious and moral questions. The Catholic tradition has consistently recognized that the truth about specific moral questions differs considerably from the truth about the ultimate meaning of human existence. To its great credit, the Catholic theological tradition has insisted on the importance of mediation—the divine is mediated in and through the human. In the area of moral theology and dealing with moral questions, one must examine in great detail all aspects of the complex human reality before coming to an answer to a complex moral question about what should be done in a particular situation.[17]

The Catholic tradition has argued against going immediately from a truth of faith or a scriptural citation (for example, love of neighbor or concern for the poor) to a specific conclusion such as multinational corporations are immoral. One must know all the complex human realities before coming to arrive at such a specific moral conclusion. The Catholic tradition has often used casuistry as a way of trying to deal with specific moral issues, thus showing how important it is to consider all the details of the situation.[18] Too often the papal encyclicals employ truth in the univocal sense, which fails to recognize that truth is an analogous concept.

Second, problems also arise when the encyclicals recognize the analogous nature of truth and describe the different kinds of truth. In their descriptions of truths of faith, moral truths, and truths of social teaching, they do not explicitly recognize the limitations involved in these three different types of truth and also fail to appreciate the different levels of certitude involved. On the level of moral truth, the Catholic tradition has consistently recognized a difference between moral truth and speculative truth. Moral truth deals with practical matters. As Thomas Aquinas pointed out, speculative truths are always true. Thus, for example, a triangle always has 180 degrees even if some people, because of their poor background or knowledge, do not always recognize this fact. But secondary precepts of the moral law oblige generally, but they admit of exceptions precisely because of the myriad circumstances that can enter in.[19] Thus, John Paul II should have recognized explicitly the limits on truth and certitude especially in the moral area which is the proper concern of this essay.

Third, a discussion of truth in these documents raises the age old epistemological problem—what is truth and how do we know truth? A detailed examination of this question lies beyond the scope of this essay. But the papal documents seem to have a classicist notion of truth as something out there, which is then knowable by all. A more historically conscious understanding of truth sees it always in relationship to persons seeking truth and imbedded in the historical and cultural circumstances of time and place.[20] Margaret Farley in her many writings from a feminist perspective strongly opposes essentialism and abstract universalism while still recognizing obligating features of all persons based on their autonomy and relationality.[21] Thus, the concept of truth in the papal encyclicals suffers from significant deficiencies in the light of the Catholic tradition.

THE CHURCH

The encyclicals of John Paul II address the understanding of the church in many different contexts with two, *Redemptoris missio* and *Ut unum sint*, concentrating on the church as such. The encyclicals frequently refer to the magisterium as charged with the task of authentically interpreting the word of God with authority exercised in the name of Jesus Christ (for example, *Veritatis splendor* 27.3). The magisterium's reply to questions raised by people's consciences "contains the voice of Jesus Christ, the voice of truth about good and evil" (*Veritatis splendor* 117.2). The encyclicals, however, as one would expect, do not develop in detail an understanding or theology of the magisterium. Our focus thus concerns the general understanding of the church and the magisterium as teaching the truth about humankind.

The basic role and mission of the church for John Paul II was very clear as has already been pointed out. Thanks to the gift of the Holy Spirit the church continues in time and space to carry on the mission of Christ the Redeemer in teaching the truth about humankind. But more specific aspects help to flesh out the above understanding of the role and mission of the church.

Grace and Truth Outside the Catholic Church

Yes, the church carries on in time and space the redemptive message of Jesus, but God's grace also exists outside the boundaries of the church. The church remains distinct from both Christ and the Kingdom but "the church is indissolubly united to both. . . . The result is a unique and special relationship which, while not excluding the action of Christ and the Spirit outside the Church's visible boundaries, confers upon her a specific and necessary role; hence the Church's special connection with the Kingdom of God and of Christ which she has 'the mission of announcing and inaugurating among all peoples'" (*Redemptoris missio* 18.3). This basic understanding grounds the necessity for the evangelizing mission of the church as developed especially in the encyclical *Redemptoris missio*. Yes, the Spirit exists and works outside Christ and the church, but this work of the Spirit is linked both to Christ and to the church. The Spirit both develops gifts in all peoples but also works by "guiding the Church to discover these gifts, to foster them, and to receive them through dialogue. Every form of the Spirit's presence is to be welcomed with respect and gratitude, but the discernment of this presence is the responsibility of the Church, to which Christ gave his Spirit in order to guide her into all the truth (cf. Jn 16:13)" (29.3). The recognition that the Spirit, grace, and even religious truth exist outside the Catholic Church does not take away from the church's mission to teach the truth about humankind to all and to discern the presence of the Spirit even outside the Catholic Church.

What about the Catholic Church's relationship to other churches? *Ut unum sint* deals precisely with the question of ecumenism to which John Paul II is definitely committed. In this context he cites the position enunciated in Vatican II that "the Church of Christ 'subsists in the Catholic Church . . .' and at the same time acknowledges that 'many elements of sanctification and of truth can be found outside her visible structure'" (10.2).

In ecumenical dialogue, truth remains the ultimate principle. Ecumenical dialogue rests on "a common quest for the truth" (33). "The obligation to respect the truth is absolute" (79.3). As mentioned above, the famous distinction between the truths of faith and their expression opens the door for ecumenical dialogue. In *Ut unum sint*, John Paul II cites his own previous documents pointing out, "(W)e are aware as the Catholic Church that we have received much from the witness borne by other Churches and Ecclesial Communities to certain common Christian values" (87).

As an example of the need for dialogue to be connected to the truth, the pope recognizes that the office of papacy and its concomitant gift of infallibility constitute a difficulty for many other Christians. John Paul II clearly insists on the need for papal primacy and infallibility as a part of the papal office but also recognizes that the papal office must be carried out in a theology of communion. He then asks non-Catholics to help him find ways of exercising his office that will not be an obstacle to Christian union (88–97).

John Paul II admitted that the Catholic Church has learned from the ecumenical dialogue, but some passages seem to play down this learning by implying that the Catholic Church learns from other Christian churches something that the Catholic Church in its fullness already has. The pope explicitly recognizes that there is not an ecclesiastical vacuum outside the boundaries of the Roman Catholic community, but then goes on to say: "Many elements of great value, which in the Catholic Church are part of the fullness of the means of salvation and of the gifts of grace which make up the Church, are also found in the other Christian Communities" (*Ut unum sint* 13.3). But still he has acknowledged that the Catholic Church has learned from other churches and ecclesial communities. However, it is true to say that his recognition that the Catholic Church has learned from other churches in no way denies or modifies his basic understanding of the Catholic Church as called by God to teach the truth about humankind and to discern the presence of that truth.

Nature of the Church

What precisely is the nature of the Catholic Church? John Paul II sees both a divine and a human element in the church—"the very essence of her divine-human constitution" (*Dominum et vivificantem* 61.1). In the light of this understanding of the "divine-human constitution" of the church, the shortcomings, failures, and even sins come from the human element in the church but not from the church itself, which also includes the divine element. In his very first encyclical, John Paul II inveighs against an overly critical attitude toward the church that often existed immediately after Vatican II. But he quickly recognizes the need for some criticism in the church—"While it is right that . . . the Church also should have humility as her foundation, that she should have a critical sense with regard to all that goes to make up her human character and activity, and that she should always be very demanding on herself, nevertheless criticism too should have its just

limits" (*Redemptor hominis* 4.1). The church knows trials and tribulations but is sustained and "strengthened by the power of God's grace
promised to her by the Lord" (*Redemptoris mater* 35.1). "The Catholic Church acknowledges and confesses *the weaknesses of her members*,
conscious that their sins are so many betrayals of the obstacles to the
accomplishment of the Savior's plan. . . . At the same time she acknowledges and exalts still more *the power of the Lord*, who fills her
with the gift of holiness, leads her forward, and conforms her to his
Passion and Resurrection" (*Ut unum sint* 3.1). Notice here how the
human and the divine element in the church work. Such an approach
prevents John Paul II from saying that the church itself has sinned or
done wrong. Only the human part or the members of the church do
wrong and sin. The divine element assures that the church knows the
truth about humankind.

But many Catholic theologians take a different tack. The church
is a sinful church—always in need of reform and repentance.[22] John
Paul II's ecclesiology sees the divine element as a separate element in
the church and never completely merging with the total reality of the
church. However, in fairness to John Paul II, more than any other
pope, he often called attention to the sins and injustices committed
by members of the church and asked for forgiveness even though his
ecclesiology prevented him from saying that the church itself has committed sin or is a sinful church.[23]

Metaphors of the Church

John Paul II's metaphors for the church also cohere with his understanding of the church as continuing the teaching mission of Jesus and
having a divine element and a human element. John Paul II's favorite
metaphors for the church tend to highlight the divine element of the
church as being something always present. In his writings before becoming pope, his primary metaphor for the church was the Mystical
Body of Christ.[24] His very first encyclical includes three references to
the church as the Body of Christ (*Redemptor hominis* 7.3, 18.1, 21.2).
The church as the Mystical Body of Christ "makes the Church as a
body, an organism, a social unit, perceive the same divine influences,

the life and strength of the Spirit that come from the crucified and risen Christ, and it is for this very reason that she lives her life. The Church has only one life: that which is given her by her Spouse and Lord" (18.1).

John Paul II as pope mentioned many of the metaphors of the church found in Vatican II's Constitution on the Church, but the encyclicals emphasize the understanding of "the Church as a kind of sacrament or sign and means of intimate union with God, and of the unity of all humankind" (*Redemptor hominis* 7.3, as quoted from *Lumen gentium* 1). Such an understanding of the church fits in very well with his basic thesis of the church as continuing the mission of Jesus to teach the truth about humankind. The very beginning of *Redemptor hominis* describes the church as the Body of Christ and then goes on to develop this concept in the light of Vatican II's understanding of the church as sacrament or sign of two realities—intimate union with God and of the unity of all humankind (7.3). *Redemptor hominis* also quotes in full *Lumen gentium* on the church as sacrament (18.4). *Redemptoris missio*, which deals especially with the role of the church in redemption, devotes an entire paragraph to "the church sign and instrument of salvation" citing *Lumen gentium* 48 and *Gaudium et spes* 43 (9). Later the same encyclical refers to the church as "the sacrament of salvation for all humankind," citing *Gaudium et spes* 39. *Dominum et vivificantem* devotes an entire section of three paragraphs to "the church as the sacrament of intimate union with God" (61–64).

Other Vatican II metaphors of the church stress more the lack of complete identification between the church and the risen Jesus and also do not identify the church with the divine element in the church. Perhaps the most popular metaphor of the church in the post–Vatican II era has been the church as the people of God. This metaphor is the title of chapter two of *Lumen gentium*, the Constitution on the Church. Such a metaphor, as mentioned earlier, does not support a sharp distinction between the divine and the human element in the church to the extent that the sins and shortcomings are those of the members of the church and not of the church itself. The church, as the people of God on earth, cannot be separated from the members of the church. The encyclicals of John Paul II do not neglect the metaphor of the people of God. In fact, *Redemptor hominis* uses the metaphor almost twenty times. But the encyclicals of John Paul II do not develop this metaphor and fail to adopt this metaphor in dealing with the sins and shortcomings of the church.

Another metaphor, that of the church as the pilgrim people of God, recognizes the tension between the imperfect and sinful church of the present and the eschatological fullness. The metaphor of the pilgrim church serves as the basis for Vatican II's recognition that the church is always in need of change and reform. In the light of the eschatological tension, the pilgrim church will always fall short. The pilgrim church is in constant need of conversion and forgiveness and never possesses the fullness of sanctity and truth. John Paul II develops the metaphor of the pilgrim church in chapter two of *Redemptoris mater* with its title—"The Mother of God at the Center of the Pilgrim Church." But in this section the description of the pilgrim church does not include a recognition of the church either as a sinful church in need of conversion or a recognition of the church growing in its understanding of the knowledge of the truth. Mary and her *Magnificat* serve as a model for the pilgrim church because Mary, like the church, lives by faith. Mary proclaimed "the undimmed truth about God" (37.1). "The Church which even 'amid trials and tribulations' does not cease repeating with Mary the words of the *Magnificat,* is sustained by the power of God's truth, proclaimed on that occasion with such extraordinary simplicity. At the same time by means of this truth about God, the Church desires to shed light upon the difficult and sometimes tangled paths of humankind's earthly existence" (37.2).

A third metaphor of the church, as the herald or servant of the reign of God, also recognizes eschatological tension. The church is not the reign of God but points to the reign of God. The tension between the church at present and the fullness of the reign of God will always be present and felt. In *Redemptoris missio* (12–20), John Paul II deals in some depth with the relationship of the church and the kingdom (his word). He chides those who have separated the kingdom both from Jesus and from the church. "It is true that the Church is not an end unto itself, since she is ordered toward the kingdom of God of which she is the seed, sign, and instrument. Yet, while remaining distinct from Christ and the kingdom, the Church is indissolubly united to both" (18.3). John Paul II tends to downplay somewhat the eschatological tension between the church and the reign of God.

Fides et ratio recognizes the eschatological tension between the fullness of truth and the truths taught at the present time (2). In this context, the encyclical acknowledges that the church is on a "pilgrim way" and that the believing community is "a partner in humanity's shared struggle to arrive at truth." But, on the other hand, the church has "her duty to serve humanity" as "the *diakonia* [servant] *of the truth.*" This service "obliges the believing community to proclaim the certitudes arrived at albeit with a sense that every truth attained is but a step toward the fullness of truth which will appear with the final revelation of God." Here there seems to be some tension between the recognition of humanity's shared search for the truth and the role of the church as the *diakonia* of truth for humankind. However, the eschatological tension based on the fullness of truth as coming only at the end of time does not take away from the certitude of the truth that the church teaches humanity today.

The understanding of church found in John Paul II's encyclicals thus fits in very well with his thesis that the church continues in time and space the work of the risen Jesus in teaching the truth about humankind without explicit recognition of the shortcomings and limitations of both the church and the truth it teaches about humankind.

The Church as Learner of the Truth

These encyclicals never explicitly address a basic question: how does the church learn or acquire the truth? The encyclicals frequently refer to the deposit of faith. Especially in the nineteenth century this term signified the propositional truths of faith that were handed over to the church and that the church preserves. Thus the church has the deposit of truth and simply draws on these truths when needed. But even with regard to the truths of faith, John Paul II himself has recognized the difference between truth and the expression of truth. For that reason and many others, including historical consciousness and the recognition of the development of doctrine, the deposit of faith cannot be conceived as a deposit of verbal propositions handed over to the church that she preserves and applies.[25] Thus, even with regard to the truths of faith, the church itself has to learn these truths. Take, for example, the Trinitarian (three persons in one God) and Christological (two natures in one person) doctrines. The church came to a knowledge of these truths as expressed this way in the course of history. Likewise, as mentioned, only in the second millennium did the church acknowledge the existence of seven sacraments.

In the moral area we are not dealing with truths that belong to the deposit of faith or with truths of faith at all. These truths by John Paul II's own recognition are often based on natural law. So here it is obvious that the church has to learn these truths before it can teach them. But how does the church learn these truths? One can appeal to the assistance of the Holy Spirit, but how does the Spirit work? In keeping with the Catholic notion of mediation and God working in and through the human, the assistance of the Holy Spirit means assistance in the human ways of acquiring truth, but the assistance does not substitute for the human process.[26] As already noted, the truth about the condemnation of direct abortion or direct killing depends on a philosophical distinction that arose in the late nineteenth century between direct and indirect, which, at the very minimum, is somewhat controversial.

History reminds us that over the centuries and the years the church has changed its teaching on a number of significant issues such as slavery, usury, freedom, religious freedom, human rights, democracy, the right of the defendant to remain silent, the death penalty, the intention and role of procreation in marital sexuality, the nature of the family, and the role of women in society.[27] Such changes remind all that the church has learned its moral teaching and moral truths from a multitude of different human sources while helped by the assistance of the Holy Spirit.

To explore thoroughly how the church learns the truth that it teaches goes well beyond the scope of this paper. For our purposes, it is sufficient to point out that John Paul II's encyclicals fail to recognize that the church not only teaches the truth about humankind but must also learn these truths. The church is both learner and teacher.

It is fitting that the last word in this essay should come from Farley. She has recently insisted on this learning process within the church. The temptation for office holders in the church is to grasp for certitude. Farley insists that the church as a whole and the hierarchical magisterium need the gift of the Spirit she calls "the grace of self-doubt." Obviously, self-doubt can have pejorative meanings, but Farley insists on a graced self-doubt that recognizes epistemic humility as the basic condition for communal as well as individual moral discernment. "If all co-believers are to participate in the moral discernment in the church, and if the limited contribution of each requires the participation of the others, then all—laity, clergy, theologians, church leaders—have need of the grace of self-doubt."[28] Thus, Margaret Farley sees the grace of self-doubt as a very important factor in the learning process of the church and its official teachers.

This essay has examined the understanding of Pope John Paul II in his encyclicals that the church teaches the truth about humankind. Such an understanding needs to be nuanced. Thus, the church should strive to teach the "truth about humankind," but there are different types of truths with different types of certitude connected with them, and, above all, the church itself must learn these truths before it teaches them.

NOTES

1. For perspectives on Karol Wojtyla's philosophy, see Rocco Buttiglione, *Karol Wojtyla: The Thought of the Man Who Became Pope John Paul II* (Grand Rapids, MI: Eerdmans, 1997); Kenneth L. Schmitz, *At the Center of the Human Drama: The Philosophical Anthropology of Karol Wojtyla/Pope John Paul II* (Washington, DC: Catholic University of America Press, 1993); George Hunston Williams, *The Mind of John Paul II: Origins of His Thought and Action* (New York: Seabury, 1981).

2. Charles E. Curran and Richard A. McCormick, eds., *John Paul II and Moral Theology*, Readings in Moral Theology 10 (New York: Paulist Press, 1998), 237–375.

3. Ibid., 137–234.

4. Margaret A. Farley, *Compassionate Respect: A Feminist Approach to Medical Ethics and Other Questions* (New York: Paulist Press, 2002); Margaret A.

Farley, "Response to James Hanigan and Charles Curran," in *Sexual Orientation and Human Rights in American Religious Discourse*, ed. Saul M. Olyan and Martha C. Nussbaum, 101–9 (New York: Oxford University Press, 1998).

5. Antonin Scalia "God's Justice and Ours," *First Things* 123 (May 2002): 17–21.

6. For one volume containing all these encyclicals with introductions, see J. Michael Miller, ed., *The Encyclicals of John Paul II* (Huntington, IN: Our Sunday Visitor, 2001). Future references to these encyclicals will put the appropriate paragraph number in parenthesis in the text itself. In this way, one can use any available source for consulting the encyclicals. I have changed the language to be inclusive. Thus, for example, "man" is usually written as "humankind."

7. Ibid., 18.

8. John Paul II frequently cited the documents of Vatican II, but often reinterpreted Vatican II in his own way; see Mary Elsbernd, "The Reinterpretation of *Gaudium et spes* in *Veritatis splendor*," *Horizons* 29 (2002): 225–39.

9. For the history of how marriage became the seventh sacrament, see Theodore Mackin, *The Marital Sacrament* (New York: Paulist Press, 1989), 274–323.

10. For the nineteenth- and twentieth-century developments leading to the present understanding of direct and indirect abortion, see John Connery, *Abortion: A Development of the Roman Catholic Perspective* (Chicago: Loyola University Press, 1977), 225–303.

11. Thomas Aquinas, *Summa theologiae* I-II, q. 94, a. 4.

12. Congregation for the Doctrine of the Faith, "Declaration on Procured Abortion (November 18, 1972)," in *Medical Ethics: Sources of Catholic Teachings*, ed. Kevin D. O'Rourke and Philip Boyle (St. Louis: Catholic Health Association, 1989), 39n19.

13. For further development of the teaching on dissent in the Wojtyla papacy, see Congregation for the Doctrine of the Faith, "Instruction on the Ecclesial Vocation of the Theologian," *Origins* 20 (1990): 117–26. For my understanding, see Charles Curran, *The Catholic Moral Tradition Today: A Synthesis* (Washington: Georgetown University Press, 1999), 215–28.

14. For the Vatican II development on religious liberty and John Paul II's understanding of it, see Hermínio Rico, *John Paul II and the Legacy of "Dignitatis humanae"* (Washington: Georgetown University Press, 2001).

15. Paul E. Sigmund, "Catholicism and Liberal Democracy," in *Catholicism and Liberalism: Contributions to American Public Philosophy*, ed. R. Bruce Douglass and David Hollenbach, 217–41 (Cambridge: Cambridge University Press, 1994).

16. Patrick Granfield, "The Right to Silence: Magisterial Development," *Theological Studies* 27 (1966): 401–20.

17. For my understanding of the role of mediation in Catholic moral theology, see Charles Curran, *The Catholic Moral Tradition Today,* 11–13 and passim.

18. James E. Keenan and Thomas A. Shannon, eds., *The Context of Casuistry* (Washington: Georgetown University Press, 1995).

19. Aquinas, Summa theologiae I-II q. 94, a.4.

20. Michael Vertin, "Truth," in *New Dictionary of Theology*, ed. Joseph A. Komonchak, Mary Collins, and Dermot Lane, 1062–63 (Wilmington, DE: Michael Glazier, 1988).

21. Farley, *Compassionate Respect*, 21–23; and Margaet Farley, "A Feminist Version of Respect for Persons," *Journal of Feminist Studies in Religion* 9 (1993): 183–98.

22. Bradford E. Hinze, "Ecclesial Repentence and the Demands of Dialogue," *Theological Studies* 61 (2000): 207–38.

23. Pope John Paul II, *Tertio millennio adveniente*, nn. 33–36, in *Origins* 24 (1994): 410–11; *Incarnationis mysterium*, n. 11, in *Origins* 28 (1998): 450–51; "Jubilee Characteristic: The Purification of Memory," *Origins* 29 (2000): 649–50. See also John Ford, "John Paul II Asks for Forgiveness," *Ecumenical Trends* 27 (December 1998): 173–75; Francis A. Sullivan, "The Papal Apology," *America* 182, no. 12 (2000): 17–22.

24. Schmitz, *At the Center of the Human Drama*, 110.

25. Nancy C. Ring, "Deposit of Faith," in Komonchak, Collins, and Lane, *New Dictionary of Theology*, 277–79.

26. Richard R. Gaillardetz, *Teaching with Authority: A Theology of the Magisterium in the Church* (Collegeville, MN: Liturgical Press, 1997), 131–58.

27. Charles E. Curran, ed., *Change in Official Catholic Moral Teachings,* Readings in Moral Theology 13 (New York: Paulist Press, 2003).

28. Margaret A. Farley, "Ethics, Ecclesiology, and the Grace of Self-Doubt," in *A Call to Fidelity*, ed. James J. Walter, Timothy E. O'Connell, and Thomas A. Shannon (Washington: Georgetown University Press, 2002), 68.

Chapter Fifteen

Neither Thick nor Thin

Politics and Polity in the Ethics of Margaret A. Farley

William O'Neill, S.J.

In this essay, I wish to develop the political implications of Margaret Farley's ethics of "compassionate respect"[1] against the backdrop of what Michael Sandel calls the liberal "politics of rights" and the rival communitarian "politics of the common good."[2] I shall first explore Farley's fusion of a Kantian claim of "respect for persons" with a feminist ethics of care, and then argue that her reconstructive criticism offers a *via media* between liberal and communitarian warrants of public reasoning and their respective "thin" or "thick" backings or justifications.[3] Finally, I argue that an ethics of compassionate respect, while resolving an apparent antinomy in modern Roman Catholic social teaching, that is, its rights-based rendering of the common good, nonetheless poses critical questions for the church as polity in the (post)modern world.

COMPASSIONATE RESPECT

"Claims to autonomy," writes Farley, "have been important bulwarks in women's struggle against exploitation and oppression."[4] Liberal feminist philosophy, in particular, has given pride of place to impartial respect for "every human person" qua autonomous moral agent, and the derivative claim rights that would ensure recognition "of the full humanity of women."[5] Since the publication of Mary Wollstonecraft's *Vindication of the Rights of Women* (1792), such "mainstream feminism" has tempered liberal political philosophy, in Farley's words, by "(a) 'adding' insights drawn from women's history and experience; (b) claiming for women a 'sameness' with men as human persons and as full citizens; and (c) asserting the autonomy of individual women and the rights of self-determination for women as members of a group."[6]

Yet liberal feminism has itself been subject to feminist critique. The liberal ideal of the rationally autonomous individual in Kantian philosophy, say its critics, is "disembedded, and disembodied."[7] In the name of abstract impartiality, women are subsumed into a "generalized other," divested of their "social histories and concrete, specific bonds."[8] The consequence is not only attenuation of women's moral subjectivity, for example, the cognitive role of affections,[9] but the tacit generalization of the male *autos*, belying the putative impartiality of liberal rights. Indeed, the narrow and pinched sense of the rights of sovereign selves, that is, "negative" liberties enjoining duties of forbearance, neglects the concrete demands of women's welfare and need. Women's experience, for example, the gendered division of labor, thus becomes epiphenomenal to the moral "point of view," relegated to the private sphere, while liberal rhetoric of impartiality (sameness) veils the systemic "alienation" of women "in sexual relations, child rearing, and the support services of ordinary housework."[10]

Feminist critics such as Carol Gilligan and Nel Noddings propose an alternative "ethics of care," one devoted rather to "the needs of others, the sustenance of relationships, concreteness, particularity, respect for differences, and narratives (the stories of persons' whole lives, not only their discrete moments of decisional crisis)."[11] Here ethical identity emerges in gendered difference: "woman-identified emotion in relation to reason, embodiment in relation to transcendent mind, and caring in relation to abstract principles of justice."[12] Responsibility for the "concrete other" precedes individual rights, limiting not only the scope of rational autonomy, but the very "possibility of a solely

self-generated personal self."[13] Social relationships thus figure consti-
tutively in identity formation; as the circle of such constitutive relations is progressively enlarged, race, ethnicity, class, age, and sexual
orientation overlap in "social constructivist views of the self."

In Marxist and especially contemporary socialist feminism, one
can no longer speak of the "sameness" of women's experience. "Essen-
tialist" interpretations of the moral self (women's "nature") give way
to a multiplicity of concrete others, fragmented in their diverse social
roles and historical communities. Yet, as Marilyn Friedman notes, the
ascendency of communitarian philosophy is finally "a perilous ally for
feminists."[14] For "caring" may itself betray a traditional hermeneutic of
patriarchal dominance, that is, the gendered roles assigned to women.
So privileging "traditional communities and relationships," says Farley, is to "risk perpetuating the tyranny of unchosen roles, patterns
of domination and subordination, and overall normative complacency
regarding the inhumanity of individuals and groups in relation to one
another."[15] In excluding "those who are different," and suppressing
"the differences of those who are considered the same," illicit generalization is merely localized.[16] No less than the primacy of the sovereign
self in philosophical liberalism, an "uncritical focus on community"
devalues the concrete other.

So we come full circle. And it is precisely here that Farley's originality emerges, for her ethics of compassionate respect weaves together the various strands of feminist theory in a rich, reconstructive
critique. I will develop her "feminist version of respect for persons"
in two stages (and will propose a third in the next section). Although
Farley draws upon the Kantian heritage of moral philosophy, she differs from modern liberal theorists, such as John Rawls and Jürgen
Habermas, in favoring what Kant calls the "material" formula of the
categorical imperative.[17]

Now while Rawls and Habermas work variations upon the "formal"
or "canonical" formula enjoining abstract impartiality, Farley grounds
her ethics in the material and complete determinations. Universality
is thus, at least implicitly, specified in the respect due each unique,
irreplaceable agent as an "end" in a "realm of ends." Reading Kant
thus enlarges our moral repertoire, for "autonomy is not fulfilled in

Hobbesian self-protectiveness, but in a 'kingdom of ends'; human dignity translates into equality, with respect inclusive of the self as well as others, adversaries as well as friends; there are positive duties to persons as well as negative, duties of caring as well as of noninterference."[18] In the *Doctrine of Virtue*, writes Farley, "embodied diversity," for example, "age, health, sex, wealth, etc.," factor in the interpretation, if not justification of respect.[19]

Yet only traces of such embodiment appear in Kant, so that his interpretation of respect for persons "remains inadequate."[20] Building upon the "complete determination," Farley enriches the Kantian notion of respect by incorporating the complex set of relationships ("relationality") that configure the moral self. For dignity is always in local garb: the moral dictates of autonomy are not *subsequently* embodied or embedded, for example, in lifting the Rawlsian veil of ignorance; rather, autonomy is embodied *ab ovo*. On Farley's interpretation, the generalized attitude of respect (expressed in Kant's "material" formulation of the categorical imperative) is not tantamount to respect for a generalized other (as in G. H. Mead's interpretation of the "formal" formulation).[21]

What Kierkegaard says of love as embracing "everyone in particular but no one in partiality" pertains no less to the attitude of mutual respect.[22] For inasmuch as the virtue of respect presumes my sympathetic identification with the particular attitudes and beliefs of other agents, I respect not the abstract identity of a generalized other, but the *concrete* universality of embodied selves.[23] Impartial *respect* thus bids us regard moral persons as "concrete others," "embodied and social beings," in Charles Taylor's words, who though "situated" are never merely reduced "to a function of objectified nature."[24] As Farley concludes,

> An obligation to respect persons requires that we honor their freedom and respond to their needs, that we value difference as well as sameness, that we attend to the concrete realities of our own and others' lives (reminded, if need be, by the power of the most deeply embedded universal).[25]

An ethics of "just and fitting care," moreover, is enriched by the quality of mercy or compassion. Compassion bids us attend to what

Walter Benjamin once called "the suffering or passion of the world."[26] For if the "cognitive structure" of compassion "leads us within and beyond the requirements of respect," so the latter mediates a "fitting" response to the concrete other in need.[27] And so it is, "like Aristotle's description of 'sympathetic consciousness,'" a "loving knowledge," passes into a "knowing love"[28]—a love, as Farley says, that is finally cruciform: "Respect is the Cross for compassion, the sword to its heart that allows its life to pour forth."[29]

RIVAL POLITICS

The foregoing sketch, limited as it is, must suffice as a backdrop for our inquiry into the political implications of Farley's ethics of compassionate respect. She has, of course, addressed the political import of her critique on numerous occasions, most notably in her presidential address to the Catholic Theological Society of America, "The Church in the Public Forum: Scandal or Prophetic Witness."[30] And her extensive writings in the areas of medical, bioethical, and sexual ethics, and of the impact of the HIV/AIDS pandemic on African women, underscore her astute assessment of the political background of the church's prophetic witness. But it is the latter I wish to bring into relief now, for, as adumbrated above, our politics bequeaths us a Hobson's choice: between the "thin" Kantian lineage of the politics of rights, or the "thick" communitarian politics of the common good beholden rather to Hegel. Let me touch briefly on these rival warrants of public reason (reflected or refracted, we have seen, in feminist thought) before proceeding to consider Farley's critical riposte.[31]

The liberal metanarrative

For liberalism as a philosophic doctrine, the very irreconcilability of our comprehensive conceptions of the (common) good leads us to cherish the "liberties of the moderns" as our foremost rights.[32] "The only freedom which deserves the name," writes J. S. Mill in a justly memorable phrase, "is that of pursuing our own good in our own way." Our liberty, in turn, is parsed as our several immunities or negative rights, limited principally by duties of forbearance; we must, says Mill, *respect* others' like liberty, neither depriving them of their own good, nor impeding "their efforts to obtain it."[33] Under the banner of negative freedom, heirs of the liberal tradition appeal to their individual liberties as warrants, while relegating positive de-limitations of liberty, such as claim rights to adequate nutrition, to an inferior sphere, if not dismissing them as mere rhetorical license. Our negative liberties, says Robert Nozick, "fill up the space of rights."[34]

With the apotheosis of the sovereign self, social bonds, once derived from the ethical ideal of the common good (the positive, teleological determination of freedom or *libertas)* must now be "constructed" through exercise of individual will (*liberum arbitrium*), whether of Locke's fiduciary contract or the imperious fiat of Hobbes' Leviathan. Where communitarian rhetoric appeals to a thick narrative tradition, philosophical liberalism thus finds its backing in a thin procedural in-terpretation of justice. In his magisterial account of justice as fairness, for instance, John Rawls recurs to the heuristic device of a social con-tract in which mutually disinterested agents select the principles of justice under a "veil of ignorance."[35]

Fairness is achieved by bracketing agents' knowledge of their par-ticular cultural roles, economic status, natural and acquired abilities, and particular desires, goals, and so forth. In Rawls's thought experi-ment, self-interested choice under the veil of ignorance is thus tanta-mount to fairness or impartiality once the veil is lifted. So reflecting modernity's skepticism regarding a comprehensive conception of the common good, what Hans-Georg Gadamer describes as our "preju-dice against prejudice," perfectly prudential agents, says Rawls, would prefer an increment of liberty (immunity from interference) to that of any other social good.[36]

The communitarian narrative

Harking back to the Romantic critique of the empty formalism of Kantian morality (*Moralität*), communitarian critics as diverse as Tay-lor, Sandel, and Alasdair MacIntyre envision the self as constituted in the ensemble of social relations, the distinctive mores of Hegelian ethics (*Sittlichkeit*), albeit bereft of "Reason's cunning."[37] Knit together by shared history and sentiments, our moral rhetoric appeals to what Edmund Burke called the "latent wisdom" of our particular traditions.[38] Our cherished liberty "has a pedigree" sharply distinguishing members of the body politic from strangers.

Rhetorical warrants in communitarian philosophy rest less in the politics of rights than in the politics of the common good.[39] Indeed, for Richard Rorty, philosophy holds a mirror, not to nature or natural rights, but to our cultural mores. To the "thoroughly enlightened" postmodernist, the "natural, inalienable, and sacred rights" of the individual are a supreme fiction. In Rorty's agnostic piety, rights are redeemed, not as self-evident or sacred verities but as "local and ethnocentric" customs—their backing deriving from "the tradition of a particular community, the consensus of a particular culture."[40] Rights' talk, like edifying discourse generally, would be "relative to the group to which we think it is necessary to justify ourselves—to the body of shared belief which determines the reference of the word 'we.'"[41]

The rhetorically circumscribed "we" need not, of course, be xenophobic or racist, although such prejudices cannot be ruled out *tout court*. For if the primary virtue of liberal metanarrative is *respect* for the negative liberty of abstract, sovereign selves, then the virtue distinguishing communitarian philosophy is *recognition* of difference, for example, the identification of members and strangers, which as Walzer observes, "structures all our other distributive choices: it determines with whom we make those choices, from whom we require obedience and collect taxes, to whom we allocate goods and services."[42] And since these seemingly incommensurable virtues inspire our differing politics, one wonders if the Catholic Church has read the "signs of the times" aright, or if its belated rapprochement with modernity is, in Rorty's words, merely "quaint." For in a characteristically irenic turn, Pope John XXIII resolves the antinomy of rights and the common good by stipulative fiat: *Pacem in terris* glosses the premodern teleology of *Mater et magistra* (depicting the common good as "the sum total of those conditions of social living, whereby [we] are enabled to achieve [our] own integral perfection"[43]) in deontological terms of human rights.[44] "It is agreed that in our time the common good is chiefly guaranteed when personal rights and duties are maintained."[45]

A critical riposte

As Farley argues, however, the issue cannot be settled by merely adding or grafting the modern (deontological) rhetoric of rights to the premodern (teleological) ideal of the common good.[46] Yet precisely in enriching the Kantian notion of respect by showing its object (or subject) to be the concrete, socially embodied "other," Farley offers a critical *via media*. For in thickening the Kantian claim of respect, Farley implicitly thins what Burke called the latent wisdom of our particular narrative traditions. Recognition of "particularity and diversity is not criterionless,"[47] inasmuch as "the content of the obligation to respect persons provides the norms, the criteria for true caring,"[48] and, by implication, interpretation of tradition.

Respect for the concrete other, then, "cannot be separated from the obligation to respect and to care for their bodies (or better, for them as embodied)."[49] Such an integral understanding of the relationship of the moral/hermeneutical virtues of respect *and* recognition, as I argued in the preceding section, emerges from the first two stages of Farley's criticism of the Kantian critique, that is, after initially specifying *universality* in terms of the moral agent as a self-existent end, she proceeds to specify the *moral agent* as concretely embodied in the ensemble of social relations.

Now it is these stages or steps of argumentation that warrant a third stage in *recognizing* the concrete conditions of embodying autonomy; for in redeeming the virtue of *respect* in our narrative traditions, we may further specify the criteria of a "just and fitting care." Thus to respect the concrete, narratively embodied "other" is, implicitly, to respect the conditions of her exercising narrative agency, that is, her agential capabilities. And as Martha Nussbaum and Amartya Sen have persuasively argued, these comprise both "negative" civil-political liberties and "positive" claim rights to the satisfaction of basic needs, such as security, adequate nutrition, potable water, basic education, and so forth.[50] Such rights, of course, are particularly germane to the majority of women who are so often systemically deprived of the most basic agential goods.[51]

Since even negative claim rights entail positive duties of systemic protection and provision, we may think of establishing a rights regime as a fitting narrative *telos* (or regulative ideal): how, that is, a particular cultural narrative may be woven and rewoven, in Mercy Amba Oduyoye's words, to incorporate the basic rights of women, including a fortiori their rights as narrative weavers themselves.[52] Such an understanding of a "basic set of rights and responsibilities for all human persons"[53]—precisely as entailed by compassionate respect—thickens what Rawls calls our "sense of justice," underscoring the systemic, institutional requirements of society's basic structure. By integrating respect and recognition, that is, the common good provides for the culturally fitting instantiation of a basic rights regime. But this, after all, is precisely what the Roman Catholic Church proposes in its modern reading of the common good, that is, as "the set of social conditions" presumed in our diverse polities for the realization of dignity and basic human rights.

POLITICS AND POLITY

Much more, of course, might be said, but it is perhaps fitting to end on an irenic note—for it is Farley's feminist critique of Kant that permits us to resolve the apparent antinomy besetting the church's politics. In this final section, I wish to explore the implications of this resolution for the church's own politics in both its extramural and intramural dimensions.

Extramural Politics

As we noted above, the "turn" in her social teaching from a perfectionist, eudaimonistic teleology to a rights-based conception of the common good permitted the church to speak to complex, pluralist societies in the modern world. In *Pacem in terris, Gaudium et spes,* and *Dignitatis humanae,* the church recognizes the basic rights and correlative duties of moral persons: rights to security, subsistence (including health care and basic education), and liberties of effective participation in the social, economic, political, and cultural realms, including religious liberty.[54] These rights, as *Pacem in terris* proclaims,[55] are internally limited and hence legitimately restricted by the like rights of others in the shared political reason of pluralist polities. Further restrictions upon agents' liberty or welfare rights, as Farley observes, must be persuasively redeemed in public discourse; reasons offered, that is, must be internally (rationally) persuasive to the agents affected.[56]

Such a discursive conception of the terrestrial common good implies, in the words of *Dignitatis humanae*, that "the freedom of the human person be respected as far as possible, and curtailed only when and in so far as necessary." Believers are admonished to "avoid any action which seems to suggest coercion or unworthy persuasion."[57] Just such a compassionate respect for an integral and comprehensive set of human rights and duties guides our public deliberation:[58] policies, that is, are (a) governed by basic rights as deontic side-constraints[59] in terms of negative duties of avoiding deprivation, and (b) subject to consequential evaluation in terms of positive duties of protection and provision.[60] And since satisfying these duties will be relative to prevailing political, social, and cultural circumstances, we may ask: of the set of policies deemed feasible, which will *best* satisfy persons' mutually implicative basic rights, for example, to civil liberties, security, or adequate nutrition, all things considered?[61]

Consider the implications of such a "consequentially sensitive" rights regime for population policy and HIV/AIDS prevention. In the church's public reasoning, such policies must themselves be viewed integrally and comprehensively. Population policy must, that is, be incorporated into equitable development strategies ensuring not only voluntary family planning (as in the liberal politics of rights) but also the cognate prerequisites of exercising agency, such as women's health care, education, intra-familial rights, and so on.[62] Now, inasmuch as sustained, equitable development generates social incentives to reduce fertility even as it enhances women's agency, for example, through provision of education, voluntary family planning is warranted by the church's rights rhetoric.[63] Yet such rights, in preserving capabilities rather than specific functionings, are underdetermined with respect to their particular object or end, such as "the full truth of the sexual act," which Pope John Paul II invokes "as the proper expression of conjugal love" in proscribing artificial contraception.[64]

In view of the tenor of rights' discourse preserving personal and familial liberty, such restrictions on the means of voluntary family planning must be submitted to the tribunal of public reason, and it is precisely here that the magisterial exercise of political power may be questioned.[65] As Karl Rahner observed of Paul VI's *Humanae vitae,* "[i]n all respects we shall surely have to say that on these questions a specific position has indeed been adopted, but this is merely stated rather than explained or proved in any effective sense. It becomes clear in the encyclical itself that the real and primary reason for adhering to this position is the need that is felt to hold firm to the traditional teaching of Pius XI and Pius XII."[66] Acceding to traditional teaching might be laudable; yet in so far as the reasons for assenting to *Humanae vitae's* condemnation of artificial contraception depend for their suasive force upon the "prophetic" inspiration of the magisterial tradition, or the privileged role of the magisterium in interpreting the natural law, in other words, as perfectionist teleology,[67] we must concede they fail, prima facie, the test of public reason.[68] Such a failure need not, of course, impugn the potential validity of the argument. It is rather a question of extension or scope: the arguments pertain to the intramural deliberations of the church rather than the prerequisites of what Murray termed "public order."[69] And though negotiable as public reasons, further consequentialist claims, for example, that artificial contraception eo ipso fosters "conjugal infidelity," "the general lowering of morality," the deprecation of women, or governmental "imposition" of population controls[70] have yet to be vindicated in our shared, political reason. Nor, in general, do they apply to the use of condoms in HIV/AIDS prevention.

Here, too, the analogy with John Courtney Murray's defense of religious liberty is apposite. For in differing with his "integralist" opponents, Murray did not so much deny the older perfectionist doctrine as limit its applicability to the realm of public reason.[71] The state, argued Murray, must preserve the mundane common good, that is, the prerequisites of political life or "public order" (justice, public peace, the minima of public morality, and public prosperity), yet lacked the proper competence to pronounce on matters of true religion.[72] In the public order marked by deliberative tolerance, the church must enjoy the liberty to promote her understanding of abstinence and of fidelity in the public realm; but this very liberty is disciplined by the "grammar" of public reason.[73] The ecclesial polity may, that is, adopt an attitude of tolerance regarding practices (of the civic polity) it deprecates but that do not, as such, fall under public, discursive censure.[74] Indeed, where alternative policies would entail a coercive suppression of basic rights, such as forced abortion, sterilization, or China's "one-child" policy, the church has good reason to promote voluntary contraceptive policies, even when such choice embraces artificial contraception.[75]

In a similar vein, there is good reason for promoting an integrated policy of HIV/AIDS prophylaxis that incorporates the use of condoms where alternative, feasible policies fail to protect the basic rights of the most vulnerable.[76] The use of condoms, of course, is far from a panacea—abstinence and fidelity remain morally exigent—and, consistent with compassionate respect, any effective policy must be culturally fitting. And yet to insist solely upon abstinence and fidelity, de facto, leaves vulnerable populations at risk. For just as forced sterilization or abortion deny persons' basic human rights, so a state of affairs in which women and children are involuntarily infected with HIV constitutes a grave violation of such rights.[77]

Under such conditions, the church, I believe, can promote an integrated policy of prophylaxis without abdicating its overriding commitment to fidelity and abstinence.[78] And since such policy is fittingly described in terms of public reasons, neither would promotion of AIDS prophylaxis belie the church's "nonpublic" criticisms of artificial contraception.[79] For though admittedly falling short of the ecclesial ideal, an integrated prophylactic policy is consistent with the basic human rights of the most vulnerable and may well represent, from a consequentially sensitive perspective, the best feasible policy that would preserve such rights.[80]

All things considered, what John Paul II called a "firm and perse-vering determination to commit oneself to the *common good*"[81] makes it morally incumbent upon us to prefer such policies, even as we seek through civil discourse to enlarge the number of viable alternatives.[82] Failing to play the language game of public reason, whether by revert-ing to premodern, perfectionist arguments or by neglecting the inte-gral, mutually implicative character of agents' basic rights, conversely, undermines the church's own "worthy persuasion."[83] Such failures of political imagination, says Farley, engender a "scandal of compromised credibility," exacerbated by intramural practices and policies, such as repression of "internal discourse."

Intramural Politics

In assessing the "consequences of repression and division within the church for its political ministry,"[84] Farley invokes the historic doctrinal developments of Vatican II, comprising notably, in the words of John Courtney Murray, the "principle of doctrinal progress" itself.[85] Inter-pretations of doctrinal development are, of course, vexed.[86] Viewed as a formal, quasi-axiomatic system, doctrine may "develop" inferentially, by showing that novel premises are implied by the cognitive content of prior premises, or casuistically, by subsuming novel cases, for ex-ample, in bioethics, under prior premises or rules. Yet recognition of a right to religious liberty, once abjured in magisterial teaching, falls perspicuously under neither rubric.[87] Indeed, the cognitive content of such a right appears to contradict earlier doctrinal premises, for ex-ample Gregory XVI's 1832 denunciation of religious freedom in *Mirari vos arbitramur* as a "crazed absurdity" (*deliramentum*).[88]

Since introducing such contradictory premises reduces a formal, axiomatic system to semantic nonsense, a richer conception of doc-trine is necessarily required; one that makes sense of the conciliar intent to "develop the doctrine of recent Popes on the inviolable rights of the human person."[89] Far from mere cognitive-propositional itera-tion, such doctrinal development represents a critical rapprochement with the "signs of the times," for example, the nineteenth-century abolitionist movement or the mid-twentieth-century enshrinement of human rights in international law. Here doctrinal coherence is less that of an axiomatic, inferential system than of a complex web of belief in which certain strands, once "taken as dispositive," are revised in light of other beliefs "already part of Christian teaching."[90] Thus just as we relativize Paul's acceptance of slavery in his Letter to Philemon in favor of his kerygmatic affirmation that in Christ "there is neither slave nor free" (Gal 3:28; 1 Cor 12:13), so revising Gregory's teaching rests on a growing experiential recognition of the "canon within the canon,"[91] such as the conciliar affirmation that "a sense of the dignity of the human person has been impressing itself more and more deeply on the consciousness" of contemporary men and women.[92]

Just where such doctrinal development might occur is, of course, no less vexed than the notion of development itself.[93] The Roman magisterium, for instance, denies that recognizing women's moral equality should raise into question its practice of not ordaining women, since the latter would be related to justice only if ordination were "a God-given right of every individual."[94] Yet the inference is hardly probative. For there are many special moral rights, for example, rights conferred through the practice of promising, which are not human rights per se, but which nonetheless derive their force from the fundamental human right to equality of respect and consideration (recognition). Might such special moral rights pertain to ordination? In proposing a "formal, existential ethics," Karl Rahner argues that vocational choices are fittingly described not only in spiritual but also moral terms. One acts in a morally and not merely spiritually responsible manner when one responds as an "*individuum ineffabile*, whom God has called by name, a name which is and can only be unique."[95] Since such moral responsibility presumes one's right to respond, we would regard practices that systemically impede an individual's response to God's election, for example, exclusion of African Americans from priestly ordination, as unjust even if there were no inherent, essential right to ordination.

The juridical determination that the church is not authorized to ordain women thus turns on the positive demonstration that no such formal, existential rights exist (or need be authenticated), since God wills only the ordination of men. And foremost of the reasons offered is "the constant practice of the church [*constantem Ecclesiae usum*]," as interpreted by the "living teaching authority [*vivum magisterium*]."[96] Other theological reasons serve to "illustrate the appropriateness of the divine provision," yet the crux of magisterial teaching is its interpretation of the divine provision itself, in other words, that in her practice of excluding women from priestly ordination, the church faithfully observes "a plan to be ascribed to the wisdom of the Lord of the universe."[97]

As intimated above, women's human rights figure in the hermeneutical criteria invoked to interpret "God's eternal plan." In John Paul II's words, "the nonadmission of women to priestly ordination cannot mean that women are of lesser dignity nor can it be construed as discrimination against them."[98] The Vatican elaborates its interpretation by insisting that "it cannot be forgotten that the church teaches, as an absolutely fundamental truth of Christian anthropology, the equal personal dignity of men and women, and the necessity of overcoming and doing away with 'every type of discrimination regarding fundamental human rights' (GS, 29). It is in the light of this truth that one can seek to understand better the teaching that women cannot receive priestly ordination."[99]

Yet, we have seen, the church's very affirmation of these "fundamental human rights" presumes a revised interpretation of what constitutes her "constant practice." So the theologians' charge—to vindicate the magisterial teaching that the nonadmission of women to priestly ordination is consistent with recognizing their equal dignity—is far from otiose. For only thus would the church's practice cohere with the "absolutely fundamental truth of Christian anthropology." And here, alas, the issue is further vexed, for it would seem that for centuries a notable reason for not admitting women to priestly ordination turned on the contrary premise: the prevailing belief that "women are of lesser dignity," for example, Aquinas's belief in the "natural subjection" of women."[100]

Curiously, the very texts cited under the rubrics of the "The Church's Constant Tradition," in *Inter insigniores* support such a reading.[101] *Inter insigniores* seeks to show that the church fathers not only condemned priestly ministry accorded to women in certain sects but did so in fidelity to "the type of ordained ministry willed by Christ and carefully maintained by the Apostles."[102] As John Wright observes, however, in their criticisms of heretical practices, Irenaeus, Tertullian, and Firmilian fail to address the question of women's ordination per se. And where women's role is broached, Origen's belief that "it is shameful for a woman to speak in church,"[103] or Epiphanius's dismissal of "women's pride and female madness,"[104] would hardly be admitted today. Where priestly ordination is addressed in the *Didascalia apostolorum*, it is "noteworthy that Jesus' way of acting is explained by the supposed natural inferiority of women. Clearly this work does not teach a distinct but equal dignity of men and women; it teaches the natural subjection of women to men."[105]

The postconciliar church, to be sure, resolutely renounced such beliefs and attitudes as morally objectionable and hence contrary to God's plan. As *Inter insigniores* observes, "modern thought . . . *rightly* reject[s]" the "undeniable influence of prejudices unfavorable to women" recurring in the tradition.[106] Aquinas's argument "*quia mulier est in statu subiectionis*," concedes the official commentary, is "scarcely defensible today."[107] So too, John Paul II memorably apologized for ecclesial acquiescence in historical suppression of women's human rights.[108] Yet inasmuch as the influence of such prejudices served de facto to explain or rationalize the reservation of priestly ordination to men, to that degree we must concede that her practice was not constantly faithful to what Christ intended. One observes here the semantic asymmetry of the propositional content of doctrine and practice, for while we may distinguish "doctrinal affirmation" from "the arguments intended to explain it,"[109] practices, precisely as intentional, are differentiated by the reasons that explain them.[110] At the very least, then, the living magisterium cannot appeal to a *constant* practice, if the reasons once explaining it cease to justify it (and a fortiori, if they are repudiated).

We may conclude: if, and to the degree the practice of not ordaining women rested on the prevailing belief in their natural inferiority, to that degree the practice does not cohere with the "obedience of faith" (Rom 1:5, 10:8–10), that is, the "constant tradition" of the church. This, of course, is not a knockdown argument in favor of women's ordination, but it does raise into question certain grounds of magisterial

opposition. For to preserve the coherence of the tradition with respect
to human rights, we must disavow traditional practices that deny them,
for example, refusing ordination to those of African descent or women
because of their supposed natural inferiority.

Must we not, then, as Farley has urged, appeal to the graces of
discernment, that is, of compassionate respect recognizing the "*individuum ineffabile*, whom God has called by name," in resolving the
question?[111] For the very fact that we can exculpate Origen, Ambrose,
or Aquinas—since the recognition of prejudice depends upon the historically contingent "signs of the times"—attests to the vital development of tradition in unfolding ecclesial experience.[112] With the historic
reappraisal of "the part that women are now taking in public life," must
we not rather concede that the question of the suitability of women to
receive priestly ordination is not merely raised anew, but that, *morally*
speaking, it is a new question?[113] As the introductory section of *Inter
insigniores* reminds us, "*Gaudium et spes*, aptly named *The Church in the
Modern World*—gives first place" to its denunciation of "discrimination
based upon sex" as "being contrary to God's plan."[114] "Curiouser and
curiouser," as Alice might say, it is the very development of doctrine,
for example, our *modern* appreciation of women's rights, which permits
us to interpret what is "fitting" with respect to God's *eternal* plan.

These issues are vexed, and my own remarks sorely limited. But
surely how we resolve them will demand our "just and fitting care."
Compassionate respect is, after all, the sine qua non of ecclesial discernment. In the babel of contending voices, we may still seek that
"love of wisdom" that, as Margaret Farley teaches us, is finally the
wisdom of love.

NOTES

1. Margaret A. Farley, *Compassionate Respect: A Feminist Approach to
Medical Ethics and Other Questions* (New York: Paulist Press, 2002).
2. Michael Sandel, "Introduction," in *Liberalism and Its Critics,* ed. Michael Sandel (New York: New York University Press, 1984), 4, 6, 10.

3. Cf. Michael Walzer, *Thick and Thin: Moral Argument at Home and Abroad* (Notre Dame, IN: University of Notre Dame Press, 1994).

4. Margaret A. Farley, "A Feminist Version of Respect for Persons," in *Feminist Ethics and the Catholic Moral Tradition,* Readings in Moral Theology 9, ed. Charles E. Curran, Margaret A. Farley, and Richard A. McCormick, S.J. (New York: Paulist Press, 1996), 165.

5. Margaret A. Farley, "Feminism and Universal Morality," in *Prospects for a Common Morality,* ed. Gene Outka and John P. Reeder (Princeton, NJ: Princeton University Press, 1993), 172–73. Farley adopts Alison M. Jaggar's typology which I follow here; see Alison M. Jaggar, *Feminist Politics and Human Nature* (Totowa, NJ: Rowman and Allanheld, 1983).

6. Farley, "Feminism and Universal Morality," 173.

7. Seyla Benhabib, "The Generalized and the Concrete Other: The Kohlberg-Gilligan Controversy and Feminist Theory," in *Feminism as Critique,* ed. Seyla Benhabib and Drucilla Cornell, (Minneapolis: University of Minnesota Press, 1987), 85.

8. Farley, "A Feminist Version of Respect for Persons," 164–65. Cf. Benhabib, "The Generalized and the Concrete Other," 85–91.

9. See Martha C. Nussbaum, "Emotions and Women's Capabilities," in *Women, Culture, and Development*, ed. Martha C. Nussbaum and Jonathan Glover, 360–95 (Oxford: Clarendon Press, 1995).

10. Farley, "Feminism and Universal Morality," 173.

11. Farley, *Compassionate Respect*, 30.

12. Farley, "Feminism and Universal Morality," 174.

13. Farley, "A Feminist Version of Respect for Persons," 165.

14. Marilyn Friedman, "Feminist and Modern Friendship: Dislocating the Community," in *Explorations in Feminist Ethics: Theory and Practice*, ed. Eve Browning Cole and Susan Coultrap-McQuin (Bloomington: Indiana University Press, 1992), 89; as cited in Farley, "A Feminist Version of Respect for Persons," 171.

15. Farley, "A Feminist Version of Respect for Persons," 171.

16. Ibid. Farley appeals to Iris Young, *Justice and the Politics of Difference* (Princeton, NJ: Princeton University Press, 1990), 12.

17. In the *Groundwork*, Kant distinguishes the form of the moral imperative that prescribes that "[m]axims must be chosen as if they had to hold as universal laws of nature," from the matter that prescribes that "[a] rational being, as by her very nature an end and consequently an end in herself, must serve for every maxim as a condition limiting all merely relative and arbitrary ends." Matter and form are united in a complete determination such that "all maxims as proceeding from our own making of law ought to harmonize with a possible realm of ends as a realm of nature." Immanuel Kant, *Groundwork of the Metaphysic of Morals*, trans. H. J. Paton (New York: Harper

and Row, 1964), 393 [436–37]. See John Rawls, *Lectures on the History of Moral Philosophy*, ed. Barbara Herman (Cambridge, MA: Harvard University Press, 2000), 162–216.

18. Farley, "A Feminist Version of Respect for Persons," 170.

19. Ibid., 170, 181n15. Cf. Immanuel Kant, *The Doctrine of Virtue*, part 2, *The Metaphysics of Morals*, trans. Mary J. McGregor (New York: Harper and Row, 1964) 141 [469].

20. Farley, "A Feminist Version of Respect for Persons,"170.

21. See George Herbert Mead, *Mind, Self, and Society from the Standpoint of a Social Behaviorist*, ed. Charles W. Morris (Chicago: University of Chicago Press, 1962), 152–64, 379–89. Cf. Benhabib, "The Generalized and the Concrete Other," 87.

22. Søren Kierkegaard, *Works of Love,* trans. Howard and Edna Hong (New York: Harper and Brothers, 1962), 10.

23. See Benhabib's criticism of "*substitutionalist* universality" as "the ideal consensus of fictitiously defined selves," in favor of an *interactive* universalism as "the concrete process in politics and morals of the struggle of concrete, embodied selves, striving for autonomy"; "The Generalized and the Concrete Other," 81 (italics in original).

24. Charles Taylor, *Hegel and Modern Society* (Cambridge: Cambridge University Press, 1970), 167–69; as cited by Farley in "A Feminist Version of Respect for Persons," 183n34.

25. Farley, "A Feminist Version of Respect for Persons," 179.

26. Walter Benjamin, *Origin of German Tragic Drama* (London: NLB, 1977), 166.

27. Farley, *Compassionate Respect*, 61, 80.

28. Ibid., 61; see Aristotle, *Rhetoric* 1385–86, *Nichomachean Ethics* 1106b.

29. Farley, *Compassionate Respect*, 81.

30. Margaret A. Farley, "The Church in the Public Forum: Scandal or Prophetic Witness," in *Catholic Theological Society of America Proceedings* 55 (2000): 87–101.

31. Cf. John Rawls, *Political Liberalism* (New York: Columbia University Press, 1993), 9–11, 212–54; and "The Idea of Public Reason Revisited," in *The Law of Peoples* (Cambridge, MA: Harvard University, 1999), 129–80.

32. Benjamin Constant, *"De la liberté des anciens comparée à celle des modernes,"* in *Oeuvres Politiques de Benjamin Constant*, ed. C. Louandre (Paris: Charpentier, 1874). I have developed these themes at greater length in William O'Neill, "Babel's Children: Reconstructing the Common Good," *The Annual of the Society of Christian Ethics* 18 (1998): 161–76.

33. J. S. Mill, *On Liberty,* ed. Gertrude Himmelfarb (New York: Penguin Books, 1974), 72.

34. Robert Nozick, *Anarchy, State, and Utopia* (Oxford: Basil Blackwell, 1974), 238.

35. John Rawls, *A Theory of Justice* (Cambridge, MA: The Belknap Press of Harvard University Press, 1971), 587, 505n30; and *Political Liberalism*, 13–14.

36. See Hans-Georg Gadamer, *Truth and Method*, 2nd rev. ed., trans. Joel Weinsheimer and Donald Marshall (New York: The Crossroad Publishing Company, 1991), 270.

37. Cf. Hegel's criticism of Kantian *Moralität* in the *Philosophy of Right*: *Hegel's Philosophy of Right*, trans. T. M. Knox (Oxford: Oxford University Press, 1952), par. 135.

38. Edmund Burke, *Reflections on the Revolution in France, 1700*, in *Works*, vol. 2 (Bohn's British Classics, London, 1872), 305–6, 412; cf., Burleigh Taylor Wilkins, *The Problem of Burke's Political Philosophy* (Oxford: Clarendon Press, 1967), 59–60, 109–10.

39. Sandel, "Introduction," 4, 6, 10; cf. Michael Sandel, *Liberalism and the Limits of Justice* (Cambridge: Cambridge University, 1982); Alasdair MacIntyre, *After Virtue*, 2nd ed. (Notre Dame, IN: University of Notre Dame Press, 1984), 204–43.

40. Richard Rorty, "The Priority of Democracy to Philosophy," in *The Virginia Statute for Religious Freedom: Its Evolution and Consequences in American History*, ed. Merrill D. Peterson and Robert C. Vaughn (New York/Cambridge: Cambridge University Press, 1988), 259.

41. Ibid.

42. Michael Walzer, *Spheres of Justice: A Defense of Pluralism and Equality* (New York: Basic Books, 1983), 31. Cf. Michael Walzer, "The Moral Standing of States," *Philosophy and Public Affairs* 9 (1980): 209–29; Michael Walzer, "Nation and Universe," in *The Tanner Lectures on Human Values XI* (Salt Lake City: University of Utah, 1990).

43. *Mater et magistra*, no. 65.

44. Cf. *Pacem in terris*, nos. 53–66, 132–41; *Gaudium et spes*, nos. 25–30; *Dignitatis humanae*, nos. 6–7; *Populorum progressio*, nos. 22–24, 43–75; *Sollicitudo rei socialis*, nos. 38–40. See David Hollenbach, *The Common Good and Christian Ethics* (Cambridge: Cambridge University Press, 2002); Charles Curran, *Catholic Social Teaching: A Historical, Theological, and Ethical Analysis* (Washington, DC: Georgetown University, 2002).

45. *Pacem in terris*, no. 60. The statement continues: "The chief concern of civil authorities must therefore be to ensure that these rights are acknowledged, respected, coordinated with other rights, defended and promoted, so that in this way each one may more easily carry out his duties. For 'to safeguard the inviolable rights of the human person, and to facilitate the fulfillment of his duties, should be the chief duty of every public

authority.'" Such a rights-based interpretation permits Pope John to extend the common good globally in *Pacem in terris*, no. 139. See Radio Message of Pius XII, Pentecost, June 1, 1941, *Acta Apostolicae Sedis* XX–XIII, 1941, 200; cf. *Gaudium et spes*, no. 26, and *Dignitatis humanae*, no. 6.

46. Farley contends that "feminism is searching for a more adequate theory of differences and a more integrative theory of universal norms"; Farley, "Feminism and Universal Morality," 181.

47. Ibid., 180.

48. Farley, *Compassionate Respect*, 39.

49. Ibid., 38. Cf. also Farley's integral account of "just love" in *Personal Commitments: Beginning, Keeping, Changing* (San Francisco: Harper and Row, 1986), 80–109.

50. See the refined understanding of needs, capabilities, and functioning as defining the moral minima of agency in the analyses of Amartya Sen, "Gender Inequality and Theories of Justice," and Martha C. Nussbaum, "Human Capabilities, Female Human Beings" and "Emotions and Women's Capabilities," in Nussbaum and Glover, *Women, Culture, and Development*, 259–73, 61–115, and 360–95 respectively.

51. Embodied agency thus both grounds *general* claim rights, e.g., to nutrition, and *specifies* the conditions of their application, e.g., the nutritional needs of pregnant women. In John Paul II's theology of the body, sexual (gender) complementarity likewise grounds *special rights* and duties deriving from the particular "dignity of women and their vocation." In accordance with Roman Catholic social teaching, however, women's general human rights to equality of respect and consideration would necessarily assume lexical priority. John Paul II, *The Theology of the Body: Human Love in the Divine Plan* (Boston: Pauline Books, 1997), 483–88. Cf. Charles E. Curran, *The Moral Theology of Pope John Paul II* (Washington, DC: Georgetown University Press, 2005), 187–95.

52. Mercy Amba Oduyoye, *Daughters of Anowa: African Women and Patriarchy* (Maryknoll, NY: Orbis, 1995), 210. "As African women, Akan and Yoruba," writes Oduyoye, "we work to shape our new world. Like our weaving our beadwork, we bring it into being as we create new patterns of life based on the old."

53. Farley, "Feminism and Universal Morality," 176.

54. The mutual learning to which I referred above is illustrated by John Courtney Murray's recognition of doctrinal development: The council's achievement in *Dignitatis humanae*, says Murray, "was to bring the Church, at long last, abreast of the consciousness of civilized mankind, which had already accepted religious freedom as a principle and as a legal institution"; John Courtney Murray, "The Declaration on Religious Freedom: Its Deeper Significance," *America* 114 (April 23, 1966): 592. Rawls cites

Murray approvingly in "The Idea of Public Reason Revisited," 166n75, 170n83.

55. *Pacem in terris,* nos. 28–33, 60–65.

56. See Jürgen Habermas, *Moral Consciousness and Communicative Action,* trans. Christian Lenhardt and Shierry Weber Nicholsen (Cambridge: The MIT Press, 1990), 43–115.

57. *Dignitatis humanae,* nos. 7, 4. See John Courtney Murray, "The Declaration of Religious Freedom: A Moment in Its Legislative History," in *Religious Liberty: An End and a Beginning,* ed. John Courtney Murray (New York: Macmillan, 1966).

58. A rights regime will be integral if it reflects the relative priority or weight of rights claims (negative *and* positive) in relation both to other rights and non-rights claims; it will be comprehensive if it preserves and protects all pertinent claim rights.

59. See Nozick, *Anarchy, State, and Utopia,* 28–35.

60. In the culturally fitting embodiment of a rights regime, teleological considerations recur, not in the perfection of discrete acts, but rather in the comparative assessment of policies.

61. Sen favors "incorporating the value of right fulfilment and the disvalue of right violation in the assessment of resulting states of affairs"; yet policies that directly deny basic rights or indirectly condone such denial, must, I believe, be treated as limit cases. Even if certain rights violations are subject to a "consequence-sensitive deontological assessment," abetting torture would never be permissible. See Amartya Sen, *On Ethics and Economics* (Oxford: Basil Blackwell, 1987), 73, cf. 47–51, 70–78.

62. Cf. Amartya Sen, *Development as Freedom* (New York: Alfred A. Knopf, 1999), 221–23.

63. Cf. Paul VI, *Populorum progressio,* no. 37; John Paul II, "Population Conference Draft Document Criticized," *Origins* 23, no. 41 (March 31, 1994): 716–19.

64. John Paul II, *Evangelium vitae,* no. 13.

65. See Farley, "Church in the Public Forum," 99. The question presumes that the forms of artificial contraception are culturally appropriate and not abortifacient.

66. Karl Rahner, "On the Encyclical *Humanae Vitae,*" *Theological Investigations,* vol. 11, trans. David Bourke (New York: Seabury, 1974), 263–87, at 266. For an illuminating criticism of the implications of the "global instinct" of faith, see John Mahoney, *The Making of Moral Theology: A Study of the Roman Catholic Tradition* (Oxford: Clarendon Press, 1987), 259–301.

67. Whether artificial contraception is properly described as "intrinsically evil" is much contested in Catholic moral theology. See Mahoney, *The Making of Moral Theology,* 259–301. Cf. Germain Grisez, *Contraception*

and the Natural Law (Milwaukee: The Bruce Publishing Company, 1964); Charles E. Curran and Richard A. McCormick, eds., *Dissent in the Church, Readings in Moral Theology 6* (New York: Paulist Press, 1988); Charles E. Curran and Richard A. McCormick, eds., *Natural Law and Theology,* Readings in Moral Theology 7 (New York: Paulist Press, 1991).

68. Cf. Paul VI's admonition to priestly obedience as exemplary for all in *Humanae vitae,* no. 28: "You know that you are bound to such obedience not more on account of the arguments proposed than on account of the light of the Holy Spirit enjoyed especially by the Pastors of the Church in expounding the truth."

69. See John Courtney Murray, *The Problem of Religious Freedom* (Westminster, MD: Newman Press, 1965), 28–30. Public reason may appeal not only to rights' rhetoric but also to cognate civic virtues, for example, justice, toleration, and prudence. Conversely, the arguments amenable to public reason in determining civic policy are but a subset of those subject to natural law (cf. Thomas Aquinas, *Summae Theologiae* I-II, ques. 96, arts. 2 and 3).

70. *Humanae vitae,* nos. 13ff.

71. Cf. Thomas Aquinas, *Summae Theologiae* I-II, ques. 96, art. 3: "[H]uman law does not prescribe concerning all the acts of every virtue: but only in regard to those that are ordainable to the common good— either immediately, as when certain things are done directly for the common good,—or mediately, as when a lawgiver prescribes certain things pertaining to good order, whereby the citizens are directed in the upholding of the common good of justice and peace."

72. See Murray, *The Problem of Religious Freedom,* 30; David Hollenbach, *Justice, Peace, and Human Rights: American Catholic Social Ethics in a Pluralistic Context* (New York: Crossroad, 1988), 101–7. Murray argued that decriminalization of birth-control statutes is "permissible and even advisable on grounds of a valid and traditional theory of law and jurisprudence." Cf. John Courtney Murray, "Memo to Cardinal Cushing concerning Contraception Legislation," in *Bridging the Sacred and the Secular: Selected Writings of John Courtney Murray, S.J.,* ed. Leon Hooper, 81–86 (Washington, DC; Georgetown University Press, 1994), 83.

73. Rawls concedes "that the Catholic Church's nonpublic reason requires its members to follow its doctrine is perfectly consistent with their also honoring public reason." Rawls likens his view to that of Murray "in regard to contraception"; Rawls, "The Idea of Public Reason Revisited," 170n83.

74. For ecclesial precedent, see John T. Noonan, *Contraception: A History of Its Treatment by the Catholic Theologians and Canonists* (Cambridge, MA: The Belknap Press of Harvard University, 1986), 400–405.

75. Traditional casuistry distinguishes formal (intentional) and material cooperation in another's wrongdoing. In our inquiry, it is precisely the external character of the preference that renders support of such public policy a form of material and mediate rather than formal cooperation. Cf. James Keenan, "Cooperation, Principle of" in *The New Dictionary of Catholic Social Thought,* 232–35; Cathleen Kaveny, "Appropriation of Evil: Cooperation's Mirror Image," *Theological Studies* 61 (2000): 280–313. It is consistent with the foregoing to allow for a "conscience clause" exempting the church from immediate cooperation in implementing public policy.

76. See Jon Fuller and James Keenan, "Introduction: At the End of the First Generation of HIV Prevention," in *Catholic Ethicists on HIV/AIDS Prevention,* ed. James F. Keenan et al. (New York: The Continuum Publishing Company, 2000), 21–29. The church's "option for the poor," as a primary expression of *recognizing* the conditions of preserving equal *respect,* underscores the primacy of the basic rights of the most vulnerable.

77. As Lisa Cahill observes, "Among the poor, women are the most poor, both materially and socially. Without transformation of the equal power relations that exist between the sexes in virtually every culture of the world, 'women will continue to be preferential targets of HIV infection and will be unable to guarantee their own safety.' In many cases women lack sexual self-determination both before and after marriage. This means that they have little choice of sexual partners, no say in the sexual practices of husbands, and no freedom to refuse sex even to a spouse who is infected. In some cases, women and girls are forced into prostitution. In many cases, women who develop AIDS are abandoned or cast out, whether they are prostitutes, concubines, or wives. Needless to say, children of these women often meet a similar fate"; Lisa Sowle Cahill, "AIDS, Justice, and the Common Good," in Keenan, *Catholic Ethicists on HIV/AIDS Prevention,* 283.

78. See James Keenan, "Applying the Seventeenth-Century Casuistry of Accommodation to HIV Prevention," *Theological Studies* 60 (1999): 492–512.

79. Criticisms of artificial contraception are not bracketed in public reasoning. Rather, inasmuch as such criticisms fail to persuade, it is public reasoning itself that shows their restricted logical force.

80. Policies approving the use of artificial, nonabortificient contraception or the use of condoms in HIV/AIDS prophylaxis differ from permissive abortion policies. Even here, however, John Paul II allowed for the limited licitness of supporting abortion legislation "in cases where a legislative vote would be decisive for the passage a more restrictive law, aimed at limiting the number of authorized abortions, in place of a more permissive law already passed or ready to be voted on"; *Evangelium vitae,* no. 73.

81. John Paul II, *Sollicitudo rei socialis,* no. 38, cf. no. 25 (emphasis added).

82. John Paul's personalist theology of mutual self-donation would seem to support such a conclusion, inasmuch as the use of condoms is not intended as contraceptive but rather as an expression of due respect for the seronegative spouse's basic well-being, in other words, the "dignity of personal communion." Indeed, the transmission of HIV would be profoundly contrary to both the "unitive" and "procreative aspect" of "the conjugal act." See John Paul II, *Theology of the Body*, 398.

83. See *Dignitatis humanae*, no. 4.

84. Farley, "Church in the Public Forum," 98.

85. John Courtney Murray, "Freedom in the Age of Renewal," in Hooper, *Bridging the Sacred and the Secular*, 185, as cited in Farley, "Church in the Public Forum," 98.

86. George Lindbeck, *The Nature of Doctrine: Religion and Theology in a Postliberal Age* (Philadelphia: Westminster, 1984).

87. "For a period of over 1,200 years," writes John Noonan, "during much of which the Catholic Church was dominant in Europe, popes, bishops, theologians regularly and unanimously denied the religious liberty of heretics; no theologian taught that faith may be freely repudiated without physical consequences, no pope extended the mantle of charitable tolerance to those who departed from orthodox belief. On the contrary, it was universally taught that the duty of a good ruler was to extirpate not only heresy but heretics"; John T. Noonan, "Development in Moral Doctrine," *Theological Studies* 54 (1993): 667. Noonan cites Lucius III, *Ad abolendam* (*Decretales Gregorii* IX, 5.7.9.). Cf. John T. Noonan, *A Church That Can and Cannot Change* (Notre Dame, IN: University of Notre Dame Press, 2005), 154–58.

88. Gregory XVI, *Mirari vos arbitramur*, in H. Denzinger and A. Schönmetzer, *Enchiridion symbolorum*, 32nd ed, no. 2730. See David Hollenbach's commentary in his *Justice, Peace, and Human Rights*, 101–7.

89. *Dignitatis humanae*, no. 1.

90. Noonan, "Development in Moral Doctrine," 669. Cf. Noonan, *A Church That Can and Cannot Change*, 17–123.

91. Here, perhaps, we might speak of the "depth grammar" of the "obedience of faith" (*hypakoē pisteōs*; Rom 1:5, 10:8–10). See Ludwig Wittgenstein, *Philosophical Investigations,* 3rd ed., trans. G. E. M. Anscombe (New York: Macmillan Publishing Co., 1958), pt. 1, pars. 497, 664.

92. *Dignitatis humanae*, no. 1.

93. Francis Sullivan, for instance, touches on the ambivalence attending nondefinitive declarations of definitive doctrine. See his "Recent Theological Observations on Magisterial Documents and Public Dissent," *Theological Studies* 58 (1997): 509–15; cf. his "Reply to Lawrence J. Welch," *Theological Studies* 64 (2003): 610–15, and *Creative Fidelity: Weighing and Interpreting Documents of the Magisterium* (New York: Paulist Press, 1992), 93–108.

94. Congregation for the Doctrine of the Faith "A Commentary on the Declaration ['*Inter insignioris*']" in *From "Inter Insigniores"* to *"Ordinatio Sacerdotalis: Documents and Commentaries* (Washington, DC: United States Catholic Conference, 1998), 76.

95. Karl Rahner, "On the Question of a Formal Existential Ethics," in *Theological Investigations,* vol. 2, trans. Karl H. Kruger (Baltimore: Helicon, 1963), 226–27.

96. John Paul II, *Ordinatio sacerdotalis,* no. 1, in *From "Inter Insigniores"* to *"Ordinatio Sacerdotalis,"* 185. John Paul II cites Paul VI's response to the letter of Rev. Dr. F. D. Coggan, Archbishop of Canterbury, concerning the ordination of women to the priesthood (Nov. 30, 1975): *Acta Apostolicae Sedis* 68 (1976), 599.

97. John Paul II, *Ordinatio sacerdotalis,* nos. 2–3. The Congregation for the Doctrine of the Faith's commentary on "*Inter insigniores*" speaks of the "constant and universal practice of the Church"; "A Commentary on the Declaration," 59.

98. Ibid., no. 3. Cf. The Congregation for the Doctrine of the Faith, "Letter to the Bishops of the Catholic Church on the Collaboration of Men and Women in the Church and in the World" (May 31, 2004), no. 16.

99. "Vatican Reflections on the Teaching of '*Ordinatio sacerdotalis*'," *Origins* 25, no. 24 (1995): 404.

100. See Thomas Aquinas, *Commentary on the Sentences,* book 4, 25, ques. 2, art. 1. Cf. Aquinas, *Summa theologiae* Supplement, ques. 39, art. 1.

101. Congregation for the Doctrine of the Faith, "*Inter insigniores,*" in *From "Inter Insigniores"* to *"Ordinatio Sacerdotalis,"* 25–27.

102. Ibid., 27. See, however, Gary Macy, "The Ordination of Women in the Early Middle Ages," *Theological Studies* 61 (2000): 481–507. Macy concludes, "For over 1200 years then the question of the validity of women's ordination remained at least an open question. Some popes, bishops, and scholars accepted such ordinations as equal to those of men; others did not" (500).

103. Origen, "*Fragmentum* in 1 Cor. 74," *Journal of Theological Studies* 10 (1908): 41–42.

104. *The* Panarion *of Epiphanius of Salamis,* 3 vols. in 2, trans. Frank Williams (New York: Brill, 1987), 2.623.

105. John H. Wright, S.J., "Patristic Testimony on Women's Ordination in *Inter insigniores,*" *Theological Studies* 58 (1997): 524. Wright concludes, "what does emerge from much of the patristic evidence cited by the CDF [Congregation for the Doctrine of the Faith] is the conviction that women by nature, temperament, and social status are inferior to men. For this reason they cannot be ordained priests. Even the practice and intention of Jesus are set within the context of this inferiority" (526).

106. Congregation for the Doctrine of the Faith, "*Inter insigniores*," 25 (emphasis added).

107. Congregation for the Doctrine of the Faith, "A Commentary on the Declaration," 59.

108. See John Paul II, "Service Requesting Pardon," *Origins* 29, no. 40 (2000): 640.

109. Congregation for the Doctrine of the Faith, "A Commentary on the Declaration," 70.

110. "The function of 'intentional' in my 'intention to perform "A"' is syncategorematic, generating action descriptions in terms of their reasons"; Donald Davidson, *Essays on Actions and Events* (Oxford: Clarendon Press, 1980), 8.

111. See Margaret Farley's moral assessment of *Inter insigniores* in her "Discrimination or Equality? The Old Order of the New," in *Women Priests: A Catholic Commentary on the Vatican Declaration*, ed. by Leonard Swidler and Arlene Swidler, 310–15 (New York: Paulist Press, 1977).

112. See John T. Noonan, "Experience and the Development of Doctrine," *Catholic Theological Society of America Proceedings* 54 (1999): 43–56. Cf. Noonan, *A Church That Can and Cannot Change*, 193–222. Noonan concludes by citing "the teaching of Paul to the Philippians": "Love must 'abound' in order to 'test what is vital' (Phil 1:9–10). Love accomplishes this task by abounding 'in knowledge and insight of every kind', that is, by empathetic identification with the other" (215).

113. Congregation for the Doctrine of the Faith, *Inter insigniores*, 21; cf. 24–25 where it is acknowledged that "we are dealing with a debate which classical theology scarcely touched upon."

114. Ibid., 21.

Selected Publications of Margaret A. Farley

1966

A Metaphysics of Being and God, coauthored with J. V. McGlynn. Englewood Cliffs, NJ: Prentice-Hall, 1966.

1974

"Liberation, Abortion, and Responsibility." *Reflection* 71 (May 1974): 9–13. Reprinted in *Inside* 6 (March–April 1975): 32–35, and in *On Moral Medicine*, ed. S. Lammers and A. Verhey, 434–38. Grand Rapids, MI: Eerdmans, 1987.

"Welfare Rights and the Civil Rights Tradition." In *Perspectives on Poverty*, by Connecticut League of Women Voters, 1974 (pamphlet).

1975

"Commitment in a Changing World," coauthored with D. Gottemoeller. *Review for Religious* 34 (November 1975): 846–67.

"Divorce and Remarriage." *Proceedings of the Catholic Theological Society of America* 30 (1975): 111–19.

"Justice and the Role of Women in the Church: Thirteen Theses." *Origins* 4 (June 1975): 89–91. Reprinted in *New Visions, New Roles: Women in the Church*, ed. L. A. Quinonez, 35–39. Washington, DC: Leadership Conference of Women Religious, 1975.

"New Patterns of Relationship: Beginnings of a Moral Revolution." *Theological Studies* 36 (December 1975): 627–46. Reprinted in *Women:*

New Dimensions, ed. Walter Burghardt, 51–70. New York: Paulist Press, 1976.

"Response to Doctor Duff." *Reflection* 72 (January 1975): 11–13.

"Testimony: Right to Health Care." In *National Health Insurance, Public Hearings Subcommittee on Health of the Committee on Ways and Means of the House of Representatives*, 680–84. Washington, DC: U.S. Government Printing Office, 1975. Reprinted in *Network Quarterly* 3 (Fall 1975): 1–4.

1976
"Ministry: Homeless and Ordained." *Reflection* 74 (November 1976): 12–13.

"Moral Imperatives for the Ordination of Women." In *Women and Catholic Priesthood: An Expanded Vision*, ed. A. M. Gardiner, 58–61. New York: Paulist Press, 1976.

"Sources of Sexual Inequality in the History of Christian Thought." *Journal of Religion* 56 (April 1976): 162–76.

Editor and principal author of *The Status and Roles of Women: Another Perspective*. Washington, DC: Leadership Conference of Women Religious, 1976.

1977
"Discrimination or Equality: The Old Order or the New?" In *Women Priests: Catholic Commentary on the Vatican Declaration,* ed. Leonard Swidler and Arlene Swidler, 310–15. New York: Paulist Press, 1977.

"Vatican Makes Symbols Absolute." *National Catholic Reporter* 13 (April 1, 1977): 9.

1978
"The Church as Christ Living in the World: What Needs Must be Ministered to Today?" In *Ministering in a Servant Church*, ed. F. A. Eigo, 73–98. Villanova, PA: Villanova University Press, 1978.

"Fragments for an Ethic of Commitment in Thomas Aquinas." *Celebrating the Medieval Heritage*, ed. David Tracy, *Journal of Religion* 58 (Supplement 1978): 40–45.

"Sexual Ethics." In *Encyclopedia of Bioethics*, 4:1575–88. New York: Free Press, 1978.

1979

"Beyond the Formal Principle: A Reply to Ramsey and Saliers." *Journal of Religious Ethics* 7 (Fall 1979): 191–202.

"Sexism." In *The New Catholic Encyclopedia*, Supplement. Washington, DC: Catholic University Press of America, 1979.

1981

"Testing the Vision," coauthored with Francine Cardman. *Network Quarterly* 9 (January–February 1981): 19–29.

Review essay of Alan Donagan, *The Theory of Morality*. *Religious Studies Review* 7 (July 1981): 233–37.

1982

"Nothing is Impossible with God." *Reflection* 79 (January 1982): 3–5.

"Power and Powerlessness: A Case in Point." *Proceedings of the Catholic Theological Society of America* 37 (1982): 116–19.

"Weep for Yourselves and for Your Children." *Criterion* 21 (Winter 1982): 19–21.

1983

"The Church and the Family: An Ethical Task." *Horizons* 10 (Spring 1983): 50–71.

"An Ethic for Same-Sex Relations." In *A Challenge to Love: Gay and Lesbian Catholics in the Church,* ed. Robert Nugent, 93–106. New York: Crossroad, 1983.

1984

Canonical Regulation of Women's Religious Communities: Its Past and Its Future. Religious Sisters of Mercy of the Union, 1984. Manuscript, Mary Austin Carroll Collection #479. Avila University, Kansas City, MO.

"Feminist Ethics in the Christian Ethics Curriculum." *Horizons* 11 (Fall 1984): 65–76.

"Institutional Ethics Committees as Advocates of Social Justice." *Health Progress* 65 (October 1984): 32–35.

"When are Third Trimester Pregnancy Terminations Morally Justifiable?" coauthored with Frank A. Chervenak, LeRoy Walters, John Hobbins, and Maurice Mahoney. *New England Journal of Medicine* 310 (February 23, 1984): 501–4.

1985

"Feminist Consciousness and the Interpretation of Scripture." In *Feminist Interpretation of the Bible*, ed. Letty Russell, 41–51. Philadelphia: Westminster Press, 1985.

"Feminist Theology and Issues in Bioethics." In *Theology and Bioethics*, ed. E. Shelp, 163–85. Boston: D. Reidel. Reprinted revised version in *Women's Consciousness, Women's Conscience,* ed. Barbara Hilkert Andolsen, Christine Gudorf, and Mary D. Pellauer, 285–305. Minneapolis: Winston Press, 1985. And in *Feminist Theological Ethics: A Reader*, ed. L. Daly, 192–212. Louisville, KY: Westminster John Knox, 1994.

1986

"Feminist Ethics." In *The Westminster Dictionary of Christian Ethics*, ed. James Childress and John Macquarrie, 229–31. Philadelphia: Westminster Press, 1986.

"From Moral Insight to Moral Choice: The Problem of Conflicting Obligations." *Reflections* 83 (Fall 1986): 1–4.

Personal Commitments: Beginning, Keeping, Changing. San Francisco: Harper and Row, 1986.

1987

"Moral Discourse in the Public Arena." In *Vatican Authority and American Catholic Dissent*, ed. William W. May, 168–86. New York: Crossroad, 1987.

1988

"Author's Response" to symposium review of *Personal Commitments. Horizons* 15 (Spring 1988): 133–40.

1990

"Divorce and Remarriage: A Moral Perspective." In *Divorce and Remarriage: Religious and Psychological Perspectives*, ed. William P. Roberts, 107–27. Kansas City, MO: Sheed and Ward, 1990.

"Divorce, Remarriage, and Pastoral Practice." *Moral Theology: Challenges for the Future*, ed. Charles E. Curran, 213–39. New York: Paulist Press, 1990.

Report of the Catholic Theological Society of America on the Profession of Faith and the Oath of Fidelity, coauthored with M. Buckley, J. Ford, W. Principe, and J. Provost. Washington, DC: Catholic Theological Society of America, 1990.

1991

"Love, Justice, and Discernment: An Interview with Margaret A. Farley." *Second Opinion* 17 (October 1991): 80–91.

"A New Form of Communion: Feminism and the Chinese Church." *America* 164 (February 23, 1991): 199–204. Reprinted in *In God's Image* 10 (Autumn 1991): 46–52.

"Response to Martin Marty on Civic Virtue." *Religious Education* 86 (Fall 1991): 528–31.

1992

"The Concept of Commitment as Applied to Questions of Marriage and Divorce." *Proceedings of the Canon Law Society of America* 54 (1992): 87–97.

"Ethical Dimensions of Informed Consent." American College of Obstetricians and Gynecologists committee opinion, May 1992. Also in *ACOG Newsletter* (April 1992).

"Forms of Faith." *The Living Pulpit* 1 (April/June 1992): 4–5.

"One Thing Only Is Necessary." *The MAST Journal* 2 (Summer 1992): 17–23.

1993
"Feminism and Universal Morality." In *Prospects for a Common Morality*, ed. G. Outka and J. Reeder, 170–90. Princeton, NJ: Princeton University Press, 1993.

"A Feminist Version of Respect for Persons." *Journal of Feminist Studies in Religion* 9 (Spring/Fall 1993): 182–98.

1994
"Family." In *The New Dictionary of Catholic Social Thought*, ed. Judith A. Dwyer, 371–81. Collegeville, MN: The Liturgical Press, 1994.

"How Shall We Love in a Postmodern World?" *The Annual of the Society of Christian Ethics* 14 (1994): 3–19.

"Pre-embryo Research: History, Scientific Background, and Ethical Considerations," coauthored with R. Cefalo, completed in ethics committee, American College of Obstetricians and Gynecologists. American College of Obstetricians and Gynecologists committee opinion, April 1994.

1995
Embodiment, Morality, and Medicine, coedited with Lisa Sowle Cahill. Boston: Kluwer Academic Publishing, 1995.

"Ethical and Religious Responses to Intellectual Disabilities." United Nations document, 1995.

Issues in Contemporary Christian Ethics: The Choice of Death in a Medical Context. The Santa Clara Lectures. Santa Clara, CA: University of Santa Clara Publications, 1995.

"Sexual Ethics." In *Encyclopedia of Bioethics,* rev. ed., 5:2363–75. New York: Simon and Schuster Macmillan, 1995.

1996

"Afterword and Retrospective." In Christopher F. Mooney, *Theology and Scientific Knowledge*, 219–26. Notre Dame, IN: University of Notre Dame Press, 1996.

"Ethics and Moral Theology." In *Dictionary of Feminist Theologies*, ed. L. Russell and S. Clarkson. Louisville, KY: Westminster John Knox, 1996.

Feminist Ethics and the Catholic Moral Tradition, Readings in Moral Theology 9, coedited with Charles A. Curran and Richard A. McCormick. New York: Paulist Press, 1996.

"Relationships." In *Dictionary of Feminist Theologies*, ed. L. Russell and S. Clarkson. Louisville, KY: Westminster John Knox, 1996.

"The Role of Experience in Moral Discernment." In *Christian Ethics: Problems and Prospects*, ed. L. Cahill and J. Childress, 134–51. Cleveland: Pilgrim Press, 1996.

1997

Tradition and the Ordination of Women, coauthored with Jon Nilson et al. Catholic Theological Society of America, 1997. Report of task force presented at the annual meeting of the Catholic Theological Society of America, June 5, 1997, Minneapolis. Available at http://ncronline.org/NCR_Online/documents/ctsa2.htm (last accessed May 2007).

1998

"Freedom and Desire." In *The Papers of the Henry Luce III Fellows in Theology*, vol. 3, ed. Matthew Zyniewicz. Atlanta: Scholars Press, 1998.

"History, Spirituality, and Justice." *Theology Digest* 45 (Winter 1998): 329–36.

"No One Goes Away Hungry From the Table of the Lord." Sermon published in *Spectrum* 18 (Fall 1998): 12–13.

"Response to James Hanigan and Charles Curran." In *Sexual Orientation and Human Rights in American Religious Discourse*, ed. Saul M. Olyan and Martha C. Nussbaum, 101–9. New York: Oxford University Press, 1998.

"Selecting Your Baby's Sex: Beware of Social Abuses." *New York Daily News*, October 11, 1998, 59.

1999

"Diversity and Community." *The MAST Journal* 9 (Spring 1999): 12–18.

"Feminist Theology and Ethics: The Contributions of Elizabeth A. Johnson." In *Things New and Old: Essays on the Theology of Elizabeth A. Johnson*, ed. Terrence Tilley and Phyllis Zagano, 1–19. New York: Crossroad, 1999.

Liberating Eschatology: Essays in Honor of Letty M. Russell, coedited with Serene Jones. Louisville, KY: Westminister John Knox, 1999.

"No One Goes Away Hungry from the Table of the Lord: Eucharistic Sharing in Ecumenical Contexts." In *Practice What You Preach: Virtues, Ethics, and Power in the Lives of Pastoral Ministers and Their Congregations*, ed. James F. Keenan and Joseph Kotva, 186–201. Franklin, WI: Sheed and Ward, 1999.

"This World and Another." Sermon, Feast of All Saints. *Berkeley at Yale* (Summer 2000): 12–13.

2000

"The Church in the Public Forum: Scandal or Prophetic Witness?" *Proceedings of the Catholic Theological Society of America* 55 (2000): 87–101.

"Postmortem Sperm Retrieval for Assisted Reproduction." *ASRM News* 34 (Summer 2000): 15–16.

2001

"Marriage, Divorce, and Personal Commitments." In *Celebrating Christian Marriage,* ed. Andrian Thatcher, 355–72. New York: T & T Clark, 2001.

"Roman Catholic Views on Research Involving Human Embryonic Cells." In *The Human Embryonic Cell Debate: Science, Ethics, and Public Policy*, ed. Suzanne Holland, Karen Lebacqz, and Laurie Zoloth, 113–18. Cambridge, MA: The MIT Press, 2001.

2002

Compassionate Respect: A Feminist Approach to Medical Ethics and Other Questions. New York: Paulist Press, 2002.

"Ethics, Ecclesiology, and the Grace of Self-Doubt." In *A Call to Fidelity: On the Moral Theology of Charles E. Curran*, ed. James J. Walter, Timothy E. O'Connell, and Thomas A. Shannon, 55–75. Washington, DC: Georgetown University Press, 2002.

"Religious Meaning for Nature and Humanity." In *The Good in Nature and Humanity*, ed. Stephen Kellert and Timothy Farnham, 103–12. Washington, DC: Island Press, 2002.

2003

"Feminism and Hope." In *Full of Hope: Critical Social Perspectives on Theology*, ed. Magdala Thompson, 20–40. New York: Paulist Press, 2003.

2004

"Partnerships in Hope: Gender, Faith, and Responses to HIV/AIDS in Africa." *Journal of Feminist Studies in Religion* 20 (Spring 2004): 133–48.

2005

"Agenda for Women in the Church of the Saints." *The MAST Journal* 15, no. 2 (2005): 3–10.

"HIV/AIDS and Our Journey in Faith." *The MAST Journal* 15, no. 1 (2005): 14–19.

2006

Just Love: A Framework for Christian Sexual Ethics. New York: Continuum, 2006.

Work Forthcoming or in Progress
The Experience of Free Choice.

"Religious Considerations in Stem Cell Research." In *Handbook of Embryonic Stem Cells*, ed. R. Lanza et. al. Elsevier/Academic Press.

Contributors

Lisa Sowle Cahill
is the J. Donald Monan Professor of Theology at Boston College.

Francine Cardman
is Associate Professor of Historical Theology and Church History at Weston Jesuit School of Theology.

Charles E. Curran
is the Elizabeth Scurlock University Professor of Human Values at Southern Methodist University.

Ada María Isasi-Díaz
is Professor of Ethics and Theology at Drew University.

Mary Rose D'Angelo
is Associate Professor of Theology at the University of Notre Dame.

Ronald R. Garet
is the Carolyn Craig Franklin Professor of Law and Religion at the University of Southern California.

Leslie Griffin
holds the Larry and Joanne Doherty Chair in Legal Ethics at the University of Houston Law Center.

David Hollenbach, S.J.,
holds the Human Rights and International Justice University Chair and is Director of the Center for Human Rights and International Justice at Boston College.

Serene Jones
is Titus Street Professor of Systematic Theology at Yale Divinity School.

M. Cathleen Kaveny
is John P. Murphy Foundation Professor of Law and Professor of Theology at the University of Notre Dame.

Brian F. Linnane, S.J.,
formerly Associate Professor of Christian Ethics at the College of the Holy Cross, is President of Loyola College in Maryland.

William O'Neill, S.J.,
is Associate Professor of Social Ethics at the Jesuit School of Theology at Berkeley and the Graduate Theological Union.

Gene Outka
is the Dwight Professor of Philosophy and Christian Ethics at Yale Divinity School.

Anne E. Patrick, S.N.J.M.
is William H. Laird Professor of Religion and the Liberal Arts at Carleton College.

Jean Porter
is the John A. O'Brien Professor of Moral Theology at the University of Notre Dame.

Letty M. Russell
passed away shortly before the publication of this volume. At the time of her death she was Professor Emerita of Theology at Yale Divinity School and Co-coordinator of the International Feminist D.Min. program at San Francisco Theological Seminary.

Maura A. Ryan
is John Cardinal O'Hara, C.S.C., Associate Professor of Christian Ethics at the University of Notre Dame.

Index